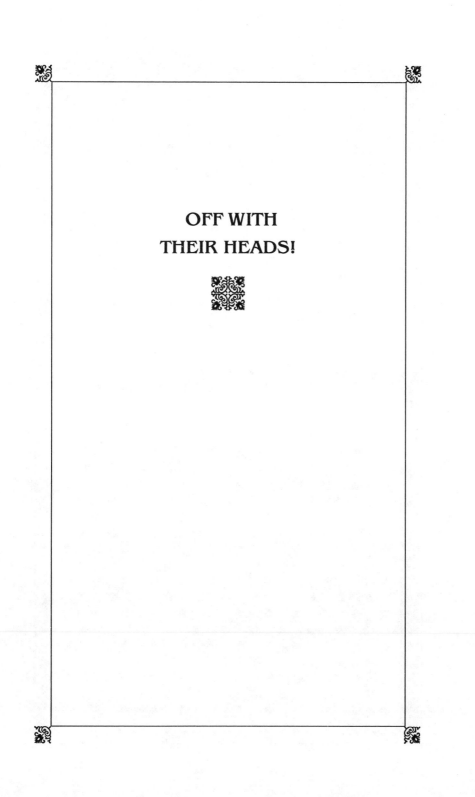

OFF WITH
THEIR HEADS!

OFF WITH
THEIR HEADS!

FAIRY TALES AND THE CULTURE
OF CHILDHOOD

Maria Tatar

PRINCETON UNIVERSITY PRESS

PRINCETON, NEW JERSEY

Library of Congress Cataloging-in-Publication Data

Tatar, Maria M., 1945–
Off with their heads! : fairy tales and the culture of childhood /
by Maria Tatar.
p.   cm.
Includes bibliographical references and index.
ISBN 0-691-06943-3
1. Fairy tales—History and criticism.   2. Folklore and children.
3. Children's stories—Psychological aspects.   I. Title.
GR550.T38   1992
398'.45—dc20   91-26470

FOR ANNA, JOHN, AND STEVE

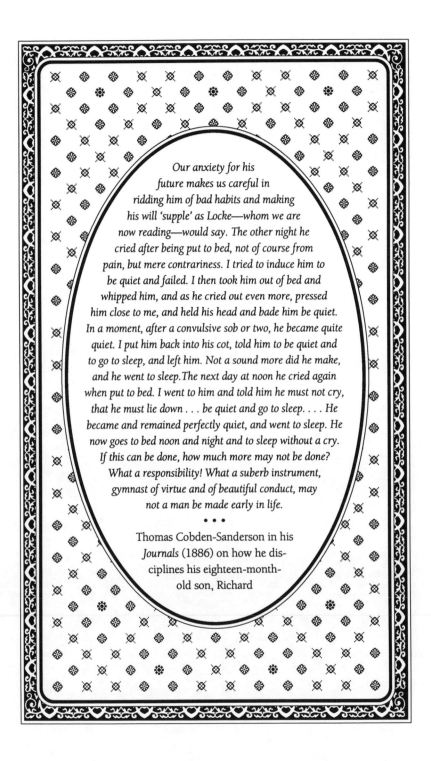

Our anxiety for his
future makes us careful in
ridding him of bad habits and making
his will 'supple' as Locke—whom we are
now reading—would say. The other night he
cried after being put to bed, not of course from
pain, but mere contrariness. I tried to induce him to
be quiet and failed. I then took him out of bed and
whipped him, and as he cried out even more, pressed
him close to me, and held his head and bade him be quiet.
In a moment, after a convulsive sob or two, he became quite
quiet. I put him back into his cot, told him to be quiet and
to go to sleep, and left him. Not a sound more did he make,
and he went to sleep. The next day at noon he cried again
when put to bed. I went to him and told him he must not cry,
that he must lie down . . . be quiet and go to sleep. . . . He
became and remained perfectly quiet, and went to sleep. He
now goes to bed noon and night and to sleep without a cry.
If this can be done, how much more may not be done?
What a responsibility! What a suberb instrument,
gymnast of virtue and of beautiful conduct, may
not a man be made early in life.

• • •

Thomas Cobden-Sanderson in his
Journals (1886) on how he dis-
ciplines his eighteen-month-
old son, Richard

❧ CONTENTS ❧

❧ LIST OF ILLUSTRATIONS ❧

✻ PREFACE ✻

And then, as to "Puss in Boots," when I came to look carefully at that
story, I felt compelled to re-write it, and alter the character of it to a
certain extent; for, as it stood, the tale was a succession of successful
falsehoods—a clever lesson in lying!—a system of imposture
rewarded by the greatest worldly advantage!—a useful lesson, truly,
to be impressed upon the minds of children!

George Cruikshank, "To Parents, Guardians, and all Persons
Entrusted with the Care of Children" in his *Puss in Boots*

WHEN LUCY of the "Peanuts" comic strip is called upon to tell
the story of "Snow White," she rises to the occasion in characteristic good form: "This Snow White has been having trouble
sleeping, see? Well, she goes to this witch who gives her an apple to eat
which puts her to sleep. Just as she's beginning to sleep real well . . .
you know, for the first time in weeks . . . this stupid prince comes along
and kisses her and wakes her up." To this strong "misreading" (to borrow Harold Bloom's term), Linus responds, "I admire the wonderful
way you have of getting the real meaning out of the story."[1]
   Getting at the true meaning of our cultural stories can be a real challenge. While some may believe, with Hemingway, that messages are for
Western Union and not for books, almost all of us turn to children's
stories with the expectation that morals and lessons will be forthcom-
ing, even in those cases where they are not spelled out in the text. For
every Mark Twain who wants to banish anyone trying to find a moral
in a book, there will be a hundred Duchesses of Wonderland who assert that "everything's got a moral, if only you can find it."[2] That moral
is not, however, a stable entity, but seems to vary dramatically with
each reader. Take the case of the popular children's classic *Curious
George*, a story that sends two conflicting, but equally persuasive, lessons about the wages of curiosity. Some will find George's curiosity
endearing and worthy of emulation because it opens the gateway to a

world of adventure.[3] Others will emphasize the way in which that particular trait constantly gets George in trouble and imperils his life. Is
Curious George an exemplary story or a cautionary tale? It is often up to
the adult reader to produce the "real meaning" that is then, in subtle or
not so subtle ways, passed on to the child.

Meaning is produced by more than the words on the page. Stanley
Fish has taught us that reading and the attendant process of interpretation engage us in an active process that creates a text by constructing its
meaning. We each belong to an interpretive community with shared
strategies "not for reading but for writing texts, for constituting their
properties."[4] The marks of those shared strategies are not always readily
apparent in our readings, in large part because the interpretive community to which we belong usually produces textual truths continuous
with our cultural beliefs. Ambiguities, disruptive moments, contradictions, and gaps are suppressed in favor of the construction of a concise,
self-evident, universal truth—"the real meaning of the tale." This true
meaning often turns out to be nothing more than an ossified and ossify-
ing bit of wisdom with little relevance to the lives of those who read—
or are read—the tales.

While the literature we read as adults (and here I refer primarily to
nineteenth- and twentieth-century novels) traditionally registers its dis-
approval of conformity and idealizes resistance to social regulation, the
literature we read to our children by and large stands in the service of
productive socialization.[5] As Roald Dahl has pointed out, adults have a
relentless need to civilize "this thing that when it is born is an animal
with no manners, no moral sense at all."[6] From its inception as a commercial endeavor with Newbery's "A Little Pretty Pocket-Book" (1744),
children's literature has openly endorsed a productive discipline that
condemns idleness and censures disobedience even as it hails acculturation and accommodation. While some stories have been so openly
and violently coercive that they lose their socializing energy, turning
instead into horror stories or surreal comedies (the German *Struwwelpeter* comes immediately to mind), the vast majority of tales from Newbery's time on have played a powerful role in constructing the ideal
child as a docile child.

Contemporary authors of children's literature have openly resisted
the disciplinary field staked out by nineteenth-century writers. In challenging a self-conscious form of didacticism that advocates industry
and obedience, these authors have tried to free themselves of an adver-

sarial relationship with the children that constitute their audience. But even though they often see themselves as conspiring with children, they are unable to escape creating new behavioral models and programs for them. In empathizing with children, for example, they are often at pains to help them work through problems by providing cathartic pleasures that, in the end, will turn them into "well-adjusted" (read: "socialized and productive") adults. Still, even if today's agenda, tipped as it is in the direction of playfulness and subversive pleasures, cannot eliminate coercive elements, most parents will find it preferable to reading "awful-warning" tales about girls who perish while playing with matches or boys who drown while torturing animals.

Children's literature in general—but fairy tales in particular—has traditionally addressed itself, broadly speaking, to two very different interpretive communities, each with its own vested interests and each in periodic conflict with the other. I refer, of course, to adults and children and, more specifically, to parents and their children. With a few notable exceptions, nearly every study of children's fairy tales published in this century has taken the part of the parent, constructing the true meaning of the tales by using the reading strategies of an adult bent on identifying timeless moral truths, folk wisdom of the ages, and universally valid developmental paradigms for boys and girls. This is true even of Bruno Bettelheim's *Uses of Enchantment*, which was published nearly fifteen years ago to great critical acclaim and still remains the authoritative study on fairy tales, despite the existence of competing books that come closer to taking the part of the child.[7] Bettelheim's study seems to capture more accurately than any other volume what our own culture has wanted to find in fairy tales, and for that reason I will focus in some detail on its conception of fairy tales to lay bare the ideological premises we bring to our reading of these stories.[8] Even the simplest fairy tale, as Harold Bloom tells us, has become a "textual jungle in which one interpretation has grown itself upon another, until by now the interpretations have become the story."[9]

Let us begin with a look at one of Bettelheim's cultural "stories," his reading of "Hansel and Gretel." In this text preserved by the Grimms, Bettelheim divines "an important, although *unpleasant*, truth [my emphasis]," namely that "poverty and deprivation do not improve man's character, but rather make him more selfish, less sensitive to the sufferings of others, and thus prone to embark on evil deeds."[10] This truth really is too unpleasant for Bettelheim to contemplate, for though he positions its enunciation in the very first paragraph of a lengthy commentary, he quickly erases the "evil deeds" of the impoverished parents to focus on the "frustrations," "destructive desires," "uncontrolled craving," "ambivalent feelings," and "anxieties" of the children in the tale. The story may ostensibly be about hard-hearted parents who abandon their children in the woods, but for Bettelheim it is really about children who engage in "denial and regression" in their effort to remain "dependent" on their parents. What the children encounter in the woods is not a cannibalistic witch, but a projection "onto their parents" of Hansel and Gretel's own desire "to eat somebody out of house and home." The happy ending of the story "force[s] the children to recognize the dangers of unrestrained oral greed and dependence" just as it "teaches . . . a valuable lesson" and trains the listeners to become "mature children." What most impresses Bettelheim about the tale seems captured in his statement about Hansel and Gretel: "As dependent children they had been a burden to their parents; on their return they have become the family's support, as they bring home the treasures they have gained." An odd message, one is inclined to add, for this tale's target audience: children ranging in age from four to eight.

Bettelheim's reading of "Hansel and Gretel" turns the children, who are viewed as burdens on the parents and strains on the family budget, into the real villains of the story; it then turns the children into agents of rescue for their oppressed parents, who need someone to provide for *them.* Hansel and Gretel's deficiencies, anxieties, and needs become the occasion for the story—the children are the ones in need of therapeutic intervention that will turn them from helpless creatures into self-sufficient adults who will take care of their unflawed elders. But as psychoanalyst James B. Hoyme has proposed, there is another way of reading and rewriting this story:

> I won't name any names of course, but if I had to chop wood for a meager living and had nothing more to look forward to at the end of each back-breaking day than two gaunt, demoralized children and a nagging, selfish woman, I can imagine that I might wish that they'd all go away, leave me in peace, and fight out their hungry rage elsewhere amongst themselves. I might even wish that my children would someday return . . . fat and rich and smiling, to report their final solution of the greedy witch problem and give me, ungrudgingly, so much money that I'd never have to chop another tree.[11]

1. Hansel and Gretel indulge their "oral greed" as a delighted witch
spies her victims. Note the serpent in the left-hand corner, a hint
by the artist that this is a story of temptation.

2. Hansel and Gretel return home with jewels in this happy ending that
reconstitutes the family by eliminating the stepmother.

Hoyme's retelling makes it evident that it is possible to construct two
mutually exclusive accounts of what goes on in the story: one "superfi-
cial" reading that focuses on the tale's manifest content (parents abandon their children in the woods and leave them at the mercy of a cannibalistic witch) and a second, "deeper" reading that looks for latent
meanings by detecting inversions, projections, and enactments of fears
and fantasies (children are terrified of abandonment and fear the consequences of their oral greed). Most adult readers are drawn to this second kind of reading, a psychoanalytic interpretation that turns the
child protagonists into egocentric villains who are forever projecting
the dark side of their fantasy life onto unwitting adults. I would submit
that we are drawn to these readings in part out of a desire to avoid

facing the "unpleasant truths" that emerge once we concede that some of the events staged in fairy-tale fictions can be as real as the fantasies they seem to represent. The "evil deeds" to which Bettelheim refers in his opening statement about "Hansel and Gretel," for example, took place with astonishing regularity in premodern Europe, where rates of child abandonment in urban areas probably ranged from 15 to 20 percent of registered births (as compared with a 1.5 percent rate for all recorded births in the United States).[12] Though the rate of child abandonment is dramatically lower in this country than it was in eighteenth-century Europe, the "abandoning impulse" is very much with us today, as Hoyme's account of patients in his psychoanalytic practice attests.

In our eagerness to analyze the childhood fantasies that are said to generate fairy-tale plots, and our reluctance to probe the role of parents in those plots, we unwittingly reshape the cultural stories we read to children. The places where we wince, cower, laugh, comment, whisper, shriek, or engage in any of the other numerous activities that mark the sites of our rewriting of a text determine the way the child perceives the story. A child's reception and response is always heavily marked by the context of relationship and performance.

But as readers of bedtime stories, we also do much more than change the story through verbal cues and body language—we also select the stories, often on the basis of anticipated therapeutic or didactic effects.[13] Bettelheim claims that the chief criterion he used in selecting stories for analysis was their popularity, but he never once stops to ponder just why certain stories became popular, or to think about the distinction between popularity and availability.[14] Our fairy-tale canon is drawn, for the most part, from collections produced by Charles Perrault and the brothers Grimm, and those collections are marked by strong rewritings (in the case of Perrault) and by repeated editorial interventions (in the case of the Grimms).[15] The handful of stories from Perrault and Grimm that have become a part of our common cultural heritage in the Anglo-American and European worlds consists of tales with an emphatic bias in favor of passive heroes and heroines—figures who start off as victims but live happily ever after because they are beautiful or lucky. These are also stories modeled on a transgression/punishment pattern that is consonant with an ideology in which the Calvinist notion of Original Sin has taken hold.

Part of what made these stories attractive to Bettelheim, I would maintain, is that they could be harnessed into service to support Freudian oedipal plots that position the child as a transgressor whose deserved punishment provides a lesson for unruly children. Stories that run counter to Freudian orthodoxy are, to a large extent, suppressed by Bettelheim or rewritten through reinterpretation. In "Little Red Riding Hood," we have the perfect example of a tale that has been subjected by Bettelheim to a Freudian rewriting. The story tells of a child who receives her "merited punishment" because she has "expose[d] herself dangerously to the possibility of seduction," spied into corners "to discover the secrets of adults," and reverted "to the pleasure-seeking oedipal child" (169–72). Bettelheim's fairy-tale heroes and heroines, as the prime movers of the oedipal plot, become tainted by blame and deserving of punishment even if, in the end, they emerge triumphant from the "trials" to which they subject their parents.

For a book that champions the interests of children by reclaiming for them a canon of stories that has come under heavy fire from American parents, educators, and librarians, *The Uses of Enchantment* is oddly accusatory toward children. "Snow White," the story of a stepmother who persecutes her helpless stepdaughter, is for Bettelheim really a story about a girl who cannot control her feelings of jealousy:

> Snow White, if she were a real child, could not help being intensely jealous of her mother and all her advantages and powers.
>
> If a child cannot permit himself to feel his jealousy of a parent (this is very threatening to his security), he projects his feelings onto this parent. Then "I am jealous of all the advantages and prerogatives of Mother" turns into the wishful thought: "Mother is jealous of me." The feeling of inferiority is defensively turned into a feeling of superiority. (204)

Note what happens as Bettelheim turns a character from a folktale into a real person stretched out on the psychoanalytic couch. If Snow White were a "real child," as Bettelheim puts it, she would have to be jealous of her mother, if for no other reason than the "fact" that filial jealousy is, like so much else in fairy tales, an "age-old phenomena" (204). This analysis, however, disregards the historical fact that, had Snow White been a "real child" at the time the Grimms published their *Nursery and Household Tales*, she would have been far more likely to be the target of angry resentment from a stepmother (who has to raise someone else's child, usually in addition to her own) than the agent of jealous rancor.

Few fairy-tale heroines fare any better than does Snow White in *The Uses of Enchantment*. Beauty, according to Bettelheim, ought to be grateful that her father has married her off to a beast. In "relinquishing his oedipal attachment to his daughter and inducing her to give up hers to him," the father clears the way for a "happy solution" to their problems (129). The wall of thorns on which Sleeping Beauty's suitors perish stands as "a warning to child and parents that sexual arousal before mind and body are ready for it is very destructive" (233). Warning six- and seven-year-olds about the destructiveness of premature sexual arousal (in however veiled a fashion) seems more than odd. It may be that parents will have sex on their minds when they read about a princess who pricks her finger on a spindle, then falls into a deep sleep, but children are unlikely to free-associate from the blood on the princess's finger to intercourse and menstruation, as Bettelheim believes they will. When the thorns on the hedge surrounding Sleeping Beauty's castle turn into flowers and the wall opens to let the prince enter, "the implied message" of the tale, as Bettelheim cheerfully enunciates it, is: "Don't worry and don't try to hurry things—when the time is ripe, the impossible problem will be solved, as if all by itself" (233).

Once we read Bettelheim's interpretations closely and critically, we begin to see that his reading produces a text that is very different from one that might be constituted by a reader with different cultural assumptions and expectations. This becomes painfully evident when we look at the way he rewrites stories about women, continually making them guilty of seductive behavior or sexual betrayal, even when the stories themselves are concerned with the rape and murder of women. Here is how Bettelheim paraphrases a description of rape and abandonment in Basile's "Sun, Moon, and Talia" (a variant of "Sleeping Beauty"): "[The king] found Talia as if asleep, but nothing would rouse her. Falling in love with her beauty, he cohabited with her; then he left and forgot the whole affair" (227). Bluebeard's wife, who is quite wise in opening the door to the room where the corpses of her predecessors are stored, is accused by Bettelheim of "sexual infidelity." Since "in times past, only one form of deception on the female's part was punishable by death inflicted by her husband" (300), Bluebeard's wives, he reasons, must have been guilty of sexual transgressions.

Notwithstanding these occasional digressions on female behavior, children remain the central subjects for Bettelheim's project of social-

ization through fairy tales. By choosing his texts carefully and bending them to his purpose, Bettelheim finds everywhere confirmation of
his view that life consists of a struggle to master unruly childhood
emotions:

> This is exactly the message that fairy tales get across to the child in
> manifold form: that a struggle against severe difficulties in life is un
> avoidable, is an intrinsic part of human existence—but that if one
> does not shy away, but steadfastly meets unexpected and often unjust
> hardships, one masters all obstacles and at the end emerges victori
> ous. (8)

For Bettelheim, that struggle inevitably turns out to be oedipal. "Fairytale fantasies," he asserts, "—which most children would have a hard
time inventing so completely and satisfactorily on their own—can help
a child a great deal to overcome his oedipal anguish."

Despite the persistence of idealized constructions of childhood as an
age of innocence, it has not been easy to see children as either victims
or heroes, particularly since Freud. Driven by narcissistic desires and
unbridled rage, they are often perceived as the real agents of evil and as
the sources of familial conflict. Freud's reading of the Oedipus story—
like Otto Rank's understanding of the myth of the birth of the hero, and
Bettelheim's interpretation of fairy tales—constructs a cultural story
driven by a child's fantasies of desire and revenge even as it suppresses
the realities of parental behavior ranging from abuse to indulgence.[16] If
a story tells of an infant abandoned by its father, for example, the abandonment, we are told, represents the distorted expression of a child's
rage toward a father. Our cultural stories are produced more or less by
self-pitying "retrograde childhood fantasies" that conceal a child's real-
life narcissism and hostility.[17]

If we read myths and fairy tales through the lens of the oedipal
drama, we will necessarily see the child as the sole target of therapeutic
intervention, for it is children who must work through the feelings of
anger expressed in the stories told to them by adults. Fortunately, this
transhistorical assumption of a disturbed child and a healthy adult has
been discredited to some extent by recent psychoanalytic literature and
historical research.[18] The need to deny adult evil—whether it takes the
form of infanticide, abandonment, physical abuse, or verbal assault—
has been a pervasive feature of our culture, leading us to position children not only as the sole agents of evil, but also as the objects of unend-

ing religious, moral, and therapeutic instruction.[19] Hence the idea that
a literature targeted for them must stand in the service of pragmatic
instrumentality rather than foster an unproductive form of playful
pleasure.

Bettelheim's *Uses of Enchantment* is of special interest for my purposes because it is so deeply symptomatic of our own culture's thinking
about children. Of course there is also much in the book that reflects
Bettelheim's own biases, and it is not always easy to separate out the
ideas specific to Bettelheim's concerns from those central to our cultural
situation. The conclusion to *The Uses of Enchantment*, however, clearly
tells us a great deal about Bettelheim's own real-life fantasies. In it,
Bettelheim, himself a parent, tells us that he feels the need to escape the
savage "generational conflicts" enacted in fairy tales and to take refuge
in a story that celebrates the "tender affection" between "parent and
child" (in reality between father and daughter). In "Beauty and the
Beast," the last of the tales analyzed in his volume, he finds that Beauty
"gives her father the kind of affection most beneficial to him"—she not
only "restores his failing health" but also provides him with "a happy
life in proximity to his beloved daughter." Beauty's devotion to her husband *and* to her father becomes the happy ending both to her own story
and to Bettelheim's meditation on fairy tales. On this wistful note of
wish fulfillment, which contains more than a hint of unresolved paternal conflicts (Bettelheim's suicide fourteen years later at age eighty-six
came after an "estrangement" from one daughter and a sense of "disappointment" when he moved to be closer to the other), the volume
ends.[20]

Once we are made aware of Bettelheim's personal history and the
way that it becomes implicated in his reading, we begin to see that
traces of the need to create the cultural construct of the dutiful daughter
who takes care of everyone's wants (the father's in particular) mark the
entire analysis. Bettelheim is, for example, full of enthusiasm for the
proposal of the dwarfs in the Grimms' "Snow White": "If you'll keep
house for us, cook, make the beds, wash, sew, and knit, and if you'll
keep everything neat and orderly, you can stay with us, and we'll provide you with everything you need." Here is Bettelheim's comment, for-
mulated without a trace of irony: "Snow White becomes a good housekeeper, as is true of many a young girl who, with mother away, takes
good care of her father, the house, *and even* her siblings" (208; my
emphasis).

It is important to note that Bettelheim also focuses intensely on stories that stage "female oedipal dramas," with the result that attention is drawn above all to a girl's sexual rivalry with her mother for the attention and affection of a father/husband. Although Bettelheim's index devotes six lines to entries under the term "stepmother," and we hear time and again about the splitting of mothers into two components (a good, dead mother and an evil, jealous stepmother), we never once learn of the existence of a story like the Grimms' "Allerleirauh," a tale in which a widower is so intent on marrying his daughter that the girl must flee into the woods. Over forty pages are dedicated to the "animal-groom cycle" of fairy tales (in which girls must prove their unending devotion to male monsters), yet animal-bride stories are totally neglected. Bettelheim provides us with a canon perfectly suited to validate and safeguard the universality of the ideas he describes. It is the canon we now mobilize for the acculturation of our children—a canon that uncritically perpetuates the cultural legacy defined by Freud.

I cannot claim immunity to a set of personal and ideological biases that infiltrate my readings of fairy tales, but I can state with certainty that my own concerns and perspective are very different from those of Bettelheim. Favoring the story over its deeper meaning often means accepting the version of events that sides with the child and validates an experiential model that is not "true to life" in the usual sense of the phrase. While I have not discounted the value of deeper meanings, I have tried also to give the stories their due. This has meant reading with the grain of traditional interpretations to find out how we have been led to construct certain meanings for "Snow White," "Cinderella," or "Beauty and the Beast," but also reading against the grain of those interpretations to see whether these tales can be reconstituted to produce different stories for us and our children. Just as every rewriting of a tale is an interpretation, so every interpretation is a rewriting. My hope is that this critical rewriting of the tales will contribute to producing new versions of stories that, for better or for worse, will have a powerful hold on our imaginations for a long time to come.

Since my story begins at the point when folktales were converted into written texts for children, the first part of this book focuses on the kinds of tales produced by the merger between folklore and children's literature and culminates in an analysis of Wilhelm Grimm's *Dear Mili,* a story that offers a telling lesson about our failure to recognize and acknowledge the cultural dissonance generated by telling nineteenth-century stories to children growing up today.

The second part of this study begins by looking at fairy-tale heroines and the ways in which they are slotted into many of the same roles occupied by children. Curiosity and disobedience, along with a variety of other vices, are seen as the besetting sins of both children and women. Courtship tales move us to the altar and show us heroines who are victims of tyrants at home—fathers relentlessly pursue them with proposals of marriage even as mothers try to turn them into domestic slaves. The social regulation of desire becomes the central issue of a final chapter that explores tales of animal-grooms, with a brief look at animal-brides.

Violence figures as the chief concern of the last section, which charts a move from festive violence as a form of social empowerment to violence as a destabilizing force within the family. Fairy tales serve as instruments of socialization and acculturation precisely because they capture and preserve disruptive moments of conflict and chart their resolution. Nowhere is this conflict more pointedly and poignantly displayed than in "The Juniper Tree," a story which gives us tableaus of aggression in its most brutish folkloric forms (physical violence and cannibalism). An analysis of this tale will serve as a springboard to a final meditation on rewriting our cultural stories.

I have tried, throughout this study, to take advantage of readings by various interpretive communities (though I am linguistically restricted to the Anglo-American and European worlds), since my own approach requires a careful weighing of previous interpretations, to see both what they do right and how they go wrong. As a result, I have resorted to an unabashedly eclectic approach, making use of whatever material is available about the folkloric, historical, sociological, literary, and cultural dimensions of the tales. Every interpretation of a tale (even the strongest misreading) can add something to our understanding of the high threshold of tolerance in these stories for editorial intervention and reinterpretation along ever-changing ideological lines.

It is nothing short of astonishing that we reflect so little on the stories read to our children—stories that so many of us acknowledge as having a profoundly formative influence on our childhood selves. As adults, we may never be able to get the stories just right for the child, but once we begin to recognize the ways in which we have failed to rewrite old stories—or failed in our rewritings of them—we may also be prepared to drop the pretense of being preachers, educators, or therapists, and to give our children stories in which they truly figure as heroes and heroines.

My children, Daniel and Lauren, reintroduced me to the world of children's literature and remind me, on a daily basis, of the power of stories over minds. Christabel, the Purple Heffalump, and Mr. Fussy, born of our familiar routines, play a decisive role in our lives with their unpredictable maneuvers and invisible interventions.

My thanks also go to the librarians and staff members of Widener Library and Houghton Library at Harvard University, of the Simmons College Library, the Cambridge Public Library, and the Boston Public Library. At an early stage in my work, research at the archives of the Brüder-Grimm Museum in Kassel and at the Kinder- und Jugendbibliothek in Munich proved invaluable, and I am grateful to the staffs there for their benevolent resourcefulness. The Disney Studio Archives offered the perfect setting for studying story conferences on "Snow White and the Seven Dwarfs" and for looking at everything from scrapbooks of film reviews to the early sketches for the animation. I am indebted to David Smith and his staff for providing access to those materials. Bob Brown, with his usual good cheer and heroic patience, moved the book through its many production stages. I was especially fortunate to benefit from the sophisticated expertise of Carolyn Fox's tactful editing before going into print.

For wit, wisdom, and counsel during the years in which this book was written, I am especially grateful to Elaine Backman, Janice Bassil, Annemarie Bestor, Sue Bottigheimer, Ellen Chances, Dorrit Cohn, Penny Laurans Fitzgerald, Bill Frank, Ed Gainsborough, Sander Gilman, Larry Gomes, Ingeborg Hoesterey, Peter Jelavitch, Perri Klass, Sandy Kreisberg, Catriona MacLeod, Jackie Panko, Judith Ryan, Marielle Smith, Melanie Tardella, Monika Totten, Gordon Trevett, Anke Vogel, and Larry Wolff.

OFF WITH
THEIR HEADS!

· CHAPTER I ·

Rewritten by Adults: The Inscription of Children's Literature

Follow children learning their fables; and you will see that when they
are in a position to apply them, they almost always do so in a way
opposite to the author's intention, and that instead of looking within
themselves for the shortcoming that one wants to cure or prevent,
they tend to like the vice with which one takes
advantage of others' shortcomings.

Rousseau, *Emile*

WHEN FOLKTALES retreated from workrooms and parlors to take up residence in the nursery, something was lost in the move. The tales may not have forfeited their hold on the imagination of young and old alike, but they did lose many of the elements that accounted for their appeal to adults *qua* adults, rather than as parents, guardians, or teachers. "Little Red Riding Hood," as we shall see, started out as a ribald story with a heroine who spends a good part of the narrative undressing while provocatively asking the wolf what to do with her bodice, her petticoat, and her stockings, and who then tricks the wolf into freeing her by asking if she can go outdoors to relieve herself. It is not difficult to imagine what a skilled raconteur could do with this story to enliven the hours spent husking corn or mending tools. But in the hands of those who turned traditional tales into literary texts, the story of Red Riding Hood came to be oriented toward a new audience and transformed into a solemn cautionary tale warning children about the perils of disobeying mother's instructions. "The Frog

King," a story rich in opportunities for risqué humor, was similarly re-
cast to produce a tale designed to issue stern lessons about the importance of keeping promises—even when it means sharing your bed with
an amorous frog. The twins born to Rapunzel materialize in magical
fashion when they appear between the covers of books for children—
not once are they connected with the heroine's daily romps with the
prince in her isolated tower.

Those who recorded folktales for a posterity that included children
as well as adults often took the path of least resistance and turned a deaf
ear to stories that showed priests hightailing it when husbands returned
home unexpectedly or that described worldly men helping naive young
women "put the devil into hell." With some imagination and ingenuity,
it was also not that difficult to alter a few details in a tale to make it
acceptable—if not necessarily appealing—children's fare. In the oldest
versions of "The Three Gifts," a boy wishes for a bow that will hit its
every target and a pipe that will force people to dance. He also asks that
whenever his stepmother glares at him, "her bum might then let go, and
crack like roaring thunder." Later versions of the story show us the boy
wishing for a bow, a pipe, and the ability to make everyone do as he
commands.[1]

Every collector, of course, had a different bias. The Frenchman Henri
Pourrat, for example, let scatalogical episodes slip into his multi-
volumed anthology of folktales but excised anything that smacked of
anticlerical sentiment or sacrilegious conduct. In his story "The Stupid
Wife," a woman hiding in a tree with her husband cannot restrain herself and defecates. The substance lands in a pot of soup being cooked
by bandits, who chant "Bubble, bubble, rich and brown, / God's own fat
is tumbling down." Pourrat had the "delicacy" to change "God's own
grace" ("la grâce de Dieu") into "God's own fat" ("la graisse de Dieu").[2]
Yet Pourrat's practice in this particular tale represents something of a
deviation from the norm, in part because he was less intent on writing
for children than on preserving rustic customs. In general, the closer we
move toward the nineteenth century, the lower the tolerance of collectors for virtually anything that touches on bodily functions.

Scholars have produced abundant evidence to show that folk raconteurs took advantage of opportunities to blend generous doses of earthy
humor into their plots and season them with sexual intrigue. The liberties they took by the fireside were almost always eliminated once the

stories reached print and moved into the realm of "official" culture. As Bakhtin has taught us, the grotesque realism of folk culture produced a boundless world of carnival humor that stood in a contestatory relationship to the official ecclesiastical and feudal order. Bodily functions were celebrated in both their degrading and reproductive aspects—the material triumphed over the spiritual as the source of life. "Grotesque realism . . . is the fruitful earth and the womb. It is always conceiving," Bakhtin asserts.[3] Laughter becomes a subversive power, undermining the stable truths of official culture and producing an irreverently playful world of change and renewal. As folktales became divested of their humorous elements, they also lost their subversive edge and became assimilated into the official canon of children's literature, which had always been more interested in producing docile minds than playful bodies.

Thanks to the efforts of certain folklorists (many of whom were considered uncomfortably close to the lunatic fringe in their own day and age), we possess unbowdlerized versions of some popular tales. Alexander Afanasev, the Russian counterpart to the brothers Grimm, had to print the bawdy tales he had collected at his own expense, in the city of Geneva, "without fanfare, in a place far from the cataclysmic events of the world, a place that the sacrilegious hand of the censor has not yet violated."[4] Even in the recent past, folklorists have felt obliged to keep their anthologies clean and to file away any "dirty" stories they may have heard from raconteurs. The American folklorist Vance Randolph, for example, published numerous collections of Ozark folktales in the 1950s, but the off-color tales he recorded were quietly deposited in the Library of Congress and in the Kinsey Institute for Sex Research at Indiana University and did not reach print until some twenty years later under the title *Pissing in the Snow and Other Ozark Folktales*.[5]

When it came to violence, the collectors of folktales put a different strategy into operation. Instead of disguising it or blotting it out, they preserved and often intensified it, though usually only when scenes of physical suffering or mental torment could be invested with a higher moral purpose. Since many classic fairy tales for children move along the path from victimization to retaliation, there was always ample opportunity to dilate on a person's misfortune. The example of the Grimms' "Cinderella" illustrates the attentive detail lavished on a heroine's trials and tribulations:

3. Fairy-tale villains often receive the punishments they have designed
for others. Here, Sleeping Beauty's mother-in-law ends up in
the barrel of snakes she had prepared for the heroine.

[The stepsisters] expected her to work hard there from morning till
night. She had to get up before dawn, carry the water into the house,
make the fire, cook, and wash. Besides this, her sisters did everything
imaginable to cause her grief and make her look ridiculous. For instance, they poured peas and lentils into the hearth ashes so she had
to sit there and pick them out. In the evening, when she was exhausted from working, they took away her bed, and she had to lie
next to the hearth in the ashes. This is why she always looked so
dusty and dirty and why they all called her Cinderella.[6]

The Grimms were astute enough to know that a fairy-tale character
obliged to do any housework at all—let alone all of it—has the immedi-

ate sympathy of most children. To turn a heroine into a tragic martyr often required little more than putting a broom into her hands.

The punishment of villains rarely called for restraint: most nineteenth-century anthologies of folktales paint remarkably vivid scenes of torture and execution. In some instances, violence was even added to stories. In the Grimms' first printed version of "Cinderella," for example, the stepmother and stepsisters are "horrified" and "turn pale" when they witness the heroine's good fortune.[7] By the time of the second edition, when Wilhelm Grimm was well aware that the collection had become a big hit with children, pigeons peck out the eyes of the stepsisters and they are "punished with blindness for the rest of their lives [for] their wickedness and malice." American versions of the tale were rarely so violent, in part because they were usually based on Perrault's version of "Cinderella," which showed the heroine ("as good as she was beautiful") setting aside apartments in her palace for her sisters and marrying them to "two gentlemen of high rank about the Court."[8] But Perrault's ending was the exception rather than the rule: other printed versions of "Cinderella" (including French ones) show the stepsisters and their mother enduring agonizing mental or physical pain. From Basile's stepsisters, who creep home to their mother "livid with envy and unable to bear the torment of their breaking hearts," through French stepsisters who are turned to stone or get jaundice and die, to Portuguese stepsisters who are put to death, we can get a rough idea of the full palette of punishments reserved for Cinderella's rivals.[9] As the old wives who tell the tales collected in Basile's *Pentamerone* observe, the stepsisters always get off too easy, for "no punishment or disaster can be too great for the deserts of pride and envy."

Why this strong moral indignation? If we look at the frame tale for Basile's *Pentamerone*, we discover that "The Cat Cinderella" is, like the other stories in the collection, "one of those tales that old women tell to amuse children."[10] We know, then, that in seventeenth-century Italy, folktales were already oriented toward children, though Basile's collection was produced with an adult audience in mind. The judgmental posture of the narrator derives, to some extent, from the need to provide a moral backbone to what otherwise might be perceived as an utterly frivolous tale. Unfortunately, not only stories like "Cinderella" (with its victimization/retaliation pattern) became grist for the mill of those who felt a relentless need to teach children lessons. "Little Red Riding Hood," which began with a prohibition followed by the heroine's violation of it, played right into the hands of those who were eager to find morals and send messages. In it, however, as in its folkloric cousins, the *heroine* (not her oppressors) meets with a violent end—only in a few versions (like the Grimms') is she rescued from the belly of the wolf. This cautionary tale makes an example of its protagonist, the very figure with which children identify, rather than of its adult villain, and thus becomes a true horror story.

Folktales began to reach print at just the point when a real commercial market was developing for children's literature. Ever adaptable, they could easily be harnessed into service as stories for children so long as a few key changes were made—changes that divested the tales of their earthy humor, burlesque twists, and bawdy turns of phrase to make room for moral instruction and spiritual guidance. Those who produced the great anthologies of folktales and fairy tales had an ever watchful eye on the models generated by the authors of children's books.

From its inception, children's literature had in it an unusually cruel and coercive streak—one which produced books that relied on brutal intimidation to frighten children into complying with parental demands. This intimidation manifested itself in two very different forms, but both made examples of children. First, there were countless cautionary tales that managed to kill off their protagonists or make their lives perpetually miserable for acts of disobedience. Then there were stories about exemplary behavior which, nonetheless, had a strange way of also ending at the deathbeds of their protagonists.

Since cautionary tales and exemplary stories were the two principal models available for producers of children's fiction and biography, they exercised a powerful influence on writers who were (sometimes intentionally, sometimes unwittingly) turning folktales into stories for children. Although transforming a folktale into a cautionary tale or exemplary story may seem like a futile exercise producing nothing more than tales graceless and contrived in their effect, the opposite, in fact, holds true. What is astonishing is the ease with which folktales could be transplanted into the flinty soil of what was once considered suitable reading matter for children.

Since the cautionary tale and the exemplary story played so instrumental a role in the revision of folktales, we need to take a short detour to explore their form and function. Let us begin with the cautionary tale, a genre that flourished in the harsh climate of nineteenth-century childrearing practices. Here we find Heinrich Hoffmann's Pauline, who plays with matches in the German children's classic *Struwwelpeter*, goes up in flames, and perishes. While she is reaching for the matches and lighting them, her cats chant warnings: "Your father has forbidden it. . . . Your mother has forbidden it."[11] Pauline's fate does not deviate sharply from that of her German antecedents and their French and British counterparts, who all suffer dreadful consequences for their lapses. When a young procrastinator tries to learn her lessons on the way to school, the British Miss Kilner lets her trip, fall on her face, and run home with blood pouring over her. "I am sorry you are hurt, still I do really think you deserve to be so for your own indolence and folly," the girl's mother announces with more than a touch of satisfaction.[12] Karl August Engelhardt recounts the story of a boy who, with no malice aforethought, pulls a caper whose consequences are spun out so broadly that they include the loss of the family home and the death of the boy's parents.[13] One false step, these tales imply, and you will perish or, better yet, suffer a thousand deaths as you watch your home put on the auction block, your father go blind, your mother die of grief, and your siblings land in the poorhouse.

Just what is this false step? Pauline's cats proclaim that the deeper cause of the girl's death lies in disobedience. The boy who mistakes arsenic for sugar and dies from eating it in countless children's stories and poems deserves his fate not because of his gluttony, but because he has disobeyed parental commands. "The little Fish that would not do as it was bid," in Ann and Jane Taylor's *Rhymes for the Nursery* (1835), makes the following speech before expiring on a fisherman's hook: "Dear mother, had I minded you, I need not now have died."[14] The cardinal sin of youth is disobedience, and it is a sin that habitually demands the death penalty. What is particularly odd about these stories is that the pedagogical program of each tale clashes so starkly with the tale's content: survival and good fortune are promoted through images of death and disaster.

The titles of eighteenth- and nineteenth-century bestsellers for children are telling: *A Tale of Warning, or, The Victims of Indolence; The Good-Natured Little Boy and the Ill-Natured Little Boy; Meddlesome Mattie; Dangerous Sports, a Tale Addressed to Children Warning them against Wanton, Careless, or Mischievous Exposure to Situations from which Alarming Injuries so often Proceed;* and *The Adventures of a Whipping-Top. Illustrated with Stories of many Bad Boys, who themselves deserve whipping, and*

of some Good Boys, who deserve Plum-Cakes. The wave of moralism that
swept through children's fiction to produce tales of the "awful-warning"
school also encroached on other areas of childhood culture. In *Rhymes
and Pictures for the Nursery and School. By a Lady*, we hear of a little girl
who insists on eating forbidden fruit:

> They went on a little, but Anna complain'd
>   Of pain in her stomach and head,
> And very soon follow'd most terrible pains,
>   She shriek'd out with anguish and dread. . . .
> She died from not doing what Ma had desired,
>   And eating the fruit of the wood.

The year 1810 witnessed the issue of the British *New Game of Virtue
Rewarded and Vice Punished*, whose game board was covered with such
attractive scenes and figures as "The Stocks," "The House of Correc-
tion," "Faith," and "Prudence."[15] The popular American children's game
Chutes and Ladders, in which game pieces landing on pictures of children eating candy, reaching for a cookie, or drawing with crayons on a
wall must slide away from the goal down a chute, while game pieces
landing on pictures of children mowing the lawn, sweeping the floor,
or baking a cake may advance up a ladder, probably evolved from its
British equivalent. There too a child is to learn "the rewards of good
deeds and the consequences of naughty ones."[16]

All these tales, rhymes, and games operate with a minimal narrative
unit that consists of a pattern basic also to folktale plots (prohibi-
tion/violation/punishment). We can see this syntagmatic unit at work in
"Sleeping Beauty," where the heroine must not touch a spindle. When
she violates the (unspoken) prohibition, the penalty consists of a death-
like sleep that lasts a hundred years. Unlike the naughty children of
cautionary tales, however, Sleeping Beauty never willfully defies an
order—in fact, she does nothing at all to merit the punishment visited
on her. There is no moral dimension whatever to her action. This could
easily be changed, and often was changed, once fairy tales were appropriated by the purveyors of children's literature. Sleeping Beauty usually remained morally unimpeachable, though one recent American
version turns her into a girl who, like Bluebeard's wife, succumbs to the
temptation of taking a key and opening the door to a forbidden chamber—one that houses a spinning wheel. On the other hand, Sleeping
Beauty's folkloric sisters (among others, Little Red Riding Hood, the

princess in "The Frog Prince," and the heroine of "King Thrushbeard") nearly all became models of bad breeding. By the middle of the nineteenth century, they had become morally reprehensible in one way or another and in some sense responsible for their fates.

Defenders of fairy tales often fall into the trap of elevating these stories into repositories of higher truths and moralities. Fairy tales, we have been taught to believe, offer comfort to children, for in them we find a moral corrective to everyday life, a world in which the good are consistently rewarded and the evil are just as consistently punished.[17] In reality, the picture is quite different. Although fairy tales often celebrate such virtues as compassion and humility and show the rewards of good behavior, they also openly advocate lying, cheating, and stealing. The heroes and heroines (who are not necessarily either "good" or "virtuous") get all the rewards while the villains (who are not always "evil" or "sinful") are dispossessed and tortured. Think of the miller's daughter in "Rumpelstiltskin," who marries a king and lives happily ever after even though she fails to keep up her end of the bargain struck with the "villain" of the tale's title. Rumpelstiltskin, by contrast, fulfills all the terms of his contract but perishes because he is moved by the queen's tears and agrees to build an escape clause into the contract.

The moral depravity of fairy-tale heroes and heroines did not escape the attention of those who had an audience of children in mind as they prepared volumes of fairy tales for publication. In order to please "every tender mother, and every gentle tutor," Benjamin Tabart had to make sweeping changes in traditional tales to produce his *Popular Fairy Tales; or, a Lilliputian Library*. His Jack, for example, does not rob the giant of his rightful possessions—he simply reclaims (as we learn in a lengthy digression) what the giant had previously stolen from his father.[18]

Once fairy tales entered the realm of children's literature, they took on a protective didactic coloring that has been virtually impossible to remove. Rather than toning down scenes of violence for children's stories, recorders and collectors often added moral lessons that, in their eyes, gave them license to emphasize or even exaggerate descriptions of punishment and death. At the same time, authors of conventional cautionary tales were learning some lessons of their own from didactic fairy tales, enlivening their often dreary depictions of virtue rewarded and vice punished by dwelling on the naughty, corrupt, and evil deeds of children and by borrowing surreal elements from folktales to add spine-chilling effects. The result occasionally added up to gratuitous cruelty, as in the case of Mrs. W. K. Clifford's *Anyhow Stories* (1882), in which a "wild woman" tempts two small children to engage in ever more naughty deeds until finally their mother can bear it no longer and turns over her children and her home to a woman with glass eyes and a wooden tail. The children flee into the woods. "They are there still, my children," Mrs. Clifford solemnly concludes. "Now and then . . . [they] creep up near to the home in which they once were so happy, and with beating hearts they watch and listen; sometimes a blinding flash comes through the window, and they know it is the light from the new mother's glass eyes, or they hear a strange muffled noise, and they know it is the sound of the wooden tail as she drags it along the floor."[19] This story, which plays on children's deepest fears about maternal abandonment, stands as the most extreme example of what could happen when an author combined naturalistic descriptions of children's behavior with surreal incarnations of punishing parents.

The anonymous author of a collection of cautionary stories entitled *Tales Uniting Instruction with Amusement consisting of the Dangers of the Streets; and Throwing Squibs* must have had a strange notion of "amusement." The readers of this volume are treated to the contrast between wellbred Edward Manly, who is always careful to watch his step, and mischievous George, who walks out into the street, is run over by a wagon, and ends up on the operating table: "The surgeon took out his instruments, cut the flesh all round with a sharp knife, cut through the bone with a saw, and thus poor George's leg was taken completely off." Then there is Tom, who throws squibs and ends up killing his father and hurting himself: "He often bitterly laments his ill-conduct, and wishes he had followed his poor father's good advice. If he had done so, he might now have been at a genteel boarding school with both his eyes safe, instead of being a chimney sweeper, and blind of one eye."[20] The stories were probably meant to amuse in the sense of "divert," yet they inadvertently produce a comic effect. When a punishment is so disproportionate to the crime, as in these cases, there is something ludicrous about the solemnity of the narrator's pronouncements.

Tales Uniting Instruction with Amusement can help us understand just why it was that cautionary tales were probably less distasteful to children than one might suspect. The gory accidents that children meet up with when they are careless or disobedient may have been meant to repel children, but the fact is that they could also prove a source of unending fascination. What child is not mesmerized by the sight of the burning dresses, lopped-off thumbs, and tormented animals in Hoff-mann's *Struwwelpeter*, a book whose appeal can be traced not just to the need of parents to coerce their children into docile behavior, but also to the desire of children to hear stories as sensational in their own way as the ones once told around the fireside. In many cases, the more carried away adult writers of cautionary tales were in their descriptions of tortures and mutilations, the more attractive the tales proved for children.

At times it seems as if some authors deliberately sabotaged the didactic aim of their stories. Mrs. Bell in Kilner's *Village School* is described as "a very good woman," a "valuable member of society," and "much beloved." Here is how she punishes one of the many "naughty" children at her school:

> She took off his coat, and beat him very much with a cane she kept on purpose to beat naughty children. She then tied his hands behind him, and his legs together, and assured him he should not go home that night; but that, when school was over, she would shut him up in some closet, where he might be safe, and not do any more mischief. (9)

It is easy enough to imagine that Mrs. Bell's death in a fire while she is concurrently nursing a sick woman and making a shirt for a neighbor whose wife is also ill is something of a relief for both author and readers. Mrs. Kilner seems almost too eager to describe the demise of her heroine, whose "flesh was so entirely consumed as to make it impossible to distinguish Mrs. Bell from the poor woman she had charitably assisted" (88). Yet when we read the sanctimonious tribute to Mrs. Bell and find that her story culminates in yet another lesson—this time "to be extremely cautious not to leave candles burning near linen"—it is hard to imagine that Mrs. Kilner's aim was parody. This would not, however, prevent young readers of *The Village School* from getting some grim satisfaction out of Mrs. Bell's death.

Exemplary stories could be just as unsparing as cautionary tales in describing scenes of suffering—in some ways they seem even crueler than stories in which boys perish because they have pulled the wings off a fly. That these stories dominated the children's book market for some time becomes clear from an observation made in the 1830s by Catherine Sinclair, when a friend residing in the country asked her to select some books for her children. On surveying what was available, it

surprised Sinclair that "a large proportion of the volumes recommended had frontispieces to represent a death-bed surrounded by the
clergyman, the physician, and the afflicted relatives of a dying Christian, the memoirs of children *especially*, which I examined, were almost
invariably terminated by an early death."[21] The most notorious example
of a book that celebrated the deaths of "good" children was James Janeway's *A Token for Children: Being an Account of the Conversion, Holy and
Exemplary Lives, and Joyful Deaths of Several Young Children* (1671–72).
Janeway is dead set against allowing children to enjoy themselves in this
world. Pleasure and joy are reserved exclusively for dead children, or,
at best, for those in their death throes. "How do you spend your time?"
he asks his audience with calculated artlessness. "Is it in play and idleness, and with wicked children? . . . Do you dare to idle and play upon
the Lord's day?"[22] We do not have to read far into the volume to discover the fatal consequences of idleness, but Janeway does not give us,
as might be expected, death scenes of wanton young sinners. The sweet
children whose deaths he documents "feared God, and were dutiful to
their parents." Now that they are in heaven, they see "glorious things,
and have nothing but joy and pleasure." For those children who are not
yet fortunate enough to experience the "ecstasy of joy and holy triumph" that the four-year-old Mary A. felt on her deathbed, Janeway
recommends a combination of "secret prayer" and weeping, with occasional pauses for quoting of scripture, expressions of gratitude for parental prohibitions, and readings in his own book, whose richness, he
asserts, will not be exhausted even after a hundred readings.

The case history of young John Sudlow has Janeway's characteristic
touch: a dreary, sanctimonious style combined with a hagiographic
tone that wears thin even on a first reading. The death of John's brother
inspires the boy "to avoid whatsoever might displease God." His interest in scripture becomes so intense that "when neighbors' children
would come and call him out, and try to entice him to go with them,
he would by no means be persuaded . . . if he had any hope that any
pious person would come to his father's house" (44–45). His temper is
so "sweet" that he is always "dutiful" to his parents and careful not to
"displease" them. Compassion for his brothers and sisters runs so deep
that he begs his parents to take better care of the souls of these siblings
"lest they should go on in a sinful Christless state, prove their sorrow
and shame, go to hell when they died, and be ruined forever" (46).
Struck down by the plague, this model child remains steadfast in his

faith even when the local minister consoles him on his deathbed by asking him whether he is afraid to die and reminding him that he is a sinner who cannot expect salvation.

The London Bills of Mortality reveal that in the period shortly following the publication of Janeway's *Token for Children*, the mortality rate of children age five and under could run as high as 66 percent.[23] Thus when Janeway asked, in the "directions for children" accompanying his volume: "Did you never hear of a little child that died?" he could count on "yes" as an answer. "If other children die," Janeway hastened to add, "why may not you be sick and die! and what will you do then, if you should have no grace in your heart, but are like other naughty children?" (94). Given the visible presence of death in the daily lives of most children growing up in the premodern era and the nineteenth century, the specter of an early death could be raised in a highly effective way by those who chose to use it in their childrearing practices.[24]

Janeway's sensationalizing dramas of children's victories over sin may, like cautionary tales, have ended in the cemetery, but they prospered with the reading public. One critic has likened the appeal of these spiritual biographies to that of romances and fairy tales, for in them sin figures as an ogre or monster against which the child struggles to emerge victorious.[25] Yet while folktales could easily absorb the ethos of the cautionary tale and transform themselves into miniature moral dramas, they proved more resistant to the spirituality of the exemplary story; accounts of pious children lacked the element of transgressive action required to generate fairy-tale conflicts. Still, one should not underestimate the attractiveness of the genre for children. P. L. Travers (author of *Mary Poppins*), for example, writes about her "great affection" as a child for a book called *Twelve Deathbed Scenes*.[26]

As we shall see, there are a number of tales that glorify the sufferings of their protagonists and celebrate the afterlife, among them a story whose most popular incarnation is found in Hans Christian Andersen's "Little Match Girl." *Dear Mili*, a tale by Wilhelm Grimm recently published with great fanfare in this country, is similarly oriented toward death, with a heroine who loses her life during a time of war and is translated into a higher sphere, where she lives with St. Joseph and plays with her guardian angel.

A culture with a high mortality rate will understandably reach for Janeway, Andersen, or Grimm in order to prepare children for death by offering the consolation of spiritual salvation. It is, after all, not easy for anyone to answer the concerns raised by a child in Lucy Cameron's *History of Margaret Whyte, or, The Life and Death of a Good Child* (1837): "'How can we tell that we shall ever live to grow up? Many children die much younger than either of us; and if we do not think of preparing for death, what will become of us?'"[27] Even Janeway seems quite tame by comparison with some of the sermons preached to British children in the early part of the nineteenth century. Here is an excerpt from one delivered by the grim Reverend Carus Wilson, author of a juvenile magazine called—in all seriousness—*The Children's Friend*:

> My dear children, the hooping [sic] cough is spreading fast; several little ones have died of it. Day after day I hear the bell tolling, and one little child after another has been buried here; and as I walk out into the villages, and the lanes, and go into schools, I see your little faces swelled, and hear you coughing; but I am pained to think how few of you would be found ready were you called to die of it. Let me beg of you, dears, to try to think about death; say to yourselves, "perhaps I may soon die, and then where will my soul go? will it go to heaven, or will it be cast down into hell, where there will be weeping, and wailing and gnashing of teeth?"[28]

There is no escaping the fact that tales like "The Little Match Girl" and *Dear Mili* use death in much the same way as do sermons like these. The goodness, obedience, and piety of the match girl and Mili secure them a place in heaven; implicitly, we know that their fate would be quite different were they to lack those qualities. It is thus more than odd that a text like *Dear Mili*, which is so firmly anchored in the cultural realities of its time, should be resurrected and hailed as a children's tale that speaks "so directly to the concerns of our time [1988] that it seems extraordinary to have it appear now."[29]

Collectors of folktales nearly always stand in awe of the stories they record. The Grimms never tired of declaring that the tales in their collection captured the authentic voice of the folk in all its purity and artless simplicity. The poetry of the people was also the poetry of nature, unsullied by the corrupting influences of culture and civilization. Yet at the same time, the Grimms called their book an "educational manual." Folktales were never meant to convey lessons, they proclaimed in the introduction to the *Nursery and Household Tales*, "but a moral grows out of them, just as good fruit develops from healthy blossoms without help from man."[30] In a sense, the Grimms were trying to have their cake and eat it too: They had a need to enshrine these tales as "natural" stories untainted by the hand of man, yet at the same time they felt compelled to stress their "civilizing" qualities. Unable to escape the influence of Rousseau, yet also children of the Enlightenment who would have applauded the view that "everything, animate or inanimate, may . . . be made subservient to moral instruction," they found themselves caught in a contradiction that characterized much of post-Enlightenment thinking about folktales.[31]

The myth of folktales as sacred, "natural" texts was deftly propagated by Charles Dickens, who brought to the literature of childhood the same devout reverence that he accorded children. Dickens, like the Grimms, hailed the "simplicity," "purity," and "innocent extravagance" of fairy tales, but he also praised the tales as powerful instruments of socialization: "It would be hard to estimate the amount of gentleness and mercy that has made its way among us through these slight channels. Forebearance, courtesy, consideration for the poor and aged, kind treatment of animals, the love of nature, abhorrence of tyranny and brute force—many such good things have been first nourished in the child's heart by this powerful aid."[32]

Dickens' paean to fairy tales was part of a crusade against the efforts of George Cruikshank, his illustrator and erstwhile friend, to produce a new breed of fairy tales. Passions ran high when the two quarreled over the issue. Cruikshank, in response to Dickens' attack on his versions of "Cinderella," "Hop-o'-my-Thumb," "Puss in Boots," and "The History of Jack & the Bean-Stalk," correctly pointed out that there was much in fairy tales that was not suitable for children. In the preface to his "Cinderella," he told readers that he had pored over several versions of the tale and found "*some* vulgarity, mixed up with so much that was useless and unfit for children, that I was obliged . . . to re-write the whole story."[33] Cruikshank could not resist the temptation to introduce "a few *Temperance Truths*" in his rewriting. When Cinderella is to be wed, for example, the father of the Prince orders "fountains of wine" to be set up in the courtyards of the palace and in the streets. Cinderella's godmother is appalled by these plans and reminds the monarch that these fountains of wine will foment "quarrels, brutal fights, and violent death." The King's belief that moderation in drink will avert violence is challenged by the godmother, who sanctimoniously states that "the history of the use of strong drink . . . is marked on every page by *excess, which follows, as a matter of course, from the very nature of their composi-*

tion, and . . . always accompanied by ill-health, misery, and crime" (25). The King is converted and orders all the beer, wine, and spirits in the kingdom collected for a "great bonfire" on the night of the wedding. After reading Cruikshank's "Cinderella," Dickens' words about the "intrusion of a Whole Hog of unwieldy dimension into the fairy flower garden" seem remarkably apt.[34]

Cruikshank, however, did not limit himself to "*Temperance Truths*." In "The History of Jack & the Bean-Stalk," he rambled on about the evils of "idleness and ignorance" and introduced a fairy who tells a reformed Jack: "I have long wished to employ you in a difficult and important matter, but I could not trust you whilst you were so careless and idly disposed; but now, that you have this day shaken off that slothful habit, and have determined to be active, diligent, and trustworthy, I no longer hesitate."[35] In "Hop-o'-my-Thumb," the hero and his brothers learn to wash themselves in "cold water (which they did winter and summer, because it is most refreshing and healthy to do so)" and to "go to bed early, which they all did, like good children, without any grumbling or crying."[36] Cruikshank's passionate drive to correct the moral vision of fairy tales is nowhere harder at work than in his remarks about Cinderella's stepmother. To preserve the sanctity of motherhood, including stepmotherhood, he represents the villain of the piece as an anomalous case. "It is the nature of woman to have children," he pontificates, "because the Almighty has appointed her to bring them up; and when little boys and girls are placed at an early age under the charge of a stepmother, it is very rarely that they feel the loss of their own mother: but there are exceptions, and it was so, unfortunately, in this case; for Cinderella's mother-in-law [sic] was proud, selfish, and extravagant, and these bad qualities led her to be unjust and cruel."[37]

Cruikshank's reinterpretations of fairy tales may have been more heavy-handed than those of most other authors and collectors, but they dramatically illustrate the way in which the ethos of the collector/editor/rewriter penetrates the moral universe of a fairy tale, even of those tales that escaped a merger with the cautionary tale or exemplary story. "Cinderella," for example, in telling of a child persecuted by her stepmother and siblings and of how the child gets back at them, was probably never really designed to illustrate the rewards of good behavior. Still, as we have seen in the case of Cruikshank's rewriting, this story of a girl's victimization and retaliation left plenty of room for moral glosses on whatever virtue or vice happened to preoccupy its recorder.

All printed fairy tales are colored by the facts of the time and place in which they were recorded. For this reason, it is especially odd that we continue to read to our children—often without the slightest degree of critical reflection—unrevised versions of stories that are imbued with the values of a different time and place. Collections like those of Charles Perrault, the brothers Grimm, and Joseph Jacobs are documents from the past, "old-time" fairy tales which, according to the author of *The Wonderful Wizard of Oz*, should now be "classed as 'historical' in the children's library." For L. Frank Baum, the time had come for "a series of newer 'wonder tales' in which the stereotyped genie, dwarf and fairy are eliminated, together with all the horrible and bloodcurdling incidents devised by their authors to point a fearsome moral to each tale."[38] We would be well advised, as Rudolf Schenda has proposed, not only to provide the old-time fairy-tale collections with prefaces about the genesis of the tales and notes about the cultural milieu in which they flourished, but, even more importantly, to think twice before reading certain stories from the collections to children.[39]

Schenda's suggestion, however sound, does not take into account a parent's unwillingness to purchase storybooks with a scholarly apparatus, let alone a publisher's horror at the thought of printing such a volume. But how, then, do we avoid throwing the baby out with the bathwater? How do we preserve the fairy-tale canon even as we divest it of the "wisdom" of another age, of cultural constructs that are irrelevant or inappropriate for the child to whom the tale is read? One obvious answer is to rewrite the stories so that they are closer to our own time and place. But such projects do not necessarily succeed in producing "better" texts—they may end by reflecting the values of one class, ethnic group, or other social segment of our own culture, but that segment may not have much appeal for those living in a culture characterized by ideological pluralism.

Rewriting is often just as likely to produce an unsatisfying text as it is to produce an improved version of the story. Consider the example of the recently issued *Princess and the Frog*, which is a self-described adaptation of "'The Frog King and Iron Heinrich' by the Brothers Grimm."[40] This rewriting does not by any means eliminate the father's intervention and his declaration that the princess must keep her promise and let a frog climb into her bed. "Go and let the frog in," the father insists. "You have made a promise and you must keep it." This new version of an old tale gives us a dutiful daughter who obeys her father, then goes along with the frog's request to let him sleep on her pillow. Instead of a princess who—in a gesture appropriately charged with fear and frustration—dashes the importunate frog against the wall, we have a girl who falls asleep three times with the frog in her bed and finally awakens, on the third morning, to find a prince. The adapter is careful, however, to position the frog on the princess's pillow, just as she replaces the girl's feelings of disgust and anger with tolerance toward her amphibian suitor. (The countless cartoons and jokes based on this story have, incidentally, almost all rewritten the scene of disenchantment: the frog is transformed by a kiss rather than by an act of violence.[41])

In prefatory remarks to "Princess Furball," a modern version of the Grimms' "Allerleirauh," the American adapter makes a point of acknowledging that she has rewritten the story and erased the theme of incest in it, yet she also asserts that she has remained faithful to the "psychological truth" of earlier tellings.[42] Trying to assess the impact of the Grimms' version of the tale and to compare it with the effect of the rewritten version is a task that must be left to the child psychologists. But the examples of the "Frog King" and "Princess Furball" remind us how a story that has been brought "up-to-date" does not necessarily give us an interpretation that is more pedagogically sound or psychologically true.

Fairy tales are not written in granite. My own experience has shown that we continue to rewrite the tales as we reread them, even though the words on the page remain the same. But it is important to remember that what we produce in our retellings and rereadings discloses more about an adult agenda for children than about what children want to hear. Thus fairy tales may not offer much insight into the minds of children, but they often document our shifting attitudes toward the child and chart our notions about childrearing in a remarkable way. It is these discursive practices, as they are embedded in children's literature, that invite reflection as we read to a child or when we put a book into a child's hands.

Maurice Sendak once stated that, as a former child, he felt fully entitled and empowered to write children's stories. In a sense, these same credentials allow all of us to retell fairy tales to our children, even if we may never be able to get the cultural script quite right. Yet while there is a child in every adult, not every adult has the power to reach that child and to engage in empathetic identification with its former self. But as Rousseau reminds us, a child's natural gift for subversion, for moving against every author's intentions, can rescue even the most solemn or dim-witted rendition of a tale and turn it into an amusing diversion, especially when it comes at the expense of its adult authors.

· CHAPTER II ·

"Teaching Them a Lesson":
The Pedagogy of Fear
in Fairy Tales

She had read several nice little stories about children who had got
burnt, and eaten up by wild beasts, and other unpleasant things,
all because they would not remember the simple rules their friends had
taught them: such as, that a red-hot poker will burn you if you hold it
too long; and that, if you cut your finger very deeply with a knife,
it usually bleeds; and she had never forgotten that, if you drink much
from a bottle marked "poison," it is almost certain
to disagree with you, sooner or later.

Lewis Carroll, *Alice in Wonderland*

O NCE UPON A TIME there was a girl who was stubborn and curious, and whenever her parents told her to do something, she would not obey them. Well, how could things possibly go well for her?" The answer is that they could not, for this girl happens to be caught between the pages of the Grimms' *Nursery and Household Tales*, where stubbornness and curiosity invite persecution and virtually guarantee a violation of the rule that all ends well for fairy-tale heroes. The case of the headstrong young girl in the passage cited above is typical. She is determined to visit a woman named Frau Trude. "'People say that there are unusual things about her house, and there are also strange things inside,'" the heroine reflects. "'All that's made me very curious.'" The sensible parents warn their daughter that Frau

Trude is known as an "evil woman" who does "wicked things," but to no avail. As the girl makes her way up the stairs of Frau Trude's house, she first witnesses a parade of ghoulish figures, then finds herself transformed into a block of wood casually tossed on the fire. "'That makes a nice, bright fire,'" Frau Trude declares with satisfaction as she warms herself by a blaze fueled by the tale's stubborn, curious heroine.[1]

There are many equally disagreeable tales in the Grimms' collection. "The Stubborn Child" also rehearses the perils of disobedience: the recalcitrant child in that story lies on his deathbed because the "dear Lord" does not "look kindly on him" (he never does what his mother tells him to do) and lets him become sick. But even in the grave the boy asserts his will by forcing one arm right through the ground, despite repeated efforts to cover it over with fresh mounds of dirt. "So the child's mother had to go to the grave herself and smack the little arm with a switch. After she had done that, the arm withdrew, and then, for the first time, the child had peace beneath the earth." Another tale, one of three "Tales about Toads," recounts the miserable lot of a child who has the nerve to bark the kinds of orders normally issued only by adults. Impertinent behavior leads the child first to lose her bright red cheeks, then to waste away. "It was not long before the owl, the bird of ill omen, began to screech in the night, and the robin gathered twigs and leaves for a funeral wreath. Soon thereafter the child lay in her coffin."[2] While most readers expect to find examples of cruel behavior in the Grimms' collection and are not surprised by scenes of violence, few fail to register shock at the grisly conclusions to these two tales.[3]

In nineteenth-century British fairy tales, disobedient children only narrowly escape the fate of their counterparts in the Grimms' collection. The six-year-old boy in "My Own Self" has been bad, we are told, "since the day he was born." When he refuses to obey his mother, she first threatens to "give him the stick," then warns him that fairies will come to fetch him. The boy laughs, and the mother, in desperation, bursts into tears and goes to bed. When a fairy actually materializes and almost spirits the boy off, he is finally frightened into good behavior—the mother is surprised to find that her son is no longer "bad" or "naughty" but "willing to go to bed whenever she liked."

Tommy in "Mr. Miacca," a grisly little tale that was reissued as a story for children as recently as 1967, almost falls victim to a cannibalistic fiend. For failing to obey his mother, he is snatched up by Mr. Miacca, who thunders: "You're rather tough . . . but you're all I've got for sup-

4. Death awaits this beaming child, who sups daily with a toad
that brings pearls, stones, and gold as a reward. After urging the toad to eat
its bread, striking it with a spoon, and betraying its existence to an adult,
the child loses its color, grows thinner by the day, and dies.

per, and you'll not taste bad boiled." Tommy survives the ordeal, but he roams too far from home a second time. This time Mr. Miacca chops off a leg and "pops it in a pot." As it turns out, however, the leg in the pot is really the leg of the sofa beneath which the boy was hiding, but readers learn that fact only after they see Mr. Miacca stirring his brew. Tommy escapes and never goes around the corner again until he is "old enough to go alone."[4]

Disobedience is generally a function of curiosity and stubbornness in the behavioral calculus of most folktale collections, and both vices are repeatedly singled out for punishment in cautionary tales. Such tales, which enunciate a prohibition, stage its violation, and put on display the punishment of the violator, are surely the most openly violent and explicitly didactic of all children's stories. They aim to mold behavior by illustrating in elaborate detail the dire consequences of deviant conduct. Charles Perrault, who recognized early on that the stories told by his ancestors to children were no "mere trifles," gave us the classic formulation of the ethical code built into them: "Virtue is rewarded everywhere, and vice is always punished." The unambiguous message and iron logic of these tales were a joy to him—children are shown the advantages of being "honest, patient, prudent, hard-working and obedient," and at the same time they discover that without these virtues they will have nothing but trouble. Perrault's description of typical plots is telling: "Sometimes there are children who become great lords for having obeyed their fathers and mothers, or others who experience terrible misfortune for having been vicious and disobedient."[5] Many of the cautionary tales to which Perrault refers include a coda in which the hero is rescued, revived, or resurrected, but there are enough that kill off their child-heroes so matter-of-factly that it becomes hard not to raise an eyebrow in bewilderment.

We do not have to look long or far to find an important source of the link between death and disobedience. Proverbs offers an endless refrain not only on the excellence of the rod but also on the perils of disobedience. In one of the more colorful passages describing the consequences of failure to honor mothers and fathers, children are advised that "the eye that mocks a father and scorns to obey a mother will be picked out by the ravens of the valley and eaten by the vultures" (Prov. 30:17). This may appear a rather harsh punishment by today's standards, but it must have seemed perfectly appropriate to the many parents who purchased one of the most popular children's books ever published: Isaac Watts's

Divine and Moral Songs (1715). One of the songs in it, entitled "Obedience to Parents," could be included in the "awful-warning" category:

> Have you not heard what dreadful plagues
> Are threaten'd by the Lord,
> To him that breaks his father's law,
> Or mocks his mother's word?
>
> What heavy guilt upon him lies!
> How cursed is his name!
> The ravens shall pick out his eyes,
> And eagles eat the same.[6]

Mercifully, the vignette accompanying the song in one edition showed
a bearded Prometheus rather than a small child suffering the consequences of disobedience.

    The degree to which the popular imagination was intent on investing
the curiosity and stubbornness of disobedient children with evil connotations becomes evident from a look at the Grimms' story "Mary's
Child." That tale, a variant of "Bluebeard," recounts the trials of a young
girl who is whisked off to heaven by the Virgin Mary when her parents
can no longer provide for her. "Everything went well for the girl there:
she ate cake and drank sweet milk. Her clothes were made of gold, and
the little angels played with her."[7] When the girl turns fourteen, the
Virgin Mary tests her by entrusting her with a key to the thirteen doors
of heaven, of which she may open twelve. Needless to say, the desire to
find out what lies beyond the thirteenth door is overpowering: it keeps
"gnawing and pecking away at her" and gives her "no peace." In the
end, Mary's Child not only succumbs to curiosity and opens the door,
but also fails to acknowledge her sin. "You've disobeyed me," the Virgin
scolds, "and you've even lied. You're no longer worthy enough to stay
in heaven." The heroine's expulsion from paradise is described in elaborate detail:

> The maiden sank then into a deep sleep, and when she awoke, she
> was lying on earth in the middle of a wilderness. She wanted to cry
> out, but she could not utter a sound. She jumped up and wanted to
> run away, but wherever she turned, she encountered thick hedges of
> thorns and could not make her way through them. She was impris-
> oned in this desolate spot and had to make an old hollow tree her
> dwelling place. . . . Roots and wild berries were her only food. . . .

5. Angels try to restrain Mary's Child from peering behind a door to which the
Virgin has given her a key but forbidden her to use. Her curiosity gets
the better of her, and—though she has promised to be obedient—
she commits the "sin" of disobeying the Virgin's command.

Before long her clothes became tattered, and one piece after the other
fell off her body. . . . She spent year after year like this and felt the
sorrow and misery of the world.

Like Adam and Eve, Mary's Child gives in to temptation and is ex-
pelled from paradise. In an interesting twist, however, she is literally
hedged in and loses her clothing so that she is left isolated and vulner-
able. Her offense becomes tainted with all the disagreeable connotations of biblical transgression and original sin: after her fall from inno-

cence and grace, she survives only by the sweat of her brow. That a child's curiosity should be linked with the Fall and punished in so severe a manner may appear odd to us, but it happens all the time in children's fairy tales. The Russian Baba Yaga, for example, warns her young visitors that "if you know too much, you will soon grow old." Worse yet, she does not hesitate to eat the "overcurious."[8] Through its forced association with original sin, curiosity in children came to be charged with evil and thus was deemed worthy of the folkloric punishments designed to remedy it.

Belief in the innate sinfulness of children was an article of faith for many in earlier ages. "When *Adam* was deceived, / I was of life bereaved; / Of late (too) I perceived, I was in sin conceived," John Bunyan's *Book for Boys and Girls* (1686) cheerfully declares. Some theologians may have exempted infants from the charge of moral corruption, but many found, like Luther, that even the newborn comes into the world tainted with sin—hence the importance of baptism. Luther himself emphasized that a child's moral condition is subject to constant deterioration: the very young do not have serious vices, but they can grow up to become the victims of all manner of deadly temptations. Bunyan summed up the prevailing wisdom of his contemporaries in his poem "Upon the Disobedient Child":

> Children become, while little, our delights,
> When they grow bigger, they begin to fright's.
> Their sinful Nature prompts them to rebel,
> And to delight in Paths that lead to Hell.

The "sinful Nature" of Mary's Child manifests itself as disobedience, set in motion by curiosity and marked with all the signs of biblical rebellion and disgrace.[9]

"Mary's Child" encapsulates two lessons for children. One has to do with the perils of curiosity, the other with the evils of stubbornness. The second phase of the story shows us Mary's Child married to a king and mother of three children, each of whom is spirited off to heaven as punishment for their mother's stubborn insistence on her innocence. Only when about to be burned at the stake does Mary's Child break down, own up to her act of disobedience in heaven, and find forgiveness. Mary's Child may have grown up, but the Virgin treats her like a child whose will must be crushed. As the first pastor of the Pilgrim Fathers in Holland exhorted parents: "Surely there is in all children . . .

a stubbornness, and stoutness of mind arising from natural pride, which must in the first place be broken and beaten down."

Around the same time as Bunyan's book appeared, Calvin was advocating capital punishment for those who disobeyed parents, though New England appears to be one of the few places that actually carried out such penalties. Luther did not even have to decree the death penalty for rebellious children. In words that remind us of the Grimms' "Disobedient Child," who wastes away and loses favor with God because he refuses to do what his mother tells him, Luther declared that "those who fail to obey [parents] will die early and not live a long life." This was, of course, little more than a reformulation in negative terms of the third commandment which warns: "Honor your father and your mother, that your days may be long in the land which the Lord your God gives you." "Mary's Child" preaches a lesson that J. H. Plumb has described as being concerned with "the repression of Old Adam, the suppression of evil, or the breaking of the will." This religious, rather than social, morality held sway in Europe well into the eighteenth century and inscribed its stern values on stories told by adults to children.[10]

In much the same way that the Grimms lent authority to their condemnation of curiosity and stubbornness with biblical allusions and a Virgin whose threshold for disobedience is exceptionally low, Hans Christian Andersen delighted in the possibilities of describing divine revenge against mortal sin and wove biblical references into his story of childish pride and willfulness punished. "The Girl Who Trod on the Loaf" features a dreadful little girl who is "proud and vain," and who commits the worst of all fairy-tale sins—she tortures animals.[11] Inger delights in catching flies and pulling off their wings or sticking beetles on pins so that she can watch them writhe in agony. One day, Inger makes the mistake of flinging a loaf of bread on the ground so that she can cross a puddle without dirtying her shoes. But no sooner has she put her foot on the loaf than she sinks down into the ground and becomes a statue at the gates of hell. The narrator expands almost endlessly on her afflictions:

> Her clothes seemed to be smeared over with one great blotch of slime;
> a snake had got caught in her hair and was dangling down her neck,
> and from each fold in her dress a toad peeped out with a croak. . . .
> Then the flies came and crawled over her eyes, to and fro. She blinked
> her eyes, but the flies didn't fly away; they couldn't, because their

wings had been pulled off. . . . That was torment for her, and as for her hunger—well, at last she felt that her innards were eating themselves up, and she became quite empty inside, so appallingly empty.

Her mother's tears of grief fail to release poor Inger from her misery; they only burn the girl, making her torment all the more intense. And what does her mother say while weeping for her child? "Pride goes before a fall—that was your misfortune, Inger. How you have grieved your mother!" The master and mistress of the house where Inger had gone to work have similar smug thoughts about the dead child: "She had no respect for God's gifts, but trod them underfoot; the door of mercy will be hard for her to open." During her trials, Inger herself begins to feel some remorse. "They should have corrected me more often," she reflects, "cured me of my bad ways if I had any." She is released at last from her misery, but not until the horrors of her sojourn in hell have been itemized in excruciating detail.[12]

For all their positive connotations, curiosity and a strong will are traits that parents rarely tolerate well in their children. As the Grimms remind us in the tales they recorded, curiosity goes hand in hand with defiance and therefore often becomes the trait that parents find most irritating. That fact alone does much to account for the vast numbers of children's stories that have sprung up in various cultures about the hazards of curiosity. The very genre "cautionary tale," while often warning of quite legitimate dangers, usually really aims to deter children from being too inquisitive about the world they inhabit and deviating in any way from behavioral norms. Using intimidation, cautionary tales persuade children to obey the laws set down by parental authority, celebrating docility and conformity while discouraging curiosity and willfulness. The consequences of this "pedagogy of fear" were recognized early on. As one French versifier put it in an attempt to serve as an advocate for children:

> To speak out for the little child
> I feel that I must scold the nurse.
> For to keep him meek and mild
> She threatens with a monster curse,
> And happy to have calmed the strife
> Leaves him fearful all his life.
>
> He's haunted by the boogey-man;
> He's haunted by the werewolf's cry.

> The dragon's coming from his den
> To gulp him down. And by and by
> The frightened child is weak and cowed,
> Surrounded by a monster crowd. . . .[13]

Cautionary tales, according to these strophes, masquerade as educational tales but are in reality sadistic stories aimed at controlling behavior. Recognizing the advantages of a docile child, caregivers create a host of monsters that discourage children from engaging in daredevil behavior while also absorbing the blame for any prohibitions issued. The economy of the cautionary tale operates in such a way as to provide maximum advantage to its teller.

It may, to be sure, be true that children need monsters and other dreadful creatures of the imagination to conserve idealized images of their parents.[14] By creating menacing figures and mobilizing them in their play, children are said to express and "master" the terror they feel when a parent is hostile, even as they protect the parent from criticism. Yet no matter what our point of view, it is coercive sadism on the one hand and forbidding hostility on the other that produces many of the monsters that haunt children's imaginations. And in each case it is parental behavior that creates the "monster crowd."

Fairy-tale collectors often put the spotlight on the morals to their stories. Each tale in the *Pentamerone*, for example, ends with a lesson that is set off from the text and italicized: "To be courteous is ever best," "To those who do good, good always comes," "Who spits at heaven gets it back in his face." But the frame-tale tells us something quite different about the immediate impact of each narrative. What the listeners find satisfying about these stories is the way in which they reward virtue and punish vice: "Everyone showed great pleasure in hearing of the consolation of the poor Prince and the punishment inflicted on the wicked women."[15] Should a villain get off the hook, there is disappointment all around; in "The Cat Cinderella," the audience feels cheated because the punishments for the stepdaughters are "too light."[16] Fairy tale collectors justified the display of cruel punishments on both pedagogical and moral grounds. If the pedagogical grounds were often a mask for sadistic impulses, the moral grounds were usually little more than a pretext for gratifying the audience's need for chilling scenes of savage violence.

In a study of lullabies, Nicholas Tucker has concluded that some of the melodies sung to children must be "exercises in controlled hatred." Caretakers seeking to induce sleep may themselves be so desperate for

sleep that, rather than singing tender words, they resort in desperation
to threats. A British lullaby is representative:

> Baby, baby, naughty baby,
> Hush, you squalling thing, I say.
> Peace this moment, peace, or maybe
> Bonaparte will pass this way.
>
> Baby, baby, he's a giant,
> Tall and black as Rouen steeple,
> And he breakfasts, dines, rely on't,
> Every day on naughty people.
>
> Baby, baby, if he hears you,
> As he gallops past the house,
> Limb from limb at once he'll tear you,
> Just as pussy tears a mouse.
>
> And he'll beat you, beat you, beat you,
> And he'll beat you all to pap,
> And he'll eat you, eat you, eat you,
> Every morsel snap, snap, snap.[17]

Similar melodies have been used to lull French and Spanish babies to
sleep, with Wellington and Bismarck, or El Coco, the Bull, or the Moor-
ish Queen standing in for Bonaparte.

Isaac Watts's "Cradle Hymn" gives a slightly different twist to menacing lullabies. Here, the mother begins on a gentle note but works herself
into a rage as she contemplates how Christ was betrayed, then finally
calms herself with thoughts of Christ as savior to her child:

> Hush, my dear! Lie still, and slumber!
> Holy angels guard thy bed!
> Heavenly blessings, without number,
> Gently falling on thy head.
>
> . . . .
>
> How much better thou'rt attended
> Than the Son of God could be.
>
> . . . .
>
> Was there nothing but a manger
> Cursed sinners could afford,
> To receive the heavenly stranger?
> Did they thus affront the Lord?

Soft, my Child, I did not chide thee,
Though my Song might sound too hard:
'Tis thy {Mother}{Nurse} that sits beside thee,
And her Arms shall be thy Guard.

Yet, to read the shameful Story,
How the Jews abus'd their King,
How they serv'd the Lord of Glory,
Makes me angry while I sing.

6. The belligerent tone of this song seems at odds with the soothing effect
   we expect from lullabies, just as it stands in stark contrast to the soft
   pastels of the illustration. Our most popular lullaby ("Hush-a-bye,
   baby, on the tree top") reminds us, however, of the way in which
   caregivers sing about all manner of calamities to the children
   they are trying to put to sleep.

> Soft my child! I did not chide thee,
> Though my song might sound too hard:
> 'Tis thy mother sits beside thee,
> And her arm shall be thy guard.
>
> Yet to read the shameful story,
> How the Jews abused their King,
> How they served the Lord of Glory,
> Makes me angry while I sing.
>
> . . . .
>
> 'Twas to save thee, child, from dying,
> Save my dear from burning flame,
> Bitter groans and endless crying,
> That thy blest Redeemer came.[18]

The way in which the mother dwells on the soft life of her child (by comparison with that of the Christ child) and expands on the misery her child has been spared makes this lullaby more than peculiar.

Happily, there is little risk of inflicting psychic damage on infants with lullabies like these, for the (often) soothing melody (what the baby takes in) stands in sharp contrast to the hair-raising text. How older siblings or any other children within earshot react to the words is less easy to calculate, though one can only speculate on a range of responses from gleeful satisfaction to nervous anxiety. It is clear, however, that the cautionary narratives embedded in lullabies represent the case in which didacticism is least important (reaching degree zero when sung to infants) and the venting of adult resentment on children is most significant.

When it comes to cautionary tales for older children, the relationship between didacticism and retaliation would seem to shift in the direction of strengthening didacticism. Even *Struwwelpeter*, that nineteenth-century answer to permissive childrearing, appears to have some sound lessons to impart. "Nasty Frederick" is cruel to animals and ends up with a dog bite; "Fidgety Philipp" rocks back and forth at the dinner table and lands on the floor; "Hans Head-in-the-Clouds" never watches his step and plunges into icy waters. Other episodes take a different turn, and it becomes difficult not to wince at the sight of the blood that flows when "Conrad the Thumbsucker" gets his thumbs sliced off by a fleet-footed tailor wielding oversized shears, or to flinch as flames engulf Little Pauline after she lights matches.[19]

On the face of it, each of the episodes recounted in *Struwwelpeter* conveys a lesson worth transmitting to children, but here, as in many of the cautionary tales in the Grimms' collection, the weight given to the punishment (often fully half the text is devoted to its description) and the disproportionate relationship between the childish offense and the penalty for it make the episode disturbing. The balance between didacticism and retaliation does not really seem to have shifted much from what it was in lullabies. Cautionary tales seem equally intent on venting adult anger about childish willfulness and on controlling behavior rather than educating. But here the adult anger has a retaliatory effect whose full force can be felt by the child. Boys or girls hearing about Conrad the Thumbsucker will probably feel a need more acute than ever for their thumbs, though it is impossible to predict the exact impact of the verses. In fact, children may—like some adults—derive a

7. Conrad the Thumbsucker makes the mistake of persisting in a bad habit
and finds himself the victim of a zealous tailor.

certain degree of pleasure from the punishments enacted in cautionary
tales.

It is not hard to guess how young readers must have reacted when
the gluttonous Tom Swallowell is tricked into eating a custard pie
mixed with cow dung in *The Memoirs of a Peg-Top* (1781).[20] We also
know how much children relish the punishments of adult villains in
fairy tales. Anthony Storr offers a telling anecdote about a child who felt
frustrated when a fairy-tale figure was rescued from a horrible death:
"'But I *wanted* him to be thrown into the cask of pitch,' sobbed the
little girl, unable to tolerate the disappointment of finding that this exciting threat was not, after all, to be put into practice."[21]

A look at what has become possibly the most famous cautionary tale
of all times may help to clarify the origins, intentions, and impact of
these tales. "Little Red Riding Hood," or "Rotkäppchen" as the Grimms
tell it, contains the customary prohibition/violation pattern of cautionary tales. Red Riding Hood's mother hands her daughter cakes and wine
for grandmother and adds a warning: "When you're out in the woods,
be nice and good and don't stray from the path, otherwise you'll fall and
break the glass, and your grandmother will get nothing. And when you
enter her room, don't forget to say good morning, and don't go peeping

in all the corners."[22] The consequences of violating the mother's pro-hibitions, as we know, turn out to be quite different from what is predicted.

When Red Riding Hood strays from the path to gather flowers for her grandmother, she lets the wolf get a head start on her, giving him a chance to devour grandmother and to don her nightclothes before Red Riding Hood ever reaches the house. That the bottle of wine remains intact despite the mother's predictions subverts the authority of her pronouncements. And whether Red Riding Hood's deviating from the path and dallying among the flowers gives the wolf more of an edge than he already has also remains questionable. The Grimms, at least, seemed to think it did, for at the end of their story Red Riding Hood says to herself: "Never again in all my life will I stray from the path and enter the woods alone, when mother has forbidden it." There is, how-ever, no clear causal connection between the violation of the mother's prohibition and its punishment by the wolf—Little Red Riding Hood encounters the wolf "as soon as" she enters the forest. And once again, the punishment hardly suits the crime.

It may seem pedantic to demand logic from a genre that traffics in the supernatural, but even fairy tales have their ground rules, and those rules assure a degree of predictability in the plot. When a father orders all the spindles in his kingdom burned to protect his daughter from a curse, we know that Briar Rose will somehow find a spindle and prick her finger. When a king instructs his servant to keep his son from a portrait, you can be sure that the son will find a way to set eyes on the forbidden image. Prohibitions lead to violations, and the consequences of these violations are generally spelled out once the prohibition has been stated. That Red Riding Hood's mother wrongly forecasts the con-sequences of her daughter's transgression suggests that something is awry in this tale. The finger of suspicion naturally points first in the direction of the Grimms. Did the brothers inject messages into this tale ("Go along properly . . . don't stray from the path . . . don't forget to say good morning . . . don't go poking in all the corners") that did not square with the story's folkloric facts?

The first place to look for an answer is in the Grimms' source for the tale. Perrault's "Petit Chaperon Rouge," despite its catastrophic ending, is the acknowledged literary antecedent of the Grimms' text. In it, the mother issues no prohibitions at all, but it becomes clear that the little girl makes the fatal error first of giving the wolf directions to grand-

mother's house, and then of amusing herself by gathering nuts, chasing
butterflies, and making nosegays while the wolf zooms off, taking a
shortcut to the house. Just to ensure that no one missed the message,
Perrault added a moral of his own: "From this story one learns that
children, / Especially young lasses, / Pretty, courteous and well-bred, /
Do very wrong to listen to strangers, / And it is not an unheard-of
thing / If the Wolf is thereby provided with his dinner."[23] This heavy-
handed didactic touch concerning the errors of Little Red Riding
Hood's ways is not to be found in the folkloric counterparts to "Le Petit
Chaperon Rouge" and "Rotkäppchen." Peasant versions of the tale simply pit a naive innocent against a predatory beast, illustrating the consequences (often both cruel and ribald in their details) of an encounter
between the two.

One of the fullest available texts faithful to oral, peasant versions of
"Little Red Riding Hood" was recorded in France at the end of the nineteenth century.[24] It too tells of a girl's trip to grandmother's house and
of her encounter with a wolf, but there the resemblance to Perrault's
"Petit Chaperon Rouge" and to the Grimms' "Rotkäppchen" ends. "The
Story of Grandmother" dispenses with the advice and warnings issued
to the heroine in its more literary counterparts—a mother simply sends
her daughter to granny with a loaf of hot bread and a bottle of milk.
Since there are no prohibitions to violate and no instructions to ignore, the heroine cannot be perceived as naughty or disobedient. Indeed, by outsmarting the wolf-aggressor, she escapes the role of hapless
victim and joins the class of clever innocents. Folk versions of "Little
Red Riding Hood" are less concerned with presenting lessons than with
entertaining an audience by rehearsing a sequence of racy episodes and
sensational events. Red Riding Hood begins by unwittingly eating the
flesh and blood of her grandmother; she then performs a striptease for
the wolf, gets into bed with him, and engages in a dialogue that leads
up to a terrifying threat; in the end she escapes by pleading with the
wolf for a chance to go outdoors and relieve herself.

For centuries, adult audiences depended on the telling of tales such
as "The Story of Grandmother" to shorten the hours devoted to repeti-
tive household chores or harvesting tasks. Is it any wonder that they
demanded fast-paced adventure stories filled with bawdy episodes, violent scenes, and scatalogical humor? Neither Perrault nor the Brothers
Grimm shows us the protagonist of "Little Red Riding Hood" relieving
herself outdoors or stripping before the wolf, but each works hard to

build tension in the scene that unfolds in the bedroom right before the wolf pounces on his unwary victim. More importantly, both Perrault and the Brothers Grimm saw to it that the victim was not without blame. Little Red Riding Hood may not deserve her fate, but she is responsible for it nonetheless. By speaking to strangers (as Perrault has it) or by disobeying her mother and straying from the path (as the Grimms have it), Red Riding Hood courts her own downfall.

For every brutal act that befalls the hero of a folktale, it is easy enough to establish a cause and to implicate the hero in it. A chain of events that might once have been linked in a totally arbitrary manner to create burlesque effects can easily be restructured to produce a "morally edifying" tale. This was certainly the case with "Little Red Riding Hood." Readers of Perrault, as of the Grimms, speak with virtually one voice when it comes to judging the tale's heroine. Jack Zipes finds that Perrault's story is one of "discipline and punishment"—Red Riding Hood is presented as "pretty, spoiled, gullible, and helpless" and is seen to collaborate in her own rape. According to Bruno Bettelheim, the Grimms' Red Riding Hood has reverted to the "pleasure-seeking oedipal child." The wolf's swallowing of the girl is nothing more than "the merited punishment for her arranging things so that the wolf can do away with a mother figure."[25] These readings are in no way idiosyncratic—both are based on textual indicators that consistently construct a sybaritic heroine rather than a rapacious wolf.

Red Riding Hood fared even worse in later adaptations of her story. Nineteenth-century literary retellings of the tale consistently stressed the importance of restraining natural instincts and adhering to social norms set by adults. An anonymous verse melodrama from the end of the century is characteristic in the way that it underscores the conflict between self-indulgent idleness and compliant obedience to parental law:

> But the pretty flowers that in the wood
> Bloomed gay and bright on either hand,
> So lured the maiden to gaze and pluck
> That she quite forgot the strict command.

Red Riding Hood fails to heed her mother's instructions—instead of heading directly for grandmother's house, she dallies in the woods, thereby becoming responsible for her grandmother's death and narrowly escaping the wolf's clutches:

> To her mother's words, ever after this,
> Red Riding Hood gave better heed;
> For she saw the dreadful end to which
> A disobedient act may lead.

Or, as Red Riding Hood's father puts it in a prose version of the tale by Sabine Baring-Gould,

> A little maid,
> Must be afraid
> To do other than her mother told her.

This was the lesson that one nineteenth-century Red Riding Hood after another learned.[26]

The shift from violence in the service of slapstick to violence in the service of the didactic added a moral backbone to folktales, but it rarely curbed their uninhibited display of cruelty. The Grimms' Little Red Riding Hood may be rescued (when a hunter slits open the wolf's belly!), but not before we are treated to two scenes in which both girl and grandmother are attacked and devoured—those are, significantly, the scenes to which illustrators habitually call attention.[27] In their best form, the folktales that entered the sphere of children's literary culture preserved the burlesque humor of the original tales even as they taught lessons; in their worst, they promoted a pedagogy of fear and terror.

Curiosity and disobedience came to be highlighted and charged with negative meanings only relatively recently in the history of folktales—specifically, with their transformation into children's literature. Nine-teenth-century rewriters of "Frau Trude," for example, had no trouble turning the protagonist of the story into a strong-willed, impudent girl who deserves to come to a terrible end. But a survey of versions closer to oral sources and therefore probably of less recent vintage reveals that disobedience never really figured prominently in the story.[28] These versions give us daredevils who court danger by entering households that are both forbidden and forbidding. Never once do we find in them condescending judgments about the weak or evil character of their heroines. Many variants of "The Household of the Witch" (the tale type in the comprehensive Aarne/Thompson classification system for folktales to which "Frau Trude" belongs) do not even feature a young girl as protagonist.[29] They show us a woman visiting her sister, a mother paying respects to her child's godmother, or a spinner knocking on a neighbor's door to borrow embers for a fire. Each time the woman visited turns out to be allied with demonic powers. One class of tales even veers off from the demonic into the comic when it describes a terrified Frau Leberwurst (Mrs. Liversausage) hightailing it out of the house of Frau Blutwurst (Mrs. Bloodsausage), who is armed with a long knife as she chants: "If I had you, / How I'd like to / Take a knife and- / Do you get my meaning?"[30]

"The Household of the Witch" was probably originally designed to send chills down the spines of its listeners. Its lavish description of the horrors housed in the witch's abode—one tale shows us piles of human heads, fingers, feet, torsos, and hair—along with its attention to the protagonist's growing awareness of the menace lurking there, mark it as a tale of terror. Once we enter the world of the tale and witness its events from the protagonist's point of view—and a skillful raconteur can arrange it so that we identify with the demon's victim—the tale becomes imbued with pathos. However, when the primary actors are themselves stick figures (as is the case with Frau Leberwurst and Frau Blutwurst), melodrama slides into slapstick. We may still have a horror story, but it is no longer horrifying.

That variants of "The Household of the Witch" moved out of the melodramatic and comic modes to take a turn in the direction of moral edification is unfortunate, for they thereby instituted a death penalty for such character traits as curiosity and audacity. Once "The Household of the Witch" ceased to function as a source of entertainment for adults, it began to deteriorate into a frightening story about the way in which the deviant behavior of children is punished with death.

"The Household of the Witch" is only one of a host of tales that lost more than they gained while making the transition from adult oral entertainment to literary fare for children. The Italian "Caterinella" also offers a striking example of the way in which a folktale once full of earthy humor could be converted into a heavy-handed text with a pedagogical agenda. In the process, the surreal violence of the original was converted into a frightening punishment for a relatively minor transgression. "Caterinella" tells of a girl sent by her mother to borrow a pan from a neighbor. The neighbor turns out to be a witch, ogre, or wolf—often masquerading as an aunt or uncle. Caterinella gets what she needs, but the sinister lender of each tale variant makes her promise to return the pan with a generous portion of whatever was prepared in it.

On her way back with the pan, the girl gets hungry and eats up the entire offering. She tries to outwit Uncle Wolf or his like by replacing the treat with animal excrement (cows, horses, and donkeys provide the substitute for the cake). When liquids are involved, urine usually does the job. The witches, ogres, and wolves all fall for the trick at first, but once they see through it, they rush to the heroine's home, track her down in her bed, and devour her. Most versions of the tale end with Caterinella's slaying; only a small number stage the heroine's rescue in scenes reminiscent of (and probably influenced by) the Grimms' "Little Red Riding Hood."

It is interesting to observe the ease with which folklorists classify this story as a cautionary tale. Caterinella is invariably described as "disobedient," although she displays nothing more than the healthy appetite of a perfectly normal child. Like most children, she starts off with one small bite, continues with larger portions, then finds herself obliged to destroy the evidence by eating the entire cake in the pan or drinking the entire bottle of wine. She then covers up her deed in a way so transparent that it can only lead to discovery. One commentator observes that "for educational reasons, it is important for Caterinella to be punished for her greed and deceit."[31] By turning gluttony into greed, and a childish attempt at a cover-up into full-blown deceit, this critic tries to make an example of the tale's heroine. But is it really such a bad thing to outwit a creature who makes a habit of devouring human beings? Moralizing readings of "Caterinella" miss the point of the story even as they fail to appreciate its scatalogical humor or, for that matter, any of the tale's comic possibilities. Much of the humor may seem crude to our ears, but it surely could have made for high entertainment among rural audiences, for whom animal dung was a powerful part of everyday life.

Caterinella's only real mistake is that she gets caught. But even the conclusion to her story is not necessarily tragic or frightening. In the proper hands, the tale can easily end by provoking gales of laughter, for the greed of the ogre, a grotesquely magnified and distorted form of gluttonous urges, can be acted out in a fashion that promotes a cathartic rather than a savagely frightening effect. The teller of a tale can indulge in the same kind of playful cavorting that goes on between children when they mock their own fears about being devoured by playing games in which ogres and witches are taunted.[32] The final episode of

"Caterinella" touches on one of our deepest fears (the idea of being devoured can be a source of anxiety for adults and children alike), but
that episode can be told in a way that works through those fears by
mobilizing an animated playfulness rather than intensifying them with
a tone of moral earnestness. Humor, along with verbal markers emphasizing the status of the tales as fantasy and not reality, prevents "Caterinella" (a tale that has flourished in oral form) from turning into a horror story. This is patently not the case with latter-day versions of "The
Household of the Witch"—these "children's stories" remain dead
serious in the punishment of protagonists whose curiosity, audacity,
gluttony, and willfulness make them easy targets of identification for
virtually every child.

If the basic narrative unit of the cautionary tale consists of a prohibition and its violation, the fundamental move of the exemplary story
involves a command and its fulfillment. In exemplary stories, dutiful
obedience to the point of subservience and servitude is enshrined as the
highest value. In this context, it is important to bear in mind that the
male protagonists of European classic fairy tales possess two virtues that
set them apart from others: humility and compassion. Humility makes
for a meek docility that earns rewards from adults; compassion is generally lavished on animals who repay kindness with assistance in carrying
out tasks. For fairy-tale heroines, by contrast, the combination of a ser-
vile attitude and hard work pays off by attracting a groom who offers
social promotion through marriage.[33] The Grimms' Allerleirauh, for example, demonstrates extraordinary self-effacing fortitude by agreeing to
do "all the nasty work," which includes hauling wood and water, tending the fires, plucking fowl, cleaning vegetables, and sweeping the
ashes.

Exemplary stories, like cautionary tales, combine didacticism with
melodrama to create powerful dramatic tableaus. The spectacles of suffering we witness in cautionary tales are often excessively cruel and unusual, but they are usually embedded in a brutal context where the lex
talionis prevails. Far more disconcerting than the severe punishments
visited on transgressors of explicit or implicit interdictions are the
penalties imposed on those who adhere to the spirit and letter of what
one would imagine to be "good behavior." Obedient paragons of virtue
often suffer more than the most hardened young criminals. We have
seen that the numbers of arrogant, disobedient, and vain children

make for a wealth of tales in which both the protagonists and the lis-
teners/readers of the tale are taught lessons even as they are treated to
pungent scenes of crimes and punishments. There are not many meek,
modest, and dutiful counterparts to these ill-bred creatures, but the
ones that do make an appearance in fairy-tale volumes inevitably fare
badly, at least for the major part of the tales that recount their trials and
tribulations.

The Grimms' "Star Coins" offers a revealing example of the way in
which exemplary stories celebrate suffering. The tale, which combines
hagiography and pedagogy in a remarkable manner, recounts the fate of
an orphaned girl who has nothing more than a crust of bread and the
clothes on her back, but who is so "good" and so "pious" that the bread
goes to a hungry man and every last item in her meager wardrobe is
bequeathed to various children shivering from the cold. Just at the
point when this paragon of compassion is bereft of all material possessions, coins shower down on her and she finds herself clothed in a
dress of the finest linen: "She collected the coins and stayed rich for the
rest of her life."[34] Virtue is rewarded with cold, hard cash. The story's
glorification of selflessness may seem extreme, but that does not appear
to have affected its popularity. "The Star Coins" was one of fifty tales
that appeared between the covers of the Grimms' *Kleine Ausgabe*, an
abridged edition of the tales that enjoyed tremendous popular success
over the years.[35] Its position as the final tale in that anthology suggests
that the Grimms had made a point of putting it in an especially prominent place, and indeed the story remains among the best known in the
collection, having found many admirers among both children and
adults. It is no accident that countless editions of the *Nursery and
Household Tales* boast a frontispiece showing this girl reaping heavenly
rewards for her selflessness and humility.[36] For the duration of her
story, this orphan girl's virtues do nothing but promote her misery and
deprivation. Manna may rain down from heaven and the girl may live
prosperously ever after, but at what price? The story displays her sufferings so ostentatiously and at such length that they remain with us much
longer than the single concluding sentence that documents a rise in
the heroine's fortunes.

Misery and suffering are nowhere more brilliantly apotheosized than
in the tales of Hans Christian Andersen. Andersen's genius for hum-
bling the proud and displaying the sufferings of the humble is unparal-

8. The heroine of "The Star Coins" is rewarded for her compassion
with coins that fall from heaven in the form of stars.

leled. His "Little Match Girl" numbers among the most extreme examples of tales that idealize wretchedness and deprivation as a state that
leads to genuine happiness: the match girl dies out in the cold "with a
smile on her lips." Andersen's tale may dispense with the supernatural
intervention we see in "The Star Coins" (here the stars fail to turn into

coins), but adds a dimension of such passionate sentimentality that many readers of the story will rub their eyes in disbelief. "It was so dreadfully cold!" the tale begins.[37] On New Year's Eve, just on the evening when there is "a lovely smell of roast goose" everywhere, a poor little girl "with bare head and naked feet" wanders the streets. Andersen mobilizes all his descriptive resources to emphasize the hopelessness of the girl's plight. "The poor little thing" is "hungry and frozen." She dares not return home, where the wind whistles through the cracks in the walls, for her father will beat her when he finds her matches unsold. There is no stopping Andersen, who punctuates his narrative packed with grim observations about the girl's life (Granny, the only person who ever spoke a kind word to the girl, is dead) with increasingly urgent pronouncements about the dropping temperature. The girl's welcome into heaven by her dear old granny may be painted in brilliant visionary hues, but the stark image of "a dead little body," a girl "dead, frozen to death," haunts the final paragraph of the tale.[38]

When Andersen was approaching age seventy, his admirers planned to erect a statue in his honor. The sculptor August Saabye brought the author preliminary sketches that showed him seated in a chair reading to a crowd of eager children. Here is Andersen's reaction:

My blood was boiling, and I spoke clearly and unambiguously, saying: "None of the sculptors knew me, nothing in their attempts indicated that they had seen or realized the characteristic thing about me,—that I could never read aloud if anyone was sitting behind me or leaning towards me, and even less if I had children sitting on my lap or on my back, or young Copenhagen boys leaning up against me, and that it was only a manner of speaking when I was referred to as 'the children's writer.'"[39]

What makes this passage remarkable is not the strength of feeling about the sculptor's mistake but the undisguised pedophobia expressed in it. The anecdote goes farther than almost any other biographical detail of Andersen's life in illustrating why the Danish writer was quite correct in stating that his books were really not for children.

"The Steadfast Tin Soldier" is also expansive in its description of suffering. Here again, Andersen creates an exemplary tale that details the protagonist's misery and builds up to a stunningly morbid death scene. Missing a leg but "steadfast" in his posture, the tin soldier makes a virtue of silent suffering. The little match girl's endurance of cold weather is paralleled by the soldier's stoic tolerance of humiliating assaults. Street urchins use his body to make a boat, which they send down the gutter; a water rat harasses him with requests to see his passport; a fish swallows him; and finally, after a miraculous rebirth from the fish's belly, the soldier is casually tossed into a fire: "He felt himself melting, but he still stood steadfast with his rifle on his shoulder."[40]

It is not only in cautionary tales and exemplary stories that children suffer cruel and unusual punishments or die slow, painful deaths. Events in the ten "Legends for Children" appended to the Grimms' *Nursery and Household Tales* are shocking in their brutality. In one, a girl is stung to death by snakes and lizards. In another, five children starve to death along with their mother. A third recounts the fate of twelve boys who, one by one, die of starvation. In a fourth, a woman dies while reflecting on the loss of her two young sons, her husband, and every one of her friends and relatives. "The Rosebud" charts the simultaneous opening of a flower and death of a child. That these tales were targeted specifically for children seems astonishing until we reflect on the social realities of the age in which they were told. In the premodern era, death stood at the center of life. As Lawrence Stone reminds us, it was a "normal occurrence in persons of all ages, and was not something that happened mainly to the old."[41] As late as 1900, when Freud published *The Interpretation of Dreams*, he noted that half of the human race fails to survive the childhood years.[42] That so many of the ten legends portray death as a release and as the path to a better life suggests that adults living in earlier centuries felt that children needed such stories to help them cope with some of the brutal facts of their everyday lives.

Those living in the premodern era probably also had a higher tolerance for descriptions of brutal behavior and violent deaths owing to the hardships to which they were exposed on a daily basis. These were times of famine and plague. Infanticide was regularly used as a method of "population control"; abandonment of children was not at all uncommon for reasons ranging from callous self-interest to an altruistic desire to better a child's chances for survival.[43] Public displays of corporal punishment and physical abuse were not uncommon. That children were routinely required—not just encouraged—to attend public executions is a telling commentary on seventeenth- and eighteenth-century modes of childrearing. One of the most prominent experts on parenting in late eighteenth-century Germany wrote eloquently (and probably convincingly) about "the pedagogical value of executions." "Despite the feelings of compassion and the unpleasant sensations that may be aroused by the sight of the execution of this criminal," Christian Felix Weisse wrote to his children, "I hope, indeed I insist, no matter what effort it may cost you, that you be present." Because these executions gave an example of the price of criminal behavior, it was all the more important that children attend them. As a postscript, Weisse noted that his children followed his instructions and "forced themselves" to witness the execution. "They did not regret it, for afterwards the event became the occasion for many edifying discussions among us and our friends."[44] Hans Christian Andersen, in his autobiography, tells about an execution that was to haunt him for years after he witnessed it. A farmer's wife, daughter, and man-servant were to be executed for their roles in conspiring to murder the farmer. "The day was like a holiday," Andersen recalled. "The Rector dismissed the upper class from school, and we were to go and see the execution, for it would be a good thing for us to be acquainted with it, he said."[45]

Earlier ages had few reservations about displaying the body in pain or in death—as the victim of nature or as the casualty of social justice. Decaying corpses, decapitated torsos, mutilated limbs, diseased parts, faces disfigured by illness—children were rarely spared the sight of physical suffering or of the body in a state of decomposition. The *History of the Fairchild Family*, the first volume of which was published in 1818, forcefully reminds us how some parents even went out of their way to expose children to the biological aspect of death. When Mr. and Mrs. Fairchild take their children to view the corpse of the "old gardener" John Roberts, they see this event as a real opportunity for religious instruction and moral enlightenment. The children find the assault on their olfactory and visual senses almost more than they can bear:

> When they came to the door, they perceived a kind of disagreeable smell, such as they never had smelt before: this was the smell of the corpse, which, having been dead now nearly two days, had begun to corrupt; and as the children went higher up the stairs, they perceived this smell more disagreeably. . . . The face of the corpse was quite yellow, there was no colour in the lips, the nose looked sharp and long, and the eyes were closed, and sunk under the brow. . . . The whole appearance of the body was more ghastly and horrible than the children expected.[46]

[39]

The CHILD.

Man that is born of a Woman, is of few Days, and
full of Trouble. He cometh forth like a Flower,
and is cut down: He fleeth also as a Shadow, and
continueth not.

JOB xiv. 1.

Man, who conceiv'd in the dark Womb,
    Into the World is brought,
Is born to Times with Mifery,
    And various Evil fraught.

And as the Flow'r foon fades and dies,
    However fair it be,
So finks he alfo to the Grave,
    And like a Shade does flee.
                    E 2

9. Vulnerability to disease and famine made death a central fact of life
    for children living in an earlier age. Ghoulish reminders of the way
    in which death strikes the young were not at all uncommon.

Mr. Fairchild seizes the chance to launch into a sermon on "the taint and corruption of the flesh," "the exceeding sinfulness of sin, and its horrible nature," and on the way in which the sinful body must dissolve and "fall to dust in the grave." To all of this the bereaved widow responds by exclaiming: "Oh, sir! It comforts me to hear you talk."

The Fairchilds' attempt to use death as the occasion for a lesson has an artificial quality to it, in part because the parents go so far out of their way to inflict the corpse on their children and to frighten them into an avoidance of sin. But those who lived under different circumstances in an earlier age were repeatedly exposed to the kinds of horrors that the Fairchilds sought out, but that we make a point of avoiding. These horrors of everyday life, particularly in times marked by war, famine, or disease, are faithfully reflected in folktale collections the world over, where they become the stuff of melodrama, black humor, or tragicomedy. It is only in relatively recent times, in certain cultures, that harshly brutal scenes have retreated from center stage to become a less visible part of the drama of daily life. Once the violent events in folktales ceased to function as mirrors (however distorted) of reality, they often began to be taken figuratively as events with a deep psychological resonance. A girl going to grandmother's house, for example, was no longer the potential prey of wild beasts but became the likely, and deserving, target of male seduction.

With its need to find a motive for everything, the Age of Reason hastened the process of identifying psychological causes for brutal or tragic effects. It is no accident that fairy tales underwent a profound metamorphosis in the eighteenth and nineteenth centuries. That era marked the rise of the cautionary tale as we know it today. Everything became motivated: A child devoured by a wolf was guilty of self-indulgence, idleness, and disobedience. A girl punished for opening a door was seen as suffering from excessive curiosity. Another girl, turned by a witch into firewood, is censured for disobedience and audacity. Representations of what had previously functioned in many cases as the random, senseless violence of a world in which human beings were hostage to powers beyond their control were mobilized to serve the purpose of moral education.

Even as the cautionary tale indulges in a gruesome spectacle of physical pain, the exemplary story mounts long, drawn-out scenes of both mental and physical suffering. But its protagonists wear their misery as if it were a badge of merit—which indeed it is. The pitiful match girl's reward may be deferred, but she wins it in the end. Other patient sufferers also reap their rewards only in heaven. As the Grimms put it in the title to one of their "Legends for Children": "Poverty and Humility Lead to Heaven"—even to sainthood in some cases. Twelve brothers who starve to death one after another are, to cite just one example, reincarnated three hundred years later as Christ's apostles. These tales may have had some value as a consolation for the death of siblings and friends, but many also openly advocate self-abnegation as the path to happiness. "Put on my tattered clothes," one old man tells a king's son. "Wander about the world for seven years, and learn all about its misery. Do not take any money, but when you're hungry, ask for a piece of bread from kindhearted people. This is how you'll find the way to heaven."[47]

Both cautionary tales and exemplary stories evolved in directions that are less than salutary. When the lessons preached in them are combined in reward/punishment tales, they have a powerful impact—one that will be explored in the next chapter. As soon as the collectors of fairy tales looked to children's literature as a model and assimilated from it the didactic mode, the stories made a bold move back to their original function as adult entertainment—but this time a grimly solemn version of it that could only be satisfying to those intent on seeing the child as the target of lessons. Hans Christian Andersen's description of the genesis of his fairy tales is revealing. Often he relied on stories he had heard in his childhood to craft these tales, but the best stories, in his view, emerged in the following fashion: "I dip into my own bosom, find an idea for the older people and tell it to children, but remembering that father and mother are listening!"[48]

Some adults may profit from exemplary stories, and they may even get some perverse satisfaction from cautionary tales, but such narratives are not really intended for children's ears. Is it any wonder that Lucy Sprague Mitchell rejected such stories not merely for their violence, but for other reasons as well? Tales that try to teach children lessons cannot but misfire. "We are utilitarian, we are executive," Mitchell complained of her generation. "We are didactic, we are earth-tied, we are hopelessly adult!"[49]

· CHAPTER III ·

Just Desserts:
Reward-and-Punishment Tales

*Since our thoughts and endeavors are permeated with evil from
childhood onward, and since the human sins and errors that deserve
punishment are manifold and varied, a chapter on punishments would
have to take up a great deal of space. When it comes to rewards and
recognition, we can be brief. For the true, the good, and the excellent
are uncomplicated; and for that reason rewards, recognition,
and praise can be handed out in plain and simple ways.*

A. Matthias, *Raising our Son Benjamin*

READING about childrearing practices in earlier centuries reminds us just how important it was to secure a strong causal link between corporal punishment and the salvation of a child's soul. Mr. and Mrs. Fairchild provide the following gloss on a story about a child who goes up in flames because she has disobeyed her parents by carrying lighted candles about the house:

> "Had this poor child been brought up in the fear of God, she might now be living, a blessing to her parents and the delight of their eyes. 'Withhold not correction from the child! for if thou beatest him with the rod, he shall not die; thou shalt beat him with the rod, and shall deliver his soul from hell.'"

Mrs. Fairchild reminds her children of just how lucky they are to have parents who punish them in the here and now and thereby save them not only from a premature death but also from damnation in the hereafter. When we read the following prayer, recommended not only for the Fairchild children but also for young readers of their story, it becomes evident that all the talk of piety and salvation is in fact geared toward producing children who will, above all, obey their parents:

> O Almighty Father! thou who didst command all children to honour their parents . . . give me a heart to keep this law. I know that I ought to do all that my father and mother and masters bid me to do. . . . Sometimes I rise up in open rebellion against my parents; and sometimes I try to disobey them slyly, when I think that they do not see me: forgetting that thine eye, O Lord God, is always upon me. . . . O holy Father! I am sorry for my disobedience. I know that disobedient children, unless they repent, always come to an ill end; there is no blessing on such as do not honour their parents. . . . Teach me to be obedient to my parents, and to honour and respect them; that I may be blessed in this present life, and may . . . be received into everlasting glory in the world to come.[1]

Johann Georg Sulzer, one of the most respected and "enlightened" authorities on childrearing in eighteenth-century Germany, was considered a real moderate when it came to punishing children. Yet reading his "Essay on Rearing and Educating Children" (1748) suggests that he was anything but tolerant when it came to unruliness or intractability. "Happy are the parents," he declares, "who scold their children in earnest and use the rod to crush stubbornness, for they will have obedient, compliant, and well-behaved children, to whom a good education can be given."[2] It is hard not to flinch in disbelief when we read in the same paragraph that all this scolding and whipping must take place before the child reaches the end of its first year so that parents can get on with the more important matter of teaching children to obey. "Obedience is so important," Sulzer insists in a stunning tautology, "for a child's entire education is nothing more than the cultivation of obedience." Inculcating obedience is not an easy task; however, fortunately for parents, there is a great advantage to making children obedient early on (preferably during the first two years of their lives), for in those years "one can use force and compulsion." As time goes by, children forget about the severe treatment: "If you can break a child's will, it soon never even remembers that it ever had a will in the first place, and the harsh treatment that you had to use is therefore of no serious consequence."[3] Stubbornness and disobedience, Sulzer never tires of declaring, are flaws that must be eradicated before they have a chance to take root and "corrupt" a child.

Reading through eighteenth- and nineteenth-century childrearing manuals and children's stories, one cannot but be astonished by the emphasis on blunting the will of stubborn children and punishing disobedient ones.[4] Brutal corporal punishments and threats of eternal damnation seem to have stretched the limits of the parental and pedagogical imagination in those times. It is not so much the need to punish as the lack of self-consciousness about the need that is astonishing—the bible, with its many exhortations not to spare the rod is frantically cited in an effort to justify the most abominable treatment of children. What seems to drive these teachers and preachers of bodily punishment is less a real concern for the welfare of the child than a hardened pedophobia that makes them deeply resent the child as a representative and reminder of everything that is unruly, untamed, and uncivilized.

Just as childrearing manuals spend page upon page expanding on the degree and duration of punishments and on what occasions they should be applied—even as they virtually pass over the subject of rewards—so most reward-and-punishment folktales show extraordinary inventiveness when it comes to punishing villains, yet are terse and to the point when rewarding heroes and heroines. What is a shower of gold coins compared to a shower of pitch? Who can help but be more fascinated by a girl who expels a toad or piece of animal dung with every word she utters than by a girl from whose mouth gems and flowers drop? How can the description of a forehead with a donkey's hoof or testicle attached to it compete with the description of a smooth one? Who wants to marvel at gems when there is a chance to snicker about a person who breaks wind at just the wrong moments? And how can a happy return home rival the depiction of a decapitation?

"The Kind and Unkind Girls" (AT 480) is probably the most familiar of all reward-and-punishment tales.[5] An Italian version of the tale gives us its main contours. A woman has two daughters: one her own, the other a stepdaughter. The stepdaughter enters the woods in search of chicory and finds a cauliflower, which, once uprooted, leaves a hole the size of a well. The girl descends to find a house full of cats and is put to work sweeping, washing, drawing water, and putting bread into an oven. For her efforts and her modest choices when offered rewards, she is given silk gowns and satin slippers. Before leaving, she puts her fingers through designated holes and finds them adorned with ornate rings. When the girl returns home and the stepmother sees her finery, she sends her own hopelessly lazy daughter on the same errand. Here is her reward:

> The girl went out, thrust her fingers into the holes, and countless worms wrapped around them. The harder she tried to free her fingers, the tighter the worms gripped them. She looked up, and a blood sausage fell on her face and hung over her mouth, and she had to nibble it constantly so it would get no longer. When she arrived home in that attire, uglier than a witch, her mother was so angry she died. And from eating blood sausage day in, day out, the girl died too.[6]

If we move from Italy to Germany, we find that the story of the kind and unkind girls moves in the same key. The Grimms' "Mother Holle" tells of a widow who has a dutiful and beautiful stepdaughter and an ugly, lazy biological daughter. In addition to doing "all the housework," the stepdaughter also has to spin until her fingers bleed. One day, she leans over into a well to rinse her bloodied reel and lets it fall into the water. Prodded by her stepmother to jump in after it, she descends into the well and awakens in a beautiful meadow. There she must carry out one household chore after another. An apple tree full of ripe fruit asks to be shaken, and the heroine not only shakes the tree, but gathers up the apples and puts them in a pile. Finally, the girl arrives at a small cottage, where an old woman tells her: "Stay with me, and if you do all the housework properly, everything will turn out well for you." In the end, the heroine is showered with gold as a reward for her industrious domesticity; her lazy counterpart gets a bath of pitch that sticks to her for the rest of her life.[7]

A British version of the tale is also driven as much by the opposition between hard-working/lazy and dutiful/disobedient as by the contrast kind/unkind. Here one girl's unloading of an oven, milking of a cow, and shaking of a tree pay off, for the oven, cow, and tree all help her out when she flees the house of a witch, taking with her a sack of money. Her sister, in too much of a hurry to acquire the rest of the witch's wealth to do any work, is chased away and returns home empty-handed.[8] In a Russian tale, the kindness of the heroine secures the assistance of animals, who discharge the tasks assigned by the bony legged Baba Yaga. The heroine returns home in triumph and inspires her stepsister to serve Baba Yaga. But this selfish girl never accomplishes the tasks set forth, for instead of sharing her food with animals, she scolds

10. The punishment of the lazy girl becomes the tale's highlight.
Note the pleasure registered on the faces of the animals and of Mother Holle.

them and hits them with a rolling pin. Baba Yaga is enraged by the girl's failure to do the chores: she breaks her into pieces and sends the bones home in a basket.[9]

Like many other versions of "The Kind and Unkind Girls," "Baba Yaga" probably served as a cautionary tale for girls, who were often sent away from home at an early age to go into service at other households. Like Baba Yaga and her folkloric cousins, the mistress of a household was a fearsome, threatening presence, yet also the one person empowered to reward a girl, if not as generously as Mother Holle or Baba Yaga. The lesson about the rewards to be reaped from hard work, humility, modesty, and kindness while in the service of an all-powerful female figure was surely pertinent, if not always valid, for the many girls whose household apprenticeships formed the basis for their livelihoods.

Much as the tale variants described thus far all emphasize the redemptive power of hard work, there are many versions of the story that celebrate a good character. When the heroine of Perrault's "The Fairies" gives a drink of water to a fairy masquerading as a thirsty old woman, the fairy tells her: "You are so pretty and so polite that I am determined to bestow a gift upon you." Each time the girl speaks, a flower or precious stone falls from her mouth. Her sister, "ill-mannered," "disagreeable," and "arrogant," hopes to win the same prize, but for her "lack of courtesy," a snake or toad drops out of her mouth whenever she speaks.[10] The heroine of the Italian "Water in the Basket" also does not toil for her salvation, but displays an unerring sense of tact and extraordinary modesty. When an old woman asks her to inspect her back to get rid of what is biting her, the girl kills vermin "by the hundreds." To avoid embarrassment, she tells the old woman that her back was covered with pearls and diamonds. Later, faced with the choice of a silk gown or a cotton dress as reward, she offers evidence of her unassuming nature by asking for the cotton dress. Her callous stepsister expresses disgust at the sight of the fleas on the crone's back, chooses a silk gown as her reward, and ends up with a donkey's tail on her forehead.[11] Whether a tale exalts the value of hard work or praises any of a host of virtues ranging from kindness to *politesse*, it imparts specific lessons by instituting a system of rewards for one type of behavior and punishments for another.

Not all renditions of "The Kind and Unkind Girls" are as explicitly didactic as the ones cited here. If we look at the various versions of the story available to the Grimms, we find that they chose to anthologize the one that had a pedagogical agenda. One version of the story, recorded in the Grimms' annotations, tells of two girls—one beautiful, the other ugly. The beautiful one falls into a well and lands in the same lush meadow described in "Mother Holle." But rather than discharging various chores assigned to her, she is the one who gives the orders and who engineers a happy ending for herself. She tells a tree to shake itself; she directs a calf to bend down; and she asks an oven to bake her a roll. Later she comes across a house made of pancakes, louses the old women who lives in it, and flees with a dress of gold when the old woman falls asleep. Her unattractive companion duplicates her every deed, but finds herself wearing a dress covered with dirt when the old woman catches up with her. In this story it does not help to be kind, modest, hardworking, or polite. Beauty, bossiness, and deceit are rewarded; ugliness is punished.

It is easy to understand why the Grimms, who openly acknowledged the educational value of their collection, favored a story that commended the virtues of hard work over a tale that credited beauty with winning all the prizes. The story of the girl who is rewarded because of her looks rather than her good conduct simply could not be harnessed into service for indoctrinating children with the right values. It is more difficult, however, to reconcile the Grimms' striving for folkloric authenticity with their choice of "Mother Holle" over other tales. The oldest tales, and hence those probably most faithful to folk traditions, tend to reward those endowed by nature with desirable qualities rather than those who cultivate specific virtues.

Beauty proves to be a great advantage in fairy tales, but—oddly enough—it also helps to be a stepchild or a child abused by one parent or another. Ludwig Bechstein's "Garden in the Well" mounts the contrasting fates of two boys—one a stepson, the other the biological child of the tale's villain. Both boys fall into wells and find themselves in beautiful gardens with flowers and trees. The stepson gets fruit and gold when he orders apple trees to shake themselves; the other boy gets sour apples with worms and has pitch poured over him, even though his conduct conforms to the letter of his brother's behavior. The fate of the stepson, who lives happily ever after with his father, contrasts sharply with that of his brother. That boy's mother scolds him and beats him when he returns, then tries to remove the layer of pitch covering his body by putting him in the oven. But when she forgets to take the boy out, she finds that he has "suffocated and burned to death."[12]

There is nothing in this boy's character or looks that warrants such a punishment; he has merely had the misfortune of being born to the wrong woman.

Early versions of "The Kind and Unkind Girls" (Bechstein's tale is one of a very small number featuring boys) tend to take a fatalistic view of the world—some children are privileged, others deprived. Basile enunciated this outlook on life through one of his narrators, who tells of a mother with three daughters, "two of whom were so unlucky that everything they did turned out badly, all of their plans went awry and all their hopes came to nothing." The third is lucky, "even in her mother's womb" and "all the elements combined to endow her with the best of all things."[13] Good fortune was seen as a basic fact of life, and fairy tales show us again and again how those favored by fortune do well no matter how flawed their character and regardless of the odds against them. The attempt of a parent to overturn this "natural" order of things by favoring one child over another always backfires. And no matter how the children conduct themselves, the one privileged by nature and deprived by a parent always wins out in the end.

All of this changed as fairy tales reached print and came to be placed in the service of acculturation and education. Storybooks emphasized the way in which toil leads to salvation. Kindness and good manners can also do the trick, as in Perrault's "Fairies" where these qualities bring the heroine pearls and diamonds. It is noteworthy that even as reward-and-punishment tales celebrate kindness and compassion, they are notoriously uncharitable when it comes to fixing the fate of their unkind protagonists. In one such tale, a girl sits in a room waiting for a sack of gold to come flying in (as it had for her sister), when a little gray man whisks into the room and "lops her head off her body."[14] That punishment must have gone a long way toward discouraging the cruelty to animals practiced by the unkind sister. Another story is even more graphic in illustrating the consequences of a girl's failure to share her porridge with a little old man: "When the girl finished eating, the little man took her, tore her into a thousand pieces, and hung them up in the trees." We are treated not only to a description of her punishment, but also to the mother's reaction to the sight of her daughter: "When she got to the place where the pieces of her daughter were hanging, she thought that her daughter must have hung her wash there. But imagine her shock and horror when she got closer and saw what had happened. She fainted dead away, and I have no idea whether she ever got back home again."[15] The scene is so extreme in its grisly detail that it begins to shift into the mode of surreal comedy rather than grim horror. Still, there is something odd about the way in which reward-and-punishment tales advocate kindness toward animals and strangers in a context that champions violent retaliatory punishments for members of the hero's immediate family. This incongruity forms the basis for the suspicion that reward-and-punishment tales began as retaliatory stories (based on sibling rivalry) and became, only later in their development, didactic tales.

There are other serious inconsistencies in the messages sent by these tales. Consider, for example, the way in which rewards for kind heroines nearly always come in the form of gold and precious stones. One girl is showered with gold; another gets a sack of gold; a third receives gowns and jewelry. With their notoriously frank drive toward gold, jewels, and wealth, fairy-tale plots begin to resemble blueprints for enterprising young capitalists rather than for self-sacrificing do-gooders. Yet the tales repeatedly emphasize and enshrine the importance of indifference to wealth and worldly goods: The heroine who chooses the cotton dress over the silk one is rewarded; the one who elects to leave by the gate of pitch rather than the gate of gold is showered with coins; the girl who chooses to eat with the cats and the dogs rather than with her prosperous host wins in the end. As Ludwig Bechstein puts it in the conclusion to his version of "Gold-Maria and Pitch-Maria," the unkind sister is punished "because she was so keen for gold."[16]

The story of the kind and unkind girls sets up gold as the highest possible value and reward, even as it attempts to train children to disdain it. In nearly every such tale, gold purchases a happy ending, but the more recent versions of the tale also stress the importance of acting as if the goal had no value. If modesty and austerity make for virtue, as these tales tell us, and if virtue prospers, as we also learn, then modesty and austerity must also lead to prosperity, which breeds vice. This contradictory message—which is implicit in numerous books of nineteenth-century children's fiction where the generosity of poor, virtuous children always pays off—suggests that most rewriters of fairy tales took the easy way out when it came to incorporating lessons into their stories.[17] Instead of integrating a moral into the plot, they simply superimposed a lesson on a story that, in its original form, often just told how beauty triumphs over ugliness or how the underdog can turn the tables on the privileged.

This is even more the case with the extended form of "The Kind and Unkind Girls," a tale type that has been designated as "The Black and the White Bride" (AT 403). One such story, the Italian "Water in the Basket," also contrasts the fate of a privileged daughter with an abused stepdaughter, but it adds a coda in which the stepmother tries to block the "kind" girl's marriage to a prince. Before the king's son comes to fetch the girl, the stepmother asks for one last favor. She begs the girl to get into a barrel (ostensibly to help wash it out), then prepares a kettle of boiling water to scald her to death. The ugly sister happens to pass by, demands to take the girl's place, and is killed by her own mother. What we have are really repetitions of one and the same tale: "The Kind and Unkind Girls" gives us the basic model, "The Black and the White Bride" repeats it in a matrimonial context.[18]

In some versions of the extended form, the groom also acts as the heroine's tester: he asks for food, proposes tasks, or extracts promises. These tales are especially extraordinary for the way in which they fuse the cautionary tale with the exemplary story to offer, despite their happy endings, a double spectacle of pain. In the Grimms' "Hans My Hedgehog," for example, the hedgehog of the title tests two girls whose good and bad behavior provide the matter for the tale's moral.

The birth of Hans My Hedgehog can be traced, as is so often the case in fairy tales about monstrous births, to an unthinking wish uttered by a person without children. "I want to have a child, even if it's a hedge-hog," a farmer says one day after he has been ridiculed for having no children.[19] Shortly thereafter, his wife gives birth to a child "whose upper half was hedgehog and bottom half human." To the relief of his parents, Hans leaves home at age eight to tend donkeys and pigs in the forest. Over the course of many years Hans meets two kings, both of whom, in return for directions, agree to give him the first thing they meet on returning home. In both cases, the kings are greeted by their daughters, one of whom is delighted to learn that her father has de-ceived Hans by writing on his agreement whatever came into his head ("The princess was happy to hear that and said it was a good thing since she would never have gone with him anyway."). The other princess, whose father has signed the agreement honestly, agrees, out of "love for him," to wed Hans whenever he wishes to fetch her. Hans, who must lay seige to the first king's realm to get what was promised to him ver-bally, victoriously drives off with the "deceitful" princess:

> When they had gone a little way, Hans My Hedgehog took off her beautiful clothes and stuck her with his quills until she was covered with blood.

"This is what you get for being so deceitful!" he said. "Go back home. I don't want you."

Then he sent her away, and she lived in disgrace for the rest of her life.

The other princess may have agreed to keep her father's promise and to marry a hedgehog-man, but she can't help being "startled" and "frightened" when the repulsive creature arrives at her father's castle sporting bagpipes, and with a rooster as his mount. But her every apprehension is eclipsed by an extraordinary sense of filial duty: "There was nothing she could do, so she thought, for she had promised her father to go with him." After the marriage ceremony is performed and it is time to get into bed with her singular groom, is it any wonder that

11. Hans My Hedgehog puts on his bagpipes, harnesses up his cock, and goes off in search of a bride.

the young woman is "quite afraid of his quills"? Hans turns into a human being right before he climbs into bed, but the ordeal of the princess up to this point should not be underestimated.

There is an interesting way in which this tale, for all its fantastic qualities, slides into the didactic mode. Two kings are maneuvered into promising their daughters to a being who is half human, half animal. The father who does everything in his power, including enlisting military support, to prevent the marriage is considered wicked and deceitful, while the one who is only "sorry" that his daughter happened to be the first to meet him on his way home, and who turns the girl over to the hedgehog-man, is extolled as a man of admirable qualities. The kinds of pacts made between Hans My Hedgehog and the two kings may be seen as binding in the logic of the tale and of the myths from which the tales evolved, but they can hardly be seen as contractual models for real life.

The heroine of the Italian story "The Devil's Breeches" offers a view refreshing in its candor. When the girl's father promises her to a man who looks like an animal, she stands up to him and refuses the match: "Father, I wouldn't have thought you capable of giving your daughter in marriage to a brute," she rightly protests. "Now I know how much you really love me." The heroine's boldness backfires, for she is soon fetched by the devil: No matter what the promise made by a father, it must be kept.

Just as remarkable as the Grimms' use of scare tactics for didactic purposes is the sliding of moral responsibility from parents onto their children. The princess punished in "Hans My Hedgehog" does nothing more than play along with her father's deceit (a perfectly reasonable act given her role), yet she is the one who suffers brutal assaults and is shamed for the rest of her life. We hear nothing about the punishment of the king. In other tales, the Grimms make a point of mobilizing parental authority to articulate moral clichés that often have very little to do with the crisis facing hero or heroine. "The Frog King, or Iron Heinrich" engages in endless preaching about keeping one's word, no matter what the circumstances. "If you've made a promise, you must keep it," the King tells his daughter. "It's not proper to scorn someone who helped you when you were in trouble!" he tells her when she bridles at the prospect of letting a frog sleep in her bed.[20] It is telling that in the earliest version of the Grimms' tale the king does nothing but issue orders; by the time the *Nursery and Household Tales* reached print, how-

ever, he was teaching lessons to readers as he was telling his daughter
what to do.

Other versions of "Hans My Hedgehog" lack the strong didactic undercurrent moving through the Grimms' tale. Straparola's "Pig Prince,"
one of many stories contained in the *Facetious Nights*, also mounts a
bride-test, showing the punishment of those who fail and the reward
for those who pass. The protagonist named in the title insists on marrying a human, despite his beastly form and brutish habits. When he first
sets eyes on his prospective bride, he is "filled with joy, and, all foul and
dirty as he was, jumped around about her, endeavouring by his pawing
and nuzzling to show some sign of affection."[21] Not surprisingly, the
girl recoils in disgust, then quite logically asks herself: "What am I to do
with this foul beast?" She makes the mistake of plotting his death out
loud to herself and is attacked that night by her groom, who drives his
sharp hooves into her breast and kills her. One of her sisters also falls
victim to the pig's wrath; however, the third and youngest sister feels
honored by the pig's proposal and ends by becoming the wife of the
"handsome and well-shaped young man" beneath the pig's skin—but
not before she too has weathered certain ordeals. Before his metamorphosis, the pig, "filthier and more muddy than ever," shows the kind
Meldina even more affection than he had displayed to her sisters.

Straparola made every effort to tap the tale's comic potential. Take,
for example, the scene that follows the hero's birth. How does a mother
react after giving birth to an animal that is unmistakably porcine? Here
is Straparola's answer:

> The child . . . , being nursed with the greatest care, would often be
> brought to the queen and put his little snout and his little paws in his
> mother's lap, and she, moved by natural affection, would caress him
> by stroking his bristly back with her hand, and embracing and kiss-
> ing him as if he had been of human form. Then he would wag his tail
> and give other signs to show that he was conscious of his mother's
> affection.

Even more extraordinary is the description of the hero's wedding night,
for bride number-three is not at all reluctant to spend the night with a
pig, and is even remarkably responsive to her groom's advances:

> When the maiden had finished speaking, the pig prince, who had
> been wide awake and had heard all that she had said, got up, kissed

her on the face and neck and bosom and shoulders with his tongue,
and she was not backward in returning his caresses; so that he was
fired with a warm love for her. As soon as the time for retiring for the
night had come, the bride went to bed and awaited her unseemly
spouse, and, as soon as he came, she raised the coverlet and bade him
lie near to her and put his head upon the pillow, covering him carefully with the bed-clothes and drawing the curtains so that he might
feel no cold.

The description stops short of any additional intimate details, but it is
amazing nonetheless. This is the part of the story that must have captured the attention of its audience. Once the tale draws to its conclusion in the *Facetious Nights*, we return to the frame narrative to learn
that "the whole company broke into laughter at the notion of the pig
prince, all dirty and muddy as he was, kissing his beloved spouse and
lying by her side." Here we are clearly in the realm of Bakhtin's grotesque realism.

Straparola's stories, printed in the sixteenth century, are products of
an era that had a relatively high tolerance for frankness in the depiction
of sexual matters. Since then, in the name of "civilization," "culture,"
and "refinement," the threshold of embarrassment and shame about
bodily functions has steadily advanced. Norbert Elias observes that feelings of shame about sexual relations have increased considerably in the
past few centuries; this shame manifests itself in the "difficulty experienced by adults . . . in talking about these relations to children." An
1857 manual on educating girls is characteristic in pointing out that
"children should be left for as long as is at all possible in the belief that
an angel brings the mother her little children."[22] In his magisterial *History of Sexuality*, Foucault identifies the nineteenth century as the age
that witnessed the full refinement of a new cultural code regulating
sexuality:

At the beginning of the seventeenth century a certain frankness was
still common, it would seem. Sexual practices had little need of se-
crecy; words were said without undue reticence, and things were
done without too much concealment; one had a tolerant familiarity
with the illicit. Codes regulating the coarse, the obscene, and the in-
decent were quite lax compared to those of the nineteenth century. It
was a time of direct gestures, shameless discourse, and open trans-

gressions, when anatomies were shown and intermingled at will, and knowing children hung about amid the laughter of adults: it was a period when bodies "made a display of themselves."[23]

Foucault may overstate the real situation when he talks about anatomies "shown and intermingled at will," but he is quite correct to point out that sexual matters were not hidden from children as rigorously and systematically as in the nineteenth century.

The need to shield children from the simple biological facts of life became a matter of considerable urgency at just the time when collecting folktales became a critical item on a variety of national agendas. As collectors went about their mission, they could not help but collaborate in the cultural project of silencing sexuality and suppressing all allusions to bodily functions. In translating oral tale into printed text, many collectors, wittingly and unwittingly, eliminated bawdy episodes or scatalogical humor, or they anthologized only those versions of a tale that had already been revised for children. Needless to say, the scholarly, often solemn gentlemen who took down the tales usually received cleaned-up versions from the very start. While the great collectors invariably toned down or eliminated whatever off-color episodes they picked up from living informants and literary documents, they also capitalized on or created opportunities to turn the tales into object lessons or to add morals that did not necessarily square with the facts of the text.[24]

"The Pig Prince" may be a literary text rather than a true oral narrative, but it is more in the spirit of folkloric sources than the Grimms' "Hans My Hedgehog." It depicts the facts of life directly and frankly, drawing on physiological matters for laughs and investing erotic encounters with comic elements whenever possible. There are also no holds barred when it comes to mounting scenes of punishment. But in the absence of a high moral tone and the presence of irony at every narrative turn, the punishments in "The Pig Prince" seem less forbidding and frightening than those in "Hans My Hedgehog." Only at one point does "The Pig Prince" begin to veer off in the direction of the didactic, and even then it does not take a full turn in the direction of the cautionary tale: Once the pig-groom is "sure of his wife's discretion and fidelity," he divulges the secret of his true identity to his bride. Like so many brides of animal-grooms, Meldina's obedience to her husband's command that she tell no one his secret is tested. Yet even though she fails the test and follows the impulse to tell her in-laws the happy truth, Meldina suffers no punishment whatsoever for her indiscretion. The fact that she has wed a pig is sign enough of loyal devotion to her husband.

"Hans My Hedgehog" vividly demonstrates the problems that arise when a moral script is superimposed on tales that started out as good, if not always clean, fun. The simplistic messages sent by the Grimms and many other rewriters of this tale become garbled, for they rarely penetrate the cultural density of the stories. It is a mistake to try to teach children about the importance of keeping a parent's promise, or of agreeing to the demands of a social superior, in the context of stories that once dealt with a complex array of psychosexual matters. Since reward-and-punishment tales offer a double dose of pain and torture in the scenes that build up to the reward for patient suffering and in the spectacle that caps the punishment, it is no minor feat to transform these tales into didactic stories with positive messages.[25] One girl may win in the end, but at a cost that will inspire few listeners and readers to emulate her. The virtual impossibility of generating positive messages did not, however, stop most collectors, who went right ahead driving out sexual episodes and replacing them with didactic elements.

In a study surveying over nine hundred versions of "The Kind and Unkind Girls," Warren Roberts found only a handful of tales with male protagonists.[26] The two main figures of the tale type may be (half) sisters, cousins, neighbors, or in-laws, but they are almost always female. There seems to be no exact male counterpart to AT 480. Still, this does not mean that there is a dearth of tales in which brothers with good qualities are lined up against brothers of bad character. In tales featuring three sons, we repeatedly encounter a contrast between two older and wiser, but cruel, boys and their young, foolish brother.[27]

The Grimms' "Golden Bird" (AT 550) gives us the main features of the tale type and offers some telling contrasts to "The Kind and Unkind Girls." The hero of the story, the youngest of three brothers, passes only one character test in order to earn his passport to good fortune. Once he shows compassion by sparing the life of a fox and displays good judgment by heeding his advice on one occasion, he can do no wrong, even when he constantly ignores interdictions and violates commands. No matter how often the fox reminds the boy of the importance of following his advice, the hero disobeys. "You don't deserve my assistance," the fox finally cries out in desperation.[28] Still, the boy succeeds

in winning a princess and a kingdom, and it is hard to escape the conclusion that disobeying orders and making errors in judgment are part
of the hero's key to success. This is so strikingly at odds with what we
find in tales about kind and unkind girls that we must take a closer look
at stories contrasting two older boys with their younger sibling.

In almost all tales of three sons, a character test follows each of the
boys' decision to launch a quest. In "The Golden Bird," the fox tests for
compassion, rewarding the boy who spares his life. In the Grimms'
"Water of Life" (AT 551), a dwarf asks each boy about his destination.
"You meddling twirp," the two oldest reply, "that's none of your affair!"[29] The dwarf becomes enraged and casts a spell on both brothers;
the youngest, by contrast, is rewarded for being polite to the dwarf.
"Since you've behaved yourself in a proper manner and are not arrogant like your faithless brothers," the dwarf tells him, "I'll tell you how
to get to the Water of Life." Where his brothers failed, the hero succeeds
and brings his father the elixir he needs for a full recovery. He may not
heed the dwarf's warning about the treachery of his brothers, but he
carries out other instructions to the letter.

In tales of two girls and in stories of three boys, the protagonists must
demonstrate compassion, humility, gratitude, and kindness. In addition, girls are often required to carry out a variety of household tasks or
farm chores, ranging from taking bread out of an oven to milking a
cow. Their male counterparts rarely toil for their rewards. This is not to
say that they do not have to perform some kind of task, but the assign-
ments they are given often require superhuman strength or energy
rather than elbow grease. Building a fully furnished castle overnight,
devouring a mountain of bread, or fetching a thousand pearls from the
depths of the ocean are among the impossible tasks imposed on male
heroes. The animals, dwarves, or fairies to whom the hero has shown
compassion take care of these tasks and enable the hero to win the hand
of a princess.

In much the same way that tales of kind and unkind girls, with their
reward/punishment system, were made to move in the didactic mode,
so tales of three sons leave room for extensive moralizing. Here too,
however, the hero rewarded suffers trials and tribulations that make it
difficult to square the actual facts of the text with the moral imposed on
it. A Greek tale of three brothers gives us what must rank as one of the
most heavy handed attempts to turn an adventure story into an object
lesson. In it, the youngest of the boys triumphs over his elder brothers

by agreeing to sacrifice his only child to cure a leper. He and his wife
plan to incinerate the child's body in order to produce a healing dust,
but they find their child alive and well when they open the oven where
he was to burn:

> In one hand he held a basket all full of diamonds and brilliants, of
> gold and of silver, and in the other little hand was a golden book
> lying open and the boy writing in it in fine big letters: *He who receives*
> *in his house and serves the stranger and the poor man, he receives and*
> *serves God Himself.* For it seems that the old man was an angel and did
> all these things to show us that the worst of all actions is ingratitude
> and hardness of heart, and also that whoever does good, to him in
> recompense God grants the same and even more.[30]

The moral is writ large in this tale, which has been transformed into a
parable of Christian charity, even as it retains the savage episode requiring the sacrificial slaughtering and incineration of a child. Here, as
with tales of kind and unkind girls, it is difficult to square the story's
message with the details of its plot. Even if we take note of the way in
which biblical accounts require a parent to consent to sacrifice a child
(think of Abraham and Isaac), the alacrity with which the parents in the
Greek tale put their son into the oven makes it difficult to see them as
models of charitable behavior.

Tales of two brothers differ sharply from those featuring two sisters,
or for that matter from stories about three sisters or brothers. Folklorists have often observed that rivalry flourishes only in those folktales
where siblings are of the same sex, e.g., "Cinderella" or "The Golden
Bird." When siblings are of the opposite sex, as in "Hansel and Gretel"
or "Little Brother and Little Sister," the two generally face hardship as
allies rather than adversaries. Oddly enough, this rule does not hold
true when it comes to tales of two brothers, in part perhaps because
these stories are so often about twins, boys who think and act exactly
alike in the logic of the folktale. Contrasts in character are suppressed
in favor of contrasting fates—the two brothers part at one point and are
reunited later only after one of them has married. A conflict erupts near
the tale's conclusion, but it is swiftly disposed of, and the two live happily ever after.[31]

That the brothers in these stories are twins makes them kindred spirits, doubles of one another, but it also introduces the possibility of duplicity into the tale. Even though one brother has every opportunity to

deceive the other (his twin's wife mistakes him for her husband), he forfeits the chance and takes special precautions to avoid physical contact with his sister-in-law. Only the brother's false suspicion that his twin has taken advantage of his absence drives a wedge between the two. When the jealous brother decapitates his twin, the damage is quickly repaired with a balm that heals wounds, with the root of life, or with some such remedy. More importantly, no moral judgment is ever weighed against one young man or the other.[32]

Tales with two female rivals tend to work with the contrasting attributes lazy/industrious, polite/rude, and kind/unkind. Stories of male rivals, even when they are not modeled on "The Kind and Unkind Girls" tend to work with the oppositions faithful/treacherous, polite/rude, and kind/unkind. Since the first pair of opposites in each series functions as the primary one, it also sets the basic tone of the tales. Heroines are, then, faced time and again with the task of demonstrating their domestic competence. Whether sweeping the house, making beds, spinning, cooking, building a fire, washing dishes, milking cows, feeding hens, or cleaning a stable (these are among the actual tasks that appear in versions of the tale), they earn rewards. Heroes, by contrast, are challenged with tasks and missions that lead them on the road to high adventure.

Because of this intrinsic difference, stories of girls were easier to transform into didactic lessons in which virtue and hard work were rewarded, while vice and laziness were punished. Hence, these were the tales canonized by nineteenth-century collectors. And, just as the opposition between laziness and industry was seen as conducive to teaching lessons, the contrast between faithfulness and treachery generated intrigues that instead lent themselves well to action-packed narratives. Lessons may have been superimposed on these adventure stories, but they did not leave the vivid impact of reward-and-punishment tales, which teach not only through the power of words and of deeds, but also through the spectacle of punishment.

Wilhelm Grimm / Maurice Sendak: *Dear Mili* and the Art of Dying Happily Ever After

Now children! I have only one piece of serious, important advice to give you all, so attend to me! —Never crack nuts with your teeth!

Catherine Sinclair, *Holiday House*

WHEN HENRY SHARPE HORSLEY published *The Affectionate Parent's Gift, and the Good Child's Reward* in 1828, he felt that the "sincerity of intention" behind his efforts separated this collection of poems and essays for children from the vast quantities of frivolous reading matter available to them:

> It is an acknowledged fact, and much to be lamented, that the greater part of the Books published for the use of children, are either ridiculous in themselves, unfit to instruct or inform, or are of an improper tendency, calculated only to mislead the susceptible and tender minds of youth; and, consequently, ought to be rejected by the parents and guardians of children with as much indignation, as a proffered poisonous ingredient for mixture or infusion into the food of their children.[1]

Horsley never names any of the "objectionable and contaminating" volumes against which he rails, but we can infer, after a reading of his own poems, that he is probably alluding to stories without any apparent didactic thrust. His own stories do not seem to deviate materially from the reward-and-punishment model that dominated children's literature at the time of his writing. "I have endeavored to portray vice in its heinous character, and its evil tendencies," he writes, "to picture the milder virtues of the mind, as being alone worthy of cultivation." Predictably, he has also "endeavored to enforce obedience, and inculcate sincerity and truth."

Horsley's book is breathtaking in its sweep. There are the usual meditations on idleness:

> An idle girl, or idle boy,
> Is hated as a pest;
> Like dirty pigs, they always love
> In slothfulness to rest.

But Horsley also includes a poem about the death of a mother, in which the woman's dying words are recorded:

> "Soon your mother will be lifeless,
> For you I'd wish but to be spar'd;
> Ah, why this wish, I n'er shall have it,
> Never see my children rear'd."

Fathers are also mortal, and so we are treated to "The Death of a Father" with a well-pointed moral:

> Children, prize a tender father,
> Best protectors of the young;
> Never let your conduct grieve them,
> Never vex them with your tongue.

There are also poems about visits to Newgate "just for example's sake," trips to an asylum for the blind where "all hands are busy in their rooms," a stop at the lunatic asylum to see "the throngs of those who don't possess their reason," meetings with orphans who are "clad in rags and patches," and an encounter with a crippled girl who affords "gen'rous Mary" the chance to make a show of her compassion.

Horsley makes a point of exposing children to the misery of everyday life in a fashion characteristic of nineteenth-century writers. Beggars, blind men, and thieves have one sole purpose in life, which is to teach lessons or to remind children to be grateful for what they have. The admitted aim of *The Affectionate Parent's Gift, and the Good Child's Reward* (the title's unintentional irony speaks volumes) is to awaken "sentiments of gratitude, obedience, and humanity" in children. If Horsley

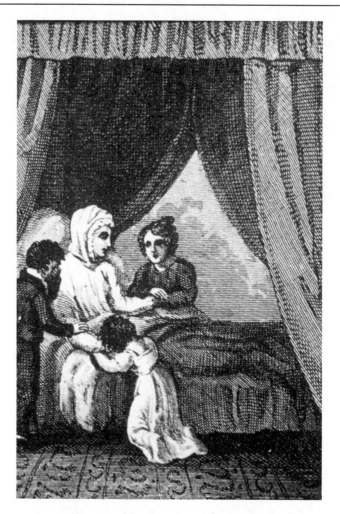

12. This illustration for "The Death of a Mother,"
which ends by admonishing children to be "grateful" to their
parents and to remain "worthy" of their love, must have
made a strong impression on its viewers.

and his contemporaries erred in the direction of exposing children to
too many of the harrowing scenes of everyday life (for all the wrong
reasons and in all the wrong ways), there were those who moved to the
opposite end of the spectrum and presented idealized and sentimental-
ized versions of reality. Here we have books like *The History of Little
Goody Two-Shoes* or stories like "The Schoolgirl," which feature a heroine "playful and innocent as the dove."[2]

13. The rhyme that accompanies this illustration of two boys
visiting an asylum tells us that "the Father of two little boys, / Resolved
one day to take / A walk through Newgate with the lads, /
Just for example's sake."

For Maurice Sendak, Goody Two-Shoes and her literary cousins are
the real villains in the history of children's literature. Even today many
writers of children's books embrace "the great nineteenth-century fantasy that paints childhood as an eternally innocent paradise" and create
hopelessly dull stories that have one purpose alone—"they don't
frighten adults."[3] False sentimentality, with its denial of the emotional
complexities of childhood, evades the very issues that children's books

ought to represent and enact. What Sendak aims to do, in his books for
children, is to "reconstruct and defuse dreadful moments of childhood"
(210).[4] In *Outside Over There*, for example, Sendak claims to have created a narrative whose subtext was his own childhood anxiety about the
Lindbergh case ("In it, I am the Lindbergh baby, and my sister saves
me") and his sister's resentment about being stuck all the time with the
care of baby Maurice. Writing the book helped Sendak in a wonderfully
economical way to master his childhood fears about being kidnapped,
to discharge the guilt in his relationship with his sister, and to make
peace with a mother who had transferred responsibility for her son to
her daughter in all too light a fashion. Sendak sees children's literature
as a therapeutic form of play in which author, character, and reader
participate to purge themselves of childhood anger, resentment, fear,
frustration, and confusion. Max, Kenny, Martin, and Rosie, like his
other fictional creations, "all have the same need to master the uncontrollable and frightening aspects of their lives, and they all turn to fantasy to accomplish this" (152).

The rhetoric of mastery that permeates Sendak's writings about children's books dovetails neatly with the therapeutic model for fairy tales
developed by Bruno Bettelheim in his *Uses of Enchantment*. Bettelheim,
too, deplores the fallacy of innocence that informs children's literature.
With the best of intentions, adults expose children "only to the sunny
side of things," drawing attention away from what troubles the child
most, "nameless anxieties" and "chaotic, angry, and even violent fantasies." That fairy tales "give body to anxieties" is precisely what makes
them so beneficial for adults and children alike. As the tales enact wor-
ries and fears, they also "relieve" them (hence the "uses of enchantment"), often "without this ever coming to conscious awareness."[5]

That representation can take an interventionist turn and lead to the
resolution of conflicts stands as the cornerstone of Sendak's philosophy
of children's literature just as it informs Bettelheim's model of psychological growth through identification and abreaction. Sendak insistently
celebrates fantasy as an empowering mode, enabling children to tame
"ungovernable" and "dangerous" emotions by providing a healthy catharsis: "Through fantasy, Max [the hero of *Where the Wild Things Are*]
discharges his anger against his mother, and returns to the real world
sleepy, hungry, and at peace with himself."[6] Children's stories become
miniature Aristotelian dramas that secure a child's identification with
their protagonists and promote a cathartic effect. Is it any wonder that

Sendak used the very term *catharsis* to describe the powerful feelings that overcame him once he had finished *Where the Wild Things Are*?

> When I write and draw I'm experiencing what the child in the book is going through. I was as relieved to get back from Max's journey as he was. . . . It's only after the act of writing the book that, as an adult, I can see what has happened and talk about fantasy as catharsis, about Max acting out his anger as he fights to grow.[7]

Sendak's observations raise a number of questions, among them one that an early commentator on children's literature framed by asking, "Do children need horror in stories? If so, how much and how soon?"[8] Sendak would probably not ask about the proper dose and its timing, but about the disease that the medicine is meant to cure. Take the case of Carlo Collodi's *Pinocchio*, a story that, in Sendak's own words, does not suffer from "whimsicality or sentimentality" yet is nonetheless "a cruel and frightening tale" built on a "sickening" premise.[9] Collodi creates a world in which children are inherently lazy, disobedient, and dishonest—the same world we encountered in cautionary and reward-and-punishment tales. At every bend in the road, evil forces, exponents of the ethos of "Playland" (which was to become Walt Disney's "Pleasure Island"), stand ready to seduce the child and to turn him into the little beast he really is. That the text is punctuated with stern lectures about the importance of hard work, obedience, and truth (always just after Pinocchio has realized the error of his ways and just before he slips once again into a "naughty" mode) makes it a dreary story, designed more to satisfy adults than children. "From now on I shall lead a different life, and become an obedient boy. I have learnt the lesson that disobedient children never prosper, and never gain anything," the backsliding boy declares to himself in a pathetic speech delivered without a great deal of conviction.[10]

Collodi's tale, with its emphasis on the importance of suppressing the desire to play and have fun in order to find salvation through hard work, conforms almost to the letter with our understanding of the ethical world of nineteenth-century children's literature. Yet despite its endless harping on the evils of "Playland," the book's focus is on adventure—on a sequence of breathtakingly exciting brushes with death framed by scenes at home—and this, even more than Walt Disney, has given the book its staying power. The structure of the adventures is not so different from the one Sendak himself uses in *Outside Over There*,

Where the Wild Things Are, and *Mickey in the Night Kitchen*. But where Collodi uses moral glosses to set things right, lest the reader perceive the book as a mere celebration of adventure, Sendak never spells out a single lesson. As one might expect from a man who sees himself above all as an illustrator and interpreter of children's books, Sendak sends powerful messages through the images and between the lines of his stories. Take the case, once again, of Max. Fantasy has for him a real instrumental value. Once he has discharged his anger against his mother through fantasy, he is "at peace with himself" and returns to his bedroom, where a "still hot" supper that includes a generous slice of layer cake awaits him. What Sendak does not tell us, but what is crucially important, is that Max must also be at peace with his mother and therefore less likely to be defiant or disobedient, those same traits that we have identified as the nineteenth-century's cardinal sins of childhood.

Both Sendak and Bettelheim argue for the instrumentalization of fantasy (whether in adventure books or in fairy tales) even as they deplore children's literature that takes an explicitly didactic turn. Stories can convey lessons and purify children of "ungovernable" (Sendak's term is telling) emotions, but they must never put those lessons into words. Twentieth-century children's literature has witnessed a gradual fading of the (adult) judgmental narrative voice that was so strident a presence in books such as *Pinocchio* and in the great nineteenth-century collections of fairy tales. Jacqueline Rose has observed that there was a time when children's books were "*only* justified by the presence of the adult, who laid out for that other adult presumed to be buying the book exactly what he or she was doing."[11] A book without a lesson was hardly worth the paper on which it was printed.

Bettelheim takes essentially the same line on fairy tales that Sendak adopts for his books by placing an equal sign between didacticism and repression, while making the case for the vanishing adult: "Explaining to a child why a fairy tale is so captivating to him destroys . . . the story's enchantment. . . . With the forfeiture of this power to enchant goes also a loss of the story's potential for helping the child struggle on his own, and master all by himself the problem which has made the story meaningful to him in the first place."[12]

Bettelheim's diction is telling. Even as he concedes the power of a text to manipulate its reader—a story is "captivating" and has the "power to enchant"—he claims autonomy for the child reader, who

struggles "on his own" to "master" a story "all by himself." Let us
bracket for the moment whether it is really a good thing for, say, a
five-year-old child to struggle "on his own," in order to ask whether the
child really does struggle "on his own" with the problem that makes the
story so attractive. Early on in *The Uses of Enchantment*, Bettelheim celebrates fairy tales as vehicles of a "moral education which *subtly*, and *by
implication* only, conveys to him the advantages of moral behavior, not
through abstract ethical concepts but through that which seems tangi-
bly right and therefore meaningful to him" (my emphasis).[13] Bettelheim's fairy tales do not seem able to escape what Roger Duvoisin
ascribes to most literature written by adults for children: "that little
sneaking desire to teach and to moralize, to pass on to children what we
think of our world."[14] Bettelheim endows children with a power over
the text that they do not in reality possess. The fact that fairy tales guide
feelings and control responses gives the lie to the notion that children
work their way from dependence to autonomy through literature.

   With their insistence on a noninterventionist policy on the part of
adults who read to their children, Sendak and Bettelheim privilege the
text, extending its power, while affecting that children control the text
as they work their way from powerlessness to autonomy. This privileging of the text may work for Sendak's stories, but it is particularly
wrong-headed when it comes to fairy tales. Forgetting that fairy tales
originally circulated as oral stories that showed extraordinary flexibility
as they were reshaped by tellers from different cultures, Bettelheim
writes: "The true meaning and impact of a fairy tale can be appreciated,
its enchantment can be experienced, only from the story in its original
form."[15] Once again, Bettelheim transfers authority and power to a stable, ideal text that in reality is nothing more than one of many constructs created by adults.

   When it comes to folktales (of which fairy tales are a subcategory),
there is no "original" text, only an infinite number of variants, each
anchored in a specific time and place. For this reason, the reading of
fairy tales is precisely the activity that invites adult intervention, for the
"original version" that has been captured between the pages of a book
has the "power to enchant," but perhaps in a way that may not be appropriate for the time and place in which it is being retold. Do we really
want to tell our children about "Frau Trude," the woman in the
Grimms' *Nursery and Household Tales* who turns disobedient children
into logs and warms herself as they burn? How will girls react to the

heroine of Perrault's "Bluebeard," who prostrates herself before her husband "asking his pardon with tears, and with all the signs of a true
repentance for her disobedience?"[16] Can we expect our children to
realize how odd it is for a woman whose husband is a mass murderer
to reproach herself for opening the door that contains the evidence of
his crimes? Are we really that keen to recite to our children the catalog
of horrors ("slimy toads," "fat snakes," and "great fat waddling spiders")
that plague the proud Inger in Andersen's "Girl Who Trod on the Loaf"?
Nowhere is selectivity more vital than when an adult decides to use
fairy tales for bedtime reading. Much as Bettelheim sees himself as the
advocate of children in his effort to sanctify their literature by purging
it of the evils of adult interpretation (an impossible task since children's
literature is produced by adults), his efforts misfire when it comes to
fairy tales.[17] Some fairy tales may appear to be a form of literature uncontaminated by adult didacticism, but they nonetheless remain the
creation of adults.

The ideal of a text that is as innocent and unreflecting as the child to
whom it is read has haunted the children's literature industry since its
inception. For this reason, fairy tales, which seem to represent both the
childhood of fiction and the fiction of childhood, occupy a special position in the hierarchy of children's literature. But the notion of childlike
innocence and naturalness implies an adult world tainted with corruption and artificiality. Is it therefore any wonder that writers and critics
of children's literature seem eager to keep the adult out of the picture
and out of the story? Yet to declare that adults should stay out of children's literature is utterly unrealistic—adults write the books, publish
them, review them, buy them, and read them[18]—and to argue that
adults should not interfere in the reading process is as misguided as
arguing that they should not intrude on children's lives. Letting children be wholly on their own as the readers of a story can, in some
situations, count as a not-so-benign form of neglect that leaves children
without any sort of compass to guide them as they enter, pass through,
and exit a world of fiction.

Sendak's child characters are experts in the art of fending for themselves in the world of fantasy, just as Bettelheim's child readers do not
need a road map to chart a path through enchanted woods. To achieve
autonomy (the ultimate goal in the process of mastery), the child must
give up relying on helpers and guides on the way to independence and
integration. This male developmental model defines the self through

separation and mastery, in contrast with Carol Gilligan's female model of affiliation and dependence and with the actual facts of many of the fairy tales analyzed by Bettelheim.[19] Heroes and heroines alike must sever ties to their family, but through the helpers and donors they encounter en route to a second home, they enter an intricate weave of relationships that envelops and protects them. The fairy-tale world is a world in which compassion counts—the good deeds of hero and heroine single them out from their siblings and mark them as the beneficiaries of helpers and donors. No matter how trivial a favor may seem, it is repaid in generous terms. The boy who spares the life of an ant and the girl who shares her crust of bread end by ruling over a kingdom. But rather than acting autonomously, fairy-tale heroes again and again depend on help from sources of the most improbable kind in order to reach the goal of reaffiliation symbolized by marriage and social integration.

Bettelheim's views on the "lessons" of "Cinderella" reveal how he typically divides fairy-tale life into two phases, each marked by a clear sense of separation from community—being "on one's own," as Bettelheim habitually puts it: "'Cinderella' guides the child from his greatest disappointments—oedipal disillusionment, castration anxiety, low opinion of himself because of the imagined low opinion of others—towards developing his autonomy, becoming industrious [note how the work ethic inadvertently slips in], and gaining a positive identity of his own."[20] The very sense of isolation and lack of affiliation experienced by the heroine at the tale's beginning is repeated in a conclusion that "elevates" her to a condition of "glorious" autonomy. Even so sensitive a critic of Bettelheim as Jack Zipes, who faults the child psychologist for attempting to construct "static literary models to be internalized for therapeutic consumption," comes down in the end (though for different reasons) on the side of "greater individual autonomy" for fairy-tale recipients.[21] Readers and protagonists alike must all march relentlessly down the royal road that leads to autonomy.

Given Sendak's penchant for telling tales in which children retreat into a world of fantasy to master unruly feelings on their own, and his distaste for tales that send explicit messages, it is surprising to find him drawn so strongly to the Grimms' *Nursery and Household Tales*, and in particular to the "recently discovered" Grimm tale *Dear Mili*. To be sure, Sendak has had a long love affair with the *Nursery and Household Tales*, beginning with his illustrations in 1973 for *The Juniper Tree and Other*

Tales from Grimm, translated by Lore Segal.[22] That he and Segal, who collaborated in selecting twenty-seven tales from the collection, chose to call the anthology *The Juniper Tree* is telling in that it suggests a desire to resurrect and rehabilitate precisely those tales that our culture has turned away from, in large part because of their open display of family conflicts, domestic violence, and illicit sexual desire. Virtually no other collection of this size, with the exception of the Grimms' own *Kleine Ausgabe* (the abridged edition of fifty tales), includes "Thousandfurs"— a story in which a king wants to marry his own daughter—and "Frau Trude"—a tale that we have already looked at for the alarmingly cruel way in which it punishes the curiosity of its protagonist.

Sendak's literary preferences and his choice of authors to illustrate suggest that it may not be so strange that he chose to collaborate with translator Ralph Manheim to produce the spectacular publishing success *Dear Mili*—a story that does not, by any stretch of the imagination, paint childhood as an "eternally innocent paradise": its heroine is exposed to perils that exceed a child's worst fears, and the story ends with the death of mother and child. But *Dear Mili* also has a didactic overlay deeper and denser than almost any text in the Grimms' *Nursery and Household Tales*. Before we look more closely at the logic of Sendak's three-year labor of love in producing the illustrations for *Dear Mili*, we need to take a closer look at the origins of the Grimms' text and to examine its status as a "lost" text.

On September 28, 1983, a front-page headline in the *New York Times* announced: "A Fairy Tale by Grimm Comes to Light." "After more than 150 years," it dramatically declared, "Hansel and Gretel, Snow White, Rumpelstiltskin and Cinderella will be joined by another Grimm fairy-tale character." This new character did not come cheap, but the "substantial five-figure price" ($26,000 according to later newspaper reports) paid by Farrar, Straus and Giroux for the tale carried with it a certificate of authenticity. The Schiller Company, a firm specializing in rare children's books, guaranteed in writing that the manuscript had never been published and promised to refund the purchase price "if this is ever found not to be the case." As John M. Ellis has noted, it was "very strange" that this unique manuscript had been available since 1974 but had found no buyers. "The first and only addition to a collection that is one of the major documents of Western culture, the first and only fairy tale manuscript in Wilhelm Grimm's hand since 1810 . . . and no one is interested?" he declared in mock astonishment. Ellis concluded that the tale recorded in the pricey manuscript did not stand out in any way from the masses of published and unpublished folkloric material not included by the Grimms in the 210 numbered texts of their *Nursery and Household Tales*.[23]

While the article in the *New York Times* conceded that there were "brief elements in the story of an earlier Grimm tale, 'Saint Joseph in the Woods,'" it avoided pursuing the point by veering off, in midsentence, to a non sequitur warning readers that the new tale, like other stories by the Grimms, "does not admit to easy interpretation or analysis." In fact, *Dear Mili* contains much more than "brief elements" from another tale—it comes very close to being a conflation of two texts from the ten "Legends for Children" that form the coda to the *Nursery and Household Tales*.

Before taking a closer look at the two texts that were merged to form the basis for *Dear Mili*, let us pause to examine the matter and the manner of the narrative itself. *Dear Mili* is not a complicated narrative. It tells of a young girl whose mother sends her into the woods to save her from the turmoil of war. There the pious, obedient girl meets Saint Joseph and stays with him for what she believes to be three days, but what turns out to be thirty years. Saint Joseph instructs the girl to return home with a rosebud, telling her not to be afraid, for she will return to him once the rose is in full bloom. Reunited with her aged mother, the girl spends the evening with her, then goes to bed "calmly and cheerfully." In the morning, neighbors find the woman and her daughter dead: "They had fallen happily asleep, and between them lay Saint Joseph's rose in full bloom."[24]

Just what is it about this tale that led Maurice Sendak to describe it as "wonderful, beautiful and touching"? When you "make an excavation," he added, "you don't expect to find Pompeii."[25] But here was, for him, the Pompeii of fairy-tale digs. Not surprisingly, what Sendak generally likes about the Grimms is that they tell rather than show or comment: "[The Grimms] did not punctuate everything with morals or messages; that's why they are so good."[26] This remark seems more than odd in the context of *Dear Mili*, a text that may not state one clear message but that forcefully guides the reader through the story by constantly passing judgment on the heroine's behavior and commenting on the events that befall her.

Dear Mili is prefaced with a letter, penned by the author. In it, the storyteller builds a bridge between himself and his epistolary partner.

Though he has never set eyes on Mili, "his heart goes out to her"; it reaches her and is thus able to tell the story set forth in his letter. The prefatory remarks draw attention to a topic close to Wilhelm Grimm's heart—the rift between man and nature—and contrast the ease with which flowers floating in separate brooks can drift toward each other when the streams converge with the difficulty humans encounter in their efforts to meet: "Great mountains and rivers, forests and meadows, cities and villages lie in between . . . and humans cannot fly."[27] Nature is thus privileged in its ease of communication, with no natural or artificial barriers blocking communion between its constituent parts.

Though the narrator claims to have sent his heart out to Mili and that this heart "speaks" even as Mili "listens," it is in fact the written word— that most artificial of signifiers—that bridges the gap between him and the girl. The narrator's insistence on turning the word into the agent that overcomes the barriers separating one person from another reminds us of the degree to which the Grimms and others unwittingly divested language of its artificiality and invested it with natural qualities when it was placed in the service of telling stories, in particular children's stories. The preface thus enunciates the naiveté of the text and declares it to be an unreflected and direct narrative lacking the stylized self-consciousness of "literary" works, which are products of culture rather than nature. We are misled to believe that the voice of nature, speaking in a register at once timeless and universal, addresses us, rather than the voice of Wilhelm Grimm, a narrator who is anchored in a specific time and place and intent on sending certain messages constructed by his culture.

Dear Mili begins on a less than cheerful note. We are introduced to a widow who lives at the edge of a village with her one surviving daughter: "Her children had died, all but one daughter, whom she loved dearly." The girl is a model of good behavior: "She was a dear, good little girl, who was always obedient and said her prayers before going to bed and in the morning when she got up." The effect of all this goodness becomes immediately apparent to the reader, who learns in the very next sentence that "everything she did went well." "When she planted something in her little garden patch, a clump of violets or a sprig of rosemary, it took root so well that you could see it growing"—a truly amazing consequence of being dear, good, and obedient. More importantly, we learn that the heroine must have a guardian angel, for "when danger threatened the little girl, she was always saved." After the girl meets up with Saint Joseph, she is more tractable and agreeable than ever, if that is at all possible. Not only does she share her Sunday cake with him and cook his food, she also volunteers to sleep on the floor ("A little straw on the floor will be soft enough for me") and happily follows his instructions to take charge of gathering food in the forest ("It was because he didn't want her to be idle that he had sent her out to work"). To be sure, the girl does get a chance to play (with her guardian angel) after the two have dug up the roots that are to constitute dinner, but she has to work surprisingly hard in view of the fact that she has died.

Sendak is right on one count when it comes to *Dear Mili.* "You have to be careful about reading things into the Grimms' stories," he warns. For *Dear Mili* this is especially the case, in part because the tale sends mixed signals to the reader and, as a result, produces a message that is almost hopelessly garbled. The heroine, we recall, is a "dear, good little girl" blessed with good fortune. But all her prayers and good behavior seem to backfire, for not only does war break out around her, but her mother decides to send her into the woods for "three days" to protect her from "wicked men." While the girl is in the woods, it begins to dawn on the reader that she is spending time at a way station to heaven. When the heroine returns home, we learn that "her mother had thought wild beasts had torn her to pieces years ago." In fact, it is possible that the girl perished in exactly that way in the forest, then entered the domestic paradise ruled by Saint Joseph. Observe what happens on the girl's first night away from home while she is contemplating the stars: "One by one the stars came out, and looking up at them the child said: 'How bright are the nails on the great door of heaven! What a joy it will be when God opens it!' Then suddenly a star seemed to have fallen to the ground. As the child came nearer, the light grew bigger and bigger until at length she came to a little house and saw that the light was shining from the window." Can there be any doubt that the girl has entered a celestial abode, from which she emerges briefly to fetch her mother?

Why, then, is it that the mother favored sending her daughter on her own into the woods, where the chances for survival must have been slim, over keeping her at home, where the risks were obviously not as grave? The question becomes an urgent one, not because children's literature must adhere to an iron logic of naturalistic motivation, but because most children who read the story in its new incarnation and real-

ize that the heroine dies while the mother survives will be puzzled by
the mother's decision to send her daughter away and will not be satis-
fied with the mother's misplaced faith in Providence ("God in His
mercy will show you the way," she tells her daughter at the edge of the
woods).

The significance of the mother's decision nonetheless pales by comparison with the weightiness of the final image and final page in the
book. With outstretched arms and eyes that seem blinded by age, the
mother greets her daughter, who marches homeward, rosebud in hand,
against the background of a brilliant sunset. Here is the verbal rendition
of the tale's "happy end": "All evening they sat happily together. Then
they went to bed calmly and cheerfully, and next morning the neighbors found them dead. They had fallen happily asleep, and between
them lay Saint Joseph's rose in full bloom." The blossoming of the rose
presumably offers the promise of eternal life, for Saint Joseph had
handed the rose to the heroine with the reassurance of a return when
the flower came to full bloom. This orientation to otherworldly salvation is very much in keeping with the story's overlay of religious piety.
The heroine not only spends a great deal of her time praying, but also
appeals to God whenever she is in need ("Oh, dear God, help your
child to go on") and is confident that he will provide for her ("God is
feeding his sheep with roses, why would He forget me?").[28]

In one sense, *Dear Mili* delivers a consistent message, for it can be
read as a Christian parable in which eternal life stands as the reward for
piety and goodness. But at the same time, as a story that draws on fairy-
tale conventions and as a text selected by Maurice Sendak for illustration, it arouses specific expectations, at least on the part of adult readers. Returning to Saint Joseph may be some people's idea of a reward,
but it does not correspond to what most fairy-tale heroines acquire
once they make their way out of the woods. What of the earthly rewards usually stored up for the protagonists and the eternal punishments reserved for the villains? It is hard to believe that children can
find in death an ending more satisfying than wealth and a return home
to *live* happily ever after. And why is it that Maurice Sendak, who usually gives us adventure stories that end with the hero's return to the
here-and-now and reconciliation with mother, suddenly chooses to
spend three years on a text that promises the reward of eternal salvation? Even leaving Sendak out of the picture, looking at the text alone,
it remains difficult to square the otherworldly orientation of this particular story with the secularity of children's literature today. There are

good reasons why we do not begin stories with descriptions of widows who have lost all their children but one, or end them with images of mother and daughter lying down and dying. This is not to say that children should be shielded from descriptions of material hardships and death, only that they are not necessarily better off when entertained with stories that reflect or take as their point of departure the social and cultural realities of a time and place other than their own.

Let us, at long last, look at the textual traces of the tale's origins. When Wilhelm Grimm wrote to Mili in 1816, he had not yet published the ten children's legends appended to the *Nursery and Household Tales*. These ten legends appeared for the first time in the second edition of the tales published in 1819. "Saint Joseph in the Woods," the first of the ten stories, is, as the Grimms themselves noted in their annotations to the tale, a variant of "The Three Little Men in the Woods." Both stories are shaped by the reward-and-punishment pattern characteristic of stories about kind and unkind girls. But "Saint Joseph in the Woods" deviates slightly from the norm by plotting the fortunes of three girls—the oldest is "mischievous and wicked," the second is "much better," while the third is a "pious and kind child." More importantly, the benevolent figure that all three girls meet is very different from the gnomes and witches who usually take up residence in the woods to test or to take in fairy-tale heroines. But the Saint Joseph of this particular tale rewards the "pious and kind child" in typical fairy-tale fashion. After demonstrating her willingness to work and to sacrifice her own comfort to ease the lot of others, the young girl retires for the evening. She awakens to find her virtues rewarded:

> She got up and searched for [Saint Joseph], but he was nowhere to be found. Finally, she noticed a bag with money behind the door, and it was so heavy that she could barely carry it. A note on the bag said that the money was for the girl who slept there that night. So the girl took the bag and hurried straight home with it to her mother. She gave all the money to her mother as a present, and the woman was totally satisfied with her daughter.[29]

The youngest child, whom the mother once "could not stand," has now found favor in her mother's eyes. Saint Joseph gives the girl exactly the reward she needs in order to live happily ever after. But just as he rewards virtue, so he punishes vice. The oldest daughter also makes the journey to Saint Joseph, who quickly determines that she is a selfish opportunist and punishes her by attaching a second nose to her face.

The girl, mortified by the disfiguring effect, pleads with Saint Joseph to relent and remove the nose, which he does. But when the wicked girl returns home, her mother takes her back to the woods to find the bag of money to which she feels entitled. Here is how Saint Joseph punishes evil:

> Along the way . . . they were attacked by so many lizards and snakes that they could not protect themselves. The wicked girl was finally stung to death, and the mother was stung all over her feet for not having raised her daughter in a proper way.

This narrative combines exemplary story with cautionary tale to produce the classic reward-and-punishment pattern. The child-victim turns the tables on her oppressor, just as the child-transgressor is punished. This is very different from *Dear Mili*, which shows us the good child as victim coming to an unhappy end. In this sense, *Dear Mili* stands as an anomaly in the world of the Grimms' fairy tales in particular and of children's literature generally, for it shows us a heroine who, for all her goodness, hard work, and obedience, comes to a sad pass. Of course, there are some who would argue that the heroine's death is more reward than punishment, and theirs would be a reading that conforms precisely with the story's authorial intent. Wilhelm Grimm surely wanted children to get that very message about the afterlife.

In the second text that influenced Wilhelm Grimm's letter to Mili, we have a classic example of the consolatory tale, a story designed to provide comfort to those whose parents or children had suffered an untimely death. "The Rose," the third of the "Legends for Children," tells of a poor woman with two children. The younger of the two must go into the forest every day to fetch wood. There the child is protected and aided by his guardian angel who, one day, brings a rosebud for the child. The mother puts the rosebud in water: "One morning her son did not get out of bed. So she went to his bed and found him dead, but he lay there looking very content. And the rose reached full bloom that very same morning."[30] This tale, as observed earlier, may have served a useful, indeed therapeutic, function in an age when the death of small children was an occurrence of distressing frequency, but it seems less than appropriate as a bedtime story for children in certain cultures of our own age.

What Wilhelm Grimm did in drafting his letter to Mili amounts to a clumsy attempt to cross two different types of tales. "The Rose," a consolatory tale, was grafted onto "Saint Joseph in the Woods," a reward-and-punishment tale oriented very much, despite the figure in the title, to this world and its rewards. The result is an impossible hybrid form, one that tries to reward a good child with something that most children can only think of as a punishment.

Dear Mili is, of course, not unprecedented in its status as a children's book that celebrates the death of a child. But we do have to go back to James Janeway's *Token for Children* (1671) and to Cotton Mather's *Token, for the children of New-England* (1700) to find comparable texts. Judging by the number of editions printed, these books were immensely popular with adults. There is also some evidence that children read them, if only to please their parents. For instance, when the eight-year-old Sarah Camme died in Westmoreland in 1682, her parents, Thomas and Anne Camme, took it upon themselves to write a brief biography of the child. In it, they described Sarah's favorite books. While alive, she "delighted much in reading the holy Scripture; . . . she took great Delight to read the Testimony of Friends to the Appearance of God's Power in Young Children, whether in their Health, or on their Dying Beds; and had got several printed Books that had relation thereto." Sarah may have been as delighted as the Cammes allege, yet it is important to bear in mind that we have nothing more than the testimony of her parents—both of whom happened to be Quaker preachers—to substantiate her love of scripture and biographical narratives.[31]

Janeway, as F. J. Harvey Darton has charitably pointed out, had the best of intentions when he published his stories.[32] From Janeway's point of view, it was a sacred duty to salvage the souls of those who are "not too little to go to Hell."[33] The exemplary stories in *A Token for Children* were also designed to provide comfort to children faced with the tragedy of a sibling's death or confronted with their own mortality when visited by some dread disease. At age 2½, Maurice Sendak himself had just this kind of brush with death—in the form of a thirteen-week bout with measles followed by double pneumonia—that left him frail for most of his childhood and also marked him psychologically. "I remember being terrified of death as a child," Sendak observed. "I think a lot of children are, but I was scared because I heard talk of it all around me. There was always the possibility I might have died of the measles or its aftermath. Certainly my parents were afraid I wouldn't survive."[34]

Sendak's childhood preoccupation with death is further reflected in the vivid recollection of a story told by his father. Of the many "beautiful" and "imaginative" stories Maurice Sendak heard as a child, this one remained fixed in memory. The tale begins with a child taking a walk with his parents. Here is how Sendak retells the rest of the story:

> Somehow he becomes separated from [his parents] and snow begins to fall. The child shivers in the cold and huddles under a tree, sobbing in terror. Then, an enormous, angelic figure hovers over him and says, as he draws the boy up, "I am Abraham, your father." His fear is gone, the child looks up and also sees Sarah. When his mother and father find him, he is dead.[35]

Sendak's admitted "obsession" with his own childhood, his need to replay it and hence defuse some of the powerful emotions associated with it, determines to a great extent not only the plots of the tales he tells but also the kinds of stories he chooses to illustrate. The mystery of Sendak's fascination with *Dear Mili* partially unravels with a look at his own childhood and its texts.

The agenda of children's literature has always been fixed by adults. From its inception, with ABC primers that proclaimed "In Adam's Fall, we sinned all," children's literature moved in the theological/ redemptive mode only to shift gradually, with the introduction of discipline through instruction, into the didactic/moralistic mode. The nineteenth century, which witnessed the great flowering of children's literature, placed, with some notable Victorian exceptions, an unprecedented premium on sending messages to children through literature even as it nervously sought to preserve the notion of childhood as a wide-eyed, innocent, uncontaminated stage of life. Consider, for example, the Grimms' preface to their *Nursery and Household Tales*, where the brothers write about the purity that "makes children appear so marvelous and blessed," then proceed to tell stories about stubborn, obstinate, strong-willed children who are put to death.[36]

The nineteenth-century celebration of childish innocence and the creation of a special literary preserve characterized by naturalness and naiveté were shadowed by a didactic mode anchored in the culture of surveillance so convincingly mapped by Michel Foucault in *Discipline and Punish*.[37] We need look no further than the popular childrearing manuals of the time, with their medieval restraining devices and projects for discipline, to recognize the extent to which manipulation feeds

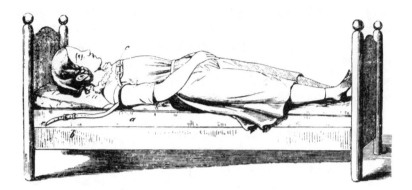

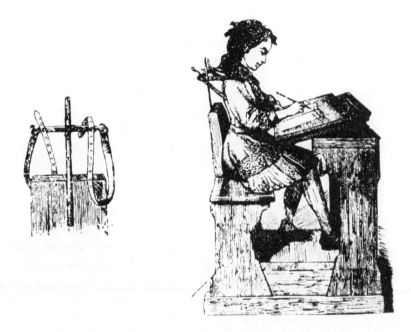

14. The German E. Vogt designed these orthopedic devices to harness children in both at their desks and in bed.

on idealization. For many parents, however, control could be exercised more effectively through visual means than through either words or material forms of restraint.

Children's books first became implicated in a culture of surveillance by propagating the threat of an all-seeing and vengeful God. "Remember," warns Mrs. Teachwell in a work tellingly entitled *The Fairy Spectator; or, the Invisible Monitor*, "that He, who sees all you do; who knows all you say, or think, will either reward you if you be good, or punish you if you be wicked."[38] In "The Child's Instructor," a young girl vows to herself: "I will always behave well, even when I find myself in the greatest solitude; recollecting that, wherever I am, the eye of my Creator is upon me; and to HIM I must look for that blessing which is the reward of a virtuous life."[39] The notorious Fairchild children of Mrs. Sherwood's nineteenth-century children's classic learn to recite a prayer addressed to a "great and dreadful God! who seest every thing and knowest everything; from whom I cannot hide even one thought of my heart; whose eye can go down into the deepest and darkest place!" But they are also kept under the strict supervision of their parents. Mr. and Mrs. Fairchild never seem to take their eyes off their children—when their daughter Lucy boasts that she and her siblings have been exceptionally well behaved and not punished for a long time, Mrs. Fairchild responds by quoting scripture about the evils of boasting and adds: "If you have not done any very naughty thing lately, it is not because there is any goodness or wisdom in you, but because your papa and I have been always with you, carefully watching and guiding you from morning till night."[40] This watchful parental eye was forever trained on the child, seeking to control with punishments, gazes, words, pictures, and whatever else could be added to the arsenal of parental weapons.[41]

Our own culture has moved into yet another mode of telling children's stories, one that might best be described as empathetic/cathartic, resting as it does on a therapeutic model.[42] Any adult who has read stories to children knows how readily they slide into the role of a tale's main character, absorbing all the pains and privileges attending the role of primary actor. The ease with which children identify with storybook characters encouraged Bettelheim and Sendak to endorse children's stories that enact the pains of childhood and help children face and work through their deepest anxieties. But even Bettelheim concedes that "we cannot know at what age a particular fairy tale will be most important to a particular child" and that therefore "we cannot ourselves decide which of the many tales he should be told at any given time or why."[43]

Through a process of trial and error, an adult can eventually determine which stories have special meaning for a child and promote identification and abreaction. Adults, in short, do need to intervene, even if, for Bettelheim, only in a rather haphazard process of selection. Sendak, by contrast, delegates even responsibility for selection to the child. To a mother who insisted, despite her daughter's protests, on reading *Where the Wild Things Are* with her because it was a "Caldecott book," Sendak wrote: "If a kid doesn't like a book, *throw it away*. Children don't give a damn about awards. Why should they? We should let children choose their own books. What they don't like *they will toss aside* [my emphasis]."[44] This is all well and good, but Sendak seems unwittingly to acknowledge adult control even as he repudiates it. Forgetting that the adult has the real power to throw a book away (the girl in question evidently had to suffer through at least ten readings of *Where the Wild Things Are* before her mother wrote to its author for advice), Sendak mistakenly claims that the child can elect to toss a book aside.[45]

It may seem churlish to mount a critique of those who wish to restore to children what seems rightfully theirs and who have done so much to steer us away from the self-righteous and often cruel didactic tales of an earlier age. Both Bettelheim and Sendak have directed our attention to the desires and needs of the child, but it is important to recognize that those desires and needs remain an eternal mystery to adults, who have the real power when it comes to determining what is to constitute children's literature. Adults produce the texts passed on to children, and, as Sendak himself acknowledges, it is *their* childhood anxieties and fears that are reconstructed and mastered through the writing of the texts—though there is also always the chance that the adult will get it right and capture the feelings and experiences of the child. "It may be that in projecting how I felt as a child onto the children I draw I'm being terribly biased and inaccurate," Sendak admits with admirable candor. "But all I have to go on is what I know—not only about my childhood then but about the child I was as he exists now."[46] Children's literature is today still really as much for adults as it is for children. "There was a time in history," Sendak has observed, "when books like *Alice in Wonderland* and the fairy tales of George Mac-

Donald were read by everybody. They were not designated as being 'for children.' The Grimm tales are about the pure essence of life—incest, murder, insane mothers, love, sex—what have you."[47] Jacob Grimm himself stated that the *Nursery and Household Tales* were not recorded for children, but he was delighted to find that they had become avid readers of the book.[48]

This simple fact of children's literature as a product of adult reconstructions of childhood's realities does much to unravel one of the mysteries of fairy tales. Why is it that tales originally written by adults for adults so insistently take the child's point of view and are so obsessed with such childhood matters as fear of abandonment, the dread of being devoured, a sense of helplessness, sibling rivalry, and so on? The answer is Sendak's answer to why he writes children's stories: because they "reconstruct" childhood anxieties and "defuse" their explosive power. The real issue does not turn on the question of why adults remain preoccupied with their past, but on why we have turned the Grimms' tales and other such folkloric monuments into literature that is targeted almost exclusively for children.[49] If those tales helped adults work through anxieties that developed during childhood by mobilizing humor and imagination, why did they then lose their sense of humor (along with their adult audience) in our own day and age? Sendak's description of the genesis of his books reminds us that the line separating children's literature from "adult literature" is really somewhat more fluid than we imagine it to be. His stories, more than those of any other contemporary author, resurrect the burlesque humor and grotesque realism of the folk culture celebrated by Bakhtin and reposition adults as members of the story's implied audience.

Decisions about what makes a good storybook shift dramatically from one era to another, though it is possible to find important continuities between each of the phases I have identified. Janeway's readers, for example, must surely have experienced something of the catharsis that marks the intended effect of many modern children's stories, just as awful-warning tales that move in the didactic/moralistic mode could be punctuated with warnings about a God who sees and hears everything.[50] Whenever a book is written by adults for children, there is a way in which it becomes relentlessly educational, in part because the condition of its existence opens up a chasm between the child reader and the older, wiser adult who has produced the book. Our current agenda and the wisdom of our time may seem vastly superior to Janeway's sanctimoniously lurid descriptions of dying children, or Dr. Heinrich Hoffmann's unforgettable images of thumbsuckers getting their digits sheared off, but they are ultimately our own adult ideas about what is "for their own good."

· CHAPTER V ·

Daughters of Eve: Fairy-Tale Heroines and Their Seven Sins

For whatever the fine ladies of our age may think of the matter,
it is certain, that the only rational ambition they can have,
must be to make obedient daughters, loving wives, faithful friends,
and good Christians.

James Burgh, *The Dignity of Human Nature* (1767)

Would men but generously snap our chains, and be content with
rational fellowship instead of slavish obedience, they would find us more
observant daughters, more affectionate sisters, more faithful wives,
more reasonable mothers—in a word, better citizens.

Mary Wollstonecraft, *A Vindication of the Rights of Women* (1792)

THE NUMBERS of children who go up in flames in nineteenth-century storybooks is nothing short of extraordinary. *Little Truths, for the Instruction of Children* (1802) begins its second volume with the illustrated story of Polly Rust—"*Yes: she was one day left alone, and, I think, playing with the fire; her clothes were burnt off her back, and she so scorched as to die the next morning in great pain.*" Little Pauline, we recall, perishes in Dr. Heinrich Hoffmann's *Struwwelpeter* because she played with matches. A pair of shoes, "so pretty and fine," along with a pile of ashes, are all that are left of her. Then there is poor Augusta Noble, who is found "in a blaze, from head to foot" after carrying a lighted candle into her bedroom in *The History of the Fairchild Family*

15. This illustration for the verse "Playing with Fire" reveals the cause
of the girl's "dread scar" and explains that "she went and did /
A thing her mother had forbid."

(1828). Even those who survive the conflagrations they have set off
must endure months of torment, as does a little girl featured in *Select
Rhymes for the Nursery* (1808):

> For many months, before 'twas cur'd,
> Most shocking torments she endur'd;
> And even now, in passing by her,
> You see what 'tis to play with fire![1]

As cruel as these nursery rhymes and stories may seem, they are not
completely devoid of merit, for they offered children a program for survival in an age where ubiquitous open fires and flames made the dangers of being burned to death far more acute than they are today. Some
of the cautionary tales and verse may dwell too long on the consequences of playing with fire, and others may try to exploit the prohibition against playing with fire by enlarging on the evils of disobedience,
but most have at least a kernel of wisdom to them. The same could be
said for the many cautionary tales designed for women, young and old.

In harping on the evils of pride, disobedience, stubbornness, and curiosity, these tales indulge in the same need to promote a safe docility while also participating in the cultural project of stabilizing gender roles. As folktales dropped contestatory stances and adopted the conciliatory mode of cautionary tales, they sought to provide (in however misguided and coercive a fashion) models of successful acculturation while supplying women with what conventional wisdom perceived as the correct program for making and preserving a good marriage. Women who did not accommodate themselves to these patterns would indeed be playing with fire.

Moving from the culture of childhood to the world of women and their marriages does not require a giant step. Fairy tales with children as heroes and heroines often culminate in marriage, and the gap between the behavior expected from children and the conduct demanded of wives is not, as we shall see, as great as one might expect. Like children, women—by nature volatile and unruly—were positioned as targets of disciplinary intervention that would mold them for subservient roles, making more visible forms of coercion superfluous.[2]

Many of the stories treated in this chapter can be seen as replayings of one biblical masterplot: the Genesis account of the Fall. For several centuries now, standard interpretations have identified Eve as the principal agent of transgression and have infused her act of disobedience with strong sexual overtones. Eve not only "disobeys" commands but also "tempts" and "seduces" Adam. She has become the real serpent in the garden. Kierkegaard, as Margaret Miles has pointed out, revealed the missing link between what goes on in the biblical text and what critics have made of it. "Eve is a derived creature," Kierkegaard writes. "To be sure, she is created like Adam, but she is created out of a previous creature. To be sure, she is innocent like Adam, but there is, as it were, a presentiment or a disposition that indeed is not sinfulness but may seem like a hint of sinfulness that is posited by propagation." Eve's body indelibly marks her (despite Kierkegaard's hedging about "a hint of sinfulness") as a creature of transgressive sensuality. That Kierkegaard locates Eve's insubordination in her role as agent of propagation, in her ability to reproduce, is especially striking in light of his insistence that Eve is also "a derived creature." What seems to irritate him more than anything else is that, while Eve must suffer the pains of childbirth, she also receives the reward of giving life.[3]

Blue
Beard.

The young wife turns the forbidden key
And, horror of horrors! what does she see?
The luckless victims of Bluebeard's crime,
But she herself is rescued in time.

16. That women are classed with children as agents of disobedience
becomes evident in this illustration showing Bluebeard's "wife"
succumbing to curiosity.

What orthodox readings of the episode from Genesis make clear is that a predominantly male interpretive community has relentlessly projected onto women a kind of innate hypersensuality and seditiousness that must be contained to prevent the human race from falling into a state of deeper sin. The biblical punishment for Eve's act of defiance takes the form of pain in childbearing along with perpetual subordination to her husband. Woman must henceforth live under the sign of labor and obedience—her untamed, unstable nature must be held in check through physical degradation and the demand for blind submission. The biblical authority that established Eve as subservient to Adam was gradually converted to natural law that admitted no contestation; it was "a hidden law of nature" or man's privilege "by nature" that fixed male superiority in the hierarchy of gender.

It is one of the lesser-known facts of folkloric life that women are rarely as virtuous as they are beautiful. Cinderella and Snow White may combine good behavior with good looks, but they are exceptional in that respect. Wherever we look in folklore, we can find disagreeable heroines. There are princesses who cannot bring themselves to crack a smile, undutiful daughters, lazy peasant women, gluttonous girls, and unfaithful wives. Among the many sins of folkloric heroines, vanity and pride—traits that breed a willful self-sufficiency—figure especially prominently. Oddly enough, these traits rarely discourage suitors; quite to the contrary, they seem to send a powerfully attractive message, in the form of a challenge, to men. Often, however, we read that beauty overrides all other considerations. In a Norwegian tale, a king's daughter "puts on airs," but suitors nonetheless flock to the manor, for the "hateful shrew" is "very pretty."[4] Beauty breeds a sense of superiority that spells disaster for suitors—think of the countless princes who line up one after another to lose their heads at the castles of proud beauties who spurn alliances. It is left to heroes to design prenuptial rites of passage that will turn these arrogant girls into marriageable women— women who are as humble and deferential as they are beautiful.

No condition is better designed to put a woman in her "proper" place than pregnancy. What better way to humble a patronizing princess than by turning her body into a visible sign of her sexual condescension, particularly when she is unmarried. An entire set of folktales shows us women subjected to physical and social mortification in order to prepare them for a life of meek subordination.

Like many a humbled heroine, Cinziella, in Basile's "Pride Punished," learns her lesson so well that she considers herself the basest of creatures and welcomes all manner of insults. She is the first to admit that she has gotten exactly what she deserves: "The miserable Cinziella, agonised at what had befallen her, held it to be the punishment of Heaven for her former arrogance and pride, that she who had treated so many kings and princes as doormats should now be treated like the vilest slut." Her fall, engineered by the King of Belpaese, is a dramatic one. Scorned by the haughty Cinziella, whose every "dram of beauty" is counterbalanced by "a full pound of pride," the king swears revenge. He masquerades as a gardener in order to make his way into the service of Cinziella's father, then, by appealing to Cinziella's vanity with offers of magnificent jewelry and apparel, succeeds in installing himself first in her apartments, then in her antechamber, and finally in her bedroom. There the wily gardener labors in the "fields of love" and gathers the "fruits of his love." Sexual conquest and attendant impregnation do not, however, satisfy the King of Belpaese's appetite for revenge. He continues to keep his identity secret, installs Cinziella in his stables, and encourages her to engage in petty thievery, always ensuring that she will be caught so she may be mocked and jeered at by her social inferiors. The pain of her humiliation becomes so unbearable that Cinziella goes into labor and delivers twin boys. Only after the King has seen his two sons does he finally declare a truce, largely because there is no need for further abasement. From that time on, his wife never forgets "to keep her sails low, bearing in mind that *Ruin is the daughter of Pride*."[5]

"The Crumb in the Beard," recorded in Bologna, tells a similar story of seduction and humiliation as the disciplinary route leading to marital accord. A princess named Stelle calls the hero a dirty fellow because a crumb remains in his beard after he has dined. Wounded vanity leads the young man to vow "vengeance" and to conspire with his own father and the father of the princess to "punish Stelle for her pride." Disguising himself as a baker's helper, the prince enchants the girl with his music, elopes with her, and subjects her to a life of poverty and other humiliations. When Stelle finally faints dead away from shame at one particularly mortifying moment, her mother-in-law intervenes, proclaiming that her son has avenged himself sufficiently. From that day on, Stelle was "never haughty, and had learned to her cost that pride is the greatest fault."[6]

Seduction is the quickest way to conquer proud Italian heroines.

Peruonto, "the greatest idiot and the most perfect boor that nature had ever produced," works faster than most men. All he must do to avenge himself when a princess named Vastolla laughs at him is to shout "Oh, Vastolla, may you become pregnant by me!" and the princess first misses her periods, then experiences "certain attacks of nausea and palpitations," as Basile pointedly states.[7] The princess is not only publicly humiliated, but also socially humbled, and therefore becomes a suitable match for a handsome young prince imprisoned in the body of a boor. This is also the case in the Grimms' "Hans Dumm," a story that was deleted from the first edition of the *Nursery and Household Tales* because of its bawdy plot. Hans Dumm can team up with the princess of the story only after he has impregnated her by wishing her with child. He then lifts her back to her former social station by turning himself into a clever young prince.[8]

The tales of Peruonto and Hans Dumm are both lighthearted in tone, in part because both stories elevate the power of the word over the deed. These are racy stories, but their actors remain innocent, since mere words function as causal agents for physical transformations normally requiring sexual contact. This contrasts starkly with what happens in a darker version of the tale type—one that attributes the pregnancy of the female protagonist to rape. This is no laughing matter. The humiliated suitor in an Arabic story, for example, gets even with the tale's proud heroine by violating her.[9] Whatever the technique—seduction, curse, or rape—the result is always the physical, emotional, and social degradation of the heroine.

The Grimms may have found "Hans Dumm" inappropriate for a collection of children's stories, but they did include in the *Nursery and Household Tales* the story of a proud princess's humiliation at the hands of her husband. Side by side with adult tales detailing the seduction and humiliation of a haughty heroine (with special attention to a woman's public mortification through her pregnancy) exists a second tradition depicting proud women coerced into carrying out demeaning acts of physical labor. The princess of the Grimms' "King Thrushbeard" is a case in point. She makes a habit of mocking every one of her many suitors, especially King Thrushbeard, who has a crooked chin. Forced by her father to marry the first beggar to appear at the door (who happens to be King Thrushbeard in disguise), she lives with him in a wretched hut, where she must tend fires, cook, and clean. When she fails miserably in carrying out these domestic tasks, and shows herself equally inept at weaving baskets, spinning, and selling crockery, she finally lands in the palace kitchen where she is obliged to do utterly disagreeable work. Like Cinziella, she is quick to recognize her failings and to reproach herself: "She thought about her sad fate and cursed the pride and arrogance that had brought her so low and made her so poor." After being treated to a scene of public disgrace, with courtiers laughing and jeering as scraps stolen from the kitchen come tumbling out of her pockets, she is rescued from further obloquy by King Thrushbeard, who has removed his beggar disguise. But demeaning physical labor and public humiliation have operated in tandem to produce just what King Thrushbeard wants: a deferential wife. In the end, the tamed heroine regains her dignity, but only by renouncing any claims to self-esteem: "I've done a great wrong and I don't deserve to be your wife."[10] The scandal of the wife's public humiliation along with a self-proclaimed acknowledgement of her inferiority becomes a *rite de passage* in the ceremony of courtship and marriage.

The not-so-hidden agenda of "King Thrushbeard" remains remarkably stable from one telling to the next. Yet the tale could also quickly be transformed from a gender-oriented to a class-oriented cautionary tale. One version of the tale begins by emphasizing the heroine's beauty and pride, but ends by teaching her a lesson about the hardships faced by the poor. "I did all this to you," King Drosselbart declares, "because you were so proud. I wanted you to know how the poor have to work to get their bread, how hard it is for them to work for their bread."[11] The same narrator turns "The Frog King, or Iron Heinrich" into a story about a princess who is so proud that she does not even deign to look at her servants. After the transformation of the prince, she casts off her arrogant manner, "and from then on she liked her servants and the poor and helped them as much as she could."[12] These versions of the two tales highlight the ideological instability of folk narratives by demonstrating the way in which a few quick strokes can reorient a story to produce a message consonant with an audience's need to correct everyday life.

Hans Christian Andersen seems to have understood more keenly than anyone else the innate contradictions of "King Thrushbeard." That the tale's relentless abasement and trivialization of its heroine might put her on a collision course with her future husband rather than turn her into the ideal marriage partner seems to have escaped the attention of most rewriters. Andersen's literary version of the tale type, however,

17. "I've come to despise you," this prince tells a princess as he
shuts and bolts the door to his kingdom. Hans Christian Andersen's
"Swineherd" reverses the usual order of events in fairy tales by
concluding with a scene of abandonment and degradation.

frankly admits the possibility that a woman who has humiliated herself
by revealing her frivolously false sense of values may be beneath con-
tempt rather than desirable. As in a number of Scandinavian folktales,
a passion for material possessions gets the heroine of Andersen's
"Swineherd" in trouble. But while popular versions of the tale show the
heroine trading her chastity for objects made of gold, Andersen eliminated the bawdy element in one quick stroke by turning the exchange
into kisses for magical toys. More importantly, however, his princess,
despite her remorse, is in the end deserted by the prince/swineherd,
who states with a depth of acerbic vehemence unparalleled in folktales:
"I've come to despise you. An honest prince you rejected. The rose and
the nightingale were not to your taste. But the swineherd—you could

kiss him for the sake of a musical box. Now you can have what you asked for!" The tale ends with the deserted princess sitting in the rain, regretting her foolish pride and mourning her desolate state. Andersen's ending demystifies the message that degradation can spell happiness for a woman.[13]

In many tales women themselves conspire to create a balance of power tilted in favor of their husbands, thus revealing the degree to which social codes could become internalized and self-regulated. The Grimms' "Little Hamster from the Water" tells of a princess who is "proud," refuses to "subject herself" to anyone, and rules her kingdom "singlehandedly." The test that ninety nine of her hundred suitors fail requires them to hide so well that she cannot find them. The hundredth suitor outwits her and never reveals how he did it. "That way she looked up to him, for she thought he had done it all on his own and said to herself: 'He's smarter than I am.'" Here, instead of a husband who has to prove his physical or moral superiority, we have a bride who deliberately seeks out a husband who has earned the badge of intellectual superiority and is thus entitled to have the upper hand in the marriage. The autonomous female subject who resists subordination to men at the start of this tale ends by mobilizing her intelligence to devise a plan designed to subject her to domination.[14]

The folktale's tenacious emphasis on the evils of female pride becomes evident when we see that virtually every inflection of female frailty contains within it an element of arrogance. Take, for example, the sad predicament of the many folkloric princesses who cannot laugh. Interestingly, the solemnness of these young women, which stands in sharp contrast to the derisive style of proud princesses who belittle and make sport of their suitors, is often traced to arrogance. In the Norwegian "Taper-Tom Who Made the Princess Laugh," the princess takes herself "so seriously" that she can never laugh. She is also "so haughty" that she rejects all suitors. "She would not have anyone, no matter how fine, whether he was prince or gentleman."[15] The challenge facing her suitors, as the Norwegian folktale makes clear, is to make her laugh— an act that will function as a sign that she has ceased to consider herself above-it-all.

Vanity and pride stand, then, as the cardinal sins of women in folktales. These vices make for the strong will (familiar enough to us from fairy tales about children) that must be broken before a woman is sufficiently obedient to qualify for matrimony. That the horrors of haughtiness can be inscribed on virtually any tale is amply documented by Ludwig Bechstein's "Proud Bride." Bechstein takes a tale that, in its oral renditions, celebrates female ingenuity in the face of chilling dangers and turns it into a moral lesson on the hazards of female vanity. "The Robber Bridegroom" (AT 955) gives us a heroine who discovers that her betrothed leads a band of ruthless criminals. She witnesses the murder of a girl and watches in horror from her hiding place while one of the robbers chops off the girl's finger in order to release a ring on it. When the robbers leave, the heroine takes the severed finger and uses it as evidence to convict her betrothed and his accomplices.

Most variants of this tale type celebrate the courage and craft of a heroine who singlehandedly gets the better of a team of murderers. Bechstein, in his *Book of German Fairy Tales* (1845), would have none of that. The heroine of his "Proud Bride" is beautiful, but vain and disobedient. While most of her counterparts in the tale type "The Robber Bridegroom" are depicted as innocent victims who come face-to-face with unspeakable atrocities, the protagonist of Bechstein's tale is held responsible for the perils she faces. "You are going to die," the robber groom tells the girl whose murder the heroine witnesses. "And soon you'll have company. A pastor's daughter, a proud young thing like you, will follow you." From her hiding place, the heroine silently swears to herself that, if she survives this hideous ordeal, she will never again act arrogantly. In the end, she is indeed "cured" and settles down to become the "good wife" of a clergyman.[16]

When Bechstein points out in this tale that it is "a well known fact that by telling a woman not to do something that she ought to do, you can get her to do it," it becomes clear that no female figure of his, no matter how heroic, could possibly escape the charge of disobedience: woman is by nature a transgressor. More importantly, by enunciating a "general truth" about the way in which women have to be treated like children in order to get them to "behave," Bechstein reveals that tales like his are out to belittle the women who read the story as much as the heroine whose story is told. The degree to which this holds true becomes evident as one teller after another of cautionary tales about proud women engages in an emphatic denial that the specific case related has anything to do with women in general. This is all too reminiscent of seventeenth-century marriage satires which, after regaling the reader with pictures and texts about shrewish wives oppressing their husbands, routinely end with hollow disclaimers emphasizing that few women are really like this, least of all "the gentle female reader." One broadsheet, for example, ends with a "Protestation to all honest, pious and gentle wives": "The above verses refer only to shrewish wives, not good ones. So I beg that no female reader should imagine that she is intended." This formulaic ending only fully affirms and underscores the extent to which the entire sex comes under fire.[17]

Bawdy tales of proud women brought to a fall by spurned suitors focus on the problem of getting even and restoring the "natural" order in the hierarchy of gender. From an initial position of social inferiority, the heroes succeed in recovering their social status while at the same time putting brides in their proper places—somewhere beneath them. Cleaned-up literary versions of these tales also show old scores being settled, but they so sharpen the didactic point in these narratives of revenge that the characters themselves teach and preach. Heroines ceaselessly blame themselves for their degradation and are forever declaring their own worthlessness. By the time they reach the altar, they have learned their lessons so well that they recite them, often in detail, for the reader. The proud heroines of this tale type are always taught lessons in humility, but the lessons are spelled out with increasing clarity as one moves from the earliest narratives—whether oral or literary—to later stylized literary texts.

Arrogance, haughtiness, and pride—whatever the name, it runs in the blood of most royal fairy-tale women and motivates a plot that relentlessly degrades women and declares them to be social misfits until they have positioned themselves as wives in subordinate roles to husbands. That King Thrushbeard and other folkloric monarchs succeed in driving out those gender-inappropriate traits is consistently presented as a credit to their ingenuity and as a happy ending that stabilizes the "natural" asymmetry of gender relationships. Husbands in folktales of an earthier quality have a different but equally formidable task—one that has aptly been captured in the tale type index by the Shakespearian formulation "The Taming of the Shrew." Humble folk must work just as hard as their royal counterparts to reform their brides who, though commoners, can be just as uppity as princesses.

A Danish version of "The Taming of the Shrew"—a folktale that is widely disseminated across the American and European folklore map and that existed in both oral and literary forms well before Shakespeare's play—gives us the essentials of the tale type and reminds us of the degree to which these stories authorize men to restore the divinely ordained hierarchy of gender relationships by adopting the very traits that they so ardently wish to banish in women.[18] In "The Most Obedient Wife," a wealthy farmer marries off two of his daughters, but hesitates with the third and oldest, a girl who is described as "stubborn," "quarrelsome," "obstinate," "violent," and "ill-tempered." One suitor insists on the match despite the girl's reputation, marries, and returns home on horseback with his new wife. When the pet dog accompanying the couple ignores a command, the husband shoots him outright. (Some versions show the husband giving the dog two chances before shooting him for a third show of disobedience.) The same fate befalls the horse, and the wife cannot but get the message that she had better shape up. In the versions that show the animals shot after three acts of misconduct, the husband frightens his wife into submission by declaring "That's once!" after she has stepped out of line in one way or another. The Danish tale ends with the once recalcitrant woman becoming "gentle" and "obedient" even as her husband has become the double of the "obstinate," "violent," and "ill-tempered" woman he has now tamed.[19]

Some versions of the tale type further celebrate obedience by adding a coda in which a woman wins a prize from her father by being the fastest to respond to a call from her husband, thus offering both a program for instilling blind obedience and a tableau displaying the desired results. This relentless foregrounding of women's vices and virtues successfully suppresses consideration of the way in which men are viewed as admirably reasonable and responsible at the very moment when they adopt the traits seen as untoward in the "shrews" they are taming.

American versions of "The Taming of the Shrew" generally take the form of a pointed anecdote that, by making fun of a woman's fall from notorious willfulness to abject subservience, is doubly invested in a move that degrades women. As Jan Harold Brunvand has shown, these stories have entered and flourished in the sphere of jokelore rather than folklore. As abbreviated forms of their fuller European counterparts, and with a snappy punchline ("That's once!"), they have become so popular a form of entertainment that they recently found their way into a "bedside book" for guests at Hilton hotels. Like their European counterparts, American versions of the tale usually make a point of underscoring the wife's obedience ("Went home, and she made him a good wife") or of emphasizing that henceforth the husband will be in charge ("There was only one pair of britches in the family, and it was Creekmore that wore 'em"). But they often also add a scene that goes beyond the idea of enforced psychological submission by displaying a woman's physical degradation as part of her permanent married condition. One recorded version illustrates a wife's physical subservience by showing her with the saddle from the dead horse on her back and with reins around her neck. A literary version inspired by popular accounts also ends with the wife literally (and voluntarily) in harness: the wife "trotted to the fallen horse, stripped the traces off, and pulled the buggy to the church steps by holding to the ends of the shafts. Leaping up and standing in the buggy, Ezra cracked the whip above his wife's head, and they drove out of the churchyard." The real point of this tale seems to be that once a woman is treated like an animal, she will work like a horse. While the American "jokes" focus on physical degradation as the mark of a successful taming, the European tales tend to limit themselves to a less spectacular and less corporal form of coercion. Neither inflection of the tale type is especially subtle in its reproduction of grotesquely bullying variants of sanctioned social practices.[20]

The coercive tactics dramatized in "The Taming of the Shrew" thrive on exaggeration for the production of a humorous effect. But hyperbole can also be placed in the service of pathos—a woman can, for example, take obedience to such an extreme that she becomes positioned as a martyr whose suffering stirs our emotions even as her moral superiority sets impossibly high standards for all women. Take the case of that female Job known in Western literature by the name Griselda. Her story does not, strictly speaking, belong to the fairy-tale canon, but it is firmly rooted in traditional literature. Of the many versions of "Griselda," those by Boccaccio, Petrarch, and Chaucer are probably the best known. But Perrault, who was more profoundly under the influence of fairy-tale traditions than the other three authors, has the version that provides the most legitimate grounds for comparison with the tales under discussion here.

In announcing that Griselda stands as a "perfect model" for women everywhere, Perrault not only declares self-effacing masochism to be woman's most noble project, but also shifts the target of disciplinary intervention from his heroine (for whom lessons are superfluous) to his female readers. "Patient Griselda" tells of a prince who believes that happy marriages are based on the dominance of one partner over the other. "If you wish to see me wed," he declares, "find me a young beauty without pride or vanity, obedient, with tried and proven patience, and, above all, without a domineering will of her own."[21] A young shepherdess catches his fancy and, once she agrees to comply with his every wish, he marries her. With time, Griselda's devotion begins to rankle him, and he decides to test her love by first separating her from her child, then communicating to her a false report about the child's death. As if this were not enough, he dispatches Griselda back to her humble cottage where she resumes her duties tending sheep. Finally, to deepen her humiliation and display his complete mastery of her will, he recalls her from exile so that she may attend his new betrothed. "I must obey," Griselda tells herself. "Nothing is nearer to my heart than to obey you completely," she says to her husband in a gesture of subordination so extravagant as to effect her own mastery of the situation. Griselda's long-suffering patience has been celebrated as the virtue that wins back her husband (this may seem more punishment than reward), but there is a way in which her patience can also be seen as a powerful social currency that buys for her a form of grim satisfaction through suffering. That message, more forcefully than the manifest lesson that blind obedience and slavish devotion pay off in the end, is probably what has reached most readers of the tale.

In its repeated disavowals of any sort of didactic agenda, the story of Griselda denies its disciplinary intent and aims to enlist the consciousness of its readers in the effort to foster patient suffering as the preferred modality of power for women. Boccaccio's narrator asserts that the deeds of Griselda's husband represent a "mad piece of stupidity."[22] Chaucer's version of "Patient Griselda" concludes with a strong disclaimer about the heroine's value as a role model: "This story does not mean it would be good / For wives to ape Griselda's humility, / It would be unendurable they should." Instead of offering a model for husband/wife relations, the tale symbolically dramatizes the relationship of man to God: ". . . everybody in his own degree / Should be as perfect in his constancy / As was Griselda."

It may well be that for Chaucer's Oxford student narrator, life on earth was nothing more than an allegory rich in implications about man's relationship to his maker. But it is also interesting that he shuttles with such evident ease from a story about husband and wife to a lesson about God and man. Christian theology clearly organizes the two sets of relationships in analogous fashion. As if this covert declaration of woman's ordained subordination to her husband were not enough, Chaucer's envoy adds a tongue-in-cheek exhortation to all women to "take the helm" and "trim the sail" even if their husbands "weep" and "wail." Here is his mock advice about husbands:

> Never revere them, never be in dread,
> For though your husband wears a coat of mail
> Your shafts of crabbed eloquence will thread
> His armour through and drub him like a flail.
> Voice your suspicions of him! Guilt will bind
> Him down, he'll couch as quiet as a quail.[23]

The pervasive irony of the passage subverts the earlier critique of Griselda as a model for women, for what comes under the heaviest fire here is not the transgressing husband but the shrewish wife who is forever abridging her spouse's freedom and coercing him into silent submission.

In Boccaccio's tale, Griselda's husband justifies his actions by explaining that all along he has had an end in view: "namely to teach you to be a wife"—as if Griselda ever needed lessons in deference and obedience. Katherina, the "tamed shrew" of Shakespeare's play, tells us (not without an undercurrent of irony) exactly what being a wife implied in the age of Boccaccio and Shakespeare. After Petruchio has provided evidence of Katherina's "new-built virtue and obedience," he charges her to tell the assembled women "what duty they do owe their lords and husbands." In her speech, Katherina recites the lessons she has learned and preaches submission to husbands:

> Thy husband is thy lord, thy life, thy keeper,
> Thy head, thy sovereign; . . .
> And craves no other tribute at thy hands
> But love, fair looks, and true obedience—
> Too little payment for so great a debt.
> Such duty as the subject owes the prince,
> Even such a woman oweth to her husband.
> And when she is froward, peevish, sullen, sour,
> And not obedient to his honest will,
> What is she but a foul contending rebel
> And graceless traitor to her loving lord?
> I am ashamed that women are so simple
> To offer war where they should kneel for peace,
> Or seek for rule, supremacy, and sway,
> When they are bound to serve, love, and obey.
>
> (*The Taming of the Shrew*,
> V.2.144–45,151–63)

Disobedience can stand on its own as a vice, but it can also be seen as the effect of deeper causes, among them stubbornness and curiosity (as was the case in fairy tales about children). Russian folklore is especially rich in tales about stubborn women. "The Bad Wife" tells of a woman who makes life "impossible" for her husband because of her perverse ways: "She disobeys him in everything." There is also "The Mayoress," in which a woman is cured of ambition, gives up her aspirations to public office, and ends by "obeying her husband."[24] Tales about pig-headed women, even more than tales about disobedient wives, took special hold in Russian folklore. "The Stubborn Wife," like many Russian tales, boldly illustrates the lengths to which a woman will go to have the last word:

> Once a peasant shaved his beard and said to his wife: "Look how well I have shaved." "But you haven't shaved, you have only clipped your beard!" "You're lying, you wretch, I have shaved." "No, it's clipped." The husband thrashed his wife and insisted: "Say it's shaved, or I'll drown you!" "Do what you will, it's still clipped." He took her to the river to drown her. "Say it's shaved?" "No it's clipped." He led her into the water up to her neck and shoved her head in. "Say it's shaved!" The wife could no longer speak, but she raised her hand from the water and showed by moving two fingers like a pair of scissors that his beard was clipped.[25]

Exaggeration in the service of a comic effect makes it impossible to take this traditional tale too seriously without looking like a fool, but it is telling that capital punishment is represented as the natural penalty for female stubbornness, just as it is repeatedly depicted as the appropriate form of retaliation for disobedience. As in many other tales, the woman's vice is foregrounded, exaggerated, and mocked, even as the husband's behavior is neutralized—here, by virtue of the contrast with a willingness to die rather than give in on a wholly trivial point. This is, after all, the story of the "stubborn wife," not the "stubborn husband who first beats then drowns his wife."

Charles Perrault's "Bluebeard" makes the point, more forcefully than any other tale, that female curiosity can lead to no good. It is important, however, to bear in mind that "Bluebeard" began to impart that lesson only in its latter-day versions, when it fell into the hands of those who saw it as a platform for preaching and teaching. Perrault, who decried frivolous stories and insisted on including a "useful moral" in every tale, launched the tradition with his judgmental pronouncements on the tale's characters.[26] Bluebeard's wife, who cannot resist the temptation to disobey her husband, becomes the transgressor, even when the man she "betrays" turns out to be a serial murderer. Here, female curiosity becomes implicated (notwithstanding Perrault's oversimplifying commentary) in a knot of productive contradictions, for Bluebeard's wives would be engaging in a self-effacing gesture tantamount to suicide were they to suppress their curiosity to know what lies behind the door to the forbidden chamber. Yet by opening the door, they willfully insert themselves into an infamous genealogy that can be traced to Eve, even as they play into the hands of a husband who is ready to execute them for discovering his secrets.

"Bloody key as sign of disobedience"—this is the motif that folklorists customarily and insistently refer to in their explications of "Bluebeard." But for many critics, the bloodstained key takes on a momentous relevance for the way in which it points to a double conjugal transgression—one that is both moral and sexual. It becomes a sign of "marital infidelity"; it marks the heroine's "irreversible loss of her virginity"; it stands as a sign of "defloration." For one critic, the forbidden chamber is "clearly the vaginal area," while the bloody key is a "symbol of the loss of chastity." If one recalls that the bloody chamber is strewn with the corpses of Bluebeard's previous wives, this reading becomes willfully idiosyncratic in its attempt to produce a stable ideology. The story itself offers no grounds for connecting the heroine's act of opening a door with sexual betrayal.[27]

Curiosity, along with stubbornness, occupies a privileged position in the pantheon of female sins. Since female curiosity is so often tainted with evil, while male curiosity is enshrined as a virtue, it is not suprising to find many more daughters of Eve than sons of Adam in fairy tales. Joseph Jacobs' "Son of Adam" in his *English Fairy Tales* is exceptional in this respect.[28] The story tells of a worker who learns from his master that Adam, the man whom the worker holds responsible for the curse of labor, was not unique in his susceptibility to curiosity. The master gives his servant the following instructions: "Now you can eat as much as ever you like from any of the dishes on the table; but don't touch the covered dish in the middle till I come back." Like Bluebeard's wife, who gets similar instructions about the rooms in her husband's castle, the servant can't resist the temptation to take a peek at the forbidden dish. When he lifts its lid, a mouse pops out. "Never you blame

Adam again, my man!" his master proclaims. Oddly enough, a failing
usually attributed to the daughters of Eve is in this text assigned to their
male counterparts. This British son of Adam would seem to be a striking exception to the rule that in folklore curiosity becomes infused
with negative connotations only when associated with women and children. Yet if we consider that Adam is a *servant* and that, like women
and children, he has been schooled in the art of submission, it becomes
clear just why his curiosity gets him in trouble rather than getting him
ahead.

In one folktale collection after another female disobedience is condemned in terms so harsh that it is reassuring to find at least one story
that celebrates disobedience. Basile's "She-Bear" commences with a
brief sermon on the merits of refusing to carry out commands:

> The wise man spoke well when he said that one cannot obey gall with
> obedience sweet as sugar. Man must only give well-measured com-
> mands if he expects well-weighed obedience, and resistance springs
> from wrongful orders, as happened *in the case of the King of Roccaspra*,
> who, by asking for what was unseemly from his daughter, caused her
> to run away at the peril of her life and honour.

That the king asks for something "unseemly" figures here as an understatement—what he demands is the hand of his own daughter in
marriage. Here at last is one case in which a women is deemed undeni-
ably right to protest an order and to resist obeying it. The narrator thus
validates female disobedience, though under circumstances so extreme
that it would cause a public scandal to comply with the command
(hence, perhaps, the term "unseemly"). Furthermore, his praise of disobedience is embedded in a context that reviles women for their cunning and deceit. Only a few lines before female disobedience is given a
small degree of validity, female trickery and manipulative skill are described in baroque detail:

> Woman is full of artful tricks strung like beads by the hundred on
> every hair of her head: fraud is her mother, lying her nurse, flattery
> her tutor, dissimulation her councillor and deceit her companion, so
> that she twists and turns man to her whim.[29]

What initially appears to be a discourse on the legitimacy of disobedience and a woman's right to resist coercion gradually becomes part of
a successful effort to condemn women in general.

The narrator's terms are instructive, for they forcefully remind us that, ever since Eve, woman has been seen as the chief agent of dissimulation and deceit. It is she who introduced evil into the world by tricking Adam into taking the apple, and she who continues to control and coerce despite the biblical words about being under her husband's rule. To wax on about woman's treachery in a tale describing a man's premeditated attempt to seduce his daughter and her spontaneous resistance invites some skepticism about the narrator's declarations, though few signs point to the presence of ironic inversions.

While Basile's tale of female disobedience makes a point of associating woman with artifice and art, Perrault's monument to female obedience sees in its female heroine the incarnation of "Nature in all its simplicity and naiveté."[30] Disobedience is the mark of woman's defection from nature; once a woman repeats Eve's sin, she enters the realm of culture, where she relentlessly employs deception and artifice to secure an "unnatural" superior position in the gender hierarchy. In folktales, women's roles are so starkly polarized that we have either dutifully obedient figures aligned with nature, or foul, contending rebels whose every act is tainted with corrupt and corrupting deceit.[31]

The vices highlighted thus far—pride, disobedience, curiosity, stubbornness, and infidelity—are all constructed as shading into each other and can be seen as symptomatic of impudently unbecoming behavior. These brazen marks of self-assertion are supplemented by a cluster of sins that stand under the sign of self-indulgence: licentiousness, sloth, and gluttony.[32] As with the sins of self-assertion, here too there is no clear line of demarcation separating one vice from the other. The licentious woman, for example, indulges her appetite for food and drink even as she evades her household chores. Stories illustrating these vices belong, for the most part, to the earthy variety of comic folktales that give license to licentiousness. Rather than serving as solemn cautionary narratives warning of the evils of various forms of behavior, they give us the facts of life in crude, ribald strokes. Rarely do they pass judgment on the tale's actors, preferring instead to display and celebrate the failures of productive discipline and repressive social codes.

The pleasures of the flesh are obviously not a subject for children's books, but this did not prevent the Grimms from including one toned-down version of a popular bawdy story in the *Nursery and Household Tales*. "Old Hildebrand" gives us the familiar folkloric triangle of a simple peasant, his hot-blooded wife, and a philandering village priest. The wife and priest want to spend "a whole day" together—"having a good time," as the Grimms discreetly put it. The two conspire to trick the peasant into taking a journey, but halfway to his destination, the man learns of their deception. He returns to witness the following scene: "The woman had already slaughtered whatever she could find in the barnyard and had also baked a lot of pancakes. The priest had also arrived and was strumming on his fiddle." This good clean fun is interrupted by the peasant, who has returned home on the advice of a wiser and worldlier neighbor. He gives the priest a "good beating" and presumably cures his wife of her "generosity."[33]

Not all folktale collections present the weaknesses of the flesh in so subtle and tame a fashion. Thanks to the efforts of Friedrich Krauss, who opened the pages of his journal *Anthropophyteia* (1904–1913) to all manner of bawdy folklore, we have ten substantial volumes of off-color items from various regions and cultures. *Kryptadia* (1883–1911), the French counterpart to this Viennese journal, offers twelve, more compact volumes of "obscene" tales from Italy, France, Great Britain, Russia, Germany, and the Scandinavian countries. On the basis of the tales in these collections, we can often reconstruct motifs suppressed in the Aarne-Thompson tale type index. Tale type 1420G (*Anser Venalis - Goose as Gift*), for example, remains cryptic in its details ("the lover regains his gift by a ruse [obscene]") until we discover an entire set of tales in which lusty young peasants bribe women for sexual favors, then mercilessly tease them until the women are prepared to return the original bribes in exchange for sexual satisfaction.

The *Kryptadia* gave its readers a privileged look at documents that had never before reached print in the Western world. It was the first to publish *Russian Secret Tales*, collected by Alexander Afanasev as a supplement to his *Popular Russian Tales*. Womanizing priests, priapic peasants, and lascivious women fill the pages of Afanasev's collection, which contains stories explicit in their sexual detail. In these most unexpurgated of all folktales, adulterous wives are rarely judged and condemned, but shown to be especially resourceful when it comes to outwitting their husbands or getting the better of their lovers. In "The Blind Man's Wife," a woman takes advantage of her husband's infirmity to deceive him with a lawyer's clerk. A miracle occurs, and the blind husband recovers his sight just in time to catch the guilty parties in flagrante. The wife does not, for a moment, lose her composure: "How glad I am, my dear," she tells him gleefully, claiming that, in a dream the night before, a voice had told her: "If you commit adultery with such and such a lawyer's clerk, the Lord will open your husband's eyes." Not one to miss an opportunity, she immediately takes credit for the miracle. "Thanks to me, God has restored your sight."[34]

While a number of Russian tales celebrate female inventiveness and its power to turn virtues into vices, others glorify adultery as a stratagem for getting ahead in life. In "The Cunning Woman," a "pretty wife" conspires with her husband to entrap her suitors (the local priest, deacon, clerk, and sexton). One by one, she lures them into the house, persuades them to undress, then tells them to hide in a chest of soot when her husband "unexpectedly" returns home. The story concludes with the husband earning five hundred roubles for displaying to a wealthy lord the devils hiding in his chest. In another version of the tale, the wife collects twenty roubles from the priest, the churchwarden, and a gypsy in exchange for an evening rendezvous. As each of the three suitors descends into the house through the chimney, the woman's husband, a blacksmith, awaits them "with red hot pincers" applied to their private parts. A second rendezvous results in similar tortures. In the end, the blacksmith and his wife make bets and take bribes that net them enough roubles to live "a little more comfortably."[35]

Bawdy folktales typically show women indulging with great zest in promiscuous behavior and adulterous relationships.[36] Their heroines relish the prospect of the sexual act itself and use sexual liaisons to turn one kind of profit or another. The presentation of female sexuality in these tales, which rarely reached print and which circulate today in the form of dirty jokes (oriented toward a male audience), stands in stark contrast to the picture of sexuality in stories about female infidelity. Cautionary tales rarely concern themselves directly with adultery, in part because they engage in a form of self-censorship that blocks representations of cuckolded husbands. As in marriage satires, the wife's "besetting sin" is pride rather than lust, and the tales are designed more or less to secure a woman's obedience before she gets into any real trouble.[37] This did not, however, prevent listeners and readers from implicating willful women—Bluebeard's wife is the most obvious example—in sexual transgression, thus creating stern cautionary texts against infidelity as a corollary of disobedience.

Gluttony and sloth, the final two items in our catalog of sins, are closely allied. Where there is a well-fed heroine, you can be sure that there will also be a lazy one. The belief that plenty goes hand in hand with laziness—even breeds it—is one that permeates the folklore of virtually every culture. The Italian tale "Jump into My Sack" succinctly formulates the relationship between the two. In it, the hero uses a magical sack to feed the inhabitants of a village struck by famine: "He did this for as long as the famine lasted. But he stopped, once times of plenty returned, so as not to encourage laziness."[38] At the time that these tales were being told, life for the great majority was an unending struggle for survival. "To eat one's fill . . . was the principal pleasure that the peasants dangled before their imaginations, and one that they rarely realized in their lives," Robert Darnton has asserted.[39] If a full stomach signaled the fulfillment of dreams, it also marked an end to struggling for advancement, and the consequent onset of sloth. Hence the constant equation in folktales between hunger and hard work on the one hand, gluttony and idleness on the other.

Nowhere is the equation between gluttony and idleness worked out in greater detail than in stories about marriageable women. In "And Seven!" (an Italian version of "Rumpelstiltskin"), the heroine is "big and fat and so gluttonous that when her mother brought the soup to the table she would eat one bowl, then a second, then a third, and keep on calling for more."[40] By the time the girl has downed six bowls, the mother gets fed up and responds to the request for a seventh by whacking her daughter over the head and shouting "And seven!" A handsome young man hears the phrase and, after asking its meaning, learns that it refers to the seven spindles of hemp spun in one morning by the woman's daughter. The girl seems to be so "crazy about work" that the young man has no reservations about taking her as his bride.

In one version of "Rumpelstiltskin" after another, we find a heroine who succeeds in getting married because an expression of astonishment at her greed is taken as praise for her industry. Just as "The Brave Little Tailor" succeeds in getting ahead because the world misreads the declaration of his accomplishments ("Seven at one blow!"), so too the heroines of various versions of "Rumpelstiltskin" climb the ladder to social success when the description of their deeds is misinterpreted. In this context, it is interesting to note that brave little tailors become desirable matches for the daughters of kings once the world sees them as men of courage rather than as weaklings, while the heroines of "Rumpelstiltskin" become attractive marriage partners as soon as they are perceived to be hard workers rather than big eaters.

The vices that folktales attribute to women are not entirely without a referential relation to real life. To be sure they are often exaggerated, as in the case of the Russian wife who insists with her last dying gasp that her husband's beard has been clipped rather than shaved. But many vices, in particular the sins of self-indulgence, are ordinary human traits that women seem to share equally with their male counterparts in folktales. When it comes to sins of self-assertion, however, women come out far worse than men. Women are the ones who suffer from pride, curiosity, disobedience, stubbornness, and infidelity—traits to be driven out, not cultivated or enjoyed for the pleasurable gains they can produce.

Far more troubling than the negative valorization of pride, curiosity, disobedience, stubbornness, and infidelity, whenever they are attached to female characters, is the consistency with which women are punished with death, threats of murder, and cruel physical abuse for displaying those traits.[41] Time and again, brute strength is used to tame shrews, as in Ludwig Bechstein's "Rage Roast," in which a woman who is not tamed after being beaten every day for a week is finally subjected to a surgery in which the "rage" is sliced off her hips.[42] The hero of the

18. A knight prepares to slice a woman's "rage" off her body.
Since the woman encouraged her daughter to disobey her husband,
she is considered an appropriate target for physical punishment.

Italian "Animal Talk and the Nosy Wife" takes his cue from the animal kingdom when it comes to dealing with his wife. Once he magically acquires the ability to understand the speech of animals, he compares notes with them on how to manage women. From a rooster, who rules his roost with an iron claw, he learns that "the hens must do as I say, even if there are great numbers of them. I'm not like you who have only one wife. You let her rule you." Like the rooster, who drives his hens away whenever they want anything, the husband discovers the advantages of resorting to physical violence, especially when his wife becomes too curious: "The husband took his belt and lashed the daylights out of her."[43] In folktales and fairy tales, physical coercion becomes a legitimate, even pleasurable, form of disciplinary action.

For pride, curiosity, disobedience, and stubbornness, a good lashing usually does the trick, though there are many occasions on which death threats are required for good measure. Adulterous wives in a small number of tales that do not conform to the contours of the bawdy tales described earlier call for more extreme measures, not so much for their sexual indiscretion as for their defiant and deviant behavior. In the Italian folktale "Solomon's Advice," a man lodges for one night at a house where a blind woman is kept in the cellar. In the evening, the woman emerges from her underground abode to have a bowl of soup, then returns to the cellar. The master of the house explains: "That is my wife. When I used to go away, she would receive another man. Once I came back and found them together. The bowl she eats out of is the man's head; the spoon is the reed I used to gouge out her eyes."[44] In the Grimms' collection, a treacherous wife is put to death by her father when she betrays her husband—she is sent out to sea with her accomplice in a boat filled with holes.[45] At the end of another story, a king declares the appropriate punishment for a deceitful wife, without realizing that he is pronouncing the death sentence for his own unfaithful spouse. "Hang her first," he insists, "then burn her, then throw her ashes to the wind."[46]

In folktales and fairy tales, laziness, gluttony, and licentiousness are taken to such comic extremes that they are less vices than subversive negations of a regime that requires continuous productive exertions to sustain life. The plots of stories recounting the consequences of these attributes may move in a realistic mode, but they take advantage of hyperbole to slide into the surreal. When it comes to depicting sins of self-assertion, however, we find an entirely different set of laws at work.

Women who display arrogance, curiosity, disobedience, and stubborn-ness, along with those who engage in adulterous behavior that is less good, clean fun than a flagrant sign of defiance, are the protagonists of tales that take a tragic turn. Here it is not so much the vices that are shown taking an extreme form as the punishments for the vices—the act of transgression that authorizes the presentation of the punishment is, in fact, often trivial. Even the harshest penalties remain unchallenged when women begin breaking all the rules in the book of feminine be-havior by taking steps in the direction of acquiring knowledge and power.

· CHAPTER VI ·

Tyranny at Home: "Catskin" and "Cinderella"

Anna will never marry until she finds a man exactly like her father.

Martha Freud

IN "THE MAIDEN WITHOUT HANDS," the Grimms made a spirited effort to mask a father's desire for his daughter. Where most European versions of the tale type (including many of the Grimms' own sources) show a father so enraged by his daughter's refusal to marry him that he chops off her hands (and occasionally her breasts or tongue as well), the Grimms' story places the father in the dreadful—but by no means scandalous—situation of having to choose between forfeiting his own life or maiming his daughter. That he chooses the latter may make him cowardly, graceless, and mean-spirited, but it emphatically removes him from the class of ruthless fiends that his folkloric cousins join when they first court their daughters, then lift the sword against them.

The miller in the Grimms' "Maiden without Hands" makes a pact with the devil. In exchange for untold wealth, he promises to give the devil whatever is standing behind his mill—his daughter, as it turns out, and not the apple tree on which the miller had counted. The doomed maiden succeeds in protecting herself from satanic advances by cleansing herself, first in bathwater, then in tears. In a rage, the devil orders the miller to chop off his daughter's hands or to face perdition. When the terrified miller elects to sacrifice the girl's hands and begs her to forgive him for the injury he is about to inflict on her, his dutiful daughter replies: "Dear Father, do what you want with me. I'm your child."[1] The girl's tears miraculously sanctify her wounds, thereby thwarting the devil's designs on her soul, but she is left with dismembered hands that she binds to her back before setting out on a journey that culminates in her accession to a throne.

Slotting the devil rather than the father into the role of villain in "The Maiden without Hands" was a brilliant move on the part of the Grimms. A tale of family conflict in which a father's sexual desire is turned on his daughter, and thereby instantly demonized, turned into a plot about devilish, rather than human, agency. What was once a frightening, sensational story about a father's illicit passion became a religious exemplum about the devil's drive to capture a girl's soul. In the Grimms' version of the tale, the father is absolved of serious blame and turned into a well-meaning though cowardly figure—one not unlike the fathers in "Hansel and Gretel," "Snow White," and "Beauty and the Beast."[2]

We can see this same tendency to blot out all signs of a father's obstructed incestuous desires as the motive for mutilating his daughter in the Italian tale "Olive." In that story, a Jewish widower leaves his daughter with devout Christians, who promise to raise the girl while he is off on business in distant lands. Not until Olive is eighteen does her father return to claim her, and by then she has become so thoroughly assimilated that she evidently cannot resist reading a copy of the Office of the Blessed Virgin on the sly. In punishment, Olive's father cuts her hands "clean off," then has her taken into the woods and abandoned.[3] Here the sexual conflict is transformed into a contest between the daughter's faith and the father's will, with the Jew, in an interesting example of projection, guilty of religious intolerance. In making the father a Jew who abandons his daughter to Christians, the tale probably suggested to its audience that this father's cruelty and willfulness were uniquely deviant, not at all homologous with the behavior of most fairy-tale fathers and their real-life counterparts.

In most unadulterated versions of "The Maiden without Hands"—including several collected by the Grimms—the heroine is the victim of a father who first demands her hand in marriage, then chops both hands off in retaliation for her refusal of his proposal. Even the literary rewritings of the folktale cannot fully conceal what is behind the father's violent mutilation of the daughter's body. The maiming episode is generally reported in the dispassionate, factual style of the folktale, with no searing descriptions of pain and no particular explanation pro-

vided for the mutilation of the arms. It is tempting to argue with Alan
Dundes that "since the father is after his daughter's hand, he takes it
literally," especially in view of the highly charged meaning of a woman's
hand as reflected in the church marriage ceremony of Western tradition
dating from the thirteenth century[4]—a service in which the father relin-
quishes power over his daughter by transferring physical possession of
her hand to her husband (he must stand and observe the priest placing
the bride's hand into that of the groom).[5] But it is not particularly satisfying to rely on an explanation for mutilation that rests on a linguistic
foundation alone. Besides, what are we to make of variant episodes that
show a father cutting off his daughter's breasts or cutting out her
tongue? In point of fact, the latter two acts square more closely with the
psychological twists and turns taken by the tale. Removing the breasts
(think of the martyrdom of Saint Agnes and Saint Barbara) would symbolically de-sexualize the daughter and hence diminish the number of
rivals in competition with the father.[6] Cutting off the tongue (think of
Tereus's rape and mutilation of his sister-in-law Philomela in Ovid's
Metamorphoses) would silence the daughter and prevent her from
broadcasting her father's base deeds.[7]

In "The Girl with Maimed Hands," Basile goes to such great lengths
to motivate the removal of his heroine's hands that we get a vivid sense
of the motif's problematic opaqueness. Basile's Penta is beside herself
when her brother (an occasional substitute for the father in this tale
type) reveals his plans to marry her. Once she has collected herself, she
demands to know just what it is that stirs her brother's desire for her.
He replies with a speech so extraordinary in its baroque detail that it
deserves to be cited in full:

> "My Penta, you are lovely and perfect from the crown of your head to
> the soles of your shoes, but above all things it is your hands that
> enchant me; that hand, like a fork, draws the entrails from the caul-
> dron of my heart; that hand, like a hood, lifts up the bucket of my
> soul from the well of this life; that hand, like pincers, grips my spirit
> while Love works on it like a file. O hand, O lovely hand, ladle which
> pours out sweetness, pliers which rend my desires, shovel which piles
> on coals to make my heart boil over!"[8]

Penta cuts his speech short, summons a servant, and orders him to
sever her hands from her body. After placing the hands in a porcelain

bowl covered with a silk cloth, she sends a message to her brother, entreating him "to enjoy what delighted him most" and "wishing him good health and fine sons."[9]

"The Maiden without Hands" gives us the extreme form of a heroine disempowered by a coercive male—usually a father. We shall see that the many stories about beauties and beasts ("The Search for the Lost Husband" [AT 425]) illustrate the perils of forced marriages, unions in which women must submit unquestioningly to matches made by their fathers and must follow a standard cultural script that privileges filial obedience over the free choice of a sexual partner.[10] "The Maiden without Hands," by contrast, violates every cultural script, if we are to believe, as Freud and Lévi-Strauss assert, that the incest taboo marks the beginning of social organization and signals the passage from nature to culture.[11] With hands severed from their arms, the heroine's body stands as an emblem of disempowerment, helplessness, and victimization. Deprived of the very appendages that have served the creation of culture, she has been moved, through a double violation—the mutilation of her hands as well as the attempted assault on her body—into the realm of nature, the sphere traditionally associated with women by virtue of their privileged biological role and assigned social role in the reproductive process. As Simone de Beauvoir concluded some years ago, the female is "more enslaved to the species than the male, her animality is more manifest."[12] When we learn how the maimed heroine pathetically shakes an apple tree with her body to reap its harvest, or nibbles at pears hanging from low branches, we realize the extent to which her bodily state has forced her to become a foraging creature and reduced her to pathetic dependency on nature's bounty.

The heroine's status as victim is doubly enacted in the tale. In the second phase of the plot, the heroine marries the king in whose garden she had sought nourishment, but becomes the target of a jealous mother-in-law's evil designs while the king is at war with a neighboring land. (The Grimms' version, once again, veers away from family conflict by resurrecting the devil as the source of mischief in the second part of the tale as well as the first.) When the queen gives birth, the mother-in-law writes her son that a dog or some kind of monster has been delivered, whereupon the king orders that his wife and child be abandoned or murdered (the queen is then sent into the forest with her nursing infant bound to her back). If it is not the devil who engineers the mur-

19. Without hands, the heroine is obliged to forage for food like an animal.
This illustration adds a religious touch in the guardian angel.

der of queen and child, it is almost invariably a female figure, usually
the king's mother but in some cases his sister.

The girl without hands thus becomes the fairy-tale victim par excellence, the prey of paternal power run wild and of maternal jealousy that

knows no limits. Bent by the burden of the child bound to her back, and with two stumps for hands, she represents a supremely abject portrait of helplessness. Yet this pathetic figure, who has no sooner escaped incestuous violation than she is driven out of her marital home by a fiendish mother-in-law, has been read by folklorists as the real villain of the story. What Alan Dundes has to say succinctly summarizes their argument:

> The maiden without hands is *a girl who wants to marry her father*, but this taboo cannot be expressed directly. So through projective inversion, it is the father who wants to marry his daughter. This is not to say that there may not be fathers who are sexually attracted to their own daughters, but only that in fairy tales, it is the daughter's point of view which is articulated. . . . Since . . . *it is the girl who is guilty of the original incestuous thought*, it is appropriate that it is the girl who is punished for this thought. [p. 61; my emphasis][13]

For Dundes, a story that describes the tyrannical demands of a father on his daughter is, in reality, nothing more than the pretext for a plot detailing a daughter's desire for her father. Dundes bases his argument on the assumption that fairy tales "represent the child's point of view" and are thus constantly turning parent-victims into parent-oppressors, a line of thinking similar to the one followed by Freud in his qualified rejection of patients' stories about incestuous seduction.[14] (Our earlier look at children's literature has shown us just how "successful" adults have been in capturing the child's point of view when they create stories about children for children.) The "guilty" child simply projects its own sins and transgressions onto the "innocent" parent. Were this so consistently the case as Dundes would have us believe, then "Hansel and Gretel" would be a story that is ostensibly about children abandoned by their parents in the woods, but in reality about parents who are left to starve by their children. Or, more to the point for our context, "Beauty and the Beast" would not really be about a girl who is forced into marriage with a beast by her father, but about a father who is forced into an undesirable marriage by his daughter. That the propositions are so preposterous for these two tales suggests something amiss in Dundes' model of projective inversion.

Dundes' interpretation of "The Maiden without Hands" is a perfect illustration of the hazards of giving too much weight to "hidden meanings" while neglecting the significance of a tale's manifest content. A

fairy tale's surface events often work in tandem with latent undercur-
rents to generate the productive ambiguities that engage our attention
as listeners and readers. In "The Maiden without Hands," the father's
sexual desire for his daughter may elicit her repudiation of his advances
in the chain of the tale's events, but that desire has deep psychological
resonances that implicate the daughter in all her vulnerability. To see a
daughter as wholly detached from the drama of her father's desire is
just as absurd as labeling her "guilty of the original incestuous thought"
when it is the father who makes the advances. Dundes makes the error
of ignoring textual realities that unequivocally show us a father (who as
male parent stands in the most asymmetrical possible power relationship to a female child) taking coercive action against his daughter.[15]
Dundes sees "The Maiden without Hands" as a text that blames the
victim, when in fact he himself engages in the very practice he identifies
at work in the psychological dynamics of the tale.

Stories of father/daughter incest invariably show the father as aggres-
sor, with the daughter as successful resister or unwilling victim. But
note how a daughter becomes tainted by her father's evil no matter
what the circumstances. Here is how Gower tells the story of the King
of Antioch in Shakespeare's *Pericles:*

> This king unto him took a peer,
> Who died and left a female heir,
> So buxom, blithe, and full of face,
> As heaven had lent her all his grace;
> With whom the father liking took,
> And her to incest did provoke:
> Bad child; worse father! to entice his own
> To evil should be done by none.
>
> (*Pericles*, prologue: 21–28)

The father may be the instigator of the incest and may be condemned
in the harshest possible terms, but his daughter, by responding to the
"provocation," becomes by implication a "bad child."[16]

The Aarne/Thompson tale type index fails to note the obvious links
between "The Maiden without Hands" (AT 706) and "The Dress of
Gold, of Silver, and of Stars" (AT 510B), a tale type that—following the
practice of Marian Roalfe Cox—I will henceforth refer to as "Catskin."[17]
Both tale types dictate the presence of a father intent on marrying his
unwilling daughter and chart the successful evasive action she takes.

They also illustrate the perils of excessive paternal devotion and stand in sharp contrast to "Cinderella," the story paired with "Catskin" in the tale type index as AT 510A. In place of the overly affectionate father in "The Maiden without Hands" and "Catskin," "Cinderella" (and for that matter "Snow White" [AT 709]) gives us an insufficiently affectionate mother who withholds love from her (step)daughter.

In all these tale types, a persecuted heroine must flee home in order to escape a parental oppressor, either one who overwhelms her with too much (paternal) love *or* who punishes her with too little (maternal) love, but rarely both. The two stories give us different aspects of one plot—each demonizing only one of the two parental actors in that drama of family conflict.[18] That the two plots really constitute only one story becomes clear from the ease with which "The Maiden without Hands" can cross over from tale type AT 706 to become a "Cinderella" or "Snow White" tale.

A late nineteenth-century German variant of "The Maiden without Hands" from the region of Mecklenburg, for example, describes the fate of a girl whose father remarries after his wife has died. After the death of the father, the heroine's stepmother runs an inn and becomes enraged by the attention paid to her stepdaughter by guests. She takes the girl down to the cellar and gives her a choice between two grisly options: "to be burned with sulfur or to have her arms and feet cut off (the arms right up to the elbows, the feet right up to the knees)."[19] The remainder of the tale charts the heroine's sufferings and redemption, capped by the obligatory punishment of the stepmother who is "torn into pieces by four oxen." The ease with which the stepmother moves into the slot of villain in "The Girl without Hands," without for one moment altering the motivation for her hatred of the heroine, illustrates the essential unity of what has turned into one plot about fathers driven by incestuous desires and another about stepmothers whose murderous schemes are fueled by sexual jealousy.

Interestingly, however, our own age has suppressed tales of paternal incestuous desire even as it has turned stories about maternal evil into cultural icons.[20] Given the radical shift in audience for fairy tales as they moved from the workroom into the nursery, it is easy enough to understand why the forbidding theme of incest—along with any sexually-charged matters—would be erased as quickly as possible. As early as 1816, when Albert Ludwig Grimm (no relation to the brothers) published *Lina's Book of Fairy Tales*, the father in "Catskin" was declared innocent. The court councillors in Grimm's "Fairy Tale of Brunnenhold and Brunnenstark" are the ones to blame, for they are intent on arranging a marriage between father and daughter. The morally unimpeachable king tries to defy their orders and delivers stern lectures on the duties of a monarch: "He explained . . . that such a thing would be a sin in the eyes of man and God, for it had never before happened that a father wanted to take his daughter for a wife, and even as a king he could not allow himself what no man had ever done."[21]

In an age that accepted the biblical wisdom of husbands as gods ("Wives submit yourselves unto your own husbands, as unto the Lord" [*Ephesians* 5.22]) and told young women that "to you your father should be as a god," it was near sacrilege to depict a father whose conduct was so shocking as to sanction disobedience.[22] But it is less obvious why "Catskin" came to be used as an opportunity to dilate on maternal malice. The tale type offers an interesting case study of the way in which rewriters of a tale ingeniously exonerated fathers and shifted the burden of guilt for a father's crimes to the mother.

Let us begin with what is perhaps the best known of all versions of "Catskin": Perrault's "Donkey-Skin" ("Peau d'Ane"). The tale begins with a dying queen's last words to her husband: "'Promise me that if, when I am gone, you find a woman wiser and more beautiful than I, you will marry her and so provide an heir for your throne.'"[23] The king, who is "inconsolable in his grief," is not eager to remarry, but his courtiers urge him to find a new wife. As it turns out, only the king's daughter has "a charm and beauty that even the queen had not possessed," and so the king is maneuvered by his dead wife's pronouncements into proposing an incestuous union to his daughter. The story clearly implies that it is the queen who has engineered the alliance and thus removes much of the blame from the father/king. To ensure that no one could ascribe malice to the tale's "innocent" monarch, the narrator observes that the king's grief has also so "confused" his mind that he imagines himself to be a young man and believes his daughter to be "the maiden he had once wooed to be his wife."

Like Perrault, most of the men who produced written versions of this tale implicate the wife in the father's bid for his daughter's hand. Fidelity to the wishes of a dying spouse thus comes to supplant incestuous desire as the motive for the father's attempted seduction of his daughter, and the heroine's mother rather than her father becomes the villain of the piece. In "La Peau d'Anon" (a tale recorded at the close of the nineteenth century in France), the prince/father explains his peculiar dilemma to his daughter with pointed Gallic logic: "I want to remarry, but your mother made me promise that I would marry only a woman who looked liked her. Therefore I can only marry you."[24] Under the circumstances, it becomes difficult to blame the man for turning to his daughter. The text goes beyond suggesting that the king's loyalty to his wife and distress about her death have led to his mad proposal of marriage; here, the king becomes the *victim* of his wife's unreasonable demands. Some versions of the tale make it clear that the wife has targeted one and only one candidate for the king's remarriage. The dying queen gives her husband a shoe or a ring—the woman who can wear the one or the other ("not too slack and not too tight") is destined to be his wife. That woman is always the daughter.[25]

In Perrault's tale, Donkey-skin turns to her fairy godmother for advice. This godmother, in keeping with the spirit of the tale and its conspiracy to muffle the shock of incest, suppresses the possibility of expressing outrage, shame, or fear at the father's demands. "In your heart there is great sadness," she tells Donkey-skin, in an observation that can only be seen as a wild understatement of how a girl would react to her father's proposal of marriage. "You must not disobey your father," she adds, in a sentence that flies in the face of all cultural logic. Nonetheless, the godmother gives advice on how to dodge her father's desire—first by asking him to have three impossibly beautiful dresses made for her, then by asking him for a donkey's skin. When it finally becomes clear that the king will go to any lengths to secure his daughter as bride, the godmother counsels flight from the kingdom.

Straparola also makes the king of his "Catskin" tale something of a victim of his wife's dying wishes. Throughout the tale we hear about the "evil designs of [the] wicked father," of his "execrable lust," his "accursed design," and his "wicked and treacherous passion." Yet it is his wife who decrees that the object of his lust and passion will be his daughter Doralice. On her deathbed, the queen beseeches her husband Tebaldo never to take anyone as wife whose finger does not perfectly fit the wedding ring she is wearing. Faithful husband that he is, Tebaldo "made it a condition that any damsel who might be offered to him in marriage should first try on her finger his wife's ring, to see whether it fitted, and not having found one who fulfilled this condition—the ring being always found too big for this and too small for that—*he was forced to dismiss them all without further parley.*"[26] As Tebaldo puts it, he must marry his daughter, for it is the only way "I shall satisfy my own desire without violating the promise I made to your mother." Thus husband and wife conspire in crafting this assault on the daughter.

Both Perrault and Straparola seem to use similar tactics, if for different reasons, when it comes to rewriting "Catskin." In order to retain the potentially offensive episode in which a father proposes to his daughter, they resort to the strategy of lifting blame for the desired marriage from the father and shifting it to the mother. The incestuous proposal on which the plot turns continues to exist, but without the underlying scandal of the father's incestuous wishes. It is interesting to observe how both critics and rewriters of "Catskin" come at the tale in similar ways. While critics of all persuasions bend over backwards to demonstrate that a story about a father who wants to marry his daughter is really about a seductive daughter, rewriters of the tale insist that the father's proposal of marriage is nothing more than the fulfillment of a mother's desire. Thus the seductive daughter and the collusive mother, the two major culprits for apologists of incestuous fathers, make their appearances in folktales, and in commentaries on them, long before they emerge in the psychoanalytic literature and in legal arguments.[27]

"Catskin," as recorded by the British folklorist Joseph Jacobs, goes one step further in the direction of eliminating the father as villain by replacing him with "a nasty rough old man" to whom the daughter is promised. "Let her marry the first that comes for her," the girl's father proclaims in a fashion reminiscent of the father/king in the Grimms' "King Thrushbeard." The urgency of removing all signs of incestuous desire is underscored by the narrator's move to separate father from daughter as much as possible: "Her father never set eyes on her till she was fifteen years old and was ready to be married."[28] (Interestingly, age fifteen would be precisely when a father might, for the first time, consciously take note of his daughter as an object of sexual desire, and the story here unwittingly betrays its thematic origins.) Jacobs' need to choose a variant of the tale that swerves as far away as possible from the theme of incest is also made clear in his notes to "Catskin." "A Mr. Nutt [the folklorist Alfred Nutt]," he observes, "is inclined to think, from the evidence of the hero-tales which have the unsavoury motif of the Unnatural Father, that the original home of the story was England. . . . I would merely remark on this that there are only very slight traces of the story in these islands nowadays, while it abounds in Italy."[29] Jacobs numbered among those who ensured that there remained "only very slight traces" of the story in collections of British folktales. The conclusion to his "Catskin" is, ironically, one of the few endings that reunite the heroine with her father. Catskin marries a lord, but cannot find happiness until her husband locates Catskin's father, a widower "all alone in the world . . . moping and miserable." Husband and father return to the castle, where with Catskin they form a curious trio that "lives happily ever afterwards."

In "Cinderella" tales, (step)mothers are regularly boiled in oil, rolled down hills in barrels spiked with nails, and torn to pieces by wild animals. The fate of the witch in the Russian "White Duck" shows us just how important it is to eliminate every trace of a malignant female:

> As for the witch, she was tied to the tail of a horse and dragged over a field; where a leg was torn off her, a fire iron stood; where an arm was torn off, a rake stood; where her head was torn off, a bush grew. Birds came swooping down and pecked up her flesh, a wind arose and scattered her bones, and not a trace or a memory was left of her.[30]

In view of this radical elimination of evil women in tales the world over, it seems more than odd that the fathers in variants of "The Girl without Hands" and "Catskin" almost to a man escape penalty and in many cases live happily ever after with their daughters. The Grimms' notes on "Allerleirauh" (their version of "Catskin") observe that two unrecorded oral stories did in fact end with the father's punishment: "He has to pronounce his own sentence and say that he no longer deserves to be king."[31] The gulf between this mild form of self-imposed punishment and the bodily tortures to which (step)mothers and their like are subjected could hardly be greater, but the distance is entirely predictable in view of the tendency in literary versions of these tales to exonerate fathers with incestuous intent and to make mothers responsible for the evil that befalls their daughters. The Grimms' elimination of any punishment for the father in "Allerleirauh" was part of a trend followed by virtually all who had a hand in producing the great nineteenth-century collections of folktales—the very collections that form the basis of tales read by and to children today.

Nowhere is this need to effect a reconciliation between father and

daughter more evident than in "Love Like Salt" (AT 923), a tale type
that has been recognized to be a diluted version of "Catskin."[32] The
folktale plot, which will be familiar in its tragic form to readers of *King
Lear*, begins with a test of love: a king demands declarations of filial
devotion from his three daughters. When the youngest states that she
loves her father like salt, he flies into a rage and banishes her from the
kingdom. The daughter marries a prince, invites her father to the wedding celebration, and in a finale that marks reconciliation with the father, teaches him the value of her declaration by serving him an un-
salted meal.

Variants of "Catskin" pose the very real threat of sexual violation in
its most shocking form to their heroines. In Basile's "She-Bear," the father responds in the following fashion to his daughter's protest against
their marriage: "'Stop your voice and keep your tongue quiet; make up
your mind to tie the marriage knot this very night, for otherwise your
ear will be the biggest bit left of you!'"[33] Fathers in versions of "Love
Like Salt," by contrast, never demand more than verbal pledges of filial
love, and their daughters remain devoted to them even though their
words are seen as indicators of a dearth of affection. Hence the road to
reconciliation remains open, for it is only the father's misreading of his
daughter's pledge that has driven a wedge between the two. In the end,
the daughter can reestablish warm familial relations with her father,
even in the context of marriage to another man—she can live happily
ever after as dutiful daughter *and* as loving wife. This is the same happy
ending Bettelheim praises in "Beauty and the Beast," where Beauty is
seen to transfer the oedipal love for her father to her husband, but is
still able to give her father "the kind of affection most beneficial to
him"—an affection that "restores his failing health and provides him
with a happy life in proximity to his beloved daughter."[34]

While the mother-daughter dyad in fairy tales rarely tolerates a third
element, and slips into the pairing of daughter with husband (eliminating the mother) if there is to be a happy ending at all, the triangular,
father-daughter-husband relationship can weather the most severe
strains and conflicts, as in "Love Like Salt" and even in many versions
of "Catskin." One clear sign of a cultural bias working in favor of keeping the triangle intact appears in the staging of *King Lear*, which for
many years was performed with a happy ending that reunited Cordelia
with Lear and married her to Edgar.[35] We shall see an analogous operation at work in "The Juniper Tree," a tale that culminates in an idyllic

final scene that removes the mother from the family circle to leave a trio consisting of father, daughter, and son.

We have seen the extent to which literary versions of "The Maiden without Hands," "Catskin," and "Love Like Salt" either erase, rationalize, or mute the transgressions of the father. One father becomes guilty of greed rather than of incestuous desire; another is the victim of temporary insanity; a third wants nothing more than a declaration of filial love. All of them, however, are responsible for the flight of their daughters from home into nature. That flight into the woods, with its concomitant degradation of the heroine into a creature of nature, remains the lasting mark of the father's attempted incestuous violation. The flight may not be psychologically motivated in rewritten texts (as was the case in the Grimms' version of "The Maiden without Hands"), but it remains an ineradicable trace of the tale's genealogy.

The Grimms' "Allerleirauh" (their variant of "Catskin") gives us an interesting take on the heroine's flight from her father. Allerleirauh dodges her father's marriage proposal by fleeing into a forest, where she finds a hollow tree that becomes her home. We are reminded of Mary's Child, who makes an "old hollow tree" in the forest her "dwelling place." These fairy-tale outcasts live like animals, sleeping in woodland sanctuaries and foraging for food. When the king's huntsmen discover Allerleirauh's dwelling, they report to their ruler: "'There's a strange animal lying in the hollow tree. We've never seen anything like it. Its skin is made up of a thousand different kinds of fur.'"[36] Mary's Child, who lives like a "poor little animal," must rely on her hair to cover her body when her clothing disintegrates in the course of her exile. As all remnants of culture disappear from the bodies of these heroines, they become affiliated with nature alone and take on its protective coloring.

A flight into nature offers numerous imperiled women an unlikely, but surprisingly common, refuge from sexual pursuit. Peneus, we recall from Ovid's *Metamorphoses*, turns his daughter Daphne into a laurel tree to avert Apollo's assault on her chastity.[37] Here the father intervenes to *protect* the daughter by moving her back to nature—though who can rule out the possibility that sexual jealousy motivates the "protection" to one degree or another? Yeats, in a very different context, but one that still concerns a father's desire to shelter his daughter, celebrates the transformation of girl into rooted tree in "Prayer for My Daughter":

> May she become a flourishing hidden tree
> That all her thoughts may like the linnet be,
> And have no business but dispensing round
> Their magnanimities of sound,
> Nor but in merriment begin a chase,
> Nor but in merriment a quarrel.
> O may she live like some green laurel
> Rooted in one dear perpetual place.

It took Sylvia Plath to recognize the coercive violence of these transformations from flesh into bark, of the cultural edict that places the
daughter's fate into the hands of the father, but more importantly
wedges her between violation and entrapment. In "Virgin in a Tree,"
Plath exposes the implications of the cultural story that celebrates the
transformation of woman into tree:

> . . . chased girls who get them to a tree
> And put on bark's nun-black
> Habit which deflects
> All amorous arrows.[38]

Thrown back into a state of nature through the threat of paternal
violation, Allerleirauh becomes a treed animal, a living being with no
father, no possessions, and hence no palpable exchange value. Lévi-
Strauss's observations on the incest prohibition indirectly reveal the
exact implications of the violation of the incest taboo—the woman in
question is not only coerced into an inappropriate "marriage," she also
loses her value as a gift. "The prohibition of incest," we learn in *The
Elementary Structures of Kinship*, "is less a rule prohibiting marriage with
the mother, sister, or daughter, than a rule obliging the mother, sister,
or daughter to be given to others. It is the supreme rule of the gift, and
it is clearly this aspect, too often unrecognized, which allows its nature
to be understood."[39] Once the incest taboo is violated, a woman is with-
drawn from circulation, no longer available to be "given away," as we
say even today, by a father to another man. In the case of "Allerleirauh,"
the incest taboo may never actually be violated, but the heroine loses
her exchange value—hence also her social status—once the father
makes known his desire for her. The isolation born of incest (threatened or real) is aptly captured in the formulation of one anthropological
observer: "An incestuous couple as well as a stingy family automatically

detaches itself from the give-and-take pattern of tribal existence; it is a foreign body—or at least an inactive one—in the body social."[40]

Allerleirauh returns to civilization when the dogs of a king's huntsmen follow her scent to the hollow tree in which she is sleeping. "'You'll be perfect for the kitchen, Allerleirauh,'" the huntsmen tell the heroine, who can occupy only the lowest rung on the social ladder now that she has been divested of all exchange value. In the kitchen where the king's meals are prepared, Allerleirauh toils away: "She carried wood and water, kept the fires going, plucked the fowls, sorted the vegetables, swept up the ashes, and did all the dirty work." Enslaved as a domestic, Allerleirauh suffers the same trials and tribulations that beset such fairy-tale heroines as the bride of King Thrushbeard and, most notably, Cinderella.

The story of Allerleirauh, as the Grimms tell it, is curiously disjointed. The two kings mentioned in the tale (father and master/groom) seem curiously undifferentiated (both are designated as "the king")—a fact that has led a number of critics to question whether this is really a story that charts a course from incest averted to the legitimate fulfillment of desire.[41] The first version of the Grimms' "Allerleirauh" makes it clear that the golden ring placed in the king's soup to alert him to the presence of the beloved was originally the gift of the man to whom the heroine was once betrothed and whom she marries at the end of the tale. All of this might lead us to believe that the heroine's father and master/groom are one and the same, were it not for the evidence produced by Heinz Rölleke that the many enigmas and inconsistencies in the story stem from the Grimms' reliance on a literary source unacknowledged in their notes to the tale.[42] Interestingly, the literary source begins with the flight of the heroine from a cruel stepmother, not from a menacing father. Allerlei-Rauch, in Carl Nehrlich's novel *Schilly* (1798), becomes the target of her stepmother's wrath because of the attentions of a suitor, to whom she becomes betrothed. She is abandoned in the woods, rescued by hunters, and obliged to polish boots and clean the kitchen in the castle where she takes up residence. By putting the ring given to her by her betrothed into the soup served up to him, she ensures her recognition and weds the duke.

The genesis of the Grimms' tale, its amalgamation of plot lines from both "Catskin" and "Cinderella," demonstrates the close degree of kinship between the two stories. A folktale heroine can become an outcast because of either a father's desire for her or a (step)mother's envy of that desirability. Basile's "Cat Cinderella" shows us just how closely knit the two passions are, though—like most tellers of tales—Basile does not spell out the connection between them:

> There was once . . . a Prince who was a widower, and he had a daughter so dear to him that he saw with no other eyes but hers. . . . The father, however, shortly remarried, and his wife was an evil, malicious, bad-tempered woman who began at once to hate her stepdaughter and threw sour looks, wry faces and scowling glances on her enough to make her jump with fright.[43]

This introduction allows the tale to move in the direction of "Cinderella," but it could easily be truncated to frame the opening situation of "Catskin."

Whether the heroine is oppressed by a father or a (step)mother, she finds herself in dire straits. Becoming a slave to her father's love represents an intolerable situation, and the prospect leads her to become a fugitive. Becoming a domestic slave for her mother brings abuse and humiliation, though it does not force the heroine to take immediate flight. The heroine pursued by her father may hightail it into the forest, but she eventually ends up in the kitchen, where she suffers the lot of Cinderella. In a British variant of "Catskin," the voice of the chief cook in the king's kitchen is uncannily close to that of the wicked stepmother in "Cinderella." When Catskin hints to "Mrs. Cook" that she would like to attend the ball honoring the young lord of the castle, the cook responds in familiar tones and Catskin, like Cinderella, suffers in silence as insults are hurled at her:

> "What! you dirty impudent slut," said the cook, "you go among all the fine lords and ladies with your filthy catskin? A fine figure you'd cut!" and with that she took a basin of water and dashed it into Catskin's face. But she only briskly shook her ears, and said nothing.[44]

It is at this juncture in the tale that the kinship between "Catskin" and "Cinderella" becomes most clearly evident. Cooks, as we know from looking at different variants of other tales (the Grimms' "Fledgling," for instance) often occupy the same functional slot as mothers. "The Juniper Tree," in which a stepmother chops up the hero and cooks him up in a stew, gives us clear evidence of just how readily the activity of preparing food slides into the monstrous. Cinderella's persecution by her stepmother is entirely homologous with Catskin's victimization at the hands of a cook. But where the one tale turns the mother into the chief villain and virtually eliminates the father as actor, the other—in its literary renditions—habitually tones down the father's villainy and continually allows the mother to resurface in the role of fiend.

That the drama of maternal evil (which involves sexual jealousy and domestic enslavement) came to be favored over that of paternal evil (which involves the expression of forbidden sexual desires) comes as no surprise. What is astonishing, however, is that the dual tyrannies exercised by mother and father display such stability in the manner of their representation among different eras and cultures. No matter how far and wide we look, there are just not many fathers who browbeat their daughters with requests for fresh laundry or clean floors, while the number of mothers who turn their daughters into domestic slaves is legion. By the same token, mothers never seem tempted to propose to their sons, though widowers find their daughters virtually irresistible. The domains of the father and mother are clearly marked in "Cinderella" and "Catskin." Control of marriage, and hence the regulation of desire and sexuality, are in the hands of the father; the organization of the domestic sphere, which also determines the availability and desirability of daughters, is orchestrated by the mother. It is at just the point when father and mother wield their power to wall the heroine in, to keep her "at home" through an endogamous marriage or through a form of labor that prevents exogamy (by making her as unattractive as possible), that the heroine becomes either a fugitive or a victim awaiting rescue.

"Catskin" offers the fullest depiction of parental tyranny in its description of a father who withholds the gift of his daughter and of a cook/mother who keeps the heroine at home in a perpetual state of degradation. The only hope for the heroine depends on finding the right clothes and getting a chance to sneak off to the ball. From the father, guardian of her desirability, the heroine receives the clothing that she needs to attract the prince, but only because she has succeeded in hoodwinking him. In many versions of "Catskin," it is the cook, too, who allows the heroine to slip off for half an hour to observe the festivities at the ball—an opportunity that the quick and clever heroine uses to attend the ball. Somehow, despite the control and oppression exercised by those at home, the heroine finds a way to escape and to establish a new home. That she can do so only by proving her domestic skills and presenting herself as dazzling in her physical attractiveness sends a distinct message to the tale's audience, one that has rarely been refashioned by the many cultures in which the tale has flourished.

Ironically, it is our own day and age that, in the tales of "Cinderella" and "Snow White," has intensified maternal malice while placing a premium on physical beauty as the source of salvation for a woman. Walt Disney's "Cinderella," based on Perrault's version of the tale, shows us a stepmother whose harsh, angular features and shrill, arrogant voice conspire to present a portrait of evil incarnate. While her daughters are no lambs, they are never presented as the primary movers in this version of the tale, which privileges mother/daughter rivalry over sibling rivalry. Incessantly barking orders at Cinderella, the stepmother does everything in her power to obstruct the girl's rise from ashes to throne. Cinderella's father, as it turns out, never even enters the animated portion of the movie. In stills that form a preface to the film, we learn that Cinderella's father died in untimely fashion—but he was "kind and devoted," giving his "beloved" child "every luxury and comfort." The only mistake that he made was to marry a "cold," "cruel" woman who was "bitterly jealous of Cinderella's charm and beauty" and "grimly determined to follow the interests of her own two awkward daughters."

In "Snow White," Disney went a step further than in "Cinderella" by revealing in visual terms the monstrous nature of the wicked queen. While the Grimms' stepmother dresses up as an old peddler women (Disney based his film on the Grimms' version), Disney's stepmother transforms herself into a hag of such startling ugliness that she bears no resemblance whatsoever to the wicked queen. The images of this cinematic witch's physiognomy dominate the film and give us its most arresting, and controversial, moments. So frightening was the figure of the old hag that many parents kept their children away from the film. "All over the country," Richard Schickel writes, "there were earnest debates about the appropriateness of *Snow White* for children, and everyone seemed to have a story about someone's child who had had hysterics in the theater or bad dreams for weeks after seeing the film."[45] Fifty years later the debate repeated itself when the film was rereleased to mark its anniversary.

Just as Disney gives us maternal evil in its most extreme manifestation, so too he strengthens the emphasis on female attire and physical beauty. This might seem logical in a cinematic version of these tales, but the amount of footage devoted in "Cinderella" to that perennial "female" problem of what to wear is extraordinary. Disney's subplot concerned with the relationship between Cinderella and the mice in the castle is also based almost entirely on costumes of one sort or another. Snow White may not go through any costume changes, but it is no exaggeration to say that the focus on her physical appearance, highlighted most dramatically when she lies in repose under glass, is remarkable.

The Disney version does not, however, represent a revolutionary turn in the development of these two tales, but rather the logical culmination of a trend that diminished the part of the father even as it magnified the role of the mother. We have seen just how important it was to eliminate fathers and to write large the villainy of mothers as folktales were turned into storybooks. Since then, the invisible father and the monstrous mother have come to serve as twin anchors of many fairy-tale plots and will remain stationed there until the tellers of tales receive new messages to inscribe on their narratives.

· CHAPTER VII ·

Beauties and Beasts:
From Blind Obedience to Love
at First Sight

Love looks not with the eyes, but with the mind,
And therefore is winged Cupid painted blind.

Shakespeare, *A Midsummer Night's Dream*

THE CASUAL WAY in which fairy-tale parents sacrifice their daughters to beasts is nothing short of alarming. A few may hesitate, others show signs of distress, but when the monster comes around to fetch his bride, parents surrender their offspring without much protest. In the Norwegian "East o' the Sun and West o' the Moon," a man even talks his daughter into eloping with a white bear: "[He] kept on telling her of all the riches they would get, and how well off she would be herself; and so at last she thought better of it." A woman in Straparola's "Pig King" decides that marrying her daughter off to a beast is not really such a bad thing, especially since the groom's mother has told her: "Remember that your daughter will inherit this whole kingdom when the king and I shall be dead." When wealth is not at stake, ethics plays a surprisingly prominent role. A father in the British "Small-Tooth Dog" grieves over the loss of his daughter, but "what he had promised had to be done," and he hands his daughter over to a dog to whom he had pledged his most precious possession. In Basile's "Serpent," a king pleads with his daughter—in a choice example of self-serving sophistry—to take a snake as her husband: "Finding myself, I know not how, bound by my promise, I beg you, if you are a dutiful daughter, to enable me to keep my word and to content yourself with the husband Heaven sends and I am forced to give you."[1]

The desire to increase wealth and the wish to preserve the honor of a family often motivate the perplexing, if not downright scandalous, unions of girl and beast. Yet the earliest extant literary version of the tale, "Cupid and Psyche" in Apuleius's *The Golden Ass*, stages a different scenario.[2] Psyche, a "second Venus," has so many admirers that she provokes the jealous wrath of the goddess herself, who summons her son Cupid and orders him to "cause the maid to be consumed with passion for the vilest of men." When Psyche's father, distressed that his daughter, for all her beauty, has no suitors, seeks advice from the oracle, Apollo instructs him to prepare his daughter for a ghastly marriage to a wild beast:

> King, stand the girl upon some mountain-top
> adorned in fullest mourning for the dead.
> No mortal husband, King, shall make her crop—
> it is a raging serpent she must wed,
> which, flying high, works universal Doom,
> debilitating all with Flame and Sword.
> Jove quails, the Gods all dread him—the Abhorred!
> Streams quake before him, and the Stygian Gloom.[3]

In obedience to the oracle, Psyche's parents escort their daughter to the appointed crag, where she is "surrendered to her fate" (108).

The ancient tale makes female sexual jealousy, rather than wealth or the preservation of male honor, the motive for the wedding of the heroine. Psyche must be spirited away to wed a beast because, as a "second Venus," she draws attention away from the goddess to herself. All three of the motives thus far named for marriages to beasts are consonant with the circumstances of arranged marriages and point to the possibility that this tale type dramatizes the actual twists and turns of such alliances. In agreeing to marry a suitor chosen by her parents, a young woman could bring prosperity and honor to her family even as she duly bowed out as a rival for her father's love and affection. But arranged marriages had an obviously disagreeable side to them. The woman who was to make the match had every right to feel frightened by an alliance of such sudden intimacy to a stranger; hence it is no wonder that fairy tales turn the grooms of these unions into beasts.

In facing the paradox of intimacy with a perfect stranger, the female partner in arranged marriages of an earlier era was also expected to give up any notion of autonomy. Marriage in general was seen as the "absolute surrender" of woman to man. In specific terms, it may not have meant the loss of the right "to look, to laugh, or speak," as Lady Chudleigh insisted it did in a poem of 1703, but it did entail a certain loss of liberty and of legal status.[4] In his *Advice to Young Men, and (incidentally) to Young Women*, William Cobbett revealed the extent to which women were deprived of a voice in every sense (from the literal to the legal) of the term. He began by reminding his readers of just how important it was that a wife hold her tongue. The party slandered by a married woman, he pointed out, would proceed legally against a husband, not against a guilty wife. Cobbett also wrote with candor about the typical premodern implications of marriage for women.

> [A woman] makes a surrender, an absolute surrender, of her liberty, for the joint lives of the parties; she gives the husband the absolute right of using her to live in what place, and in what manner and what society, he pleases; she gives him the power to take from her, and to use, for his own purposes, all her goods, unless reserved by some legal instrument; and, above all, she surrenders to him her *person*.[5]

Psyche's wedding ceremony offers a telling commentary on the deeper meaning of a dictated marriage. For Psyche, marriage implies banishment and loss—the event is celebrated as a funeral rather than as a wedding. Torches burn low, "choked with ash and soot," and the marriage chant modulates into "doleful howls." This lugubrious ceremony resonates with powerful symbolic meanings. Erich Neumann gives us a (somewhat overdramatized) reading of Psyche's nuptials as a compelling representation of the terrors of marriage for all women:

> Seen from the standpoint of the matriarchal world, every marriage is a rape of Kore, the virginal bloom, by Hades, the ravishing, earthly aspect of the hostile male. From this point of view every marriage is an exposure on the mountain's summit in mortal loneliness, and a waiting for the male monster, to whom the bride is surrendered.[6]

We need only look at the social construction of love and passion as reflected in our discursive practices to recognize that Psyche's marriage, even in the specificity of all its horrors, mirrors the general nature of courtship. When it comes to descriptions of passionate erotic actions, warlike metaphors appear in profusion. Men *pursue* women, deliver *assaults* on their virtue, and *conquer* them. Women are *besieged* by their admirers, put up *resistance*, and *surrender* to men. The god of love himself (not coincidentally also Psyche's anonymous groom) is an archer whose shots are nearly always fatal. What is interesting for our purposes is that the battle in which the two sexes are engaged can be seen in erotic terms to culminate in the symbolic death of *both* sides, though most frequently it is represented as the conquest of the woman.[7]

In cultures where marriages were routinely arranged by parents, the wedding/death depicted in "Cupid and Psyche" must have been charged with special relevance. What girl could escape the sense of being abandoned by her parents and turned over to a monstrous creature with repulsive desires when she was about to be wedded to a total stranger? The introductory segment of Apuleius's story, with its stark dramatization of the psychological realities attending arranged marriages to strangers, could have had a certain instrumental value in its day and age. By making a show of Psyche's courage in facing the unknown ("Lead forward, and stand me up on the rock to which the response devoted me. Why should I lag?"), and by revealing the senselessness of her fears ("She was smoothly wafted down the steep and rocky slope, and laid softly on the lap of the valley, on flower-sprinkled turf"), the tale may have subdued, if not banished, the fears of girls on the threshold of marriage.

In this context, it is interesting to observe how more recent versions of the tale type "The Search for the Lost Husband" (AT 425), of which "Cupid and Psyche" and "Beauty and the Beast" are variants, highlight the importance of obedience, self-sacrifice, and self-denial, even as they downplay the courage it takes to put these virtues into practice.[8] Like the heroine of Angela Carter's "Courtship of Mr. Lyon," the young women in these tales are "possessed by a sense of obligation to an unusual degree" and would gladly go "to the ends of the earth" for their fathers, whom they "love dearly."[9] Entering into matrimony "for their own good," they take dutiful self-denial to an extreme and are prepared to do almost anything to reverse the declining fortunes of their fathers. The Rumanian "Enchanted Pig" makes it clear that those who obey will get all the rewards. The King in that story cheerfully encourages his youngest daughter to marry the pig who has asked for her hand. "'Obey him, and do everything that he wishes, and I feel sure that Heaven will shortly send you release,'" he tells her. And to ensure that no reader can miss the lesson, the tale ends when the King declares: "'You see, my child, how wise you were in doing what I told you.'"[10]

Madame de Beaumont's Beauty also endorses the value of self-sacrifice: "My father shall not suffer upon my account," she declares. "Since the monster will accept one of his daughters, I will deliver myself up to all his fury, and I am very happy in thinking that my death will save my father's life, and be a proof of my tender love for him." Beauty's sacrifice is applauded throughout the tale, most notably when a "fine lady" appears to Beauty in a dream to congratulate her on her "good will" and to inform her that her act "shall not go unrewarded." More significantly, Beauty's own gloss on her decision to marry Beast reminds us of how important it was for Madame de Beaumont to convey lessons about who knows best when it comes to choosing a marriage partner. "Why did I refuse to marry him?" Beauty asks herself. Astonishingly, it never seems to occur to her that there was nothing wrong with refusing to marry an animal; instead, Beauty offers an extended apology for marrying for friendship rather than love:

> It is neither wit, nor a fine person, in a husband, that makes a woman happy, but virtue, sweetness of temper, and complaisance, and Beast has all these valuable qualifications. It is true, I do not feel the tenderness of affection for him, but I find I have the highest gratitude, esteem, and friendship.[11]

It is not hard to guess what Beauty means by "the tenderness of affection," and one is almost relieved to hear that she has given up the hope for that. But it is difficult for us to imagine how Beauty can renounce sexuality and submit to marriage with a beast, no matter how much "gratitude, esteem, and friendship" she may feel for him. That those feelings could overcome physical repulsion or even substitute for physical attraction becomes particularly ludicrous if we look at some of the animal grooms to whom girls are betrothed in other tales. Take the groom in Afanasev's "Snotty Goat," for example, who is described as follows: "Snot ran down his nose, slobber ran from his mouth." Or consider the "small mouse with a tail a mile long that smelled to high heaven" who becomes the betrothed of a princess in an Italian tale.[12]

For Beauty, a marriage that starts out as an act of self-sacrifice turns into the best of all possible marriages, because it comes to be based on feelings rather than appearances. This privileging of the inner over the

20. Beauty dines with a dignified Beast who is considerably less ferocious
than his counterparts in most other illustrations.

outer, the mind over the body, repeats itself throughout French versions of "Beauty and the Beast." In Perrault's "Ricky of the Tuft," a princess who is as stupid as she is beautiful consents to marry the hero of the tale's title because of his ability to bestow good sense on those he loves. Though she is thrilled to have acquired intelligence and wit, she balks at the thought of marrying a man of such exceptional ugliness until Ricky informs her that she has the power to bestow beauty on the man she loves:

> They say that the princess, as she mused upon her lover's constancy, upon his good sense, and his many admirable qualities of heart and head, grew blind to the deformity of his body and the ugliness of his face; that his hump back seemed no more than was natural in a man who could make the courtliest of bows, and that the dreadful limp which had formerly distressed her now betokened nothing more than a certain diffidence and charming deference of manner. They say further that she found his eyes shone all the brighter for their squint, and that this defect in them was to her but a sign of passionate love; while his great red nose she found nought but martial and heroic.[13]

This most unmagical of fairy-tale transformations takes place because the princess has learned to value character over looks—a truly gender-specific lesson, for fairy-tale heroes are rarely obliged to privilege personality over appearances.[14] This devilishly clever version of the tale reminds us of the emphatic need to persuade women that passion must be sacrificed to duty (as was the case in "Beauty and the Beast") or re-channeled (as in Perrault's tale).

Latter-day literary versions of "Beauty and the Beast" enlist the consciousness of their heroines in the project of socialization. The princess who marries Ricky of the Tuft does not stride "resolutely" on her own to the scene of her nuptials, nor is she coerced into marriage by a belligerent father. Acting neither under the guise of self-empowerment nor under compulsion, she has taught herself to value the very qualities endorsed by a social code and to renounce what her own subjective desires dictate. Here we are in the realm of a form of self-regulation and internalized discipline that makes issues of obedience and coercion entirely superfluous even as it fully effaces the autonomy of the subject by converting the subject's desires into those authorized by the world it inhabits.

Not all heroines of this tale type participate so earnestly in the social regulation of desire. The Italian tale "Bellinda and the Monster" shows us a self-sacrificing yet rebellious heroine who goes against her father's wishes and insists on marrying a monster "so ugly that the mere sight of it was enough to reduce a person to ashes." Bellinda reasons that "it's better for me to sacrifice myself than for all of us to suffer" and over-rules her father, who would prefer to risk the monster's wrath.[15] The same holds true for the heroine of the Grimms' "Singing, Springing Lark," whose father begs her not to put herself at the mercy of the wild lion to whom he has promised her. "'Dearest Father,'" she replies. "'If you've made a promise, you must keep it. I'll go there, and once I've made the lion nice and tame, I'll be back here safe and sound.'"[16] These two beauties give us a double display of courage, first in their determi-nation to reason with the enemies, even when they take the form of ferocious animals and horrifying monsters, then in their unraveling of paternal authority. To the confrontational policies of father and beast, which give rise to violence by affirming the law that might makes right, the daughters respond with a diplomacy of negotiation.

Although it is clear that the self-monitoring heroine in "Ricky of the Tuft" is a relatively late arrival on the site of "Beauty and the Beast," it is less easy to locate the chronological place of the dutifully virtuous daughter or the courageously defiant girl. But it is extraordinary to see how easily a tale about heroic defiance can slide into a story about the virtues of obedience to the law of the father. Literary fairy tales, as we have seen, tend to supplant the diplomatic heroics of folktale figures with qualities like obedience and humility, for collectors and writers of tales assigned heroes and heroines the very character traits they wished to instill in the young. The dutiful daughter who agrees that gratitude should be the sole guide for her marital choice, who resolves not to be swayed by appearances, and who lets herself be persuaded by her fa-ther that a "horrible beast" with a "trunk resembling an elephant's" makes a suitable husband, is an invention of Mme de Villeneuve and other writers.

The lesson in obedience now often preached through a beauty's deci-sion to wed a beast is doubled in the tale's "scene of betrayal." Most variants of "Beauty and the Beast" repeat the relationship between father and daughter in that between husband and wife. Just as latter-day beau-ties learn to defer to paternal authority, so they must also learn to submit to a husband's commands, no matter how tempted they may be to challenge them. In most cases, these beauties must shift allegiances and be prepared to transform filial obedience into uxorial fidelity.

Of the many extant versions of "The Search for the Lost Husband," "Cupid and Psyche" gives us perhaps the fullest description of the tale's scene of betrayal. Psyche's husband (unbeknownst to her, the god Cupid) limits his conjugal visits to the nocturnal hours, when his wife cannot see him, and forbids her to look at him by light. Although Cupid warns his wife of her sisters' duplicity, Psyche finds it hard to ignore their insistence that her spouse is in reality "a monstrous, twining, twisted, coiling, venomous, swollen-throated, ravenously gaping-jawed Serpent." Who can blame her for disobeying her husband and falling in with her sisters' plot when she learns that he is a "bloodthirsty beast" (119)? Psyche yields to "sacrilegious curiosity" (105–6)—the very promptings that beleaguer and indict her many folkloric cousins. As we have seen, female curiosity is rarely invested with positive worth in the lexicon of folkloric values, and figures prominently in its roster of female sins. In Apuleius's tale, however, giving in to curiosity may imply disobedience, but it also requires courage, a character trait gendered masculine by way of contrast to that thoroughly feminine trait, curiosity. Consider Psyche, just as she is about to go against her husband's command: "Then drooping in body and mind, yet fed with unusual strength by the cruelty of fate, she brought forth the lamp and seized the knife, *boldly shedding her sex*" (121; my emphasis).

Psyche's desire for enlightenment (for more than carnal knowledge of her husband) is presented as a masculine act of courage that leads to nothing more than a temporary loss. Making Cupid visible may compel him to flee, but it also stirs in Psyche a love so deep that it transcends the passion she once felt for the unseen god. She stands before the god "spellbound with insatiable delight and worship" (122). Cupid, by contrast, feels himself betrayed by a wife who has exposed what he has purposefully withheld. He punishes her by taking wing—a precedent honored by his folkloric progeny, who also take flight at the first sign of disloyalty (though usually in the form of doves rather than winged gods). For Psyche, the hand that inflicts the wound is also the hand that heals it. When she succumbs to curiosity a second time and opens a casket containing the treasure of true beauty, Cupid comes to her rescue and is reunited with her. Much as the story of Cupid and Psyche disparages female curiosity with references to "sacrilegious curiosity," "rash curiosity," and "uncontrollable curiosity," it also celebrates the revelatory power of curiosity, the way in which the desire for knowledge of the beloved can deepen passion to turn it into love.[17]

The scene of betrayal can, paradoxically, also function as the scene of love at first sight—when Psyche finally *sees* Cupid, she is in a state of sheer rapture.[18] Similarly, the heroine of "East o' the Sun and West o' the Moon" sees her spouse, "then falls so deeply in love with him on the spot that she thought she couldn't live if she didn't give him a kiss there and then." But the single act of disloyalty has, in both cases, a price— Psyche cannot be reunited with Cupid until she has completed tasks that are superhuman in their demands, and the heroine of the Norwegian tale must travel far and wide in search of her husband. Before we analyze the tasks and search that constitute the third and final act of the tale type, it is important to take a closer look at the scene of betrayal in "Cupid and Psyche."

The narrative oddity that turns the moment of deepest marital intimacy into a scene of betrayal invites further analysis. For Psyche, a move that ends with a stronger sense of affiliation is shadowed by Cupid's fears about duplicity. Paradoxically, Psyche drives away the beloved just as she is passing beyond what Bachofen denounced as "sexual enjoyment, shrouded in darkness" to what he praised as "conjugal union" with the god, "recognized in all his glory." Why is it that Cupid chooses to read betrayal into a moment of conjugal loyalty deeper than his highest expectations? As Carol Gilligan's study of female and male developmental patterns reveals, men tend to locate danger, betrayal, and deceit in the context of intimate relationships, while woman identify danger, entrapment, and rejection with situations of isolation. To be sure, Gilligan's cultural model is based on behavioral patterns observed in twentieth-century American life, but it has a surprising parallel in the psychological twists and turns of Apuleius's story.

In "Cupid and Psyche," as in folkloric variants of "The Search for the Lost Husband," the heroine feels herself imperiled at every moment of separation. Twice she suffers the pains of separation, first from her family, then from her husband. So deep are her family attachments that she cannot resist the desire to preserve intimacy with her sisters, however much Cupid warns her against contact with them. By maintaining those ties, she not only falls prey to the sisters' deceptions, but also becomes tainted by them. Here is Cupid's lecture to the Psyche who has betrayed him:

"I the world-famous archer stabbed myself with my own arrow-head. I took you for my wife—only to have you think me a wild bear and raise the blade to sever my head . . . , which bears those very eyes that loved you so fondly.

"This it was I bade you always to beware. This it was against which my loving-heart forewarned you. But as for those fine advisers of yours, they shall pay heavily for their pernicious interference. My flight is penalty enough for you." (123)

Note that Cupid locates danger and deceit primarily in the very rela-tionship where intimacy has so intensified as to eradicate the least threat to him. The treachery he attributes to Psyche existed only at the time when her relationship to him was "shrouded in darkness"—at the very point when Psyche had every reason to fear for her life. Once en-lightened about the nature of her beloved, doubt vanishes and with it the threat of duplicity.

Gilligan's model goes far toward explaining the paradoxical coexis-tence of intimacy and betrayal in this celebrated scene of "Cupid and Psyche." It also does much to explain the lengths to which Psyche is prepared to go in order to reestablish her affiliation with Cupid. While Cupid initially responds with violence and aggression aimed outward to Psyche's move in the direction of greater intimacy (punishing the duplicitous sisters with death), Psyche responds with violence and ag-gression turned inward when Cupid abandons her (flinging herself into the water). She recovers quickly, however, and refocuses her energy on performing the impossible tasks required to reunite her with her husband.

Deceit and disloyalty generally take one of two distinct forms in "The Search for the Lost Husband." A heroine, like Psyche, whose apprehen-sions are often fueled by a mother or by sisters, may feel it is high time to get a good look at the man with whom she has been spending her nights. But beauties who have already seen their husbands and are satis-fied with their appearances (even as beasts) engage in a second form of disloyalty—disloyalty engendered by overly strong family attachments. Here we find stories about women who break their promises to return to the beast because of family ties so powerful that home becomes more attractive than a marital residence. Such tales construct an opposition between own / family and foreign / beast and show the heroine resisting an exogamous union, one that will oblige her to transfer allegiance from her father to her husband. Never once do these stories show a heroine making a move in the direction of autonomy—the tales ceaselessly turn on the question of retargeting the object of the woman's devotion.

The tale type listed in the Aarne/Thompson index as "The Search for the Lost Husband" contains two plots that deviate sharply from each other in their conclusions. One shows the transformation of a beast or the reunion with a husband through an act of compassion (as in "Beauty and the Beast") or an act of violence (who can forget the way in which the king's daughter in "The Frog King" throws her amphibious suitor against the wall?). The other set of tales extends the plot by deferring the transformation—the wife's disobedience leads to a prolonged search for her husband who has fled the scene of betrayal. Since the scene of betrayal is, as I have noted, also the instant of love at first sight, the bride is prepared to (and often does) go to the ends of the earth in her search. Unlike the bride who shows compassion for her husband and in doing so turns him into the object of her desire, the wife in search of her lost husband has always been passionate about him—hence the willingness to go anywhere and do anything to be reunited with him.

This willingness manifests itself more specifically in the form of carrying out superhuman tasks, acquiring magical objects, or simply engaging in a search that requires traversing vast amounts of space. "Cupid and Psyche" gives us a model in that it shows us a heroine implicated in all three tests of devotion. The tale also shows the extent to which stories of beauties and beasts may originally have been driven by the need to stage shows of competence, cleverness, or heroism rather than scenes of eager self-sacrifice and obedient self-denial.

The first three of the four tasks imposed on Psyche by Venus build a single unit—one that challenges Psyche to display control over the essential elements needed to sustain human existence. Psyche must first sort an immense heap of corn, barley, millet, poppy seed, chick peas, lentils, and beans; the second task requires her to yank a wisp of wool from one of a flock of golden sheep; fetching an urn filled with Stygian waters from a mountain stream constitutes the third task. The seeds, the wool, and the water can be seen as metonymic representations of food, clothing, and drink, provided, in turn, by creatures of the earth, water, and air (the ants, the reed, and the eagle that serve as helpers and advisers in accomplishing each task). Interestingly, the three tasks are accomplished in ever higher spatial locations, though this should not mask the fact that they represent attendance to the most basic—and hence also most primitive—biological and cultural needs.[19]

The fourth task, by contrast, requires descent into the Underworld and obliges Psyche to take an active role in her salvation. From Proserpine she must fetch a casket filled with the treasure of divine beauty. This is not only the most complex of the tasks, requiring Psyche to carry out an intricately structured sequence of commands, but also the most challenging. Psyche must resist first the temptation to take pity on those who besiege her with cries for assistance, then the temptation to peer into the casket with its precious substance. She must deny the very urge so fundamental to salvation in "Beauty and the Beast," for it is "unlawful" for her to be moved by pity. Furthermore, she must move against the grain of all later versions of her story by renouncing the desire for beauty (the characteristic feature that distinguishes her from the crowd) and relinquishing its possession to Venus alone.

Of the four tasks, this last proves to be the impossible one. Just as Psyche could not resist the temptation to see Cupid in all his splendor, so too the thought of being seen by Cupid in all her splendor proves impossibly seductive. A second time she succumbs to curiosity: "She felt a rash curiosity mount to her head" (139). But curiosity plays less of a role than it would seem. This time Psyche does not seek to see her lover, but to transform herself into the most attractive possible object of desire. "'What a foolish carrier of divine beauty am I,'" she declares to herself, "'who do not cull the tiniest little smudge for myself, so that I may please my beautiful lover'" (139–40). The only way to defeat Venus, "the fairest of them all," is by using her weapons. Psyche is deified once she has spurned "unlawful" feeling and focused her energies on retrieving from the Underworld the gift of beautiful appearances.

The valorization of beauty at the expense of compassion makes the story of Cupid and Psyche an anomaly in the literary and folkloric history of the tale type to which it belongs. But the plots of other variants are not fueled by beauty contests between two women, the intensity of which becomes clear when Venus orders Cupid to "punish this rebellious beauty" and takes her leave by kissing him "long and fervently" with "parted lips." Instead, the initial situation of rivalry usually hinges on a contrast between greediness and modesty. The heroine is always the fairest of them all, but that fact rarely figures importantly in what is at stake. She distinguishes herself from her sisters by asking for nothing more than a bird, a twig, a flower, or whatever her father happens to find by the wayside, while her sisters demand pearls and diamonds.[20] Once the heroine marries the beast, her parents quickly find consolation for the loss of their daughter in the wealth bestowed on them by their new son-in-law. The heroine, however, languishes in worldly splendor when barred from seeing her family.

It is telling that latter-day versions of "Cupid and Psyche" require the heroine to forfeit beautiful objects—to exchange them for things of no palpable value—in order to be reunited with her husband. In addition to carrying out tasks that require superhuman strength and acquiring objects with supernatural powers, the heroine must unseat her rival (who has become betrothed to the hero) by playing on precisely the vice that plagued her sisters: greed. In the Grimms' "Singing, Springing Lark," the sun, the moon, and the night-wind each give the heroine a casket containing an object used to bribe the false bride for a night in her groom's chamber. In "East o' the Sun and West o' the Moon" the heroine has a golden apple, a golden carding comb, and a golden spinning wheel that are not for sale, "neither for gold nor for money." But she does give them up to her long-nosed rival in exchange for the chance to spend the night with the tale's hero. By trading intimacy, the false bride forfeits the groom to the heroine. Greed resurfaces as the cardinal vice that impedes attaining the very goal it sets for itself. In the end, the heroine who has renounced wealth and worldly goods wins for herself a prince and a kingdom.

The temptation to read moral lessons into fairy tales is so overpowering that even a perceptive reader like Robert Graves could turn "Cupid and Psyche," with its celebration of physical beauty and erotic love, into a "neat philosophical allegory of the progress of the rational soul towards intellectual love."[21] As the tale was retold and rewritten, it was also reinterpreted until it became something of a morality tale preaching the virtue of modesty, obedience, compassion, and so on. Countless versions of the tale begin with contrasts drawn between the heroine's modest wish and her sisters' greed and end with extended contrasts between the heroine's devotion to her husband and a false bride's passion for gold. The heroine's undemanding attachments to father and husband serve as a foil to the avarice of the sisters and false bride. But it is noteworthy that the heroine's modesty does not always serve her well—even if her wish for a rose paves the way for marriage, it also gets her father into a terrible fix. At the same time that disobedience leads to Beast's salvation, it also gets Beauty into trouble. Fairy-tale figures rarely possess the moral stability with which they are invested through high-minded judgments and pronouncements (mainly for the benefit of children) inserted into the tale itself.

No story makes more evident the absurdity of trying to find models for good behavior in fairy tales than the Grimms' "Frog King, or Iron Heinrich."[22] This story, although classified as a tale type separate from "The Search for the Lost Husband," bears a distinct family resemblance to it. Both plots begin with pacts. In one, a father enters into a bargain with an enchanted beast; in the other, a princess promises herself to a frog. Unlike Beauty, the heroine of "The Frog King" operates in bad faith, agreeing to anything so long as the frog will retrieve her golden ball, but repudiating her suitor once she gets what she wants. Only on her father's insistence ("If you've made a promise, you must keep it") does she allow the frog to enter the castle. The father/king continues to order his daughter to comply with the frog's demands: "[He] gave her an angry look and said 'It's not proper to scorn someone who helped you when you were in trouble!'" When the frog insists on sleeping in the girl's bed, she flies into a rage and hurls the determined creature against the wall. At that moment he changes into a handsome young prince. An act of passion (in its most rabidly violent form) rather than an act of compassion liberates the frog from his enchanted form.

Although the princess of "The Frog King" is selfish, greedy, ungrateful, and cruel, in the end she does as well for herself as all the modest, obedient, magnanimous, and compassionate Beauties of "The Search for the Lost Husband." Much as the Grimms tried to rewrite the tale with paternal prompts about the importance of keeping promises and showing gratitude, they could not succeed in camouflaging the way in which the tale rewards indignant rage.

It may be that "The Frog King" started out as a story illustrating the importance of keeping promises. The British variant, "Well of the World's End," certainly has that message inscribed on nearly every episode. A girl promises a frog to do whatever he asks "for a whole night long" in exchange for showing her how to stop up the holes in a sieve so that she can bring home "a sieve full of water." That very evening, a tap is heard at the door and a voice cries out:

> "Open the door, my hinny, my heart,
> Open the door, my own darling;
> Mind you the words that you and I spoke,
> Down in the meadow, at the World's End Well."[23]

21. As the princess flings her amphibious suitor across the room,
he is turned into a gallant prince who takes a bow as he lands.
This courtly representation has whimsical touches, but it steers clear
of the erotic overtones present in many illustrations.

The girl cringes with each new demand, but her disagreeable stepmother urges her to comply with the frog's requests. "Girls must keep
their promises," she declares with satisfaction as she watches her stepdaughter's growing anxiety. The girl does as she is told, but when the
frog asks her to chop his head off, she hesitates. Only at his insistence
does she decapitate him, "and lo! and behold, there stood before her a
handsome young prince."

The message encoded on this tale is impossible to decipher. While it
is true that blind obedience stands the heroine in good stead, the figure

22. Beauty's compassion for Beast will transform this ferocious-looking
creature into a handsome prince.

constantly reminding her to keep her promises is unequivocally associated with evil. Of course we could see in the stepmother's pronouncements a case of evil intentions misfiring, but that would mean missing
the obvious humor in her harping on the matter of obedience. Here
we have a story in which carrying out every command issued by a
villain leads to a happy end. The Grimms' variant of the same tale
type—whatever it tells us—shows us that defying a voice of authority
urging civility and reciprocity leads to salvation.[24] A comparison of
"The Well of the World's End" and "The Frog King, or Iron Heinrich" makes it particularly evident that in the syntagmatic scheme of

folktales, a command and its fulfillment function in exactly the same way as a command and its violation. Whether a hero obeys or disobeys does not really matter much in the narrative economy of folktales, though it makes a world of difference in the moral calculus of children's literature.

Of all the tale episodes in "The Search for the Lost Husband," the scene of betrayal lends itself most readily to moralizing readings. It is here that commands are ignored and prohibitions violated, hence the ease with which a lesson is derived about the perils of disobedience. As Jan-Öjvind Swahn, the tale type's most thorough investigator thus far, points out, "the marriage combined with a prohibition, whatever this might be, is one of the numerous related tricks of which the epical technique of the folk-tale makes use in order to carry the plot further— the appearance of a prohibition in the chain of motifs in a tale implies that someone will violate this."[25] Swahn's observations are without doubt true, but it is also clear that most tellers of the tale invest the scene of betrayal with a weightiness absent from other parts of the story.

Hardly a literary version of the tale lets the episode pass without comment. Starting with Apuleius, who was anything but a straitlaced moralist, "The Search for the Lost Husband" begins to take on the character of a morality play that harps on the evils of curiosity even as it tells a tale in which very different issues are at stake. Interestingly, the most rough-hewn versions of the tale have the least to say about the violation of a prohibition. The Grimms' "Singing, Springing Lark" (which was not subjected to extensive rewriting), for example, moves the heroine from the scene of betrayal out into the world with record speed. Clearly, oral versions are more concerned about getting on with the story than with preaching morals.

The many variants of "The Search for the Lost Husband" remind us of the strength of children's fairy tales as moral magnets, picking up bits and pieces, if never entire blocks, of a value system. But since fairy tales seem to resist wholesale assimilation of a moral outlook or ethical orientation, they tend to offer mixed signals about the way to get ahead. One tale may impart a critique of dishonesty at the same time that it shows a boy defeating his enemies by cheating them. While it is tempting to look for a certain consistency in a tale's moral code (particularly since so many fairy tales have been pressed into service to provide behavioral models), it is rarely possible to find a story that does not encode competing moral claims. "Beauty and the Beast" is no exception, though it is a story that reminds us more forcefully than most of how fairy tales can be tailored to fit prevailing social and cultural fashions.

Still, a survey of variants of "The Search for the Lost Husband" reveals a degree of stability in certain key episodes—episodes of crisis and conflict above all. Scenes of betrothal and of betrayal bring the moral dilemmas facing the heroines of these tales into sharp focus. There we see them facing choices: choices between self-sacrifice on the one hand (which means satisfying the needs of fathers and husbands) and self-indulgence on the other (which implies betraying the demands of fathers and husbands). It is telling that these moments of crisis in the life of the heroine coincide with abandonment, first when her father surrenders her to a beast, then when her spouse punishes her for an act of disobedience by fleeing. The heroine's decision to sacrifice herself in the scene of betrothal invariably leads to the happy resolution of the crisis facing her. Her father is bailed out of his embarrassing financial situation, and the heroine is provided with special creature comforts—better off, even with a beast as husband, than her sisters. A further step in the direction of self-sacrifice (the decision to marry the beast out of compassion for him) leads to ever greater advantages. By contrast, those Beauties who elect to indulge their own needs for knowledge and to press for reciprocal self-revelation find themselves in a terrifying state of unrelatedness that leaves them virtually without resources. It is only by reaffirming their willingness for self-sacrifice—wearing out seven pairs of iron shoes in their search for the beloved, filling seven jars with tears, wearing down seven iron wheels—that these women can reposition themselves in the web of social relations.[26] That moves in the direction of female self-sacrifice are invariably rewarded, while satisfaction of the need for enlightenment is nearly always censured, remains one of the enduring sad facts of this extraordinary tale.

With such a profusion of animal grooms in tales favored by our culture, it is easy to forget that women also fall under magic spells and suffer in silence as snakes, frogs, and ravens, waiting for the right man to come along. While these tales may have fallen into cultural disfavor, with few incorporated into the canon of children's literature, they are worth looking at, however briefly, to see if desire and its attendant courtship rituals are constructed differently.

Tales of enchanted brides have more in common with tales of be-
witched grooms than the Aarne/Thompson index would lead us to believe. To see just how differently the two tale types are described in the
index, let us compare the episodic structure outlined for each:[27]

AT 400	AT 425
The Man on a Quest for His Lost Wife	*The Search for the Lost Husband*
I. The Hero	I. The Monster as Husband
II. The Enchanted Princess	II. Disenchantment of the Monster
III. His Visit Home	
IV. Loss of the Wife	III. Loss of the Husband
V. The Search	IV. Search for Husband
VI. The Recovery	V. Recovery of Husband

Note that the titles already differentiate the two tale types in a remarkable way. As Torberg Lundell has pointed out, the female heroine
"*searches* as for a lost sock, while a man sets off on a *quest*."[28] Her point
might seem frivolous were it not for other indicators that the protagonists of the tale types receive different treatment at the hands of their
classifiers. The wife, for example, is wholly suppressed in the title of AT
425, even though she figures as its heroine; only the object of her
search—a man—is named in the tale's title. What happens in the titles
is repeated in the description of the tales' episodes. The heroine and
central figure of AT 425 is never mentioned in the summary of the tale's
events—her husband stands at the center of attention in all five episodes; by contrast the husband/hero of AT 400, is very much in evidence at all times.[29] In prominently displaying the role of the male in
AT 400, while effacing the presence of the female in AT 425, the
Aarne/Thompson index offers a particularly vivid example of the way in
which the most expert readers of a folktale rewrite it even as they do
nothing more than summarize its events.

Enchanted princesses, whatever form they may take, make demands
very different from those of their male counterparts. From the start,
even before the transgression of any command issued by them, they
charge their grooms with tasks. "Have you come at last, my savior?"
asks the heroine of the Grimms' "The King of the Golden Mountain."
"I've been waiting now twelve years for you. This kingdom is enchanted, and you must release it from the magic spell."[30] Breaking the
magic spell requires, in this instance, impassivity more than anything

else: again and again austerity, chastity, stoicism, and asceticism are rewarded. In "The King of the Golden Mountain," the hero must participate in a sadomasochistic ceremony that requires him to spend three nights submitting to torture (stabbings, beatings, and finally decapitation) at the hands of men in chains. In the Norwegian tale "Three Princesses of Whiteland," the hero must endure floggings, first from a troll with three heads and three rods, then from a troll with six heads and six rods, and finally from a troll with nine heads and nine rods. Weathering three stormy nights in a haunted castle, refusing food and drink, staying awake for an entire night, and sleeping next to a princess without touching her are popular *allomotifs*, or variants, of the tests of endurance mounted in these two tales.

The impassive stoicism required of male disenchanters stands in sharp contrast to the obligatory gesture of passion or act of compassion required of their female counterparts. For the nearly pathological absence of affect in one set of tales, we have a surplus or superabundance in the other. To win a bride in AT 400, a man must demonstrate physical and emotional stoicism in its most extreme form. A reward comes with the display of an unbending will and cold-blooded determination. While some of the heroines of AT 425 are as strong willed as their male counterparts (at least in their perseverance), they earn their prizes primarily by revealing themselves to be creatures of passion, moved by emotions and unable to resist the waves of revulsion or love that engulf them. Their power to disenchant derives from the bold expressiveness of their feelings.

No matter in what cultural context or epoch European tales about animal-brides and animal-grooms are told, they each present a surprisingly durable notion of female and male roles. Women, as a study of "The Search for the Lost Husband" reveals, are creatures of feeling. When obliged to marry beasts, they recoil in horror (unlike their male counterparts who seem resigned, if somewhat disappointed, by their lot in life). The desire for greater intimacy and the overvaluation of family attachments always get these women in trouble, even as their surplus of emotion (passion or compassion) gets their grooms out of trouble. And finally, the desire to meet the needs of others (represented in the carrying out of every unpleasant domestic chore imaginable) and to please their husbands (represented in repeated changes of wardrobe) shows the extent to which these fairy-tale figures are invested in becoming connected and establishing relationships.

All of this might not seem unusual without the contrasting example of "The Search for the Lost Wife" (the name I will henceforth use for "The Man on a Quest for His Lost Wife"). Here the heroes are not stereotypically brave and dashing (though they usually happen to be handsome)—their chief sign of distinction is a nearly pathological deficit of emotion. They rarely commit the cardinal sin of disobedience, and when they do it is usually because a mother or a sister (who is too attached to the hero) has engineered the act. To win a bride, they must demonstrate stoic courage, impassivity in the face of danger, and resistance to affect. When they successfully perform tasks, the rewards for their accomplishments tend to do little more than further them on their journey—only occasionally are the tasks designed to provide for others. As for their physical appearance, it is true that they are often described as young and handsome, but their clothes are at issue only when their garments are so tattered that they must don fresh ones. Not only are the heroes without passion; they are also far less likely than their partners to cultivate human attachments by doing favors or seeking approval.

One variant of "The Search for the Lost Wife" deserves special attention in this context, for it thematizes male resistance to affect even as it illustrates the way in which women, through marriage, conspire to break down that resistance. "Enchanted Princesses and Their Castles" (AT 401A) tells how a hero rescues a princess by keeping awake, keeping silent, or observing a taboo—in short, by demonstrating the ability to refrain from doing something—for three nights. In the Grimms' version of this tale, called "A Tale about the Boy Who Went Forth to Learn What Fear Is," the hero makes his way through the world, encountering one horrifying incident after another, but showing no reaction whatsoever. "Oh, if I could only shudder! If I could only shudder!" he exclaims after each attempt to feel fear misfires.[31] Luck takes him to the realm of a king who needs someone with precisely his defect—a person with the requisite lack of fear to rid his castle of the spirits haunting it. In return, the hero is given the hand of his daughter. However, even after disenchanting the castle, the hero still has not learned to shudder; it takes a chambermaid and his wife to teach him that skill. The two wait until he is asleep in the marital bed, then pour a bucket of cold water and minnows on him: "Oh, I've learned to shudder! I've learned to shudder! Now I know, dear wife, just what it means to shudder!"

Since the hero learns how to shudder in his marital bed, it is easy enough to read his previous failure to shudder as a mark of the "repression of all sexual feelings."[32] But it seems as if more than sexuality is at stake. In a French version of the tale, the hero refuses to marry until he has learned what fear is. A princess who is determined to marry him removes the last barrier to a wedding by cutting open a loaf of bread that has a live blackbird in it. Yann is frightened out of his wits, and the princess proudly declares: "Well then, since you now know what fear is, there's nothing to keep us from getting married."[33] The capacity to respond serves as the passport to love and marriage—though it may also diminish the hero's ability to move without fear from one adventure to the next. Whether the hero has made a breakthrough to a higher form of wisdom or has simply turned into a domestic coward is a point that could be endlessly debated and is in fact continuously reworked in tale variants.[34]

If "The Search for the Lost Husband" displays the trauma of separation and isolation for female characters and reveals the degree to which intimacy is charged with anxiety for male characters, "The Search for the Lost Wife" shows men earning rewards by demonstrating their impassive stoicism and women winning prizes by accomplishing daring feats of domestic skill. That we receive no real information about the marriages in which these tales culminate has a certain logic in view of the patent contradiction between living happily ever after and ceaselessly contesting intimacy. "A Tale About the Boy Who Went Forth to Learn What Fear Is" is one of the few fairy tales that dismantles the barrier dividing male and female modes of relating. In its move toward a rapprochement between male resistance to affect and female affiliation with feeling, it begins to hint that the royal couple allied at its end might truly live happily ever after.

·CHAPTER VIII·

"As Sweet as Love": Violence and the
Fulfillment of Wishes

*The Queen had only one way of settling all difficulties, great or small.
"Off with his head!" she said, without even looking around.*

Lewis Carroll, *Alice in Wonderland*

ONE OF THE MOST mystifying figures of folklore is Herr
Korbes, a man who is assaulted in his own home by a gang of
animals and household objects. The way the Grimms tell the
story, innocent Herr Korbes returns home one day to find himself the
target of a series of nasty pranks. He goes to the hearth to make a fire,
but a cat throws ashes into his face. He rushes to the kitchen to wash,
and a duck squirts water at him. When he grabs a towel to dry himself,
he is ambushed by an egg that breaks open in his towel and glues his
eyes shut. Hoping to recover, he sits down in a chair and is stuck by a
pin. In frustration, he throws himself on his bed but is stuck once
again, this time by a sewing needle lurking in the folds of his pillow.
What starts out as a series of pranks takes a deadly serious turn when
the protagonist, frightened and enraged, flees his house. Just as he
crosses the threshold, a millstone falls down out of nowhere and
crushes him to death.[1]

Edgar Taylor, the Grimms' first English translator, was so baffled by
this story—especially by the unmotivated nature of the assault on the
title figure—that he made a point of writing to the Grimms to ask just
who this Herr Korbes was.[2] He must have been reassured to learn that
Herr Korbes was another name for the *Butzemann* (bogeyman) or for
Knecht Ruprecht, that sinister figure on the lookout for naughty children

as he accompanies Saint Nicholas from house to house. For the sixth edition of the *Nursery and Household Tales*, the Grimms obliged their bewildered readers by adding a concluding line offering an explanation for the events that befall the tale's protagonist: "Herr Korbes must have been a very wicked man."

Herr Korbes is not the only seemingly innocuous figure in the *Nursery and Household Tales* to come to a bad end. An innkeeper in "Riffraff" also finds himself the target of abusive treatment from his "lodgers": a pin lurks in his towel and scratches him when he goes to dry off his face, an egg laid by a duck explodes in his face, a needle sticks him ("and not in the head") when he sits down in a chair.[3] The innkeeper of "Riffraff" is not a particularly nefarious character—in fact, he brings a certain amount of goodwill toward his lodgers, who shamelessly take advantage of him. Here we once again see renegade animals and objects

23. An innkeeper, just about to settle down for a quiet evening, is stuck by a needle—"and not in the head." He is one of many fairy-tale victims of festive violence.

lined up against a man (significantly a "Herr," or master, in the story of Korbes) who becomes their unwitting victim. Yet the events in both "Herr Korbes" and "Riffraff," rather than taking a tragic turn, veer off in the direction of surreal slapstick. These are not stories of transgression and punishment or of victimization and retaliation—instead they offer the burlesque vision of a world in which men and women are constantly subjected to the tyranny of things and to brute animal force.[4] In "Riffraff," comic touches abound—the needle and pin have had "one beer too many," the duck is harnessed up to a carriage and urged to "run as fast as you can," the innkeeper sizes up the hen, rooster, duck, needle, and pin and decides that they are "not a very distinguished looking group."

These two "fables of aggression" give us examples of what one critic has called "preposterous violence."[5] There seems to be no point to what happens here, only a ritual enactment of violence, a slapstick pantomine designed to entertain rather than to educate, discipline, or punish. It may be true that such displays of ritualized violence have a cathartic effect, a "pharmakopic" function in which the poison that causes a disease also functions as a remedy, but we have no sure evidence that this is the case. While the "poison" of ritual violence directed against secondary objects inoculates some observers against violence directed at primary objects (the real targets), it probably is also capable of infecting others. Given the prevalence of violent entertainments for young adults and children, and the obvious glee with which they respond to such amusements, understanding its function in folktales takes on a special urgency. Since many of the tales discussed here have been suppressed by our own day and age as inappropriate for children—in large part for their displays of unmotivated physical violence and its pleasurable effects—reading these tales can help us identify some of the cultural conditions that sanction and facilitate representations of brute force just as they can help build a productive contrast with what emerges in place of those same representations.

"Herr Korbes" and "Riffraff" both look quite tame when compared with such enduring popular entertainments as *Punch and Judy*, in which Punch assaults a neighbor, throws out his baby, bludgeons his wife to death, murders a doctor, beats a beggar, hangs a hangman, and finally staves off the devil. In folktales, where the underdogs often control the script, there is something safely funny about their empowerment, since ducks and pins can conspire to overthrow their oppressors only in the realm of fiction. However, it is harder to get the cultural joke when the targets of violence are those already disempowered and victimized in real life. Most people will probably laugh when Punch hangs the hangman, but they will not feel entirely at ease when he bludgeons his wife and tosses the baby into the audience.

"The Old Woman Who Was Skinned," in Basile's *Pentamerone*, shows us the extent to which humor is culturally determined, for the joke in it requires us to witness a scene of bodily torture at which many readers today would rightly cringe. Basile's tale does not show us an assault in which figures from a lower order unite to harm someone from a higher order. Instead, the physical agony of an old woman who has been led to believe that she will be rejuvenated through a skinning is spotlighted for our amusement. Here is a description of the operation, as performed by the local barber:

> He set her on a stool and began to hack away the old bark, which drizzled and dripped blood; every now and again, as if he were only shaving her, she firmly repeated, "Il faut souffrir pour être belle." He continued to send her to destruction, and she went on with the same song, and between them they kept up a counterpoint to the lutes of her body till he reached her navel. There, her strength and blood abandoning her, she gave out a strong cannonade of departure and by her mishap proved the truth of Sannazaro's verse:
> *Envy, my son, destroys itself.*[6]

Basile works hard to turn his story into a cautionary tale for old women. He has the female storyteller first tell her audience that young girls deserve blame for being too vain, then remind her listeners "how much more worthy of punishment is the old woman who, by trying to compete with the girls, draws on herself the mockery of all and her own downfall." These attempts to justify the spectacle of an old woman being skinned alive appear all the more lame when we consider that, in the very same story, the old woman's sister uses deceit to compete with young girls and is rewarded with the admiration and love of a young king. Only the sister who goes without the benefit of supernatural intervention from seven fairies courts "her own downfall." No matter how vigorously the teller insists on the skinning as nothing but the occasion for an important lesson, it quickly becomes evident that the description of the act has no other purpose than to make fun of an old woman's body and her futile attempt to revitalize it.

A variant of this tale—this one with a very different cast of characters—also mounts a grisly scene of pain and suffering for comic effect. In the Grimms' "Rejuvenated Little Old Man," a part of the rich tradition of jokes about mothers-in-law, it is God and Saint Peter, rather than seven fairies, who turn a decrepit old beggar into a young man glowing with health. A blacksmith witnesses the event and decides to replicate the operation on his mother-in-law.

> So the blacksmith made a big fire and shoved the old woman into the forge. She wriggled this way and that and cried bloody murder.
>
> "Sit still! Why are you crying and jumping around? I haven't pumped the bellows enough yet."
>
> Upon saying this, he pumped the bellows again until all her rags caught fire. The old woman would not stop shrieking, and the blacksmith thought, This isn't working out quite right. So he pulled her out and threw her into the water tub. Then she screamed so loudly that the blacksmith's wife and daughter-in-law heard it upstairs in the house. They both ran downstairs and saw the old woman, who was lying doubled-up in pain and howling and groaning. Her wrinkled and shriveled face had lost its shape.[7]

That a single folktale can represent miracles performed by a benevolent God right along with the lethal buffoonery of a blacksmith is testimony to the elasticity of the genre, which can accommodate all manner of cultural contradictions. A tale that begins by celebrating the healing powers of the Lord veers off, in an astonishing way, into a sadistic tableau of physical violence. Like Basile and others who preserved this tale, the Grimms (or their informants) must have felt uncomfortable about including this scene of suffering without providing some sort of moral justification for it. They therefore tried to turn this tale about violence directed against an old woman into an etiological story, a tale about the origins of creatures and customs.

In the version of the story printed in the *Nursery and Household Tales*, it turns out that the blacksmith's wife and his daughter-in-law are both with child. When they see the old woman howling with pain, they become so agitated that they go into labor that very night and give birth to two boys who are "not shaped like human beings but like apes." The boys run off into the forest, and "it is from them that we have the race of apes."[8] The Grimms' acknowledged source of the tale went to even greater lengths to legitimize its violence: the conclusion to Hans Sachs's

Birth of the Apes (1562) warns that pregnant women must avoid exposure to startling or frightening sights, a moral so strained that even the Grimms must have felt compelled to eliminate it, perhaps because they realized it could only be an intentionally comic pretext for telling the tale.[9]

That laughter was sanctioned as a response to this particular tale type becomes clear when we look at "Put the Old Woman in the Furnace," an Italian variant of what the Aarne/Thompson tale-type index designates as "Christ and the Smith" (AT 753).[10] There, the bungled attempt at rejuvenation is drawn out to make the old woman's death as slow and painful as possible even as witnesses to the event nearly split their sides laughing.[11] What is it that makes these descriptions of the body in pain so funny? It is hard not to ask, for starters, why that body is invariably female and why it is also nearly always maternal. The story's concern with rejuvenation, with being reborn, and its reconfiguration of the normal course of birthing events with a male (often a son) attempting to give (renewed) life to a female (often a mother) is charged with comic possibilities. But that the comedy should take as macabre and savage a turn as it does and still remain funny in its contemporary cultural context is a question that does not yield to easy analysis and challenges our understanding not only of the joke but of the culture that produced it. Notwithstanding Basile's commentary, there is more to the story than a mere mockery of geriatric vanity. It is no accident that the cast of characters in many variants of the tale numbers a male divinity who has the power to give and to take life, a female mortal with the power to give birth, and a male mortal who takes a life in attempting to give it. What is at stake here has to do in part with competing genesis stories—a myth of male creation set against the biological facts of female childbirth. Hence, perhaps, the savagery of the doubly-directed satire that makes a burlesque mockery of a man's attempt to give life even as it degrades the female body that has the power to give birth.

Few folktales are as free of preaching and as unabashed in their presentation of blood and gore as "Herr Korbes" and "Put the Old Woman in the Furnace." Liberated of moral constraints and inhibitions, these stories of class struggle and gender conflict blend sadism with slapstick to produce a form of festive violence that targets either the top dog or the underdog as victim, and that observes neither temporal nor spatial limits to its reach. Wherever Herr Korbes goes, he is assaulted by one creature or object after another and suffers "a thousand deaths"; the old women in variants of "Christ and the Smith" undergo a seemingly unending process of "rejuvenation," since the smith always redoubles his efforts whenever he perceives that his pains are coming to naught. Blood flows freely as one character after another is mutilated and murdered, without our ever being encouraged to feel sympathy for the pain of a victim or satisfaction with the sufferings of a villain. The more hairraising an event in these stories, the more comical its effect, hence my use of the term festive violence.

The fairy tales we now read to our children generally foreground the motivation for violent assaults so distinctly that we do not have to search for the deeper gender or class conflicts that breed violence in the folktales discussed thus far. The heroes and heroines of canonized fairy tales are marked as targets of virtually unmediated inter-familial jealousy or resentment. These victims of violence have no trouble turning into agents of revenge, and it is astonishing to see how vigorously and adeptly fairy-tale protagonists punish their oppressors (who usually take on the mask of stepsister, witch, or ogre) and derive pleasure from their agony. Think of the way in which the Grimms' Gretel shoves the witch into the oven, bolts its iron door, listens to the witch's howls, and waits for her to "burn to ashes." Or recall how Perrault's Tom Thumb tricks the ogre into slitting the throats of his seven daughters, or how the ogress in Perrault's "Sleeping Beauty" is devoured by the "ugly creatures" she put in a tub intended for her daughter-in-law. Although revenge can be as sweet as love for the heroes and heroines of fairy tales, today it is almost always brief in its implementation, with the punishment occupying only a single moment in time and a single point in space. We are far removed from the festive violence that turns a tale into an expansive stage for spectacles revealing tormented bodies.

It should come as no surprise that fairy-tale biographies celebrating violence as a form of empowerment would gradually disappear from the canon along with tales that allowed violence to move in a festive register. A trio of tale types—"The Table, the Ass, and the Stick," "The Knapsack, the Hat, and the Horn," and "The Dance among Thorns"—features heroes who clearly relish exercising power over others, so much so that marriage and wealth become only incidental, if that, to their quests. The weapons these figures wield—a stick, a horn, and a fiddle—are in each case instruments in the double meaning of the term. They make music (the stick beats time upon the backs of its victims) and torment (the fiddle forces people to dance) at the same time. In a sense, one could say that we are back in the realm of festive violence, where torture is so solidly wedded to pleasure that pain provides music to the ears. What invests the stick, the horn, and the fiddle with such compelling allure for each hero is their power to torment adversaries and to coerce everyone else into obedience. As these instruments of destruction and revenge annihilate or torture, they secure the true happy ending to the hero's story.

Vulnerability and powerlessness were familiar feelings to those who told such tales during the era in which they were recorded. It was probably precisely the tough struggle for survival, with its accompanying sense of defenselessness when it came to poverty and disease, that bred a folklore authorizing its heroes to acquire power at any cost. The passionate attachment of many fairy-tale heroes to power through violence is not always readily conceded, but it remains a fact of life in many of the once most popular tales, where the body becomes both object and target of power through ceremonies of torture between hero and villain.[12] Here the hero is always in control, and it is he (our three tale types all feature boys and men) who is charged with disciplining bodies and administering justice.

The justice dispensed in the stories to be reviewed here stands under the sign of what Foucault has called monarchical law. Under its technology of power, punishment is a ceremonial rite performed for a sovereign who requires that the bodies of the victims be marked with the signs of revenge. The heroes of these three tale types each revel in a form of absolute empowerment, entitlement, and invincibility that allows them to slip into the role of regent even in those cases where they never rise above their original humble social station. In punishing their enemies, they create a theater of revenge in which they can relish the beatings inflicted by a cudgel, watch dispassionately as walls crumble to the tune of a horn, and witness with glee the painful contortions of those forced to dance to a fiddle. The moment that power is transferred from villain to hero, the display of pain and suffering affords untold satisfactions. A Siberian fairy tale concludes by telling us that a husband and wife are "so overcome with joy that they die."[13] These heroes are so elated when their persecutors are killed that their stories end—after a spectacle of punishment that is designed both to humiliate the villain and enthrone the hero.

Why have these tales slipped into obscurity?[14] It is not difficult to answer this question if we review the way in which those who produce literature for children have labored with such intensity to turn the heroes and heroines of fairy tales into models of docile behavior. The beautiful, hard-working girl marries; the modest yet resourceful boy wins a kingdom. However, the hero who owns a cudgel, a horn, or a fiddle thumbs his nose at the world. He flaunts a mode of coercive violence so transparent in its aim that it stands in sharp contrast to the devious forms of social regulation mobilized by those who rewrote fairy tales in an attempt to internalize in their youthful readers a constraining set of disciplinary regulations and ideological codes. Distasteful as the violent scenarios in some of these tales might be, they are worth looking at in greater detail to see how they manage a social and psychological economy of power that allows the hero to wipe out his enemies by inflicting on them the most agonizing tortures, yet remain a hero and monopolize the audience's empathetic identification.

"The Table, the Ass, and the Stick" bears out the suspicion that inflicting pain can prove a source of unending gratification for fairy-tale heroes. The three sons in this tale each receive a magical object at the end of their apprenticeships. The oldest receives a table that covers itself with food and drink; the second son is given a donkey that discharges gold pieces "from the front and behind"; the third and youngest son finds himself the owner of a cudgel that jumps out of a sack and beats people on command. It is interesting to observe that the most highly prized object of the three is the stick—even unlimited supplies of food or money pale by comparison to the power derived from unrestrained aggression. In the Grimms' version of this tale, the pleasure that accompanies the physical punishment of enemies is spelled out clearly. When the master hands over the stick to his apprentice, he tells him:

> "If someone threatens to harm you, you just have to say, 'Club, come out of the sack,' and the club will jump out at the people and *dance* on their backs so *merrily* that they won't be able to move a bone in their body for a week. And the club won't let up until you say 'Club, get back in the sack.'" [my emphasis][15]

If anyone has the audacity to step on the hero's toes or threaten him in any way, the cudgel "dances a jig" on his back. This is the instrument that eventually recovers the magical objects stolen by a greedy inn-keeper from the two other brothers and enables the father to live "in joy and splendor" with his three sons.

The Grimms themselves gave greater prominence to the tale's central spectacle of aggression as they revised the story for successive versions of their collection. In the first version of the *Nursery and Household Tales*, the encounter between the story's hero and the innkeeper who has confiscated his brothers' possessions is brief:

> The turner placed the sack under his pillow. When the innkeeper came and pulled at it, he said: "Cudgel, come out of the sack!" The cudgel jumped out of the sack and attacked the innkeeper, danced with him, and beat him so mercilessly that he was glad to promise to return the magic table and the gold donkey.[16]

The second edition of the *Tales* paints a more detailed portrait of the innkeeper's punishment:

> At bedtime [the turner] stretched out on the bench and used his sack as a pillow for his head. When the innkeeper thought his guest was fast asleep and that no one else was in the room, he went over and began to tug and pull very carefully at the sack, hoping to get it away and to put another in its place. But the turner had been waiting for him to do exactly that. Just as the innkeeper was about to give a good hard tug, he cried out: "Cudgel, come out of the sack!" In a flash the little cudgel jumped out, went at the innkeeper, and gave him a good sound thrashing. The innkeeper began screaming pitifully, but the louder he screamed the harder the cudgel beat time on his back, until at last he fell to the ground. Then the turner said: "Now give me the magic table and the gold donkey, or the dance will start all over again." "Oh no!" said the innkeeper. "I'll be glad to give you every-thing, if only you'll make that little devil crawl back into his sack." The journeyman answered: "This time I will, but watch out for fur-ther injuries." Then he said: "Cudgel, back in the sack" and left him in peace.[17]

The cudgel not only possesses magical properties but is also extraordi-nary in its efficiency as an instrument of justice. Like the most exqui-site instrument of torture, it simultaneously extracts a confession and inflicts a punishment even as it preserves a safe distance between crim-inal and avenger. The turner may speak the words that activate the

24. The thieving innkeeper takes a beating while the
tale's hero watches from behind the door.

cudgel, but he stands at one remove from the agent of punishment, able
to witness with unalloyed pleasure the inflicting of pain precisely because he can profess not to be its immediate cause.

Schadenfreude—the pleasure of witnessing the pain of others at a safe
remove from it—is not a trait uniquely German. The Russian tale "Two
out of the Sack" gives us a domestic variant of "The Table, the Ass, and
the Stick." In this story there are only two providing objects: a "kindly"
sack containing two men who furnish unlimited food and drink, and a
"punishing" sack containing another two men who use brute force to

crush the enemies of their owner. The hero secures both sacks, returns home with them, and—here is where the tale deviates sharply from other variants—puts both sacks to use. Most heroes lay their cudgels and sticks aside once they return home, but not this Russian husband. To cure his wife of her abusive ways and scolding manner, he leaves the punishing sack on a hook and waits for her to recite the words she has overheard her husband say to the kindly sack. No sooner have those words left her lips than two men with big sticks climb out of the sack and start to beat her:

> They thrashed her so hard that she could bear it no longer. She called her husband: "Old man, old man, come into the hut, the two men are beating me up!" But he walked around, laughing and saying: "They'll show you how it's done!" The two men thrashed the old woman even harder, repeating: "Don't thrash your husband! Don't thrash your husband!"[18]

The husband's reaction to the beating shows us the extent to which these tales make of violence a hilarious spectator sport.

The fantasy of unrestrained violence expressed in "The Table, the Ass, and the Stick" becomes especially appealing because it allows the hero to settle old scores even as it frees him of direct blame for punishments inflicted. In the Grimms' tale it is the cudgel that goes out of control, dancing merrily on the back of the innkeeper. "Two out of the Sack" also makes the husband innocent—the wife brings the punishment on herself by pronouncing the words that summon the louts, and she is accused of doing the beating even as she is thrashed. The Grimms' hero responds to the innkeeper's screams of agony by ordering the cudgel back in its sack. "'Mercy shall prevail over justice this time,'" he declares as a sign of his leniency.[19]

An Italian version of "The Table, the Ass, and the Stick" reminds us, however, that revenge against specific personal enemies or against villains of every stripe is not the most important element of the tale type. The satisfaction of possessing an instrument that endows its owner with sheer brute power is a pleasure in and of itself. In "The North Wind's Gift," a box containing two men who beat others up with their clubs is described as "solid gold," "beautiful," and "glittering."[20] The child-hero of "The Ass that Lays Money" receives from his uncle a stick that responds to the command "*Beat, beat!*" "Imagine how joyfully the boy took the stick!" we read. "It was a handsome polished stick, with a gold handle, and delighted one only to see it."[21] When the boy sets the instrument in motion, he does so not just to punish a thieving innkeeper, but to stage a dazzling scene of destructive violence. The innkeeper gets a beating, but so do innocent spectators—not to mention the room's furnishings: "Suddenly blows were rained down without mercy; everything broken to pieces, the chest of drawers, the looking-glass, all the chairs, the glass in the windows; and the landlord, and those that came at the noise, beaten nearly to death." This Italian version of the tale expresses in unvarnished form the joy of possessing and cultivating to excessive lengths the power to injure and destroy.

This ability to annihilate on a grand scale is the subject of a related tale type. If the heroes of "The Table, the Ass, and the Stick" usually content themselves with battering a dishonest innkeeper, the heroes of "The Knapsack, the Hat, and the Horn" are not satisfied until they have razed everything around them. These tales, however, are less expressions of *Schadenfreude* (giving violence a grim, comic twist) than exercises in apocalyptic ruin (giving violence a tragic turn). The hero of the Grimms' version of the tale meets a princess who cheats him of all his possessions save his horn—when he blows on it, everything around him collapses. "Then he was all alone and remained king until he died."[22] This conclusion was so unrelieved in its bleak pessimism that the Grimms rewrote it in such a way that the hero has the chance to vent his anger, but also ends as a monarch with subjects to rule over:

> He still had the horn, however, and his rage was so great that he blew it with all his might. All at once everything collapsed—the walls, the fortifications, the cities, and the villages—and the king and his daughter were crushed to death. If he had not stopped blowing at that point, everything would have been devastated, and not a single stone would have remained standing on top of another.
>
> After that nobody dared to oppose him, and he made himself king of the entire country.[23]

An eighteenth-century German version of "Snow White" ends with the cynical observation that "revenge can be as sweet as love."[24] That wish fulfillment can be found more readily in power, violence, and aggression than in the accumulation of wealth and the repetition of marriage vows receives its fullest illustration in "The Dance among Thorns" (AT 510). Let us look first at a French version called "The Three Gifts." The hero of that story belongs to an unusual folkloric species: a *male*

25. "All heads off except mine!" declares the hero, and heads roll
as he decapitates each and every subject in the land.

child abused by a stepmother. By demonstrating compassion for those
less fortunate than he, the boy receives the right to request the three
things that will give him "the most pleasure." His first wish is for a
crossbow that will fire without missing, his second for a flute that will
make everyone dance ("whether they want to or not"), and his third for
the most remarkable thing of all: "He had a little trouble deciding on
the third wish; but in thinking back on all the cruel treatment he had

received from his stepmother, he wanted to have vengeance and wished that everytime he sneezed she would not be able to resist letting out a loud fart."[25] The boy uses his power to humiliate his stepmother at home, at the *veillée*, and in church. When the priest scolds the boy, the lad responds by shooting a bird with his crossbow and sending the priest to fetch it from a patch of brambles. No sooner has the priest reached the thorny area than the boy takes out his flute and strikes up a tune on it. The priest begins to whirl and dance so rapidly that his cassock gets caught in the thorns and is torn to shreds. His subsequent efforts to mobilize the legal system to punish the boy misfire—the boy takes out his flute before the priest, clerk, and justice of the peace, who begin to shake their legs in so lively a fashion that the courtroom looks like "a dance hall."

The hero of "The Three Gifts" seems content to make fools out of his stepmother, the priest, and the court officials. He is not out to inflict physical punishment, but he is eager to humiliate his persecutors, each of whom is invested with the authority of family, church, or state. By contrast, one German version of the tale, "The Jew in the Thornbush," gives us a hero who delights in adding physical injury to public insult, this time to the Jew of the title, rather than to a priest. In comparing these two versions of one tale, it is important to bear in mind the circumstances under which each came to be recorded. The French variant captures in print a folktale told by a nineteen-year-old peasant boy of Upper Brittany and recorded in 1878. The German version was recorded at an earlier date, but it was based on both oral and literary sources, then substantially reshaped and rewritten by the Grimms from one edition to the next. Let us look first at the final version of the Grimms' "Jew in the Thornbush"—at the text as it appears in most English translations of the Grimms' *Nursery and Household Tales*.

The tale's hero is an honest servant who is cheated out of three years' wages by "an old miser." So good-hearted and compassionate is this young man that he gives his last three farthings to a beggar, who rewards him by granting three wishes. The servant asks for a gun that will hit every target, a fiddle that will make everyone dance, and the power to compel people to accede to his every request. Back on the road, he meets a Jew "with a long goat's beard" and shoots a bird for him. The servant instructs the Jew to fetch the bird, which has fallen into thorn bushes. What follows is a scene remarkable in the degree to which it makes sport of suffering:

[The Jew] got down on the ground and worked his way into the bush. Just as he was right in the middle, the servant was overcome by a mischievous spirit, and he took out his fiddle and began to play. All at once the Jew began to lift his legs high and leap in the air. The more the servant played, the better the Jew danced. But the thorns ripped the Jew's coat to shreds, combed his goatee, and scratched and pricked his entire body.

"My!" exclaimed the Jew. "What's the sense of all this fiddling? Please stop all this fiddling, sir. I have no desire to dance."

The servant kept playing nevertheless, for he thought, You've skinned plenty of people, so now the thorns will give you some of your own treatment in return. He continued fiddling so that the Jew had to leap higher and higher, and parts of his coat remained hanging on the thorns.

"Woe is me!" cried the Jew. "I'll give the gentleman whatever he demands, if only he'll stop fiddling! You can have a whole bag of gold."

"Well, if you're going to be that generous," said the servant, "then I'll gladly stop my music. But I must hand it to you, your dancing is something special." Upon saying this, he took the bag of gold and went his way.[26]

Anxious to recover his money, the Jew rushes to a judge, who finds the servant guilty of theft and orders him hanged. But at the gallows, the servant takes out his fiddle and soon has the entire town dancing—even the dogs join in. "And the longer the servant played, the higher the dancers leapt so that they bumped their heads against each other and began screaming in a dreadful way." Once again the hero uses his instrument to stage a violent burlesque, one that operates with a triple economy resulting in the punishment of his enemy, the extraction of a "confession," and his own release. "I stole it, I stole it!" the Jew shouts, desperate to stop dancing. "But you earned it honestly." With that, the Jew is taken to the gallows and hanged as a thief.

It is worth pausing here for a moment to take a closer look at this tale before considering how it challenges the positive moments of empowerment and catharsis that seem characteristic of festive violence. To begin with, the issue of anti-Semitism raised by the German text must be addressed head on. Robert Darnton has observed that "it would be abusive to take this tale as evidence that anticlericalism functioned in

26. All must dance to the fiddler's tune, but note that the Jew occupies center stage.

France as the equivalent of anti-Semitism in Germany."[27] Yet even as he denies the validity of the comparison, he makes it and insists that comparing folktales "helps one to identify the peculiar flavor of the French tales." This may be true, but the conclusions drawn from comparing two specific tales need to be backed up with a comprehensive look at French and German variants. Darnton fails, for example, to note that numerous German oral and literary variants of this tale type, including the ones that the Grimms used to construct their story, cast a cleric in the role of the Jew; nor does he point out that the Grimms' tale was subjected to what one expert on the tales has called "careful editing."[28] The Jew is steadily vilified from one edition of the *Nursery and Household Tales* to the next until he becomes an avaricious, vindictive thief, while the servant becomes ever more "honest" and less of a swindler, until in the end it is he who has "earned" the money stolen from the Jew.[29]

The Grimms also made a point of strengthening the link between the servant's master, a man who cheats the hero out of three years' wages, and the Jew. The last edition of the tales describes the master as "rich" and "greedy." He deliberately cheats the hero, who is so good-natured and unworldly that he has no idea that three farthings are inadequate pay for three years of labor. The Grimms' attempt to blacken the character of the master and to make him a double of the Jew appears to be part of a concerted effort to justify the servant's sadistic pranks and introduce logic into a tale otherwise filled with contradictions.[30] The Jew's confession about the money ("I stole it, I stole it! But you earned it honestly") makes no sense unless we begin, as the Grimms evidently did, to connect the underhanded master with the grasping Jew. Once we see the two, if not as identical, then at least as doubles of each other, the tale's inconsistencies, as cataloged by Bottigheimer, resolve themselves immediately.[31]

As astonishing as the Grimms' demonization of the Jew is their readiness to include this particular version of the tale in their collection when other available variants lacked the anti-Semitic elements. In their annotations to the second edition of the *Nursery and Household Tales*, the Grimms take note of two versions in which renegade monks occupy the slot of the villain. They not only preferred the anti-Semitic tale to these other versions, but actually intensified the anti-Semitic elements, allegedly to achieve the "dramatic effect" referred to in their annotations.[32] Furthermore, the Grimms even made a point of including this tale in the pages of their enormously popular abridged edition (*Kleine Ausgabe*), which comprised fifty tales selected for their appeal to a larger audience, specifically to children. Thus it was not at all antiquarian interest, the desire to record the uncensored voice of the people, that led the Grimms to choose "The Jew in the Thornbush" over other versions of "The Dance among Thorns." The principle of selection that guided their hand in putting together their abridged edition was, as Heinz Rölleke has pointed out, to some extent pedagogical. Popular folktales like "The Brave Little Tailor" and "The Magic Table, the Gold Donkey, and the Club in the Sack" never made it into the abridged edition because they did not send the right messages.[33] What made "The Jew in the Thornbush" especially attractive, even when "The Magic Table, the Gold Donkey, and the Club in the Sack" was not, must have had something to do with the cast of characters, with the antagonism set up between a naively innocent German lad and a sophisticated Jewish swindler, especially since the Grimms worked so hard to sharpen the contrast between hero and villain. The attempt to present the German people with sanitized moral tales that could be used for educating children misfired in this, as in other instances, in a remarkable way. "The Jew in the Thornbush" gives us the most compelling possible illustration of how the nineteenth-century collections of cultural stories we so treasure are not necessarily appropriate reading matter for children.

"The Dance among Thorns" is particularly instructive when it comes to understanding how it is that tales of festive violence can produce effects ranging from chortling glee to offended outrage. We all rejoice to see Ulysses conquering the Cyclops, David defeating Goliath, and Jack outsmarting and killing the giant, in part because the two antagonists, so unfairly matched when it comes to size and strength, are even more polarized in their moral character. It becomes almost impossible not to sympathize with a diminutive hero who becomes the victim of a bullying giant. But the same polarization of character traits that creates a gulf between our response to the hero and our feelings about the villain also produces the possibility of quickly demonizing whatever "type" is slotted into the latter role. In some instances, this may be an old woman, in others a Jew. The folkloric record we have examined indicates that, at certain times, in certain places, there was nothing jarring about sliding old women or Jews into a position where they served as victims of festive violence. Quite to the contrary, the stories often became even funnier because they allowed some of the anxiety aroused by the perceived domestic foe or the stereotyped enemy to be discharged. However much these stories empower the weak or purge us all of savage feelings, even with evil giants slotted in the role of villain, they retain the potential for enacting the humiliations emphasized in the French versions of the tale.

Folktales like "The Table, the Ass, and the Stick," which condone retaliatory violence and celebrate its festive character, are surprisingly closely allied to tales openly critical of violence. "The Dog and the Sparrow" in the Nursery and Household Tales shows us the dire consequences of cruelty to animals, but in it the revenge against a wagoner, who has brutally run over a dog befriended by a sparrow, takes on so central a role (reminding us of the violence inherent in didactic strategies) that it engulfs the narrative in much the same way that the violent pranks of "Herr Korbes" and the beatings in "The Table, the Ass, and the Stick" take over the text. Though the text presents itself in the garb of the cautionary tale, it quickly reveals itself to be little more than the occasion for a protracted struggle to the death between unequal adversaries. The sparrow, outraged when the wagoner runs over the dog, first bores holes in the wagoner's barrels and pecks out the eyes of his horses. "Oh poor me!" the wagoner cries out, but the bird shows no mercy and responds with the words "Not poor enough yet!" The sparrow summons friends, who attack and devour the wagoner's grain supply. These are only the first in an extraordinary sequence of acts of revenge engineered by the sparrow. The full force of the conclusion can only be captured by citing all its grisly details:

> The wagoner grabbed his ax and threw it at the sparrow. But it missed the bird and merely broke the windowpane in two. The sparrow hopped inside the house, sat down on the stove, and called out, "Wagoner, it's going to cost you your life!"
>
> Now the wagoner was furious and blind with rage. He chopped the stove in two and continued to chop all the furniture—the mirror, the benches, the table—and finally the walls of the house, all in an effort to hit the sparrow, who flew from spot to spot. At last the wagoner caught the bird with his hand.
>
> "Do you want me to kill it?" his wife asked.
>
> "No," he yelled. "That would be too merciful. I want it to die a more cruel death. I'm going to swallow it."
>
> Then he took the bird and swallowed it whole. However, the sparrow began to flutter inside his body and fluttered back up again into the man's mouth. Once there he stuck out his head and cried, "Wagoner, it's going to cost you your life!"
>
> The wagoner handed the ax to his wife and said, "Wife, kill the bird in my mouth!"
>
> His wife swung the ax, but she missed and hit the wagoner right on the head, and he fell down dead. But the sparrow flew up and away.[34]

The story of the dog and the sparrow warns against brute force even as it legitimizes the retaliatory violence of the sparrow. It is not the bond of affection uniting dog with sparrow that remains memorable, but the sparrow's steady escalation of violence in his relentless pursuit of the wagoner. On the surface of things, this is not a funny story. A certain kind of recitation can, however, bring out the comic absurdity of the tale's final events. The wagoner's futile efforts to hit the bird (all the while destroying his own house), his desperate effort to kill the bird by swallowing it, and the wife's murder of her husband in place of the bird are suggestive of the cartoon humor à la Tom and Jerry that has entertained generations of American children. In the Grimms' story, however, the characters cannot rise from the dead to reinsert themselves as actors in an endless series of violent pranks. Despite its celebratory stand on violence, "The Dog and the Sparrow" does have a lesson to convey and, perhaps for that very reason, was included— despite its extravagantly destructive and brutal scenes—in the abridged edition of the tales published for children. Just as the "grateful animals" of fairy tales reward heroes for kindness and compassion, so the provoked beast, however weak and diminutive, will get even with the human adversary, however powerful.

The didactic opening in this and other stories of animal revenge on humans was an opportunity that producers of children's literature did not allow to slip by unnoticed. As early as 1693, Locke's influential *Some Thoughts Concerning Education* remarked that children who caught "any poor creature" were "apt to use it ill," often treating it "very roughly" and "with a seeming kind of pleasure." Locke recommended swift parental intervention, for "the custom of tormenting and killing . . . beasts, will, by degrees, harden their minds even towards men; and they who delight in the suffering and destruction of inferior creatures, will not be apt to be very compassionate or benign to those of their own kind."[35] Locke's observations served as a cue for storybook writers, who published such an assortment of books in which cruelty to animals inspires a stern cautionary tale unrelieved by comic touches that one critic of children's literature found it "almost inconceivable that so many small boys spent so much time as is alleged in pulling the wings off flies, throwing at tethered cocks, and tormenting puppies and kittens."[36] In these stories, too, the most passionate tirades against violence result in the most extravagant displays of cruelty.

Edward, in Mrs. Trimmer's *Fabulous Histories, or, The History of the Robins. Designed for the Instruction of Children, respecting Their Treatment of Animals* (1786), is a case in point. This eleven-year-old boy practices "horrid barbarities." When he is not plucking feathers from chickens, tying cats and dogs together, stoning cocks, and throwing cats off roofs, he is drowning puppies (while their howling mother looks on) or pulling the wings and legs off flies and delighting in the "agonies" they endure. It is amazing, at times, to see with what scrupulous detail the Mrs. Trimmers of the literary world recorded the cruel practices of young boys and how conscientiously they orchestrated their deaths.

Edward, for example, graduates from torturing animals to pinching and teasing schoolboys, then is thrown and killed by a horse whom he "inhumanly" beats.[37] One cannot but feel that the didactic point of many of these stories becomes blunted by the sensationalistic recitation of atrocities, which children are sure to have found more riveting than the moral commentaries attached to them.

William Hogarth's "First Stage of Cruelty" (1751) dramatizes more effectively than any other cautionary scene about cruelty to animals the way in which didacticism yokes anguish and pleasure by feeding on violence in order to terrorize and fascinate. This first of "four stages of cruelty" seeks to "reform some reigning Vices peculiar to the lower Class" by introducing us to Tom Nero and other street urchins while they are hard at work torturing animals. A bone is tied to a dog's tail; some cats are thrown from windows, others are strung up; and Tom himself is shown inserting an arrow into the anus of a howling dog. Brutality toward animals in the first two stages of Tom's cruelty yields to murderous impulses against humans; stage three shows Tom apprehended for cutting the throat of a woman whom he has presumably also made pregnant. This scene, "Cruelty in Perfection," shows us the woman's corpse, with gaping wounds at throat and wrist. It is in the final scene, "The Reward of Cruelty," that Hogarth stretches the limits of the genre by showing us the dissection of Tom's corpse. Tom's body is the center of attention for an anatomy lesson, and we watch in horror as the surgeon reaches into his breast cavity after disemboweling him (in a touch of macabre irony, a dog begins nibbling at one of the discarded vital organs). While the doggerel of the captions tries hard to drive home the pedagogical point that cruelty toward animals leads inexorably to crimes that merit capital punishment, Hogarth's riveting art goes far toward indulging the viewer's needs for violent delights with a violent end.

Hogarth's attempt to "reform" seems disingenuous even if it is also informed by a tradition that holds the representation of violence to be an innocuous surrogate for the real thing. It is almost impossible to take one's eyes off these scenes as long as they are in sight—the events in them are meant to hold the viewers' attention and train their gaze on a succession of horrifying images designed to deter what they represent. The violent representations thus contain a doubly coercive moment— one that arrests the gaze of viewers and consequently exposes them to the messages imparted by the images.

27. Hogarth's scenes of cruelty to animals show us "the tyrant in the boy."

The most flagrant abuse of stories about cruelty toward animals can be found, as we might expect, in a tale by Hans Christian Andersen. Unlike Hogarth, however, Andersen instrumentalizes violence by catering to a parent's need to frighten children rather than to a general fascination with brutality. "The Storks" recounts the story of boys who taunt nesting storks with threats of hanging, stoning, and burning. Their offspring, who suffer these intimidations, are determined to have their revenge: "Vengeance should be wreaked in full, they felt, on the boy who first began to mock them and who kept on at it."[38] Here is the punishment that the mother stork contrives for that boy:

"I've worked out a plan that'll be the very thing. I know where the
pond is in which all human babies are lying until the stork comes to
fetch them away to their parents. . . . In that pond lies a little dead
baby that has dreamt itself to death. We'll take the boy that one, and
he'll cry because we've brought him a dead little brother."

Once again Andersen proves himself to be a master in the art of writing
the most frightening of all children's stories. He does not train the punishment on an adult villain, nor does he indulge his reader's fascination
with violent spectacles through surreal exaggerations. Instead he makes
a "naughty" boy (the only character with whom the child-reader can
identify) the victim of a form of vengeance so repulsive that we avert
our eyes as quickly as possible from its verbal representation ("a little
dead baby," "a dead little brother"). The added detail about the baby's
death by dreaming could only be invented by someone intent on sti-
fling a child's imagination.

While much folktale violence can be described as preposterous in its
stylized exaggeration, it is anything but pointless. We have seen the way
in which the representation of violence is placed in the service of retaliatory justice, demeaning sadism, pedagogical zeal, and cathartic pleasure. But there is one class of stories that traffics in violence for no other
evident reason than to stage scenes of doom and gloom. These tales give
us either a chain of events that leads to the tragic death of a central
figure or they recount one catastrophe after another, building up to the
annihilation of all characters in the tale. In the Russian "Death of the
Cock" (AT 2021A), a hen has to run a relay race of tasks in order to
secure water for her dying mate, but by the time she has executed all
the necessary chores, the cock is "lying there quite still, neither panting
nor breathing. He had choked to death on a bean!"[39]

The Grimms' version of this story bears the title "The Death of the
Hen" and adds a coda describing the hen's funeral. The hen is carried
to her grave in a wagon holding "all the animals in the forest." While
crossing a brook, the carriage tips into the water, drowning every pas-
senger but the rooster. "So the rooster was all alone with the dead hen,
and he dug a grave for her. He laid her in it and made a mound on top.
Afterward he sat down on the mound and grieved until he too died.
And then everyone was dead."[40] This tale, unlike its Russian counterpart, can be seen as a drama of full-scale annihilation.

The Grimms seem to have made a habit of turning tales culminating in a single tragic death into apocalyptic tales staging the extinction of all life. "The Louse and the Flea" (AT 2022) normally ends with the death of the flea alone. In the Grimms' version the louse is scalded, the flea weeps, a door creaks, a broom sweeps, a cart races, a dung heap burns, a tree shakes, and, finally, a spring begins to flow. But it flows "so violently" that all are drowned—"the maiden, the tree, the dung heap, the cart, the door, the flea, and the louse, every last one of them."[41] The tale's movement toward its own extinction is unparalleled in its radicalness.

Not all cumulative tales end in so dreary a fashion, and even when they do fail to conclude on an upbeat note, their verbal playfulness often prevents them from sliding into the tragic mode of "The Death of the Hen." It is always a challenge for listeners to follow the logic of the tale or the rhyme's chain and to retain each and every item in the catalog of things or events. "The House that Jack Built" gives us perhaps the best-known example of a chain that builds on incremental repetition to produce a comic effect.[42] In addition to their value as entertainment, these tales and rhymes could also serve an important pragmatic function in preliterate societies. Learning the days of the week ("Solomon Grundy, / Born on a Monday, / Christened on Tuesday . . ."), the months of the year ("In March I make my nest . . . in August I have nothing more to do with my young"), or numbers ("At one I was born . . . at ten my child's soul was crowned in heaven") was easy enough through the repetition of these rhymes.[43]

This avoidance of a tragic effect does not hold true when we turn to cumulative tales with human actors. Here too we find tales ending with the death of a single figure or the extinction of the story's entire cast of characters, but with an atmosphere of gloom never once relieved by comic touches or verbal playfulness. The Grimms' "Misfortune," for example, recounts the fate of a man relentlessly pursued by bad luck and doomed in his efforts to evade death. Although a lesson is inscribed on the tale, it becomes clear that instruction takes a backseat to terror as each new narrow escape generates a starker threat to the life of the protagonist. In multiplying dangers, the story draws its audience into a maelstrom of surreal horrors: The tale's protagonist is so poor that he must fetch wood from the forest, but just as he is about to lift his ax, a pack of wolves charges him. He throws down his ax, dashes off, and steps onto a bridge that collapses under his weight. In desperation he jumps into the water, but nearly drowns because he cannot swim. Fishermen save him, but just as he feels secure and is about to recount his misfortunes to his rescuers, the wall against which he is leaning crumbles on top of him and kills him. The story enunciates its fatalistic message even before it stages these events: "When misfortune is after someone, that person may try to hide in all sorts of places or flee into the open fields, but misfortune will still know where to find him."[44] This pronouncement, illustrated by the assaults and accidents that follow, reveals itself to be less a moral than a message about the hopelessness of mounting a defense against anything. In this sense, "Misfortune" is probably the most antididactic of all the tales in the Grimms' collection—even though it displays its "message" more prominently than any other tale.

The chain of catastrophes in "Misfortune" is matched and surpassed in its dreadfulness by only one other tale in the Grimms' collection: "How Some Children Played at Slaughtering." In that story, children watch their father slaughter a pig, then reenact his deed with one child as butcher, another as pig. The consequences of this chilling event build a chain of disasters:

> The mother was upstairs in a room bathing another child, and when she heard the cries of her son, she immediately ran downstairs. Upon seeing what had happened, she took the knife out of her son's throat and was so enraged that she stabbed the heart of the other boy, who had been playing the butcher. Then she quickly ran back to the room to tend to her child in the bathtub, but while she was gone, he had drowned in the tub. Now the woman became so frightened and desperate that she did not allow the neighbors to comfort her and finally hanged herself. When her husband came back from the fields and saw everything, he became so despondent that he died soon after.[45]

Reading this tale reminds us of the extent to which folktales and fairy tales traffic in the sensational and melodramatic. Wilhelm Grimm had defended the inclusion of this story in the *Nursery and Household Tales* by insisting that hearing it in childhood had made him "cautious" and "anxious" ("vorsichtig" and "ängstlich") in his play with other children. Whether children should be made that nervous is a question that Wilhelm evidently did not consider. More importantly, however, the defense is at best disingenuous. "How Some Children Played at Slaughtering" unfolds a spectacle of domestic horrors for no other reason than to send chills up the spines of listeners and readers by reminding them of their powerlessness in the face of misfortune. It would be fatuous to try to read into this story lessons about cruelty to animals, about the hazards of imitation, or about the need for restraint. What we have is a world in which one tragic accident leads to a full-scale catastrophe, designed to horrify its audience.

The Italian "Three Tales by Three Sons of Three Merchants" makes it clear that the tellers of many shocking tales are responding to nothing more than the desires of their audiences. The widow in that story promises her hand to the man who can tell "the most hair-raising, blood-curdling tale."[46] She is then treated to accounts of how one merchant's son has to cut off his own finger, another is shipwrecked and must resort with his crewmates to cannibalism, and a third has to share his room at an inn with a corpse.

Cumulative tales like "Misfortune" and "How Some Children Played at Slaughtering" can be seen as forerunners of sensationalistic tabloid stories. The tale of children playing butcher did, in fact, appear in a Berlin newspaper at the time the Grimms were assembling their collection. These stories give us human actors in a realistic setting, though they often slide into the surreal as one horror is piled on another. In "Misfortune" human agency slips out of the picture to produce a world where tragedy intervenes in the most cruel, arbitrary manner, turning the tale's protagonist into an utterly helpless victim. One easy way to recuperate these stories is to mark them as exceptions to the rule, as anti–fairy tales that leave their heroes and heroines helpless instead of empowered and that give us a tragic inversion of good rewarded and evil punished.

In a post-Enlightenment age that gives children the illusion of empowerment as consolation for their true state of vulnerability by telling them stories in which they magically acquire wealth and autonomy, we are understandably reluctant to pass on to them fables of abject helplessness. Just as we have suppressed the festive violence of "The Table, the Ass, and the Stick" in favor of stories that train coercive disciplinary action on naughty children, we have also replaced the bleak pessimism of "Misfortune" with tales that encourage faith in the continual exertions of productive adventures or in a deferential, stoic patience that pays off with a happy ending.

· CHAPTER IX ·

Table Matters: Cannibalism
and Oral Greed

. . . Could you breach the gates
and the great walls yourself and feed on Priam
with all his sons, and all the other Trojans,
dished up raw, you might appease this rage!

Homer, *The Iliad* (Robert Fitzgerald)

MAURICE SENDAK, whose gift for understanding the texture of childhood experience is virtually unrivaled, once discussed the genesis of those quaintly savage monsters tamed by the boy Max in *Where the Wild Things Are*. He recalls the "dreadful Sundays" in Brooklyn when as a child he had to dress up for visits with aunts and uncles for whom he had no particular affection. "I was an ungracious and ungenerous child," he reports, "because what I really resented was that they were coming to eat our food. I never agreed for an instant that they should eat our food, or that we should share it." Sendak describes how he examined those relatives critically, making a note of "every mole, every bloodshot eye, every hair curling out of every nostril, every blackened tooth." As he and his siblings sat "for what seemed like hours" in the living room, he was haunted by the following thoughts:

> I lived in apprehension that, if my mother cooked too slowly and they were getting very hungry, they would lean over, pinch my cheek, and say, "You look so good, we could eat you up." And in fact we had no doubt that they would. They ate everything in sight. And so, in the end, it seems that the Wild Things are those same aunts and uncles. May they rest in peace.[1]

Sendak had the wisdom to admit that the autobiographical elements embedded in his work constituted only one among many layers of meaning, but he had no trouble formulating the autobiographical reading in succinct terms: "On one level at least, you could say that the *Wild Things* are Jewish relatives."[2]

Readers of *Where the Wild Things Are* will remember that its last pages show Max, seduced by the aroma of good things from "far away," abdicating his throne as King of the Wild Things and preparing to return home. As he leaves, his subjects cry out in desperation: "Oh please don't go—we'll eat you up—we love you so!"[3] The story of Max, like the story of Mickey (the hero of Sendak's *In the Night Kitchen*), spins out a fantasy about what psychoanalytic theory has solemnly dubbed "the dread of being eaten." Freud and his contemporary Otto Fenichel both used that term with reference to fears connected with mothers and fathers (the real ogres in a child's life). Fenichel, who found "abundant proof" for his speculations about the dread of being eaten in the "terrible mothers" of myth and fairy tales, would no doubt have been fascinated with the Wild Things, though he would probably have insisted that the "Jewish relatives" were really a mask for Sendak's mother and father.[4]

The dread of being eaten, when it appears as a theme in children's literature, often walks a tightrope between the terrifying and the absurd. Sendak's Wild Things, like the chefs of *In the Night Kitchen*, are at once fiends and buffoons. They may dwarf the hero and overwhelm him with their sheer physicality and multiple presence, but even their massive girth fails to intimidate once they are perceived to be at the hero's beck and call. The cannibalistic fiends of fairy tales have the same double-edged quality characteristic of Sendak's creatures, inspiring in children both horror and delight. Stories about witches who plan to feast on the flesh of small children and about ogres who relish the thought of drinking an English boy's blood rank among the most popular fairy tales, in part perhaps because no one has ever been able to turn them into stories that preach and teach.

Isaac Bashevis Singer unwittingly linked the presence of cannibalistic themes to the absence of pedagogical zeal in his observations about fairy tales and their "pointlessness." In recalling stories told to him as a child, Singer contrasted the dreary religious tales recited to him by his father—tales in which good people loaf in Paradise while bad ones roast in Hell—with the beautiful and pointless stories narrated by his mother. It is easy to nod in agreement with these remarks, but when

Singer actually describes one of the "beautiful" tales told by his mother, it becomes difficult not to flinch in disbelief. "Let's say that a bear swallows three children or something like this and then they cut open his belly and the children go free," he states. "A story like this had no meaning, but it had beauty."[5] P. L. Travers, we recall, had the same ability to see beauty in violence and horror. "The Juniper Tree" was a story that she found "most beautiful, even though others protest that it is brutal and bloody."[6] Tales about bears devouring children and about fathers feeding on their sons appear to have something so compelling about them that, despite the gruesome details of their plots, they are perceived as stories of haunting beauty.

Just what makes a tale about being devoured seem so poignantly attractive when in fact it is dreadful? Why is it that not only stories about animals eating humans, but tales about humans eating other humans have such a hold on the imagination that they enjoy almost unparalleled popularity in the realm of folklore? We can begin to answer these questions by looking at various forms of anthropophagy and, in particular, its subcategory cannibalism. Anthropologists divide cannibalism into various classes, and among them is one they call survival cannibalism. Entire cultures may sanction cannibalism because the geographical areas which they cover suffer from persistent protein shortage. The Mesoamerican ecosystem, for example, experienced serious depletion under the pressures of population growth and the intensification of agricultural production. Animal flesh was in short supply, and flesh from the victims of sacrificial rites performed among the Aztecs came to be used at critical junctures as a political reward for selected segments of the population.[7] Even in cultures with abundant supplies of food rich in protein, either an anomalous famine that strikes a region or a situation of extreme personal deprivation will yield examples of people driven to eat human flesh for want of anything else.

That famine plays a prominent role in fairy tales comes as no surprise when we consider the chronic food shortages and periods of scarcity that afflicted those who shaped these stories. The Grimms' collection of tales, in its first incarnation, contained numerous stories set in times of famine. "God's Food," for example, ends with a tableau displaying the mother of five children, surrounded by her dead progeny, sinking to the ground as she too dies of starvation. "Hansel and Gretel" begins with a vivid description of hunger and its consequences for a family of four. In "The Knapsack, the Hat, and the Horn," hunger provides the incentive for three brothers to leave home and embark on a life of adventure. "We can't go on like this," they declare when their plight has become so severe that there is nothing left to eat. "We'd better go out into the world and see if we can change our luck."[8]

Far more shocking in its stark portrayal of food shortages and starvation than "God's Food" and "Hansel and Gretel" is a tale that the Grimms printed in the first edition of the *Nursery and Household Tales* but left out of all subsequent editions. "The Children of Famine" concerns itself with the plight of a woman who cannot provide for her family. But this mother, unlike the woman in "God's Food," does not seek refuge in faith. When she runs out of food, she tells her two daughters: "I've got to kill you so I can have something to eat!"[9] In desperation, the girls pacify their mother by begging for crusts of bread, but this only buys them a temporary reprieve. Their mother eventually leaves them in peace, but they end by lying down and sleeping until Judgment Day arrives.

"The Children of Famine" achieves its ghastly effect without ever once resorting to the surreal or the supernatural. It may seem inconceivable that a mother would actually consider devouring her daughters to assure her own survival, but historical evidence reveals that cases of maternal cannibalism were not unknown in times of severe food shortages, probably because deprivation can be one of the factors leading to a state of mental derangement in which a person may be driven to eat human flesh. The authors of clinical case histories of cannibalism recorded in nineteenth-century medical journals must have perceived the two to be closely linked. On the one hand, they strained their rhetorical resources to describe the unprecedented and inexplicable nature of the crimes committed by their subjects ("Here my pen cannot continue, my heart bleeds . . . the sun has never before witnessed so hideous a crime"), but they also invariably made a point of beginning their accounts with a detailed description of food shortages ("1817 was a year remarkable for its bad harvest and for its high grain prices . . .")—in part, perhaps, to seek the false security of extenuating circumstances.[10] But documented cases of maternal cannibalism are exceedingly rare, and when legal or medical literature does report it, it is always in connection with an infant, not a grown child. "The Children of Famine" more likely gives us the inversion of a motif found in some variants of the "Cinderella" story. In an Armenian tale, for example, two girls kill and devour their mother to ward off starvation. Marian Roalfe Cox records four variants from Greece, Cyprus, and Dalmatia that also tell of daughters eating the flesh of their mother during a time of famine.[11]

While survival cannibalism plays a role in some of the collections that came to be designated as fairy tales, it takes a backseat to another more common form of folkloric cannibalism—the kind that we find in the Grimms' "Hansel and Gretel" and Perrault's "Tom Thumb," both listed as variants of "The Children and the Ogre" (AT 327). These tales are set in lean years, but the witch who fattens Hansel for a feast of flesh, and the ogre who plans to slaughter Tom and his brothers, move in a nonnaturalistic world and are driven by something more than hunger. In order to understand just what it is that gives rise to their cannibalistic urges, let us begin by looking at the relationship between the perils at the heroes' homes and the hazards of the enchanted forest.

In both "Tom Thumb" and "Hansel and Gretel," the initial "lack" on which the plot hinges concerns food. "Tom Thumb" is set in a time of famine so severe that Tom's parents agree to abandon their children in

28. The ogre is about to slaughter Thumbling and his brothers for dinner when his wife intervenes.

the forest. There is nothing in the least hard-hearted about the boy's parents as they are depicted by Perrault. The woodcutter's heart is "heavy with sorrow" when he speaks to his wife: "It must be plain enough to you that we can no longer feed our children. I cannot see them die of hunger before my eyes, and I have made up my mind to take them tomorrow to the forest and lose them there."[12] The wife consents, but only after reflecting on "what a grief it would be to see them die of hunger." In this telling, every effort is made to protect the parents, whose "tenderness" and "sensitivity," however misguided, move them to abandon their children.

"Hansel and Gretel" tells a quite different story. Here the step-mother/villain makes no effort to disguise her hatred of the two children when she declares that, once abandoned in the woods, the children will never "find their way back home, and we'll be rid of them."[13] When her husband protests, she calls him a fool and tells him to start planing the boards to build coffins for all four of them. Here it is selfishness pure and simple that motivates the stepmother's plot to lead the children deep into the forest. The father's empathy with Hansel and Gretel ("I feel sorry for the poor children") lacks the passion necessary to resist the strength of his wife's resolve—it is not long before he falls in with her plan and collaborates in the project of abandonment. Here, the children are sacrificed in part out of murderous resentment and in part to insure their parents' survival.

Whatever the motive for abandoning hungry children—be it the fear of witnessing suffering, or nothing but brutish self-interest—the result is always the same. Even when a tale half-heartedly exonerates one or both parents of malice by implying that abandoning children is the lesser of two evils, the children are left to fend for themselves because parents have been too incapacitated to provide. One way or another, the parents are to blame and begin to emerge at the least as monsters of negligence.

In the case of "Tom Thumb," where the hero's father is the prime mover of the plot to abandon Tom and his six brothers, a male ogre "who eats little children" figures as the chief threat to the seven boys. The ogre's wife, like the boys' mother, does everything she can—in her limited way—to protect the boys. In Perrault's "Tom Thumb," the parental constellation in the woods repeats the parental configuration at home, with the customary exaggeration and distortion attending the move from home to the enchanted forest. The same holds true for

"Hansel and Gretel." The Grimms' disagreeable stepmother reemerges in the woods as an evil witch masquerading as a magnanimous mother, while the children's father stands at the end of their journey, overjoyed when reunited with his children. In both stories, exaggerated self-interest and the inability to provide are distorted in the mirror of the fairy-tale world and transformed into cannibalistic hatred.

Neither of the two stories spares us details about their villains' appetites and acts. The ogre in "Tom Thumb" devours the seven boys with his eyes when he sees them and tells his wife that they will make "most dainty morsels" when cooked with a good sauce. We hear exactly how he is tricked by Tom into "[cutting] the throats of his seven daughters" and are treated to a gory scene detailing his wife's discovery of the murders. "Hansel and Gretel" is no different, with an elaborate description of the witch who traps the children with her maternal gestures: "The old woman . . . had only pretended to be friendly. She was really a wicked witch on the lookout for children, and had built the house made of bread only to lure them to her. As soon as she had any children in her power, she would kill, cook, and eat them. It would be like a feast day for her." In the woods, the hungry children become the victims of monsters who initially provide them with all the food that their parents failed to supply, but then turn the children into the main course for their own dinners. It is as if the satisfaction of oral urges had brought to life fiends whose voracious appetites outpace those of even the most famished children.

How do we account for these monsters? Are they nothing more than hyperbolic representations of the selfish parents who appeared in the tales' opening paragraphs? Do they, as Bruno Bettelheim would have it, come to life as projections of the child's own oral greed (itself emblematic of "untamed id impulses")?[14] Let us return, for the moment, to our initial example, for the adventures of Max in *Where the Wild Things Are* have instructive parallels with tales told by the Grimms and by Perrault. Max's brush with anthropophagy is shaped by the feelings that come to life when his mother decides to punish him for his mischievous ways. Sent to bed without dinner, Max retaliates by shouting to his mother: "I'll eat you up!" At the risk of obscuring a psychological mechanism whose logic is made perfectly clear by Sendak's narrative, we can draw on the language of psychoanalysis to state that oral deprivation leads to a desire for retaliation in the form of oral aggression, which in turn is projected in fantasy onto the agent responsible for the original state of deprivation.

Bettelheim's belief that children are so ashamed of their voracious appetites that they bring to life—through projection—the cannibalistic fiends of fairy tales seems at first blush the most satisfying of the various theories set forth to explain these stories. But are Hansel and Gretel, along with Tom Thumb, really guilty of "unrestrained oral greed and dependence"? Do they give in without a moment's pause to "untamed id impulses, as symbolized by their uncontrolled voraciousness"? Quite to the contrary, theirs is a life of privation marked by poverty and need. In the woods, they walk an entire day and night and are near starvation, "for they had had nothing to eat except some berries." By the time they find the witch's house, they are about to "perish of hunger and exhaustion." This seems a far cry from "unrestrained oral greed." Tom Thumb and his brothers fare slightly better because the ogre's wife takes pity on them, but they find themselves "so cowed with fright" that they are unable to eat the "splendid supper" set before them. To speak of the heroes' "oral fixation" seems preposterous in light of the facts of the story. What we have, as in *Where the Wild Things Are*, are deprived and disempowered protagonists who have to find some way to get back home and have a good meal with their dignity intact. Bettelheim, however, once again turns victims into villains, enabling himself to rewrite "Hansel and Gretel" to produce a "psychologically correct" account that culminates in the following happy ending: "Having overcome his oedipal difficulties, mastered his oral anxieties, sublimated those of his cravings which cannot be satisfied realistically, and learned that wishful thinking has to be replaced by intelligent action, the child is ready to live happily again with his parents."[15] This reading can be produced only by willfully ignoring the most basic realities of the Grimms' story—among them the fact that the children return to live happily ever after with their father alone. Worse yet, it sets up a hopelessly ambitious social and moral agenda for reforming the unoffending and unwary child listening to the story.

English and Russian folklore give us two celebrated examples of tales that challenge the notion of fairy-tale cannibalism as a disfigured form of parental aggression or a projection of the heroes' oral greed. Both of these stories never once allude to the appetites of their protagonists, yet they carefully attend to elaborate descriptions of bloodthirsty ogres and witches. Let us look first at "Jack and the Beanstalk," in the version published in 1807 by Benjamin Tabart as *The History of Jack and the Bean-Stalk, Printed from the Original Manuscript*. The story of Jack ends on a curious note, for unlike the vast majority of fairy-tale heroes, Jack does not end his adventures by marrying a princess, acceding to a throne, or winning half a kingdom. Instead his odyssey takes a moral turn, transforming him from a boy who is at the outset "indolent, careless, and extravagant" into a son who is both "dutiful and obedient": "His mother and he lived together a great many years, and continued to be always very happy."[16]

Jack's father was a "rich" and "benevolent" man who was swindled and murdered by a giant living in the area. The giant, who is described as "envious, covetous, and cruel," stands as the perfect antithesis to Jack's father. From a guardian spirit, Jack learns that he is destined to avenge his father's death by reappropriating his possessions and killing the giant. The "large and powerful Giant," who has a voracious appetite and eats nothing but human flesh, makes for a daunting adversary, but Jack, with some help from the giant's "compassionate" wife, succeeds in liberating the giant's hen, money, and harp, and slays the giant.

The wealth of attributes assigned to the characters, along with the emphasis on Jack's behavioral conversion from willfulness to obedience, makes it clear that the tale's author was keenly aware of a didactic mission as he wrote down this story. Much is made of the fact that Jack is not stealing the giant's possessions—he is simply recovering what by rights belongs to him ("Every thing he has is yours," the fairy tells him, "though now you are unjustly deprived of it"). A strong moral overlay covers nearly every aspect of this version of "Jack and the Beanstalk," turning what probably started out as a tale of high adventure into a didactic story that molds its hero into a model for children. A summary of the story by William Denslow, the illustrator of *The Wizard of Oz*, reveals how remarkable a transformation Tabart made:

> See what a perfectly outrageous thing is Jack and the Bean-Stalk. A lad gains admittance to a man's house under false pretences, through lying and deceit, imposing on the sympathy of the man's wife, then he commits theft upon theft. He is a confidence man, a sneak-thief, and a burglar. After which, when the man attempts to defend his property, he is slain by the hero (?), who not only commits murder, but mutilates the corpse, much to the delight of his mother.[17]

By converting Jack from indolence and deception to enterprise and obedience, Tabart may do violence to earlier versions, but he also introduces a certain logic into the conclusion—since the tale becomes invested with the notion of producing a docile son, it is natural that Jack should be living in peace with his mother in the end.

Still, there is one element of the tale resistant to the moralizing tendency that sweeps across the narrative. Much as the tale tries to naturalize the giant by turning him into a "gentleman" who has moved into the neighborhood, it does not divest him of his cannibalistic traits, probably because they formed too integral a part of the tale's oral tradition. What makes "Jack and the Beanstalk" especially interesting is its splitting of the father-figure into two separate entities—the benevolent, dead father and the cannibalistic giant. This splitting, so customary in tales where events are orchestrated by women, is virtually unheard of in male-centered tales and puts "Jack and the Beanstalk" in a class by itself when it comes to popular stories.

What are we to make of this singular constellation in which the hero's relationship to his mother is arrested in the mother-child dyad, while the only male figure in the tale uses oral aggression to ward off threats to his position of power? It is difficult to avoid recognizing the powerful double presence of incestuous desire and cannibalistic aggression in this tale, the one linked with the mother, the other with the father. All this might seem farfetched were it not for the fact that incest and cannibalism are habitually linked to a precultural phase marked by the inability to differentiate. That some languages employ the same term for incest and cannibalism makes the presence of the two in "Jack and the Beanstalk" all the more arresting.[18] Both Freud and Fenichel remarked on the connection between cannibalism and incest, which seemed to them, as cultural taboos, (not always explicably) related.[19]

"Jack and the Beanstalk" gives us a situation in which the fear of paternal retaliation does not take the form of an oedipal castration complex but of the pre-oedipal dread of being devoured. Here, however, the boy never transfers the heterosexual attachment to his mother to another woman, but manages to negotiate an arrangement that allows him to stay at home as a dutiful and devoted son. What is fascinating for our purposes is that the constellation of characters and distribution of roles in "Jack and the Beanstalk" are almost exactly repeated in a popular Russian tale, with the important difference that the protagonist is a female who lives happily ever after with her *father* after escaping a cannibalistic witch. In place of the asymmetry of masculine and feminine Oedipus complexes, we have two perfectly parallel versions of a single complex, a pre-oedipal masculine and feminine dread of being devoured.

"Vasilisa the Beautiful" tells of a girl who is at the mercy of a cruel stepmother after the death of her real mother. One evening, the flame

29. Vasilisa brings back light after her visit to Baba Yaga's hut.
Note the gate made of bones in the background.

goes out in the house, and Vasilisa is ordered to get light from the hut
of Baba Yaga. Baba Yaga's reputation for eating human beings "as if they
were chickens" is confirmed by one look at her abode: "The fence
around the hut was made of human bones, and on the spikes were
human skulls with staring eyes; the doors had human legs for door-
posts, human hands for bolts, and a mouth with sharp teeth stood in
place of a lock."[20] Unlike Jack, who takes possession of the giant's treasures by outwitting him, Vasilisa gets what she needs by carrying out

household chores—sweeping the yard, cleaning the hut, cooking dinner, washing linen, and sorting grain. When she announces to Baba Yaga that she has accomplished her tasks by taking advantage of the blessing of her dead mother, she is swiftly dispatched with her light. With this light, Vasilisa succeeds in eliminating her stepmother and stepsisters and living happily ever after with the tsar. But the tale does not end without bringing the father into the household: "Soon Vasilisa's father returned, was overjoyed by her good fortune, and came to live in his daughter's house."

The story of Vasilisa could be said to trace a movement from nature to civilization. Even if the story shows the heroine living with her father in the end, she has overcome an implicitly incestuous attachment and become the bride of the tsar. By bringing light (in the form of fire) to the hut and conquering the cannibalistic witch, Vasilisa becomes a cultural heroine who has decisively left behind the disorganized and disordered realm of nature. Yet this reading, as attractive as it may seem, fails to take into account numerous other tales of young girls sent on errands to the hut of Baba Yaga.[21]

Like Vasilisa, the heroine of "Baba Yaga" suffers at the hands of an evil stepmother, who hopes to rid herself of her stepdaughter by ordering her to get needle and thread from "Baba Yaga, the Bony-Legged." The girl dutifully obeys, but flees the witch's hut when she realizes that she will be the main course for breakfast. Baba Yaga jumps into her traditional mortar and goads it on with her pestle, but is unable to catch the heroine, who is assisted in her escape by the dog and cat she fed, the hinges she oiled, by the birch around which she tied a ribbon, and the maid to whom she gave a kerchief. She returns home and gives her father a detailed account of her narrow escape: "When the old man heard all this he grew angry at his wife and shot her to death; then he and his daughter began to live and prosper."[22]

Another Baba Yaga story does not end with the shooting of the stepmother, but with her moans and groans when she realizes that her stepdaughter received gifts from Baba Yaga, while her biological daughter has been broken into pieces so that nothing is left of her but a basket of bones. Here once again, father and daughter will live happily ever after without those eternal intruders known in fairy tales as stepmothers and stepdaughters.

Stories about young girls who visit Baba Yaga are surprisingly symmetrical in the contours of their plot with "Jack and the Beanstalk." In

both tale types, the cannibalistic villain of the piece occupies the slot
left vacant by the death of one parent and persecutes the child, who
emerges triumphant to live with the other parent after engineering the
villain's defeat. The examples of "Jack and the Beanstalk" and "Baba
Yaga" provide dramatic evidence that cannibalism in fairy tales must be
about more than oral greed and projection. In both tales, cannibalism
becomes enmeshed with a complex array of matters touching on the
dread of being devoured and incestuous attachment. For this reason, it
may be prudent to pause and look at some of the mythological and
psychological models for understanding cannibalism to see the way in
which the folkloric imagination and the folklore of the mind often
move along the same track.

Since the gender of cannibalistic monsters in fairy tales appears to be
evenly distributed between males and females (for every bloodthirsty
giant there is a flesh-eating witch), we must search the mythological
sources for male and female alike. For many, the first figure that comes
to mind is Cronus, that father of the gods for whom murder, incest, and
cannibalism were second nature. After learning that one of his children
was destined to overthrow him, Cronus devoured them all, save Zeus.
Cannibalism, in this case, serves a protective cause, warding off murderous assault by incorporating the enemy through oral aggression.

Cronus's attack on his sons belongs to the relatively rare category of
intentional cannibalism. Other mythological examples usually show us
victims innocently feasting on their own flesh and blood. A bacchana-
lian frenzy prevents Agave from knowing that she is tearing her son
Pentheus limb from limb. Thyestes has no idea that Atreus has served
him the limbs of his own sons, nor does the monstrous Tereus know
that he has eaten his son Itys for dinner. Tricked into cannibalism,
these figures are all targets of revenge in its most extreme form. Theirs
is not an act of aggression, but a forced incorporation and entombment
of their next of kin. This is the form of cannibalism (cooked [usually]
vs. raw, as the anthropologists would remind us) that is dramatized in
its most spectacular form in "The Juniper Tree."

For Freud, forced cannibalism proved less interesting than its premeditated counterpart. The mythological contest between a father and
his sons, as captured in the story of Cronus, could not but be attractive
to Freud, who, in his *Totem and Taboo*, interpreted cannibalism as an
efficient way of resolving the conflict between generations. It was in
Totem and Taboo that Freud offered his readers the "glimpse of a hy-

pothesis which may seem fantastic but which offers the advantage of establishing an unsuspected correlation between groups of phenomena that have hitherto been disconnected."[23] To explain the origin of the taboo on murder and incest, Freud adopted Darwin's notion of a primal horde and asserted that the brothers who had once been driven out of it banded together to kill and devour the patriarchal leader ("the father"). To atone for their crime, they created, out of a "filial sense of guilt," taboos against murder and incest (two taboos that happen to correspond to the repressed wishes of Freud's Oedipus complex) and set out on the long road leading to the social organization and moral restrictions of culture. Few scholars would quarrel with Freud's description of this hypothesis as "fantastic." Still, its positing of taboos against (cannibalistic) murder and incest as the markers of social organization is telling in the context of tales such as "Jack and the Beanstalk" and "Baba Yaga," which would give us a reconfigured return of the Freudian repressed by attributing the violation of the taboos to fathers and mothers.

Our two cultural stories—the mythological one of Cronus devouring his children and the psychoanalytic one about the children devouring their father—stand in an interesting relation. The Freudian text rewrites the classical myth, giving us the father as victim and the children as cannibalistic aggressors. After Freud's intervention, any retelling of the original story or of its Freudian revision would make it impossible to blame the father—the sons could never be victims. They are either directly and "truthfully" portrayed as aggressors, or their story enacts a victimization which is nothing more than a projection of their own murderous hostility onto the father.

The association of cannibalism with an act of male aggression (represented either through the father or his children) that has the aim of seizing or consolidating power stands as the legacy of Greek mythology and of Freud's reading of it. Interestingly, however, Freud himself found that while the dread of being eaten is often associated with the father, "it is probably the result of the transformation of oral aggressive tendencies directed upon the mother." For Freud, the mother who nourishes the child, but who also imposes "manifold restrictions" on it in the course of its development, becomes the target of the child's hostility and of a projected form of oral aggression.

Freud never constructed a maternal myth analogous to the account of the masculine primal horde and its move from nature to civilization.[24] It was left to one of his disciples, Melanie Klein, to pursue and explore the role of hostility in the mother/child relationship. Klein's elaboration of Freud's views on a child's innate oral aggression takes weaning as its point of departure. For Klein, the mother's breast begins as a source of pleasure and gratification, then becomes the target of destructive fantasies that are "of a definitely cannibalistic nature": "In his imagination the child attacks [the mother's body], robbing it of everything it contains and eating it up."[25] These fantasies are then projected onto the mother to produce the dread of being eaten. Although Klein's analysis appears compromised in its positing of breast-feeding as a near cultural universal and in its failure to accommodate instances in which fathers serve as primary caretakers, its larger contours could conceivably hold true for babies fed by men with bottles. The cultural reality of women as primary caretakers may color Klein's language, but it does not materially affect her theories about the way in which oral aggression is trained on the nurturer's body and, at a later stage, turned into the nurturer's primary characteristic.

As Susan Suleiman has pointed out, Klein writes "with great sympathy and understanding about the murderous impulses that every child feels toward its beloved mother: she does not speak about the murderous impulses that a mother may feel toward her beloved child" (355).[26] Klein's refusal to question the status of the Oedipus complex, its claim to universal validity and absolute truth, blinded her to the possibility that the traffic of love and hate between child and mother might move along a two-way street. It was virtually impossible for any of Freud's disciples to break with the exclusive focus on the child's fantasy life that developed once Freud rejected the seduction theory and developed the Oedipus complex. As Masson has pointed out, with some polemical exaggeration, "the impulses of parents against their children were forgotten, never to surface again in his writing."[27]

Right in line with a long tradition whose powerful influence we have seen at work in children's literature, the Oedipus theory positioned the child more firmly than ever as the source of conflict (revised from sin and disobedience to take the form of sexual desire and retaliatory fantasies) and as the object of adult didactic (read "therapeutic") efforts.[28] Like Freud's reading of the story of Oedipus which, failing to take into account that Laius had tried to kill his son and that he provoked Oedipus when they met at the crossroads, blames Oedipus for all that goes wrong, our readings of fairy tales focus almost exclusively on the unwritten fantasy life of the child/protagonist (on whom we project all kinds of feelings) rather than on the actual, textual facts of the story.

We will probably never be able to determine the exact extent to which the fear of being devoured can be traced to anxieties rooted in the reality of aggressive parental behavior or to guilty fantasies projected onto mothers and fathers. Clinical experience and personal observation, mythological texts and fairy tales, along with psychological case histories and psychoanalytic theories all tell us that a child's fears about being devoured are nearly always linked to parental figures—fathers and mothers seemingly invincible in their stature and power. What is important to bear in mind is that the psychoanalytic theory and its revisionist interpretation are not necessarily incompatible—they could be seen to take the form of a thesis and antithesis that cry out for a synthesis. Acknowledging the realities of children's experienced sense of parental aggression and withdrawal (no matter what form it takes) does not rule out the possibility that the child also harbors feelings of rage toward a parent. The power of parent/child relations derives its very strength from an emotional double helix, though this does not rule out the possibility that, in specific instances, the flow of hostility and aggression is stronger from one side to the other.

When adults tell children that they are good enough to eat and indulge in mock cannibal feasts, they may be exorcising a child's fears of being devoured, but they may also be fueling them. For those who cannot subscribe to the views of Freud and Klein (unrevised and revised), these adults, like Sendak's Jewish relatives, may even be creating the dread of being eaten. That this fear is solely a cultural construct seems unlikely, however, when we survey its pervasiveness in folkloric records. The giants slain by the British Jack, the witches of German folktales, and the bony-legged Baba Yaga of Russia are just a small number of the hordes of cannibalistic fairy-tale fiends that can never satisfy their craving for the flesh of children.

The degree to which orality conditions and shapes the world of folktales is at first sight astonishing. But since the tales so often represent the world from the child's actual or perceived point of view, it seems logical that food and its absence, along with conspicuous consumption and painful privations, should play a pronounced role in these stories. Still, the child's optic is not the only factor at work in representing a world where food seems to be on everyone's mind. It is important to recall once again the cultural context in which most of the tales recorded in the celebrated national collections are grounded. In many French folktales, according to Robert Darnton, wish fulfillment has more to do with the stomach than anything else: "To eat one's fill, eat until the exhaustion of the appetite (*manger à sa faim*), was the principal pleasure that the peasants dangled before their imaginations, and one that they rarely realized in their lives."[29] Food played a preeminent role in the lives of the peasants who told these tales, for it, more visibly and more repetitively than almost anything else, assured survival. It is not at all uncommon for a peasant hero, faced with three wishes, to ask first of all for a plate of steaming meat and potatoes, or to be so distracted by hunger that he yearns for a sausage while he is contemplating the unlimited possibilities before him. "What shall I command?" asks the hero of a Greek tale when told that he can have anything he wants. Without a moment's hesitation he answers the question with the words: "Food to eat!"[30] In the world of folktales, a full stomach can become the signature of success. For many a folktale heroine, it is a point of pride to have downed seven plates of noodles, seven loaves of bread, or seven bowls of minestrone.

The way in which the competition for food created a dog-eat-dog world is neatly illustrated by a fable in the Grimms' collection of tales. "The Companionship of Cat and Mouse" shows us the two animals in the tale's title setting up household and laying in a supply of fat for the winter. The cat pretends to attend baptisms on three different occasions—once for a child named "Skin-Off," a second time for one called "Half-Gone," and finally for a child named "All-Gone." When the mouse discovers that the baptisms were nothing more than occasions manufactured to eat the fat, the cat suppresses the rodent's complaints by devouring it. While the fable is ostensibly designed to illustrate the perils of keeping company with those who are by nature adversaries, it also establishes a program for survival predicated on getting to the food before anyone else does and eliminating any rivals in competition for it. Most adults will read this story from the victim's point of view and promote the lesson gleaned from that reading, but children are probably more likely to identify with the predator, whose insatiable appetite leads him first to start nibbling, then to destroy the evidence of his greed, and finally to eliminate the agent of reproaches.

The sheer number of folktales enacting eating binges suggests that few things are more satisfying than stories about indulging gluttonous urges. Many of these chain tales give a new depth of meaning to oral greed by showing a creature swallowing a series of objects that grow ever larger as the tale wears on. The Norwegian "Tabby Who Was Such a Glutton," a variant of "The Fat Cat" (AT 2027), culminates in the full recitation of the cat's diet for the day: "the man of the house, and the old woman in the cowshed, and the bell-cow in the stall, and the branch-chopper in the home pasture, and the stoat in the rock-pile, and the squirrel in the bush, and Slypaws the Fox, and Hoppity Hare, and Glutton Greylegs, and Frisky Bear, and Snappish She-bear, and Bruin Fine-Fellow, and the bridal procession on the road, and the funeral procession by the church, and the Moon in the sky, and the Sun in the heavens."[31] This predator tabby's hyperbolic gluttony is not checked until a billy goat butts her off a bridge, throwing her into the river where she bursts and ejects the entire company of ingested creatures. Similarly, in "The Cat and the Parrot," crabs swallowed by a cat liberate the five hundred cakes, the parrot, the old woman, the man and his donkey, the king, the queen, and a wedding procession with elephants and soldiers lodged in the cat's stomach.[32]

Both stories present elaborate fantasies about oral greed taken to an extreme, showing us the lighter side of the matter by keeping the victims intact until they are rescued. These tales consistently highlight the pleasure of the gluttons (rather than the anguish of the victims) and turn their eating sprees into a series of burlesque encounters whose humor is heightened as the body count rises. Any adult who has watched *Sesame Street* and observed reactions to Cookie Monster's unbridled appetite for everything from chocolate chips to hubcaps will recognize that children bring nearly unbounded goodwill and sympathy to creatures unable to resist eating everything in sight. Like infants and young children, the hungry creatures of folktales have a relationship to their social and physical world that is predominantly oral in nature.

While chain tales about gluttonous tabbies give free play to oral aggression and turn a voracious appetite into a laughing matter, other stories take the affair more seriously. The Italian "Master Francesco Sit-Down-And-Eat" offers a lesson on the grim wages of gluttony. Master Francesco, anxious to have a job that requires little work, enters the service of a lady who treats him like a prince and feeds him dainty dishes in exchange for lounging about the house. In no time at all, the former shoemaker becomes plump enough to satisfy the woman's desire for a hearty meal of human flesh: "The ogress seized him by the feet and sucked him completely up in one long gulp, without leaving a single bone."[33] Before being devoured, however, Master Francesco summons the strength to deliver a speech acknowledging the wisdom of his daughters. Spurning the easy life, these girls had told their father: "We're better off here . . . better off at home working our fingers to the bone day and night and wearing our old rags than scarcely turning a hand for good food and clothing from the ogress, who would eat us in the end!" The stern stoicism advocated in this Italian tale reminds us that the Grimms' collection was only one of many that sponsored the work ethic and spurned the "corrupt" life of luxury and leisure.

For every tale that condemns gluttony, however, there is at least one that celebrates or condones a hearty appetite. "The Seven Lamb Heads," another Italian tale, sides with the heroine Atanasia, who has shared the repast named in the title with her cat and is persecuted by a stingy granny who whispers relentlessly in her ear: "Every last one, you ate every last one . . . ."[34] Even at the heroine's wedding to a king, granny cannot restrain herself and spoils the celebration with her never-ending reproaches. At last Atanasia shouts: "She's a hungry old skinflint and even in the midst of all this royal splendor she can't take her mind off those messy lamb heads!" Outraged by the "greed" of granny, the king calls his guards and orders the woman decapitated.

When they have a moralizing twist to them, stories about oral greed either intone the now familiar rhythms of judgmental "parental" voices to condemn gluttony or they take the child's part, punishing adult misers who try to curb healthy youthful appetites. There is no consistent message to be garnered from these types of stories, though the two types of tales (cautionary and retaliatory) move along well-trodden paths. What is remarkable, however, is the degree to which cautionary tales can express power relationships in terms of control over food and turn stories about hearty appetites into vehicles for preaching on idleness, stinginess, and a host of other vices.

Nowhere is food endowed with more power than in the Grimms' "Hansel and Gretel," where the threat of death is doubled in scenes of withholding and providing food. It is easy enough, on reading the description of the children's reaction to the witch's house, to understand how Bruno Bettelheim could turn the story into a cautionary tale about oral greed, for the Grimms show Hansel and Gretel attacking the house made of bread with unrestrained gusto. The two children are so giddy with delight at the feast before them that even the witch's reprimand to them falls on deaf ears and fails to interrupt their intemperate banquet: "They did not bother to stop eating or let themselves be distracted. Since the roof tasted so good, Hansel ripped off a large piece and pulled it down, while Gretel pushed out a round piece of the windowpane, sat down, and ate it with great relish." But the story then veers off in another direction, plotting the triumphant conquest of the "godless" witch—the real incarnation of oral greed—by the children.

"Hansel and Gretel," in contrast to cautionary tales about gluttony, is more therapeutic than didactic in its aims. In showing that children can use their wits to defeat the monsters that bedevil them, it gives us a story that empowers children and helps them work through anxieties about abandonment and agression—though, here again, the premises of the "therapy" must be called into question. In the Grimms' tale, Gretel has her wits about her and tricks the witch into demonstrating the proper way to enter the oven. The hero of the Russian "Baba Yaga and the Brave Youth" escapes death by shoving Baba Yaga and her three daughters into the oven.[35] The heroine of the Italian "Garden Witch" asks for a demonstration of how to close the oven, then proceeds to grab the witch by the legs and shove her into it.[36] While the protagonists of some of these tales get into trouble because of their craving for anything from candy to cabbage, others show no interest whatsoever in food and still end up in the clutches of cannibalistic monsters. What unites them is their ability to rely on their wits to slip away from or destroy malevolent spirits.

What, then, do we make of the many cautionary tales in which children do not elude the witches, ogres, and wolves pursuing them and end up instead in their stomachs? Perrault's "Little Red Riding Hood" and the Italian "Caterinella" come immediately to mind. The more one learns about the oral versions of these two tales, the easier it is to see the kinship between them. Let us take a brief detour to examine those parallels before returning to the problem of the tales' endings. The oral forerunners to Perrault's story often not only include an elaborate striptease (excised from most literary versions of the tale), they also—as we have seen—incorporate episodes with cannibalistic and scatalogical moments in them. Italo Calvino was so shocked by the cannibalistic elements of an Italian "Little Red Riding Hood" ("The Wolf and the Three Girls") that he rewrote the story to eliminate the heroine's cannibalism—a procedure that had no doubt been performed by many other recorders of the tale. In Calvino's source, the wolf kills the heroine's mother, makes a doorlatch cord from her tendons, chops her up to make a meat pie, and pours her blood into a wine bottle. Both meat pie and blood are downed by the heroine with obvious pleasure. Calvino records another version of the same tale in which the heroine, realizing once she has gotten into bed with the wolf that Grandmother never had hairy hands or a hairy chest—let alone a tail—declares that she must "take care of a little business" before going to sleep.[37]

In "Caterinella," cannibalistic urges drive only the villain, not the heroine, of the story, whose taste runs more in the direction of sweets. The heroine's substitution of animal excrement and urine for the cake and wine that she was unable to resist eating does not at first seem analogous to Red Riding Hood's request to relieve herself, but both incidents fill the functional slot of ruses designed to divert the attention of the tales' villains. What makes these two tales particularly interesting in this context is the way in which they efface the line dividing the agent from the victim of oral aggression. Red Riding Hood seems to enjoy the taste of flesh and blood nearly as much as the predatory wolf, while Caterinella, though she spurns the offerings, is freqently invited to dine on her grandmother's teeth and ears.

If we reflect on the number of children's games that culminate in the mock devouring of one player by another, and consider the way in which children continuously rotate roles in their play, then the appeal of stories like "Little Red Riding Hood" and "Caterinella" becomes less enigmatic. Let us look at one of those games, as described by Walter Scherf. One child is designated witch; the others chant "Old wench, why are you sleeping such a long time?" The witch pretends to be awakening:

> "What time is it?" she asks.
> "Half goat's tail," is the impudent answer.
> "Why are the bells ringing so sweetly?" she asks.
> "Because your husband is dead," cry the children, with satisfaction.
> "Who has done this?" howls the witch.
> And the children, screaming "Me!" "Me!" rush away, the witch in hot pursuit.[38]

For Scherf, this is a game that, in its repetitions, helps the child to "master anxiety and the shudders of horror, and finally to wear them out." But it is important to point out that the child caught at the end is not only the witch's victim but also her successor. The child-victim thus quickly moves into the role of predator-villain.

In "Little Red Riding Hood" and "Caterinella," the heroine is not the sole figure in the tale with whom a child can identify. Heroine and villain, as we have seen, share so many traits that the contrast between them is less pronounced than it might at first seem. At the end of the recited story, when a lively teller or reader might offer a comic simulation of the devouring of the child, we have a modified, if one-sided, version of a game that children have been playing with each other in countless cultural settings. The logical conclusion to the adult's dramatization of the ending would be a role reversal in which the child takes the part of predator.

The ease with which children can identify with either the victim or the agent of oral aggression—and indeed slide from one role into the other—is best illustrated by a story with a hero and a villain who both engage the sympathies of children. "The Gingerbread Boy," in its many versions, gives us the obverse of "The Fat Cat." Here the protagonist—whether it is a Norwegian pancake, a Scottish bannock, or a Russian bun—boasts of his ability to outrun one hungry persecutor after another, until he meets his nemesis, usually in the form of a wily fox. The tale's success feeds in large part on its staging of the tension between the fear of being eaten and oral greed. The child listening to the story is engaged in a double drama through the temptation to identify with both gingerbread boy and fox.

"The Gingerbread Boy" appeared in 1875 in a landmark American journal for children's literature, *St. Nicholas Magazine.* Mary Mapes Dodge, its editor, had written two years earlier about the goal of the magazine: "Let there be no sermonizing, no spinning out of facts, no rattling of dry bones. . . . The ideal child's magazine is a pleasure ground."[39] Stories like "The Gingerbread Boy" do indeed mark something of a break with the sermonizing and moralizing of the past. Yet, though the tale contains no explicit lessons, it cannot entirely resist the relentless didactic and therapeutic demands placed on literature recited or read to children. There is bound to be someone out there who will take note of the way in which the gingerbread boy's naiveté (trusting a fox to give him safe passage) gets him in trouble.

Still, stories like "The Gingerbread Boy," along with others discussed in this chapter, are more difficult to serve up as lessons in this or that virtue or vice, in large part because their fixation on basic matters of survival (eating or being eaten) deflects attention from issues of good or bad behavior. They may not be "pointless," as Isaac Bashevis Singer asserts, but they tend to spin out fantasies rather than proclaim facts.

· CHAPTER X ·

Telling Differences:
Parents vs. Children in
"The Juniper Tree"

"She is my mother," said Colin complainingly. "I don't see why she died.
Sometimes I hate her for doing it."

Frances Hodgson Burnett, *The Secret Garden*

THE JUNIPER TREE" has long been recognized as one of the most powerful of all fairy tales. Its widespread dissemination across the map of European folklore—one monograph identifies several hundred versions of the tale—suggests that there must be something especially attractive or at least compelling about the story. That it remains popular today, though not necessarily as a bedtime story told by adults to children, means that it must speak to more than one age and generation. Even the brutal and bloody events enacted in the tale did not keep an expert like P. L. Travers from referring to it as "most beautiful," nor did it prevent Tolkien from writing about it as a story of "beauty and horror" with an "exquisite and tragic beginning."

"The Juniper Tree" begins with a stirring tableau of death in childbirth, moves to a distressing depiction of child abuse culminating in murder by decapitation, and ends with what is probably the most savage scene of revenge staged in any fairy tale. So infamous are the principal events in this particular tale that even the usually sober Aarne/Thompson index of tale types refers to this story as not only "The Juniper Tree" (AT 720) but also as "My Mother Slew Me; My Father Ate Me." The alternate title comes from the hero's lament in a song that summarizes the tale's events. The version in the Grimms' tale reads as follows:

> My mother, she killed me,
> My father, he ate me.
> My sister Marlene
> Gathered up my bones,
> Put them in a silken scarf,
> Buried them under the juniper tree.
> Keewitt, keewitt, what a fine bird am I.

The song leaves out the tale's conclusion, which shows us the step/mother in a state of alarm, her hair shooting out "like tongues of fire."[1] As she goes outdoors in an attempt to dispel her fears, "Bam! the bird dropped a millstone on her head and crushed her to death!"[2]

What we have here conforms to the classic model of a cautionary tale for adults: those who threaten and abuse children become themselves targets of brute violence. The punishment enacted in the tableau that closes the tale must have been a particularly suggestive one to the Grimms' contemporaries, who were generally better versed in scripture than successive generations of listeners and readers. These are Christ's words on the means for entering heaven: "'Whoever receives one such child in my name receives me; but whoever causes one of these little ones who believe in me to sin, it would be better for him to have a great millstone fastened around his neck and to be drowned in the depth of the sea'" (Matthew 18.5). The biblical intertext does not correlate perfectly with the Grimms' tale, but the millstone in both is an instrument of revenge that punishes adults for injuring the young and innocent. The biblical passage surely gave the millstone in "The Juniper Tree" added weightiness, just as it lent a certain authority to this canonical fairy tale about getting back at adults who mistreat children.

Like "Hansel and Gretel," "Snow White," "Cinderella," and so many other popular fairy tales, "The Juniper Tree" shows us children victimized by adults. The boy slain by his step/mother serves even before his death as the target of unrelenting physical assaults. His sister, Marlene, despite her heroic tactics to bring her brother back to life, also suffers from the savagery of adults and, as a sign of her victimization, weeps almost incessantly throughout the tale. When the step/mother chops up her stepson and cooks him in a stew, Marlene weeps so hard that her tears provide enough salt to season the meal; she continues crying while

watching her father devour the stew and while planting her brother's
bones in the garden under the juniper tree. Then her mood suddenly
shifts: the child-victim has set in motion the process of retaliation, re-
versing the effects of her villainous step/mother's deeds and exacting
revenge.[3]

When one considers that fairy tales began as adult entertainment and
made the transition to children's literature only gradually in the course
of the seventeenth and eighteenth centuries, the ending to "The Juniper
Tree" seems more than peculiar. Why would adult audiences want to
get the kind of message sent by this tale? As Alice Miller has observed
(with some polemical exaggeration), our culture has, over the centuries,
accepted a pedagogical ideology that leaves parents blameless and
makes them eternally right, even as it labels children as lazy, spoiled, or
stubborn.[4] "The Juniper Tree," probably one of the oldest, best preserved, and most widely disseminated of all fairy tales, inverts this ideology by siding at all times with the children in it. The story is by no
means unique in the economy of its role-distribution, but the adult
agents driving its plot engage in singularly monstrous acts. And instead
of mobilizing their superior strength and energy to battle fairy-tale heroes, they conduct themselves in a way that can only be described as
simple-minded or downright childish.[5]

Take first the case of the step/mother. She has two children: a stepson and a biological daughter. "Whenever the woman looked at her
daughter, she felt great love for her, but whenever she looked at the
little boy, her heart was cut to the quick." More important than her
feelings is her actual behavior: "She pushed him from one place to the
next, slapped him here and cuffed him there, so that the poor child
lived in constant fear." It does not take long for this kind of bullying to
escalate into a murderous assault on the boy. When the unsuspecting
lad reaches into a chest to get an apple, the step/mother decapitates him
by slamming the lid down on his head. Her attempt to cover up the
bloodcurdling crime is unusual—astonishingly so—in its lack of sophistication. Overcome by fear (she shows no signs of remorse), she
fetches a kerchief, puts the head back on the boy, ties the kerchief
around his neck, and seats the corpse by the door with apple in hand.
This is a distinctly childlike way of concealing a crime, but each step of
the process is carried out with the utmost gravity.

While it is true that fairy-tale characters are forever violating the conventions of human behavior (the woman in this tale exhibits decidedly
antimaternal qualities toward both stepson and daughter), just as the

events recounted in them often fail to obey the laws of nature (slamming the lid of a chest on a person's head is unlikely to result in decapitation), there is a ring of psychological truth to the step/mother's behavior once one sees it as modeled on that of children rather than adults.[6] The assault on her son may stand as an extreme expression of adult anger, resentment, and aggression, but the woman's attempt to escape blame is so artless that it can be attributed only to a child's way of thinking. It may work, but that it does reminds us of the extent to which the world in "The Juniper Tree" obeys laws legislated by a child's view of reality.

The other adult actor in the tale does not display any greater degree of sophistication than his wife. When, for example, the father notices his son's absence and learns that he will be away for six weeks, he expresses annoyance, but only because the boy failed to bid him farewell. This expression of childlike egocentricity finds its match in table manners that are innocently crude and rude. "Give me more," the father declares greedily while he is devouring the stew cooked up by his wife. "I'm not going to share this with you," he snaps. "Somehow I feel as if it were all mine." While engaging in this cannibalistic feast, he casually tosses one bone after another under the table. The anthropophagous father may come off well in contrast to his bloodthirsty wife, but he remains less than admirable in both his indifference to the lot of his children as well as a single-minded focus on his own needs.

These observations about the behavior of step/mother and father explain in part why children find the grisly events in this tale so hilarious. Raconteurs report again and again that when the boy's head rolls, when he is dismembered for the stew, and when the father dines, children respond with gales of laughter.[7] Interestingly, the laughter is rarely described as nervous, but as gleeful, in part, perhaps, because a child's worst fears about adult aggression are acted out in a wholly childlike way by the very figures authorized to monitor children and to keep *their* aggressive impulses in check. Many versions of the tale make a point of capitalizing on the slapstick possibilities of the narrative situation. In the Scottish "Pippety Pew," the father fishes a foot out of the stew, turns to his wife, and engages in the following dialogue:

"Surely that's my Johnnie's foot," said he.
"Nonsense. It is one of the hare's," said she.
Then he took up a hand.
"That's surely my Johnnie's hand," said he.

"You're talking nonsense, goodman," said she. "That's
another of the hare's feet."[8]

In the narrated events of "The Juniper Tree," children witness parental aggression and parental indifference in their most extreme forms.
The antirealistic effects (from the transformation of boy into bird to the
improbably naive behavior of the adults) mobilized throughout to stage
the child's worst fears serve to diminish the anxiety and heighten the
pleasure of the performance. When children hear about adults acting
on impulse in extravagantly ghastly ways, without any attempt to retain
their dignity by covering up their deeds, the tables really are turned. It
becomes easy to laugh about what could arouse intense uneasiness and
pain when the discourse is marked with constant reminders of its safe
distance from reality.

What marks the behavior of the various actors in "The Juniper Tree"
as especially childlike is an inability to differentiate. The father, for example, may not know that he is indulging in a feast of human flesh and
committing an atrocity that represents the most brutish form of self-
preservation, but he still has made the error of not knowing how to
distinguish human from animal flesh. Own/foreign is not a category
within which he can operate. The daughter too, even as heroine of the
tale, has trouble making distinctions. For her, this takes the form of not
being able to tell the difference between dead and alive. When Marlene
sees her brother seated by the door, she is frightened but cannot read
his condition. He may be "white as a sheet" and unable to speak, yet she
does not recognize the meaning of these signs. Even the boy, as innocent victim, falls into the trap of failing to discriminate between good
and evil when he accepts the step/mother's invitation to take an apple.
This flaw or lack on the part of all three figures is precisely what makes
them agreeable and turns them into magnets for our sympathies. Because they do not differentiate and discriminate, they become aligned
with the forces of good.

The step/mother, by contrast, is an expert in the art of making distinctions, and that expertise fuels her evil impulses, allying her repeatedly with that divider par excellence known as the devil. It is he who
"takes hold of her" and compels her to treat the hero cruelly, who "takes
possession of her" and forces her to snatch the apple from her daughter,
and who "prompts" her to slam the lid down on the boy's head. For the
step/mother, the question of own/foreign becomes the touchstone of all
decisions. The opposition is fully incarnated in her daughter and step-

30. The scarf wrapped around the boy's neck conceals the fact that
he has been decapitated by his stepmother. His sister is perplexed and
frightened but unable to determine his condition.

son. That the step/mother differentiates between the two and is forever drawing distinctions between them marks her as a villain and lends to her every act a kind of self-consciousness absent in the actions of other figures. When her stepson returns from school, she speaks to him in honied tones, tricking him into taking the apple that means his death. The obverse of a nurturing and protective figure, she mobilizes the semblance of maternal actions to trap her victims. She deludes Marlene into taking responsibility for her brother's death, and she deceives her husband by telling him that his son is paying a visit to a great-uncle when he is in fact being dished up for dinner. The step/mother may act "as innocently as a child" at times, but her behavior is motivated by the need to see differences and to assert preferences.

Other versions of the "The Juniper Tree" confirm that deception fueled by differentiation is the key tactic used by the step/mother to attain her goals. Murderous intentions are masked by maternal goodwill in order to lure the tale's heroes/heroines to their deaths. In the British tale "The Rose-Tree," a stepmother camouflages the anger she harbors toward her stepdaughter with maternal tenderness. "'Come lay your head on my lap that I may comb your hair,'" she gently proposes. The girl rests her head on the woman's lap, unaware that dissimulation is at work. What follows is a sharp reversal, starkly brutal in its depiction of maternal affection sliding into fiendish savageness:

> So the little one laid her head in the woman's lap, who proceeded to comb the yellow silken hair. And when she combed the hair fell over her knees, and rolled right down to the ground.
> Then the stepmother hated her more for the beauty of her hair; so she said to her, "I cannot part your hair on my knee, fetch a billet of wood." So she fetched it. Then said the stepmother, "I cannot part your hair with a comb, fetch me an axe." So she fetched it.
> "Now," said the wicked woman, "lay your head down on the billet whilst I part your hair."
> Well! She laid down her little golden head without fear; and whist! down came the axe, and it was off. So the mother wiped the axe and laughed.[9]

We do not have to look long or far in the Grimms' collection to find other examples of murderous intentions masquerading as maternal goodwill. The three attempts on Snow White's life all nearly work because the heroine suspects nothing when an old peddler woman offers to lace her up "properly," to give her hair a "proper" combing, and to share an apple with her. The ruses work each time precisely because they incorporate gestures openly maternal in their aim. The shock comes when these gestures are revealed to be pure artifice, when the compassion and care they imply unmask themselves as murderous hatred.

Significantly, the first step in the direction of evil in "The Juniper Tree" is taken when the step/mother offers her son an apple. Numerous commentators have insisted on connecting that apple with Eve and the Garden of Eden.[10] But to see, as they do, the step/mother (as Eve) offering the infamous apple to the stepson (as Adam) signifies a failure to recognize differences. The boy's function is not analogous to that of Adam, and, more importantly, the step/mother is not tempting the boy with knowledge, but luring him to his death. Curiosity, original sin, knowledge (the entire complex of associations connected with the biblical Fall) are absent from the thematics of this particular episode.[11] And if we look at variants of the tale, we find that few others feature apples. In a version collected by Jacob Grimm, but included neither in the *Nursery and Household Tales* nor in the notes to it, the step/mother orders the boy to get into the chest and gather up its contents.[12] As soon as he climbs in, she slams the lid down on him, and the boy suffocates. Since the apples are, by virtue of their biblical function, so closely linked with temptation and deception, it is not surprising that they were smuggled into some versions—but that does not mean that the entire range of their biblical associations was transported into the text.

What seems more significant than the step/mother's offer of an apple is her method of committing a crime and of destroying the evidence of it. She first severs the boy's head from his body, inflicting a wound that cannot, for all her efforts, be healed. Once she recognizes the irreversibility of her deed, she further mutilates the corpse by "cutting it into pieces."[13] She thus becomes a person who not only makes distinctions, but also divides what should be whole and destroys things by taking them apart. She inflicts on the body precisely those operations that she also carries out in her mind. "Der zerstückelnde Verstand" (literally: reason that cuts things into pieces) was a central metaphor of negativity harnessed by German idealist philosophy in its nostalgia for organic wholeness and unity. As a differentiator, the step/mother creates a rupture in the "natural" order of things, dividing, segmenting, mutilating, and destroying. In this regard, she bears a distinct functional resemblance to Eve, who is also linked to death through division and sin. As the apocryphal *Book of Sirach* puts it: "From a woman was the beginning of sin, and because of her we all die."[14]

While the hero's step/mother is connected with artifice and malice, his birth mother is described in terms that link her with nature and biological rhythms. When it comes to analyzing the "natural" mother and her role in the Grimms' tale, however, a word of caution is in order. The long paragraph that opens "The Juniper Tree" as it appeared in the version printed in the *Nursery and Household Tales* has correctly been viewed as suspect by folklorists. Its florid language along with its inclusion of a formulaic phrase that appears in few other versions of the tale (the mother wishes for a child "as red as blood and as white as snow") suggest that certain liberties were taken to produce as poetic a text as possible.[15]

The textual history of the Grimms' version of "The Juniper Tree" is in fact complicated. To begin with, the Grimms cannot really be credited with taking down the words of the tale. The Romantic painter Philipp Otto Runge recorded "The Juniper Tree" along with "The Fisherman and His Wife" as a sign of his willingness to collaborate in a national effort to preserve folk traditions. The tale subsequently found its way into one collection after another. The Grimms' version deviates slightly from Runge's original, yet there are no real substantive changes.[16]

Philipp Otto Runge, a master in the art of ornamental detail and decorative art, gives us a highly stylized version of the tale even as he uses dialect to convey the impression of "artless" narration. He was, no doubt, largely responsible for the expansive narrative tone that dominates the tale's first paragraph. His is the only extant version of the tale that weds the biological mother so closely to nature—once she becomes fertile and conceives, she is turned into a virtual prisoner of nature, subject to its laws of growth and decay. An elaborate narrative duet coordinates the rhythms of the child's gestation period with nature's seasonal changes. Conceived in the dead of winter after a long stretch of barrenness, the child flourishes in the spring, becomes "big and firm" like the fruit on the juniper tree, and is born at some time in the fall, at which point his mother's health declines, and she dies. (Pro)creation and death are wedded here in the conventional mythical thematics common to cults of fertility and agricultural rites.

The text's linking of pregnancy with the rhythms of nature is implicitly part of a larger project that connects mothers with Mother Nature, an association not altogether flattering, as Dorothy Dinnerstein and other feminist writers have emphasized.[17] Note how Freud, for example, writes about Nature and its hostility to the male-gendered notion of civilization (without once, incidentally, acknowledging how closely his description fits that of the preoedipal mother):

> There are the elements, which seem to mock at all human control: the earth, which quakes and is torn apart and buries all human life and its works; water, which deluges and drowns everything in turmoil, storms, which blow everything before them; . . . and finally there is the painful riddle of death, against which no medicine has yet been found. . . . With these forces, nature rises against us, *majestic, cruel, and inexorable*; she brings to our mind once more *our weakness and helplessness*, which we thought to escape through the work of civilization [my emphasis].[18]

Though the poignancy of the opening paragraph in "The Juniper Tree" is unsettled by the complexities of the biological mother's associations with nature and death, it still stands in sharp contrast to the horrors of the tale's main events, events engineered largely by the step/mother. Runge (or perhaps his informants) must have had a clear sense of the biological mother as a "natural" foil to the step/mother, who represents self-consciousness and artifice in its most dreaded and dreadful form. His introduction also establishes a pattern in which birth and death become so entwined that one is not present without the other; indeed, the birth of one person spells the death of another in the biological economy of the text. The co-presence of birth and death is inscribed on this first scene and is then doubled and repeated as rebirth and murder in the tale's subsequent syntagmatic units.

"The Juniper Tree" eliminates both stepmother and biological mother in the end, yet it is (if one may coin the word) *matricentric* from beginning to end. The mothers serve as progenitors of more than the children—they are the ones who, in their affiliation with origins and endings, generate the action that constitutes the plot and who, through their association with nature at one extreme and with artifice at the other, engender a complex chain of signification. The death of the biological mother, central as it is to the narrative, is often omitted both in

variants of the tale and in conventional inventories of the tale's stock
events. The Aarne/Thompson index of tale types, for example, lists the
following episodes as key: "The Murder," "The Transformation," "The
Revenge," and "The Second Transformation."[19] This tabulation has not
been corrected or modified by any of the tale's commentators. But a far
more satisfying, and also more revealing, list of the chief events in "The
Juniper Tree" would take into account the death of the biological
mother, as it would take note of the way in which murder alternates
with transformation.

In classic fairy-tale fashion, "The Juniper Tree" begins with a realistic
basic situation, then veers off abruptly into a world where supernatural
events and violent actions are the order of the day. Think, for example,
of "Hansel and Gretel," where the villain of the tale first appears as a
cruel stepmother at home, then as a cannibalistic witch residing in enchanted woods. The portrait of the evil stepmother may seem almost as
unrealistic in its broad contours as that of the wicked witch with her
red eyes and keen sense of smell, yet if one considers the social realities
of other cultures, the heartless stepmother is less of a stark deviation
from the norm than would appear at first sight. That stepmothers
treated the children of their husbands' first marriages badly—in part
because they wished to preserve the patrimony for their own children,
in part because they resented the idea of becoming enslaved to a previous wife's children—was more or less a fact of life in the era that gave
shape to the tales recorded in the Grimms' collection. In "Hansel and
Gretel," as in so many other fairy tales, the plausible and realistic trau-
mas of everyday life, as described in the tale's opening paragraphs, are
sharply intensified and repeated in the antirealistic nightmare of victimization and retaliation acted out in the remainder of the tale.[20]

"The Juniper Tree" takes as its starting point a scene of birth and
death that constituted a part of the life experience of large segments of
the population of premodern Europe. As Eugen Weber has observed,
"deaths in childbed and after made for high female mortality between
the ages of 20 and 39, hence an unusually high proportion of maternal
orphans."[21] The version of "The Juniper Tree" recorded by Philipp Otto
Runge is exceptionally expansive when it comes to describing the
mother's death. Many tales simply state that the mother of one of the
two children (usually the boy, but sometimes the girl) has died without
making clear the circumstances of her death.[22] The birth kills the
woman, but the text hints that she is not entirely blameless. Greed be-

comes implicated in the woman's death: "In the seventh month she snatched at the juniper berries and ate them so greedily that she grew sad and became ill." Still, it is the birth that leads directly to the death, and ultimately the child must take on the burden of guilt for the mother's death. In the second phase of action, however, the child is innocent victim more than anything else, becoming the target of the step/mother's abuse and homicidal impulses. From the child's point of view, the first two principal episodes of the tale enact the syntactical inversion of "I killed you" into "You killed me" ("I" representing the child in the tale, "you" the mother in both her incarnations). The initial situation has been reversed, with the cold-blooded slaying of a child by his stepmother far overshadowing in dramatic intensity the death of a mother from the birth of her child.

The version of "The Juniper Tree" in the *Nursery and Household Tales* lends itself to the construction of two alternative, mutually exclusive scenarios. The one registers in exaggerated form a child's very real fears about parental aggression and engulfment. The other—and this reading attests to the possibility that fairy tales give body to both fears of aggression and to fantasies of retaliation—can be read as a story responding to the distress felt by a child growing up under the weight of guilt (whether consciously registered or not) produced by the death of a mother during childbirth, or even by the symbolic "psychic" death of a mother when she gives birth. As Adrienne Rich pointedly puts it, in childbirth, "the mother's life is exchanged for the child's; her autonomy as a separate being seems fated to conflict with the infant she will bear."[23] The tale moves from a naturalistic episode of birth and death (in which the child figures as "murderer") to a supernatural inversion of this scene (in which the "mother" stands as slayer). Through this inversion, the tale's child-hero is both enshrined as victim and vindicated as murderer. It may appear crude to turn this version of a classic fairy tale into a therapeutic text for children who feel responsible, however remotely, for their mothers' deaths (real or symbolic), but there is more than a hint in the Grimms' "Juniper Tree" that the tale sought to turn morbid guilt into self-righteous innocence.

The naturalistic scene of death in childbirth is reversed and doubled in the most unnatural terms possible. The boy's murder represents a transgression of moral and legal conventions, while his rebirth as a magnificent bird violates natural law. The murder itself is so abominable, and the song that describes it so haunting and direct, that it becomes easy to erase the victim's implication in the death of his birth mother and to justify his role as a deadly agent of revenge.[24] The retaliatory murder of the step/mother, which ushers in the return and rebirth of the son, also marks the complete eradication of the mother as a threatening physical presence in her incarnation as step/mother and as a guilty memory in her incarnation as biological mother. In the end, the motherless household becomes the happy household: "[The boy] took his father and Marlene by the hand. All three were so very happy and they went into the house, sat down at the table, and ate." Grief tainted with guilt, and the fear of malice associated with domestic tyranny, have vanished with the deaths of the two mothers.

We have seen how the step/mother, as the exponent of artifice, malice, and self-conscious reasoning, serves as the agent of murderous forces, just as the biological mother, tied to the rhythms of nature, represents life-giving powers. The one seems to function as an agent of death, the other of life. Why then does the tale eliminate both in the end to culminate in the idyll of a motherless family? This is the same ending that we know well enough from "Hansel and Gretel" and countless other fairy tales. While the paradigmatic dimension of "The Juniper Tree" ostensibly introduces a sharp division between the regime of the biological mother and that of the step/mother, that opposition is overturned in the course of the narrative. The biological mother, as we have seen, becomes implicated, through her fertility and childbearing, in the cyclical rhythms of nature, which include decay and death. The step/mother, through her murder and dismemberment of the hero, becomes enmeshed in a process marked not only by death and mutilation, but also by birth and (re)creation. The murder and dismemberment of the hero constitute the events that break down the tale's elaborately constructed binary oppositions to produce continuums in which birth slides into death and destruction into creation.

When faced with the step/mother's gruesome act, critics have made it easy for themselves by referring their readers to Greek mythology, in particular to Atreus, who serves his brother a meal made up of the limbs of his sons. But the story of Atreus has little bearing on "The Juniper Tree," for it stages the shocking event of forced cannibalism as the most vicious possible form of premeditated revenge. The step/mother, by contrast, is not out to get the better of her husband or to get even—she seems to be doing little more than trying to get rid of the evidence for a crime committed in a moment of passionate rage, and incidentally passing on the burden of guilt for the murder to her husband. Given the degree to which "The Juniper Tree" focuses on birth, death, and regeneration, it seems more logical to look at her act of dismemberment in connection with various Indo-European myths of creation, where, through the ritual murder and dismemberment of a sacrificial victim (Dionysus figures as the most familiar example), the world is renewed and recreated.[25]

While it may seem incongruous to link these mythical plots with the domestic drama of "The Juniper Tree," the creation story helps us to understand the cosmic elements that slip into several scenes of the fairy tale. The birth of the bird, along with the boy's return home and transformation, are described in terms that are decidedly apocalyptic in tenor. The step/mother fears that the world is coming to an end at the very moment when Marlene and her father feel relieved and experience a joyful sense of renewal. The boy's rebirth marks the advent of a male savior who puts a decisive end to the step/mother's nightmarish reign of artifice and duplicity. Interestingly, however, it is the maternal force (now in her malevolent incarnation) who serves as agent of both death and (re)birth. Like the biological mother, she too must perish in order that the process of (re)birth be accomplished. As in the drama of cosmic renewal staged in the fairy tale told by the poet Klingsohr in Novalis's *Heinrich von Ofterdingen*, mothers must die as the precondition for a golden age of innocence and peace.

The mythical mysteries of birth and renewal through dismemberment may seem to strain the fragile domestic drama of "The Juniper Tree," yet they help us understand the way the text dismantles the very oppositions on which it builds syntagmatic and paradigmatic structures. What makes "The Juniper Tree" an extraordinary text is the way in which it remains relentlessly domestic and parochial even as it is shot through with mythical allusions and reminiscences. In the end, it remains a story about family conflicts, an allegory of development that charts the reorientation of children from their mothers to their fathers, but with a mythical signature that underwrites the tale's "sacred truths."

But let us return to the original question. Why is it that "The Juniper Tree" does away with mothers and leaves us with a tableau in which brother, sister, and father are seated at a table eating? Recent psychoanalytic literature has done much to explain the complexities of the mother/child relationship. Its emphasis on the fearsomeness of the oedipal mother, whose seeming omnipotence and whose role as an agent of prohibition create a sense of dependence, powerlessness, and resentment in the child, explains to some extent the hostility projected onto a mother by a child—this does not, of course, rule out the possibility that hostility may also be part of a child's real-life experience. In fairy tales, representations of the mother often slide into one of two categories: the omnipotent, hostile witch or the omnipotent, protective mother. "Representations of the father relationship," as Nancy Chodorow has observed, "do not become so internalized and subject to ambivalence, repression, and splitting of good and bad aspects."[26] In fact, the father often becomes, because of the "separate" and "special" status assigned him by virtue of his traditional absence from early childrearing, the representative of autonomy and of the public/social world. Development is thus traditionally defined in terms of growing away from the mother, who represents dependence and domesticity, and turning toward the father.[27] "The Juniper Tree" enacts this very process in its exclusion of the maternal component from the domestic tableau that closes the tale. The children have successfully negotiated the path from dependence to autonomy by crushing the mother and joining the father.

That the father, daughter, and son sit down to dine remains more than a curious detail in this enigmatic text. This last supper figures as an important contrast to the shocking meal in which the three participated earlier, with the son as main course. If nothing else, it signals a normalization of family relations and marks a period of banal stability leading out of the cataclysmic upheavals of the past. Yet, for all its positive connotations, this image of the motherless family participating self-sufficiently in the very activity normally arranged and orchestrated by the mother remains eerily static by contrast to the unending cycle of birth, death, and rebirth set in motion by the presence of mothers.

We will never know exactly who first told this tale and for whom it was intended. In light of the story's perspective, voice, and worldview, it is tempting to imagine a child as the tale's narrator. But as Otto Rank has observed in the context of a study about myths, heroic plots may focus on childhood experiences, but adults create them "by means of retrograde childhood fantasies"—and, we might add, in a gesture that both supplements and revises, through childhood memories.[28]

One prominent intertextual reference to "The Juniper Tree" dramatically illustrates the way in which adults continue to identify with children, even in those cases where they have passed from (child) victim into the most extreme possible form of adult oppressor. Goethe's *Faust* shows us Gretchen, imprisoned for the crime of infanticide, pathetically singing to herself:

> My mother, the whore,
> She slew me!
> My father, the rascal,
> He ate me!
> My tiny little sister
> Took my bones
> To a nice cool place;
> I became a beautiful bird;
> Fly away, fly away! (4412–20)[29]

This astonishingly revealing moment in Goethe's drama draws attention to an adult's strong identification with a child's suffering at the same time that it exposes the gesture of appropriation that accompanies feelings of empathy. What we discover in its words is that guilty adults can divest themselves of blame for their most reprehensible acts of aggression against children by identifying with the victims, then projecting their own transgressions onto other figures, and finally constructing a drama in which the self takes flight as a form of salvation. The complexities of child/parent relationships are presented with audacious simplicity in these few lines.

Adults, who may have lost the innocence and simplicity celebrated in "The Juniper Tree" (not necessarily as drastically as Gretchen), have their own reasons for telling this tale. Nostalgia—the hope of recapturing moments of childhood by reliving its high drama from a child's point of view—may make tales like "The Juniper Tree" attractive to adults. But reflexes less voluntary than nostalgia may also lead to a need to replay these childhood dramas of injured innocence and justified retaliation. Listening to "The Juniper Tree" provides young and old alike the opportunity to see and feel how a helpless victim escapes his persecutor and ultimately triumphs against all odds.

Fairy tales often address specific aspects of a child's growing pains. The version of "The Juniper Tree" in the Grimms' *Nursery and Household Tales* may in the past have proved therapeutic to children who felt that they had murdered their mothers (literally or symbolically), and it may well still serve that function today. But this tale, like so many tales of family life, also serves the more general purpose of empowering children, or at least making children feel less inferior to adults. In cultures that consistently play adult authority and privilege against childish impotence and inadequacy, these stories have a liberating power that should not be underestimated. They may lack the subversive dimension we associate with stories about diminutive giant-killers and foxy innocents, but they still appeal to that part of us that resists the notion of bowing to authority.

That ill will and evil are so often personified as adult female figures in fairy tales, even in cultures where paternal authority proves weightier than its female counterpart, raises some serious questions that threaten to invalidate the notion of the therapeutic gains we so eagerly look for in the stories we read to children. However satisfying the tales may seem from a child's point of view, however much they may reflect the psychological realities of developmental paths leading from dependence to autonomy, they still perpetuate strangely inappropriate notions about what it means to live happily ever after. "Hansel and Gretel," as noted, implies that happiness comes in the form of an enduring love triangle consisting of a father and his two children (who have defeated an evil female). Other collections show us the same constellation of figures. In Afanasev's celebrated Russian fairy tale, Vasilisa the Beautiful marries the tsar, but her story does not end until her father finds his way into his daughter's house. The hero of the Venetian "Cloven Youth" finds himself living "in harmony" with his wife and her father. Perrault lets Tom Thumb return "to his father" and purchase sinecures for him and his brothers.[30] The joy produced by the union of a brother, sister, and father in "The Juniper Tree" after the death of the step/mother is not unique to this one tale type. For this reason, it is important to bear in mind that versions of this tale and others are sacred only as cultural documents mapping the most heavily traveled developmental routes of another era. They may also capture the larger contours of patterns predominant in our own age, but that does not mean that we have to keep reading the same stories to our children today. The omnipresent, powerful mother and the distant, separate father are still the most common coordinates in the world of childrearing, but enough has changed and is changing for us to produce new cultural stories to read to our own children.

Reinvention through Intervention

Every fairy tale worth recording at all is the remnant of a tradition
possessing true historical value—historical, at least, in so far as it
has naturally arisen out of the mind of a people under special
circumstances. . . . It sustains afterwards natural changes from the
sincere action of the fear or fancy of successive generations;
it takes new colour from their manner of life, and
new form from their changing moral tempers.

John Ruskin, "Fairy Stories"

We just try to make a good picture.
And then the professors come along and tell us what we do.

Walt Disney on *Snow White amd the Seven Dwarfs*

NO FAIRY-TALE text is sacred. Every printed version is just another variation on a theme—the rewriting of a cultural story in
a certain time and place for a specific audience. For now, that
audience consists largely of children and the adults who read and tell
stories to them. Yet, although children's books and films have become
the "new matrix" for generating fairy tales, we still give very little
thought to the effect those stories might have on our children, accepting more or less what the market has to offer by way of reinterpretation.[1] This failure to question or to take the measure of what we pass on
to children is particularly surprising if we consider that fairy tales do
not merely encode social arrangements from the past, but also participate in their creation for the present and future. As Stephen Greenblatt

has observed, "the work of art is not the passive surface on which . . . historical experience leaves its stamp but one of the creative agents in the fashioning and re-fashioning of this experience."[2] As we tell these stories, we simultaneously evoke the cultural experience of the past and reproduce it in a way that will shape and structure the experience of the children to whom we speak.

Our cultural stories are the products of unceasing negotiations between the creative consciousness of individuals and the collective sociocultural constructs available to them. These negotiations may be smooth or they may be troubled, but they always leave a mark on each version of a tale. Making a new fiction means refashioning—in ways that may be conciliatory or conspiratorial, but also in ways that may be contestatory or subversive—the cultural legacy that constitutes us as individuals. Carolyn G. Heilbrun writes eloquently about the challenge of producing fictions:

> One cannot make up stories: one can only retell in new ways the stories one has already heard. Let us agree on this: that we live our lives through texts. These may be read, or chanted, or experienced electronically, or come to us, like the murmurings of our mothers, telling us of what conventions demand. Whatever their form or medium, these stories are what have formed us all, they are what we must use to make our new fictions. . . . Out of old tales, we must make new lives.[3]

We create new tales not only by retelling familiar stories, but also by reinterpreting them. Just as each age reinvents Shakespeare, constructing new meanings out of the very words read by other generations, each age creates its own folklore through rereadings as well as retellings. The prominence of certain stories is in itself symptomatic of cultural production—of the way in which culture constitutes itself by constituting us. Freud's interpretation of the Oedipus story is, for example, so firmly inscribed on our consciousness as a model of male development that its plot begins to take on the role of a self-fulfilling prophesy, reproducing the family dynamics that it relentlessly broadcasts. The absence of alternative male models or of female developmental models has led Carol Gilligan to turn her attention to a very different "old tale"—Apuleius's "Cupid and Psyche"—with the hope of resurrecting it, through a bold reinterpretive gesture, as a story of female resistance.[4]

Of the many fairy tales circulating the world over, it is not easy to pick out the ones to retell or reinterpret for our children. Which are better to start out with—the earlier, often brutal, versions that have been said to capture the "universal truths" of human experience, or the modern refashionings that speak to the specificity of our own time and place and seem more consonant with our cultural expectations? Given a choice, say, between the Grimms' "Snow White" and the dozens of modern, available versions of the story (including Walt Disney's film), which would be the "right" one for a child?

That question has no correct response, but trying to answer it reasonably well means making the effort to reflect on various versions of a particular story—their manner as well as their matter, the degree to which they empower or coerce, entertain or frighten, disrupt cultural codes or reinscribe them. It also means looking closely at the story's most stable episodes, those moments in the plot that have been most resistant to creative variation. And finally, it means identifying the particular points in a tale marked by discursive practices that are unique to one culture or another.

In thinking about the dominant fairy-tale images in our own country, the name "Disney" immediately comes to mind, for the films and books produced by the Disney Studio have more than a large corner of the American market. Let us begin by looking at "Snow White"—first at its German version (on which the Disney film is based) and then at its American cinematic incarnation. In this way, we can begin to get some sense of priorities on sociocultural agendas, however limited the sample. This in turn can help us to determine whether the specific values, ideals, desires, and sublimations transmitted by one version of a tale constitute those we wish to convey to our children.

The Grimms' first recorded version of "Snow White" is very different from what we find in standard American editions of the *Nursery and Household Tales*. In that version, which appeared in 1812 and which was heavily revised for the standard final edition of 1857, it is Snow White's biological mother, not her stepmother, who orders a huntsman to kill the girl and bring back her lungs and liver as proof of the deed. (That she boils the innards in salt and eats them is a detail the Grimms retained even after they transformed the wicked queen into a stepmother.) Even when a stepmother stands in for the mother, it has not been difficult for most readers and critics to recognize that "Snow

White" is a story about mother-daughter conflict. Yet this did not prevent modern storytellers from magnifying and intensifying maternal evil in the tale. By the time Walt Disney got his hands on the story, for example, the good, biological mother, who dies in childbirth, had been eradicated—the only maternal figure is the stepmother in her double incarnation as proud, cold, and evil queen and as ugly, dangerous, and wicked witch.[5] Disney himself, who referred to the transformation of the queen into a witch as a "Jekyll and Hyde thing," seemed unaware that there is no Jekyll component to this figure's personality, only two Hydes. We are no longer dealing with the splitting of the mother image into a good mother who dies in childbirth and an evil mother who persecutes her child—what we have here is a complete absorption of maternal figures into the realm of evil.[6]

Disney's demonization of a parent-figure might appear to be a healthy tonic to the ideological bias against children that we have seen in Bruno Bettelheim's reading of fairy tales. For Bettelheim, "Snow White" is not about a mother's murderous envy of her daughter, but about a child's wish to destroy a parent:

> Competition between a parent and his child makes life unbearable for parent and child. Under such conditions the child wants to free himself and be rid of the parent, who forces him either to compete or to buckle under. The wish to be rid of the parent arouses great guilt, justified though it may be when the situation is viewed objectively. So in a reversal which eliminates the guilt feeling, this wish, too, is projected onto the parent. Thus, in fairy tales there are parents who try to rid themselves of their child, as happens in "Snow White."[7]

But what makes Disney's "Snow White" difficult to applaud as an example of a liberating fairy tale is precisely the way in which it works too hard to efface any trace of maternal goodwill and to construct an image of feminine evil overpowering in its cinematic depth. And it was the Grimms who cleared the way for emphasizing maternal evil by magnifying female villainy in successive versions of the stories they had collected.

Since social arrangements in both the Grimms' day and in our own have positioned mothers as the dominant figure in the childrearing process, it may seem logical to locate adult villainy in female characters—be they mothers, stepmothers, or witches. Yet the "abandoning impulse" emanates from both male and female parents, and children are just as likely to feel emotionally abandoned by a father as by a mother. Some versions of "Snow White"—a Turkish tale, for example—give us a male protagonist abandoned by his father. Another tells of a princess who sits at her window sewing, learns of an enchanted prince "with skin as white as snow and lips as red as blood and hair as golden as the sun," and, with the help of three old women, frees the sleeping prince from the spell cast on him.[8] These tales along with other similarly "deviant" variants give the lie to the possibility that women have been slotted into the role of fairy-tale villains because of their greater involvement in the childrearing process. What seems more likely is that the men who recorded these oral tales—and for the most part the great collectors of the nineteenth century were male—showed, whenever they had a choice, a distinct preference for stories with female villains over tales with male giants and ogres.[9]

Yet if the fairy-tale canon vilifies mothers by turning them into characters who torment and persecute children, does it not also glorify girls by placing them in the role of heroine? Our best known fairy-tale characters are, after all, Snow White, Cinderella, Red Riding Hood, and Sleeping Beauty. If we take a closer look at the figure of Snow White to see how one representative female heroine is constructed by different cultures, the lack of variation in representing this particular character is striking. All printed versions seem to concur on her singular physical attractiveness (a necessary condition of the "beauty contest" with the wicked queen) and also on her genius for housework (Disney even turned her into a Cinderella-figure for his film's introductory sequence).

Beginning with the Grimms, it is through a combination of labor and good looks that Snow White earns a prince for herself. Here is how the Grimms, as noted earlier, describe the housekeeping contract extended to Snow White by the dwarfs:

> "If you'll keep house for us, cook, make the beds, wash, sew, and knit, and if you'll keep everything neat and orderly, you can stay with us, and we'll provide you with everything you need."[10]

But the dwarfs in the Grimms' tale are hardly in need of a housekeeper, for they appear to be models of neatness. Everything in their cottage is "indescribably dainty and neat"; the table has a white cloth with tiny plates, cups, knives, forks, and spoons, and the beds are covered with sheets "as white as snow." Compare this description of the dwarfs' cot-

tage, with the following one taken from a book based on Disney's version of "Snow White":

> Skipping across a little bridge to the house, Snow White peeked in
> through one window pane. There seemed to be no one at home, but
> the sink was piled high with cups and saucers and plates which
> looked as though they had never been washed. Dirty little shirts and
> wrinkled little trousers hung over chairs, and everything was blan-
> keted with dust.
>
> "Maybe the children who live here have no mother," said Snow
> White, "and need someone to take care of them. Let's clean their
> house and surprise them."
>
> So in she went, followed by her forest friends. Snow White found
> an old broom in the corner and swept the floor, while the little ani-
> mals all did their best to help.
>
> Then Snow White washed all the crumpled little clothes, and set a
> kettle of delicious soup to bubbling on the hearth.[11]

In one post-Disney American variant of the story after another, Snow
White makes it her mission to clean up after the the dwarfs ("seven
dirty little boys") and is represented as serving an apprenticeship in
home economics ("Snow White, for her part, was becoming an excellent housekeeper and cook").[12] The Disney version itself transforms
household drudgery into frolicking good fun—less work than play
since it requires no real effort, is carried out with the help of wonderfully dextrous woodland creatures, and achieves such a dazzling result.
Disney made a point of placing the housekeeping sequence before the
encounter with the dwarfs and of presenting the dwarfs as "naturally
messy," just as Snow White is "by nature" tidy. When she comes upon
the cottage, her first instinct is to clean up the house and surprise them
and then "maybe they'll let me stay."[13]

Reviews of the film underscore the way in which the housecleaning
sequence—"with squirrels using their tails as dusters, the swallows scal-
loping pies with their feet, the fawns licking the plates clean, the chip-
munks twirling cobwebs about their tales and pulling free,"[14] as one
enthusiastic reporter for the New York Times described it—seems to
have captured the imagination of viewers. That sequence is repeatedly
singled out as marking the film's highpoint, in large part because of its
creative élan. It is telling that this particular moment in the film became
the target of special inventive energy and wit, especially since humor is

so emphatically absent from other moments in the film. Recorded versions of the tale reveal that there was plenty of room for whimsy, even in the final scene of "Snow White." In many early versions of the story, for example, Snow White is not revived by a kiss from the prince—Walt Disney borrowed that particular motif from "Sleeping Beauty." Instead, the clumsy prince drops the coffin, and the jolt to the sleeping princess dislodges the piece of apple in her throat. Similarly, the Grimms' first published version takes us to the prince's castle, where a servant, who has to carry the coffin around all day, becomes so irritated with the sleeping princess that he declares: "We have to slave away all day long for the sake of this dead girl," then thumps her on the back so hard that the piece of apple stuck in her throat comes flying out.[15]

The success of Disney's film led one reporter to promote the idea of a new business for America: "industrialized fantasy."[16] "Industrialized fantasy sounds like something extremely complex," the reporter noted, "yet it is quite simple. Walt Disney's picture-play 'Snow White and the Seven Dwarfs' is an excellent example. Here is something manufactured out of practically nothing except some paint pots and a few tons of imagination. In this country imagination is supposed to be a commodity produced in unlimited quantities. If it can be turned out as an article of commerce which the public will readily buy, then prosperity should be—well, just around the corner, anyway." The public readily, almost too readily, bought Disney's article of commerce, along with the tons of imagination in it. As it was sold and repackaged, through its songs, through plastic figures of Snow White and the dwarfs, and through books based on the film, it came to have a powerful effect on parents and children, impressing on everyone the image of a girl who makes her dreams come true through her flirtatious good looks and her effortless ability to keep a house clean. Because the story was appropriated by what some have called the culture industry rather than "industrialized fantasy," it could also be harnessed into the service of producing cultural sentences, powerful prescriptive messages that took on the character of "universal truths" about human behavior.

Foucault has taught us the extent to which socialization produces "docile bodies" that subject themselves to self-discipline and productive labors. By internalizing a disciplinary regime in each subject, socialization staves off the need for coercive action or repressive measures. In this sense, the encoding of children's literature—of what is read in a person's "formative years"—with certain sociocultural norms plays a particularly vital role. As Western culture began prohibiting corporal punishment and eliminating disciplinary practices pertaining to the body, it made a decisive move in the direction of engendering child-rearing policies that enlisted the consciousness of its subjects in the project of productive discipline. As Margaret R. Miles has pointed out in another context, however, it is important to register the ways in which our own society has not, by any stretch of the imagination, eliminated coercion as a disciplinary practice.[17] Newspapers give us painful daily reminders of the degree to which children continue to be subjected to abusive physical treatment even as they are, by self-definition, the principal targets of socialization.

To accept Foucault's account is also to concede that the entire project of childrearing, including the telling of tales, is invested in a microphysics of power and is therefore never really in the best interests of the child. Any attempt to pass on stories becomes a disciplinary tactic aimed at control. Cultural theory will never allow us to escape this charge, but we can at least—on a pragmatic level—make the effort to identify what is transmitted in the stories we tell children and to develop a clearer awareness of how those stories can be retold or reinterpreted to produce texts that may yet be coercive, but at least will provide more pleasure.

As I observed earlier, Bruno Bettelheim has cautioned parents not to talk with children about what they read but to let them work out their feelings about a story "on their own."[18] This warning against parental intervention may well appear to attenuate the socializing energy of a story, but it can also strengthen the power of certain signals that we may not want our children to receive. We have seen how American rewritings of "Snow White" glaringly polarize the notion of the feminine to produce a murderously jealous and forbiddingly cold woman along with a girl of ideal beauty and domestic genius. Here it would not seem amiss to talk about the story, to engage in a joint interpretive effort that acknowledges the child's power to read the events, and, finally, to collaborate once again with the child in creating a new story based on the old. Working through a story by amending, excising, and transforming it creates opportunities for a new understanding of the constraints imposed on us by our culture, yet it also provides a dress rehearsal for resisting those constraints in real life.

Despite the stabilizing power of print, fairy tales can still be told and retold so that they challenge and resist, rather than simply reproduce, the constructs of a culture. Through playful disruptions, it is possible to begin transforming canonical texts into tales that empower and entertain children at the same time that they interrogate and take the measure of their own participation in a project to socialize the child. Some models exist in print, others flourish in oral form, in private exchanges between parent and child.

Roald Dahl, author of *Charlie and the Chocolate Factory*, once observed that the key to his success as an author of children's books was his ability "to conspire with children against adults."[19] Now it may well be that adults who turn themselves into co-conspirators with the child are in fact engaging in a fraudulent scheme to win the kind of affectionate loyalty that produces a docile child, but, in practical terms, it remains true that children react with glee when adults engage in the kind of behavior they try so hard to alter in children. The popular "Fairy Tale Theater" version of "Snow White," produced by Shelley Duvall, uses humor and imagination to defuse the formidable power of the wicked stepmother. That figure's narcissistic vanity is taken to such extremes that she becomes the buffoon of the story through her many expansive speeches celebrating her own beauty. Thus a figure who might, in other contexts, inspire terror becomes the laughingstock of the story.[20] Shifting the narrative centers of power becomes an effective means for diminishing the threat of adult evil and strengthening children's confidence in their ability to conquer that threat.

Defamiliarization can also go far toward breaking the magic spell that traditional tales weave around their listeners. This may take the form of a shift in perspective—retelling a story from the point of view of one of its villains—or it may take the form of an abrupt reversal in a traditional plot—showing a character resisting a proposal that is usually accepted. The "Upside Down Tales" told by Russell Shorto give us, for example, both the traditional tale and another version, "the untold story." Shorto presents the child with the Grimms' "Cinderella," then "sets the record straight" with a version of the story told from the stepsisters' point of view.[21] The effectiveness of abrupt plot reversals as devices for inducing reflection on cultural stories that have become ossified in printed form becomes evident from a reading of Rosemarie Künzler's version of *Rumpelstiltskin*, which shows the indignant reaction of the miller's daughter to Rumpelstiltskin's proposal to exchange his spinning skills for her child.[22] Jane Yolen's *Sleeping Ugly* also neatly illustrates the way in which playful reversals can produce provocatively thoughtful, rather than predictable, stories.[23] Like Bertolt Brecht, who wanted to break the magic spell of folk wisdom as captured in proverbs ("Man proposes; God disposes" became for him "Man proposes that God disposes"), some authors of fairy tales have used humor and imagination to thwart our expectations and to contest the paths taken by these stories. Their stories point the way to a folklore that is reinvented by each new generation of storytellers and reinvested with a powerfully creative social energy.[24]

🐾 NOTES 🐾

PREFACE

1. Charles Schulz, "Peanuts," United Features Syndicate, Inc. I am grateful to Doris Young for calling the strip to my attention. See her "Evaluation of Children's Responses to Literature," in *A Critical Approach to Children's Literature*, ed. Sara Innis Fenwick (Chicago: Univ. of Chicago Press, 1967), pp. 100–109.

2. Mark Twain's observation about morals appears in the prefatory notice to *The Adventures of Huckleberry Finn*, ed. John Seeyle (London: Penguin, 1985). The Duchess makes her pronouncements in Lewis Carroll's *Alice's Adventures in Wonderland & Through the Looking-Glass* (Toronto: Bantam, 1981), p. 67.

3. Alison Lurie sees subversiveness as the trait that makes children's literature worth studying. She identifies and analyzes texts that celebrate "daydreaming, disobedience, answering back, running away from home, and concealing one's private thoughts and feelings from unsympathetic grown-ups." See *Don't Tell the Grown-ups: Subversive Children's Literature* (Boston: Little, Brown, 1990), p. x.

4. Stanley Fish, *Is There a Text in This Class? The Authority of Interpretive Communities* (Cambridge: Harvard Univ. Press, 1980), p. 14. Fish's views on the way in which texts are constituted does much to diminish the distance between traditional tales (which are created by the interplay between teller and audience) and literary texts. Nina Mikkelsen describes one child's manner of reading and rewriting: "Sometimes she reads; sometimes she misreads; sometimes she extracts the essence; sometimes she proclaims the book's existence; sometimes she is building bridges connecting images; at other times she is developing new structures. . . . And as she grows and changes, the books are changing with her." See "Sendak, *Snow White*, and the Child as Literary Critic," *Language Arts* 62 (1985): 362–73.

5. On the way in which the novel tells, "with regret," how its heroes are destroyed "by the forces of social regulation and standardization," see D. A. Miller, *The Novel and the Police* (Berkeley and Los Angeles: Univ. of California Press, 1988), p. 19. Miller also emphasizes that though the novel condemns policing procedures, it reinvents them in "*the very practice of novelistic representation.*"

6. *New York Times*, 24 November 1990, p. 26.

7. On the appreciative, though not wholly uncritical, reception of the book, see the reviews by John Updike, *New York Times Book Review*, 23 May 1976; Harold Bloom, "Driving out Demons," *New York Review of Books*, 15 July 1976; Richard Todd, "In Praise of Fairy Tales," *Atlantic*, June 1976; Alison Lurie, "The Haunted Wood," *Harper's*, June 1976; Leslie A. Fiedler, "Fairy Tales—Without Apologies," *Saturday Review*, 15 May 1976; and Clare Boothe Luce, "Frogs and Freudians," *National Review*, 20 August 1976.

8. Bruno Bettelheim, *The Uses of Enchantment: The Meaning and Importance of Fairy Tales* (New York: Knopf, 1976; New York: Random House, Vintage Books,

1977). For critiques of Bettelheim's analysis, see Jack Zipes, "On the Use and Abuse of Folk and Fairy Tales with Children: Bruno Bettelheim's Moralistic Magic Wand," in *Breaking the Magic Spell: Radical Theories of Folk & Fairy Tales* (Austin: Univ. of Texas Press, 1979), pp. 160–82, and James W. Heisig, "Bruno Bettelheim and Fairy Tales," *Children's Literature* 6 (1977): 93–114.

9. Bloom, "Driving out Demons," pp. 10, 12.

10. The quotations that follow are all taken from pp. 159–66 of Bettelheim's *Uses of Enchantment*.

11. James B. Hoyme, "The 'Abandoning Impulse' in Human Parents," *The Lion and the Unicorn* 12 (1988): 32–46.

12. John Boswell, *The Kindness of Strangers: The Abandonment of Children in Western Europe from Late Antiquity to the Renaissance* (New York: Pantheon, 1988), p. 16.

13. On the difficulty of predicting the effect of literature on children, see Nicholas Tucker, "How Children Respond to Fiction," in *Writers, Critics, and Children* (New York: Agathon, 1976), pp. 177–78. Hugo Crago describes a "positive feedback loop" that focuses a child's perceptions and feeds back into the adult's performance of a text. See "The Roots of Response," *Children's Literature Association Quarterly* 10 (1985): 100–104.

14. For an explicit statement about Bettelheim's own preferences, see "Hänsel und Gretel, mein Lieblingsmärchen," in *Das Märchen - ein Märchen? Psychoanalytische Betrachtungen zu Wesen, Deutung und Wirkung der Märchen*, ed. Jochen Stork (Stuttgart: frommann-holzboog, 1987), pp. 137–60.

15. See my *Hard Facts of the Grimms' Fairy Tales* (Princeton: Princeton Univ. Press, 1987).

16. For a reassessment of these stories in light of specific cultural configurations, see Stanley Rosenman, "The Myth of the Birth of the Hero Revisited: Disasters and Brutal Child Rearing," *American Imago* 45 (1988): 1–44.

17. Otto Rank uses the phrase in "The Myth of the Birth of the Hero," in *The Myth of the Birth of the Hero and Other Writings*, ed. Philip Freund (New York: Knopf, 1932; New York: Random House, Vintage Books, 1964), p. 84.

18. Citations throughout this book will make reference to such studies. The polemical arguments of two thinkers need to be cited here, in part because their formulations, however extreme they may at times seem, cleared the way for a more balanced view of the pathology of parent/child relationships. See Jeffrey Moussaieff Masson, *The Assault on Truth: Freud's Suppression of the Seduction Theory* (New York: Farrar, Straus and Giroux, 1984), and Alice Miller, *For Your Own Good: Hidden Cruelty in Child-rearing and the Roots of Violence*, trans. Hildegarde Hannum and Hunter Hannum (New York: Farrar, Straus and Giroux, 1983). In turning their attention to the history of childhood, historians have opened our eyes to such matters as the widespread practice of infanticide and the frequent abandonment of children, as well as less publicly visible forms of child abuse in other times and places. See, for example, the exemplary study by John Boswell, *The Kindness of Strangers* (see note 12, above) which speaks specifically to the cruelties of abandonment, but also documents the ways in which certain practices that strike us as

unspeakably brutal today at one time actually insured the survival of larger numbers of children than did alternative practices.

19. It was only after I had written this preface that the disturbing revelations about Bettelheim's treatment of children at the Sonia Shankman Orthogenic School came to light. For a summary of those revelations, see "Accusations of Abuse Haunt the Legacy of Dr. Bruno Bettelheim," in the *New York Times*, 4 November 1990, the Week in Review. See also the letters in response to that article (two from former patients who confirm Bettelheim's verbal and physical abuse of children), "'Bettelheim Became the Very Evil He Loathed,'" *New York Times*, 20 November 1990, p. A20. Charges of plagiarism in *The Uses of Enchantment* followed hard on accusations of abuse. See Alan Dundes, "Bruno Bettelheim's Uses of Enchantment and Abuses of Scholarship," *Journal of American Folklore* 104 (1991): 74-83.

20. *New York Times*, 9 March 1990.

CHAPTER I

1. The early version is cited by Samuel F. Pickering, Jr., *John Locke and Children's Books in Eighteenth-Century England* (Knoxville: Univ. of Tennessee Press, 1981), p. 107.

2. "The Stupid Wife," in *French Folktales*, comp. Henri Pourrat, trans. Royall Tyler (New York: Pantheon, 1989), pp. 304–11. See also Tyler's "Introduction," p. xxiv. Jack Zipes situates Pourrat's work in the context of other collections in "Henri Pourrat and the Tradition of Perrault and the Brothers Grimm," in *The Brothers Grimm: From Enchanted Forests to the Modern World* (New York: Routledge, Chapman and Hall, 1988), pp. 96–109.

3. Mikhail Bakhtin, *Rabelais and His World*, trans. Helene Iswolsky (Cambridge: MIT Press, 1968), p. 21.

4. Cited by G. Legman, "Toward a Motif-Index of Erotic Humor," *Journal of American Folklore* 75 (1962): 227–48.

5. Even the index of tale types (a volume that classifies all folktale types according to thematic categories) suppresses a plot synopsis and gives only a tale title if a plot is obscene (e.g. AT 1110* Hans Shows the Devil How Men Are Made [Obscene]). See Antti Aarne, *The Types of the Folktale: A Classification and Bibliography*, trans. and enlarged by Stith Thompson (Helsinki: Academia Scientiarum Fennica, 1981), p. 359. In the *Motif-Index of Folk-Literature*, Thompson reserved numbers X700–799 for "Humor Concerning Sex." "Thousands of obscene motifs in which there is no point except the obscenity itself might logically come at this point, but they are entirely beyond the scope of the present work," Thompson observed. "They form a literature to themselves, with its own periodicals and collections." Oddly enough, Thompson was unable to recognize that the "obscene stories" were not separated out from folk stories until the end of the eighteenth century, when collectors either censored or suppressed them. In view of the general reticence of folklorists to publish bawdy materials, it took some courage for Friedrich S. Krauss to edit the *Anthropophyteia* (1904–1913), a journal published in Leipzig and devoted to preserving tales deemed unfit for print by most scholars. Vance Randolph

published only a fraction of the bawdy material at his disposal in *Pissing in the Snow and Other Ozark Folktales* (Urbana: Univ. of Illinois Press, 1976). On the bawdy, obscene, and scatalogical in folklore, see Herbert Halpert, "Folklore and Obscenity: Definitions and Problems," *Journal of American Folklore* 75 (1962): 190–94.

6. "Cinderella," in *The Complete Fairy Tales of the Brothers Grimm*, trans. Jack Zipes (Toronto: Bantam, 1987), pp. 86–92.

7. "Aschenputtel," in *Kinder- und Hausmärchen. Gesammelt durch die Brüder Grimm*, ed. Heinz Rölleke (Göttingen: Vandenhoeck & Ruprecht, 1986), vol. 1, p. 101.

8. "Cinderella," in *Perrault's Complete Fairy Tales*, trans. A. E. Johnson et al. (New York: Dodd, Mead, 1961), pp. 58–70.

9. "The Cat Cinderella," in *The Pentamerone of Giambattista Basile*, trans. Benedetto Croce, ed. N. M. Penzer (London: John Lane, 1932), vol. 1, pp. 56–63. The French "Cinderella" stories to which I refer appear in *Folktales of France*, ed. Geneviève Massignon, trans. Jacqueline Hyland (Chicago: Univ. of Chicago Press, 1968), pp. 147–49, and in *French Folktales*, comp. Henri Pourrat, pp. 7–14. The Portuguese tale, "The Hearth-Cat," appears in *One Hundred Favorite Folktales*, ed. Stith Thompson (Bloomington: Indiana Univ. Press, 1968), pp. 176–79.

10. Basile, *The Pentamerone*, 1:9.

11. Heinrich Hoffmann, *Der Struwwelpeter* (Volksausgabe), (N.p.: n.p., n.d.)

12. The quotation comes from Dorothy Kilner's *The Village School; A Collection of Entertaining Histories, for the Instruction and Amusement of All Good Children* (London: John Harris, 1831), p. 75. The book originally appeared in 1828.

13. Karl August Engelhardt, "Die gefrornen Fensterscheiben" (1812), in *Kinderschaukel: Ein Lesebuch zur Geschichte der Kindheit in Deutschland, 1756–1860*, ed. Marie-Luise Könneker (Darmstadt: Luchterhand, 1976), vol. 1, pp. 145–51. A similar "disaster tale" is narrated by Mary Ann Kilner in *William Sedley: or, The Evil Day Deferred* (London: n.p., 1783). There the hard-working Mr. and Mrs. Active are ruined by their "perverse and disobedient" daughters. See Pickering, *John Locke and Children's Books*, p. 181.

14. The poem is printed in *Masterworks of Children's Literature* (New York: Chelsea House, 1984), p. 250.

15. The poem is cited by F. J. Harvey Darton, *Children's Books in England: Five Centuries of Social Life* (Cambridge: Cambridge Univ. Press, 1932), p. 193. He also discusses the *New Game of Virtue Rewarded and Vice Punished* produced in 1810 (p. 153).

16. *Chutes and Ladders*, Milton Bradley Co., 1979.

17. This view was developed in its fullest form by André Jolles, *Einfache Formen* (Halle: Max Niemeyer, 1929), then modified by Max Lüthi, *The European Folktale: Form and Nature*, trans. John D. Niles (Philadelphia: Institute for the Study of Human Issues, 1982). It is resurrected in Claude Brémond's "Les Bons récompensées et les méchants punis," in *Sémiotique narrative et textuelle*, ed. Claude Chabrol (Paris: Larousse, 1973), pp. 96–121. Volker Klotz, by contrast, has emphasized that folktales move in the direction of establishing a formal rather than a moral balance; harmony rather than justice is the driving force behind the narrated events. See his "Weltordnung im Märchen," *Neue Rundschau* 81 (1970): 73–91.

18. Tabart's version appears as "The History of Jack and the Bean-Stalk," in *The Classic Fairy Tales*, comp. Iona Opie and Peter Opie (New York: Oxford Univ. Press, 1974), pp. 211–26.

19. Lucy Lane Clifford, *Anyhow Stories, Moral and Otherwise* (London: Macmillan, 1882), p. 47.

20. Cited by Gillian Avery, *Nineteenth-Century Children: Heroes and Heroines in English Children's Stories, 1780–1900* (London: Hodder and Stoughton, 1965), p. 213.

21. Avery, *Nineteenth-Century Children*, p. 212.

22. Janeway's questions and comments come from his concluding "Address Containing Directions to Children" in *A Token for Children: Being an Account of the Conversion, Holy and Exemplary Lives, and Joyful Deaths of Several Young Children* (London: Francis Westley, 1825), p. 92. Page numbers refer to this edition.

23. David Grylls, *Guardians and Angels: Parents and Children in Nineteenth-Century Literature* (London: Faber and Faber, 1978), p. 41.

24. On the role of death in children's tales, see especially Dieter Richter, *Das fremde Kind: Zur Entstehung der Kindheitsbilder des bürgerlichen Zeitalters* (Frankfurt a.M.: Fischer, 1987), pp. 81–87.

25. Pickering, *John Locke and Children's Books*, pp. 141–42.

26. P. L. Travers, "On Not Writing for Children," *Children's Literature* 4 (1975): 19.

27. Avery, *Nineteenth-Century Children*, p. 214.

28. Avery, *Nineteenth-Century Children*, p. 215.

29. *Kirkus Children's and Young-Adult Edition*, 15 Sept. 1988, p. 1403.

30. "Preface to Volume I of the First Edition of the Grimms' *Nursery and Household Tales*," in Tatar, *The Hard Facts of the Grimms' Fairy Tales*, pp. 207–8.

31. The quotation is from an 1803 review in the *Guardian of Education* and is cited by Pickering in *John Locke and Children's Books*, p. 96.

32. Charles Dickens, "Frauds on the Fairies," in *Household Words: A Weekly Journal* (New York: McElrath and Barker, 1854), pp. 97–100.

33. *Cinderella and the Glass Slipper*, ed. and illus. George Cruikshank (London: David Bogue, 1853). On the controversy between the writer and illustrator, see Harry Stone, "Dickens, Cruikshank, and Fairy Tales," *Princeton University Library Chronicle* 35 (1973–74): pp. 212–47.

34. Dickens, "Frauds on the Fairies," pp. 97–100.

35. *The History of Jack & the Bean-Stalk*, ed. and illus. George Cruikshank (London: David Bogue, 1854), p. 10.

36. *Hop-o'-my-Thumb and the Seven-League Boots*, ed. and illus. George Cruikshank (London: David Bogue, 1853), pp. 5–6.

37. *Cinderella and the Glass Slipper*, ed. Cruikshank, p. 6.

38. L. Frank Baum, introduction to *The Wonderful Wizard of Oz* (New York: Dover, 1960), n.p.

39. Rudolf Schenda, "Märchen erzählen - Märchen verbreiten: Wandel in den Mitteilungsformen einer populären Gattung," in *Über Märchen für Kinder von heute: Essays zu ihrem Wandel und ihrer Funktion*, ed. Klaus Doderer (Weinheim: Beltz, 1983), pp. 25–43.

40. Rachel Isadora, *The Princess and the Frog* (New York: Greenwillow Books, 1989).

41. Wolfgang Mieder, "Modern Anglo-American Variants of the Frog Prince (AaTh 440)," *New York Folklore* 6 (1980): 111–35, and Lutz Röhrich, *Wage es, den Frosch zu küssen! Das Grimmschen Märchen Nummer Eins in seinen Wandlungen* (Köln: Diederichs, 1987) both contain a multitude of examples.

42. *Princess Furball*, retold by Charlotte Huck, illus. Anita Lobel (New York: Greenwillow Books, 1989).

CHAPTER II

1. "Mother Trudy," in *The Complete Fairy Tales of the Brothers Grimm*, pp. 159–60.

2. "Tales about Toads" and "The Stubborn Child" both appear in *The Complete Fairy Tales of the Brothers Grimm*, pp. 380–81, 422. The German originals of both stories use the neuter pronoun "es" to refer to the children and therefore do not make it clear whether the protagonists are boys or girls. I cite from Zipes's translation, which—unwittingly or not—follows the practice of previous translators in using the male pronoun for the central figure of "The Stubborn Child" and the female pronoun for the child in "Tales about Toads." These choices are not unproblematic, but using "it" to refer to the child was, for me, not an acceptable solution.

3. On violence in the Grimms' collection, see especially Carl-Heinz Mallet, *Kopf ab! Gewalt im Märchen* (Hamburg: Rasch und Röhring, 1985); Katalin Horn, "Motivationen und Funktionen der tödlichen Bedrohung in den Kinder- und Hausmärchen der Brüder Grimm," *Schweizerisches Archiv für Volkskunde* 74 (1978): 20–40; and Lutz Röhrich, "Die Grausamkeit im deutschen Märchen," *Rheinisches Jahrbuch für Volkskunde* 6 (1955): 176–224.

4. "My Own Self" and "Mr. Miacca," in *English Fairy Tales*, comp. Joseph Jacobs (London: The Bodley Head, 1968), pp. 102–3, 156–58. The most recent edition I have found is *Mr. Miacca: An English Folktale*, illus. Evaline Ness (New York: Holt, Rinehart and Winston, 1967).

5. Charles Perrault, "Préface" to *Contes en Vers*, in *Contes*, ed. Gilbert Rouger (Paris: Garnier Frères, 1967), pp. 3–7.

6. Isaac Watts, *Divine and Moral Songs for Children* (New York: Hurd and Houghton, 1866), pp. 73–74. Arthur Paul Davis writes that, "judged by the number of its editions, *Divine Songs* has been the world's most popular children's classic." Although Davis is well aware of the content of Watts's book, he describes the verse as "tolerant, gentle and persuasive." See *Isaac Watts: His Life and Work* (New York: Dryden, 1943), pp. 78, 81.

7. "The Virgin Mary's Child," in *The Complete Tales of the Brothers Grimm*, pp. 8–11. I use the shorter title, since it is closer to the original ("Marienkind").

8. "Vasilisa the Beautiful," in Alexander Afanasev, *Russian Fairy Tales*, trans. Norbert Guterman (New York: Pantheon, 1945), p. 444.

9. "Von der Kindertaufe," in *Dr. Martin Luthers Grosser Katechismus*, ed. Gotthilf

Hermann (Gütersloh: Gerd Mohn, n.d.), 131–32. For Bunyan's verses, see *A Book for Boys and Girls: or, Country Rhimes for Children* [facsimile of first edition] (London: Elliot Stock, 1890), pp. 2, 72.

10. J. H. Plumb, "The New World of Children in Eighteenth-Century England," *Past and Present* 67 (1975): 64–93. Lawrence Stone also discusses earlier views of children's sinfulness in *The Family, Sex and Marriage in England, 1500–1800* (New York: Harper & Row, 1977), pp. 161–74. The importance of breaking a child's will is discussed by Jürgen Schlumbohm, "'Tradionale' Kollektivität und 'moderne' Individualität: Einige Fragen und Thesen für eine historische Sozialisationsforschung," in *Bürger und Bürgerlichkeit im Zeitalter der Aufklärung*, ed. Rudolf Vierhaus (Heidelberg: Lambert Schneider, 1981), pp. 279–81.

11. On the way in which cruelty to animals figures prominently in early children's literature, see Pickering, *John Locke and Children's Books*, pp. 3–39.

12. "The Girl Who Trod on the Loaf," *Hans Christian Andersen: Eighty Fairy Tales*, trans. R. P. Keigwin (New York: Pantheon, 1982), pp. 353–61.

13. Cited by Marc Soriano, "From Tales of Warning to Formulettes: The Oral Tradition in French Children's Literature," *Yale French Studies* 43 (1969): 31.

14. Dorothy Bloch has written eloquently and poignantly about the way in which disturbed children build fantasies about aggressive monsters to camouflage the real source of their terror. See her *"So the Witch Won't Eat Me": Fantasy and the Child's Fear of Infanticide* (Boston: Houghton Mifflin, 1978).

15. Basile, *The Pentamerone*, vol. 1, p.34.

16. Basile, *The Pentamerone*, 1:64.

17. The full form of the lullaby appears in *The Oxford Dictionary of Nursery Rhymes*, ed. Iona Opie and Peter Opie (Oxford: Oxford Univ. Press, 1951), p. 59. For Nicholas Tucker's observations, see "Lullabies and Child Care: A Historical Perspective," in *Opening Texts: Psychoanalysis and the Culture of the Child*, ed. Joseph H. Smith and William Kerrigan (Baltimore: Johns Hopkins Univ. Press, 1985), pp. 17–27.

18. Watts, "Cradle Hymn," in *Divine and Moral Songs*, pp. 111–16.

19. Hoffmann, *Der Struwwelpeter* (Volksausgabe), (n.p.)

20. Mary Ann Kilner, *The Memoirs of a Peg-Top* (London: Marshall, 1781).

21. Anthony Storr, "The Child and the Book," in *Only Connect: Readings on Children's Literature*, ed. Sheila Egoff, G. T. Stubbs, and L. F. Ashley (Toronto: Oxford Univ. Press, 1969), pp. 91–96.

22. "Little Red Cap," in *The Complete Fairy Tales of the Brothers Grimm*, pp. 101–5. To avoid confusion, I use the title "Little Red Riding Hood" for all variants of the tale.

23. *Perrault's Complete Fairy Tales*, pp. 71–77.

24. "Le Petit Chaperon Rouge," in vol. 1 of *Le Conte populaire français*, ed. Paul Delarue and Marie-Louise Tenèze (Paris: G.-P. Maisonneuve et Larose, 1976), pp. 373–74. An English translation of the tale can be found in *The Borzoi Book of French Folk Tales*, ed. Paul Delarue, trans. Austin Fife (New York: Knopf, 1956), pp. 230–32. See also Delarue's "Les Contes Merveilleux de Perrault et la tradition populaire:

I. Le Petit Chaperon Rouge," *Bulletin folklorique d'Ile-de-France* (1951), pp. 221–28, 251–60, 283–91; (1953), pp. 511–17.

25. The way in which literary versions of folktales tend to motivate events, giving causes where they were once absent, is discussed by Vladimir Propp. See his "Folklore and Reality," in *Theory and History of Folklore*, trans. Ariadna Y. Martin and Richard P. Martin, ed. Anatoly Liberman (Minneapolis: Univ. of Minnesota Press, 1984), pp. 16–38. On interpretations of "Little Red Riding Hood," see Jack Zipes, *The Trials and Tribulations of Little Red Riding Hood: Versions of the Tale in Sociocultural Context* (South Hadley, Mass.: Bergin & Garvey, 1983), pp. 9–10, and Bettelheim, *The Uses of Enchantment*, p. 172. Carl-Heinz Mallet's interpretation of the Grimms' story gives us an extreme example of misguided psychologizing. "A trained psychologist," he argues, "will understand exactly what the mother is after. He will translate what she says into the following words: Don't stray from the proper path, otherwise you will lose your innocence and be a fallen maiden." Needless to say, this is a strange message to send to five-year-old girls and boys. See his *Kennen Sie Kinder? Wie Kinder denken, handeln und fühlen, aufgezeigt an vier Grimmschen Märchen* (Hamburg: Hoffmann and Campe, 1981), p. 90. Carole Hanks and D. T. Hanks, Jr., describe Perrault's "Le Petit Chaperon Rouge" as a story in which "youth and innocence leave home only to be destroyed guiltless." They blame the Grimms alone for deleting the erotic elements from the story and pointing morals where there were none. See "Perrault's 'Little Red Riding Hood': Victim of the Revisers," *Children's Literature* 7 (1983): 68–77.

26. Jack Zipes incisively sums up the direction the tale took: "To live, a child had to live *properly*, restraining natural instincts according to rules established by adults. To disobey these rules or to indulge one's sensual drives for pleasure meant death." See *The Trials and Tribulations of Little Red Riding Hood*, pp. 20–31, for a discussion of the versions cited.

27. On the illustrations for "Little Red Riding Hood," see Jack Zipes, "A Second Gaze at Little Red Riding Hood's Trials and Tribulations," *The Lion and the Unicorn* 7/8 (1985): 78–109. Variants of the tale are anthologized in two collections: Hans Ritz, *Die Geschichte vom Rotkäppchen: Ursprünge, Analysen, Parodien eines Märchens* (Emstal: Muriverlag, 1981) and Zipes, *The Trials and Tribulations of Little Red Riding Hood*. For a collection of variants plus interpretive essays, see *Little Red Riding Hood: A Casebook*, ed. Alan Dundes (Madison: Univ. of Wisconsin Press, 1989).

28. See Walter Scherf's analysis, *Die Herausforderung des Dämons: Form und Funktion grausiger Kindermärchen* (Munich: K. G. Saur, 1987).

29. Hereafter, I will use the Aarne/Thompson designations to refer to tale types (Antti Aarne and Stith Thompson, *The Types of the Folktale: A Classification and Bibliography*, 2d rev. ed. [Helsinki: Academia Scientiarum Fennica, 1973]). The tale type name offers a convenient shorthand system for referring to a block of tales that have common features.

30. "The Strange Feast," in *The Complete Fairy Tales of the Brothers Grimm*, pp. 658–59. The translation is my own, since Zipes gives an abbreviated version of the sentence. The story appeared only in the first two editions of the *Nursery and Household Tales*.

31. Marianne Rumpf, "Caterinella: Ein italienisches Warnmärchen," *Fabula* 1 (1957): 76–84.

32. See the description of such entertainments in *Games and Songs of American Children*, comp. William Wells Newell (New York: Harper & Bros., 1884), pp. 215–21.

33. See my contrastive analysis of male and female protagonists in *The Hard Facts of the Grimms' Fairy Tales*, pp. 85–105.

34. "The Star Coins," in *The Complete Fairy Tales of the Brothers Grimm*, pp. 509–10.

35. Ten editions of the *Kleine Ausgabe* were printed in the Grimms' lifetimes. The volume has recently been edited and reissued by Heinz Rölleke [*Kinder- und Hausmärchen gesammelt durch die Brüder Grimm: Kleine Ausgabe von 1858* (Frankfurt a.M.: Insel, 1985)].

36. Ruth B. Bottigheimer makes this point in *Grimms' Bad Girls & Bold Boys: The Moral & Social Vision of the Tales* (New Haven: Yale Univ. Press, 1987), p. 150.

37. "The Little Match-Seller," in *Hans Christian Andersen: Eighty Fairy Tales*, pp. 121–23. I use the title by which the tale is conventionally known.

38. Andersen's preoccupation with the death of children is further documented in his poem "The Dying Child," printed in Rumer Godden's *Hans Christian Andersen: A Great Life in Brief* (New York: Knopf, 1955).

39. "The Staunch Tin Soldier," in *Hans Christian Andersen: Eighty Fairy Tales*, pp. 69–72. Here again I use the popular title for the tale.

40. Cited by Elias Bredsdorff, *Hans Christian Andersen* (New York: Scribner's, 1975), p. 272. On Andersen and his audience, see Phyllis Greenacre, "Hans Christian Andersen and Children," *Psychoanalytic Study of the Child* 38 (1983): 617–35.

41. Stone, *The Family, Sex and Marriage*, pp. 66–68. On the theme of death in fairy tales and children's literature, see Isabella Wülfing, *Alter und Tod in den Grimmschen Märchen und im Kinder- und Jugendbuch* (Herzogenrath: Murken-Altrogge, 1986).

42. Sigmund Freud, *The Interpretation of Dreams*, vol. 4 of the *Standard Edition*, trans. James Strachey (London: Hogarth, 1953), p. 254.

43. On the important though not always carefully drawn distinction between infanticide and abandonment, see Boswell, *The Kindness of Strangers*, pp. 43–45. Boswell cites the pertinent literature on both phenomena.

44. C. F. Weisse, "Der erzieherische Wert einer Hinrichtung," in *Schwarze Pädagogik: Quellen zur Naturgeschichte der bürgerlichen Erziehung*, ed. Katharina Rutschky (Berlin: Ullstein, 1977), pp. 5–9. In this context it is worth referring to the notorious moment in *The Fairchild Family* when Mr. Fairchild decides to deter sibling quarrels by treating his children to the sight of the decaying cadaver of a man who killed his brother. See the *History of the Fairchild Family*, vol. 2 in *The Works of Mrs. Sherwood* (New York: Harper, 1864), p. 56.

45. Hans Christian Andersen, *The Fairy Tale of My Life: An Autobiography* (New York: Paddington, 1975), p. 52.

46. Sherwood, *History of the Fairchild Family*, pp. 128–29.

47. "Poverty and Humility Lead to Heaven," in *The Complete Fairy Tales of the Brothers Grimm*, pp. 638–39. Zipes calls the "Legends for Children" (*Kinderlegenden*) "Religious Tales for Children."

48. The passage comes from a letter of 1843 to the poet Ingemann and is cited by Alan Moray Williams, "Hans Christian Andersen," in *Only Connect*, ed. Egoff et al., pp. 265–69.

49. Lucy Sprague Mitchell, *Here and Now Story Book* (New York: Dutton, 1921), p. 61.

CHAPTER III

1. Sherwood, *History of the Fairchild Family*, pp. 135–36.

2. Johann Georg Sulzer, "Versuch von der Erziehung und Unterweisung der Kinder," in *Johann Georg Sulzers Pädagogische Schriften*, ed. Willibald Klinke (Langensalza: Hermann Beyer, 1922), p. 129.

3. Sulzer, "Versuch von der Erziehung und Unterweisung der Kinder," p. 129.

4. Alice Miller has examined the ways in which violence perpetuates itself through childrearing practices. See her *For Your Own Good*.

5. AT 480 refers to the tale type's number in the Aarne/Thompson classification scheme cited earlier.

6. "The Tale of the Cats," in *Italian Folktales*, comp. Italo Calvino, trans. George Martin (New York: Pantheon, 1980), pp. 446–48.

7. "Mother Holle," in *The Complete Fairy Tales of the Brothers Grimm*, pp. 96–99.

8. "The Old Witch," in *English Fairy Tales*, comp. Jacobs, pp. 206–8.

9. "Baba Yaga," in Alexander Afanasev, *Russian Fairy Tales*, (New York: Pantheon, 1973), pp. 194–95.

10. "The Fairies," in *Perrault's Complete Fairy Tales*, pp. 42–46.

11. "Water in the Basket," in *Italian Folktales*, comp. Calvino, pp. 353–55.

12. Ludwig Bechstein, "Der Garten im Brunnen," in *Märchen* (Stuttgart: Parkland, 1985), pp. 440–43.

13. "Prince Verdeprato," in Basile, *The Pentamerone*, pp. 141–46.

14. "Vom Hühnchen, Hähnchen, Hundchen und Kätzchen," in *Hundert neue Märchen im Gebirge gesammelt*, comp. Friedmund von Arnim (Charlottenburg: Egbert Bauer, 1844), pp. 19–21.

15. Bechstein, "Fippchen Fäppchen," in *Märchen*, pp. 431–32.

16. Bechstein, "Die Goldmaria und die Pechmaria," in *Märchen*, pp. 79–83.

17. On this point, see David Grylls, *Guardians and Angels*, pp. 79–80.

18. "Water in the Basket," in *Italian Folktales*, comp. Calvino, pp. 353–355.

19. "Hans My Hedgehog," in *The Complete Fairy Tales of the Brothers Grimm*, pp. 393–97.

20. "The Frog King, or Iron Heinrich," in *The Complete Fairy Tales of the Brothers Grimm*, pp. 2–5.

21. "First Fable, Night the Second," in *The Facetious Nights of Straparola*, trans. W. G. Waters (London: Society of Bibliophiles, 1901), pp. 133–52.

22. Norbert Elias, *The History of Manners*, trans. Edmund Jephcott (New York:

Pantheon, 1978), pp. 169, 180. The manual Elias cites is Raumer's *Geschichte der Pädagogik*.

23. Michel Foucault, *The History of Sexuality*, trans. Robert Hurley (New York: Random House, Vintage Books, 1978) vol. 1, p. 3.

24. For Foucault, the rise of capitalism is largely responsible for the repression of sexuality, for sex is "incompatible with a general and intensive work imperative." This work ethic permeates literary fairy tales about girls' development, but it does not play as prominent a role in stories mapping out the development of boys. See *The History of Sexuality*, 1:6.

25. One noteworthy exception to the contrasting fates of kind and unkind girls appears in a story collected by Leonard Roberts: "The Gold in the Chimney." In this tale, the unkind girl visits a witch, finds a bag of gold, and flees the witch's abode. On the escape route, she encounters a cow that needs milking, a sheep that needs shearing, a horse that needs riding, and a mill that needs turning. Since she fails to respond to their appeals the animals and the mill betray her location to the witch, who seizes her gold and turns the girl to stone. Conversely, the kind girl—though she too steals the witch's gold—responds to the appeals and is protected from the witch, who is ground up in the mill. The surprise conclusion shows the kind girl turning the stone back into her sister and living "happy ever after" with her. See *Midwest Folklore* 6 (1956): 76–78.

26. Warren E. Roberts, *The Tale of the Kind and the Unkind Girls: A-Th 480 and Related Tales* (Berlin: Walter de Gruyter, 1958). On the significance of gender in fairy tales, see Kay F. Stone, "The Misuses of Enchantment: Controversies on the Significance of Fairy Tales," in *Women's Folklore, Women's Culture*, ed. Rosan A. Jordan and Susan J. Kalcik (Philadelphia: Univ. of Pennsylvania Press, 1985), pp. 125–45.

27. See Tatar, "Born Yesterday," in *The Hard Facts of the Grimms' Fairy Tales*, pp. 85–105.

28. "The Golden Bird," in *The Complete Fairy Tales of the Brothers Grimm*, pp. 216–22.

29. "The Water of Life," in *The Complete Fairy Tales of the Brothers Grimm*, pp. 356–61.

30. "Only One Brother Was Grateful," in *Modern Greek Folktales*, trans. and comp. R. M. Dawkins (Oxford: Clarendon, 1953), pp. 415–19.

31. Kurt Ranke has analyzed over 770 versions of the story in his study of the tale type. See *Die zwei Brüder: Eine Studie zur vergleichenden Märchenforschung* (Helsinki: Academia Scientiarum Fennica, 1934).

32. A related tale type, "Ferdinand the True and Ferdinand the Untrue" (AT 531), contrasts a dutiful hero with his deceitful companion. Ferdinand the True is challenged again and again by his shifty double to carry out dangerous tasks—he must fetch tapestries from the home of an ogre, embark on a perilous journey to fetch the king's bride, or undergo an experiment in decapitation. Each and every attempt on the part of Ferdinand the Untrue to do in Ferdinand the True backfires, with the result that Ferdinand the True wins one prize after another for undertaking hazardous missions. The envy and rivalry between the two protagonists serves only to elevate the one over the other.

CHAPTER IV

1. Cited in *Flowers of Delight*, ed. Leonard de Vries (London: Dennis Dobson, 1965), p. 119.

2. *The History of Little Goody Two-Shoes; Otherwise called, Mrs. Margery Two-Shoes* (London: John Newbery, 1765); William Upton, "The School Girl: A Poem," (London: William Darton, 1820).

3. Maurice Sendak, "Caldecott Medal Acceptance," in *Caldecott & Co.* (New York: Farrar, Straus and Giroux, Michael di Capua, 1988), p. 153. Subsequent page references are to this volume.

4. On fears of abandonment and engulfment in Sendak's work, see Robert J. Kloss, "Fantasy and Fear in the Work of Maurice Sendak," *Psychoanalytic Review* 76 (1989): 567–79.

5. Bettelheim, *The Uses of Enchantment*, pp. 7, 15.

6. Sendak, *Caldecott & Co.*, p. 151. Jennifer R. Waller finds that *Where the Wild Things Are* and *In the Night Kitchen* are "not therapeutic in intent." For her, Sendak's books "simply attempt to reflect and evoke the child's imaginative experience." See "Maurice Sendak and the Blakean Vision of Childhood," *Children's Literature* 6 (1977): 130–40.

7. Cited by Nat Hentoff, "Among the Wild Things," in *Only Connect*, ed. Egoff et al., pp. 323–46.

8. P. M. Pickard, *I Could a Tale Unfold: Violence, Horror and Sensationalism in Stories for Children* (London: Tavistock, 1961), p. 1.

9. Sendak, "Disney/2," in *Caldecott & Co.*, pp. 111–17.

10. Carlo Collodi, *The Adventures of Pinocchio*, trans. E. Harden (New York: Knopf, 1988), p. 67.

11. Jacqueline Rose, *The Case of Peter Pan or The Impossibility of Children's Fiction* (London: Macmillan, 1984), p. 59.

12. Bettelheim, *The Uses of Enchantment*, p. 18.

13. Bettelheim, *The Uses of Enchantment*, p. 5.

14. Roger Duvoisin, "Children's Book Illustration: The Pleasures and Problems," in *Only Connect*, ed. Egoff et al., pp. 357–74.

15. Bettelheim, *The Uses of Enchantment*, p. 19.

16. "Bluebeard," in *Perrault's Complete Fairy Tales*, pp. 78–88.

17. On children's literature as a creation of adults (hence its impossibility), see especially Rose, *The Case of Peter Pan*.

18. This point, obvious as it may seem, cannot be emphasized enough. John Rowe Townsend stresses it in his essay "Didacticism in Modern Dress," pp. 33–40, as does Penelope Mortimer in "Thoughts Concerning Children's Books," pp. 97–105. Both essays in *Only Connect*, ed. Egoff et al.

19. Gilligan, *In a Different Voice*.

20. Bettelheim, *The Uses of Enchantment*, p. 276.

21. Zipes, *Breaking the Magic Spell*, p. 177.

22. *The Juniper Tree and Other Tales from Grimm*, illus. Maurice Sendak, trans. Lore Segal, with four tales trans. Randall Jarrell (New York: Farrar, Straus and Giroux, 1973). For expert commentary from the German point of view on the illustra-

tions, see Heinz Rölleke, "Tales from Grimm—Pictures by Maurice Sendak: Entdeckungen und Vermutungen," in *Brüder Grimm Gedenken*, ed. Ludwig Denecke (Marburg: N. G. Elwert, 1975), pp. 242–45. On Sendak as illustrator, see also *Maurice Sendak: Bilderbuchkünstler*, ed. Reinbert Tabbert (Bonn: Bouvier, 1987).

23. John M. Ellis, "What Really is the Value of the 'New' Grimm Discovery?" *German Quarterly* 58 (1975): 87–90.

24. Wilhelm Grimm, *Dear Mili*, trans. Ralph Manheim, illus. Maurice Sendak (New York: Farrar, Straus and Giroux, 1988).

25. Cited in the *New York Times* article of 28 Sept. 1983 on the discovery of a new Grimm tale.

26. P. L. Travers appreciates this same lack of a didactic turn when she writes that the Grimms "spread out the story just as it was." See her "On Not Writing for Children," *Children's Literature* 4 (1975): 15–22.

27. Grimm, *Dear Mili*. The volume is not paginated.

28. On Christian elements in the Grimms' *Nursery and Household Tales*, see Heinz Rölleke, "Das Bild Gottes in den Märchen der Brüder Grimm," in *"Wo das Wünschen noch geholfen hat": Gesammelte Aufsätze zu den Kinder- und Hausmärchen der Brüder Grimm* (Bonn: Bouvier, 1985), pp. 207–19, and Ruth B. Bottigheimer, *Grimms' Bad Girls & Bold Boys*, pp. 143–55.

29. "Saint Joseph in the Forest," in *The Complete Fairy Tales of the Brothers Grimm*, pp. 634–36. I refer to the tale as "Saint Joseph in the Woods" because of the fairy-tale associations with that noun.

30. "The Rose," in *The Complete Fairy Tales of the Brothers Grimm*, p. 638. The original does not specify the gender of the child.

31. The volume is described by William Sloane, *Children's Books in England & America in the Seventeenth Century* (New York: King's Crown, 1955), p. 52.

32. Darton, *Children's Books in England*, p. 58.

33. Cited by Darton, *Children's Books in England*, p. 56.

34. Selma G. Lanes, *The Art of Maurice Sendak* (New York: Harry N. Abrams, 1980), p. 16.

35. Lanes, *The Art of Maurice Sendak*, p. 12.

36. "Preface" to the *Nursery and Household Tales*, in Tatar, *The Hard Facts of the Grimms' Fairy Tales*, p. 206.

37. Michel Foucault, *Discipline and Punish: The Birth of the Prison*, trans. Alan Sheridan (New York: Random House, Vintage Books, 1977).

38. The work, which bears no date on its title page, was penned by Ellenor Fenn (1743–1813). It is reprinted in *Masterworks of Children's Literature*, ed. Robert Bator (New York: Stonehill, 1983), vol. 3, pp. 407–23.

39. *The Child's Instructor; intended as a first book, for children*, by a fellow of the Royal Society (London: Thorp and Burch, 1828).

40. Sherwood, *History of the Fairchild Family*, pp. 68–107.

41. Mary V. Jackson notes that the newly emerging concept of childhood and family in the early 1800s produced a vision of the world "where all-powerful, all-knowing parents (increasingly mothers) examined, weighed, and assessed every thought and act in their children's lives. And in return for the means of survival, for the love and approval, as well as for this essential guidance, parents exacted strictest

obedience or, in lieu of that, extravagant repentance" (*Engines of Instruction, Mischief, and Magic: Children's Literature in England from Its Beginnings to 1839* [Lincoln: Univ. of Nebraska Press, 1989], p. 99).

42. The relationship between the didactic mode and the therapeutic becomes evident in many commentaries on children's literature. Marian S. Pyles, for example, rails against "bibliotherapy" ("literature as a means for children to solve all their emotional and psychological problems") because "didacticism simply does not work." See *Death and Dying in Children's and Young People's Literature: A Survey and Bibliography* (Jefferson, N.C.: McFarland & Co., 1988), pp. 10–11.

43. Bettelheim, *The Uses of Enchantment*, p. 17.

44. Lanes, *The Art of Maurice Sendak*, p. 106.

45. Tolkien stresses a child's powerlessness in the selection process. Children try to like whatever is given to them, he asserts, but "if they do not like it, they cannot well express their dislike, or give reasons for it." Cited by Selma G. Lanes, *Down the Rabbit Hole: Adventures & Misadventures in the Realm of Children's Literature* (New York: Atheneum, 1971), p. 4.

46. Hentoff, "Among the Wild Things," in *Only Connect*, ed. Egoff et al., p. 329.

47. Lanes, *The Art of Maurice Sendak*, p. 206.

48. *Achim von Arnim und Jacob und Wilhelm Grimm*, ed. Reinhold Steig (Stuttgart: Cotta, 1904), p. 269.

49. On historical reasons for the segregation of children's literature and adult literature, see Felicity A. Hughes, "Children's Literature: Theory and Practice," *ELH* 45 (1978): 542–61.

50. I am indebted to Alan Richardson for this insight about the effect of Janeway's books on children.

CHAPTER V

1. William Darton, *Little Truths, for the Instruction of Children* (London: Darton and Harvey, 1802), p. 1; Hoffmann, *Der Struwwelpeter* (Volksausgabe), (n.p.); Sherwood, *History of the Fairchild Family*, p. 132; Ann and Jane Taylor, "Playing with Fire," in *Rhymes for the Nursery*, vol. 4 in *Masterworks of Children's Literature*, ed. Robert Bator (New York: Chelsea House, 1984), p. 238.

2. Lissa Paul discusses the "common ground between women's literature and children's literature" in "Enigma Variations: What Feminist Theory Knows about Children's Literature," *Signal* 54 (1987): 186–201.

3. Margaret R. Miles cites the passage from Kierkegaard's *The Concept of Anxiety* in *Carnal Knowing: Female Nakedness and Religious Meaning in the Christian West* (Boston: Beacon Press, 1989), p. 113.

4. "Haaken Grizzlebeard," in *Folktales of Norway*, trans. Pat Shaw Iversen, ed. Reidar Christiansen (Chicago: Univ. of Chicago Press, 1964), p. 186.

5. "Pride Punished," in Basile, *The Pentamerone*, 2:83–87.

6. "The Crumb in the Beard," in *Italian Popular Tales*, comp. Thomas Frederick Crane (Boston: Houghton Mifflin, 1885), pp. 110–14.

7. "Peruonto," in Basile, *The Pentamerone*, 1:34–42.

8. "Hans Dumm," in *The Complete Fairy Tales of the Brothers Grimm*, pp. 659–60.

9. Ernst Philippson, *Der Märchentypus von König Drosselbart* (Greifswald: Academia Scientiarum Fennica, 1923), pp. 64–65.

10. "King Thrushbeard," in *The Complete Fairy Tales of the Brothers Grimm*, pp. 192–95.

11. "König Drosselbart," in Johannes Künzig and Waltraut Werner, *Ungarndeutsche Märchenerzähler II* (Freiburg: Rombach and Co., 1971), pp. 63–67.

12. "Die stolze Königstochter und der Frosch," in Künzig and Werner, *Ungarndeutsche Märchenerzähler II*, pp. 267–74.

13. "The Swineherd," in *Hans Christian Andersen: Eighty Fairy Tales*, pp. 90–94. A correlation between unhappy endings and moralizing tendencies is set up by Lutz Röhrich in "Märchen mit schlechtem Ausgang," in *Hessische Blätter für Volkskunde* 49/50 (1958): 239.

14. "The Little Hamster from the Water," in *The Complete Fairy Tales of the Brothers Grimm*, pp. 596–99. An Albanian version of the tale ends in disaster when the princess bursts from anger after the hero outwits her. See "Die kleine Schöne der Erde," in *Die geflügelte Schwester und die Dunklen der Erde: Albanische Volksmärchen*, trans. Maximilian Lambertz (Eisenach: Erich Röth, 1952), pp. 134–38.

15. "Taper-Tom Who Made the Princess Laugh," in *Norwegian Folktales*, comp. Peter Christen Asbjørnsen and Jørgen Moe, trans. Pat Shaw and Carl Norman (New York: Pantheon, 1960), pp. 20–24.

16. "Die hoffärtige Braut," in Bechstein, *Märchen*, pp. 460–63.

17. "Ein köstlich gutes bewertes Recept / vor die Männer / so böse Weiber haben," in David Kunzle, *The Early Comic Strip: Narrative Strips and Picture Stories in the European Broadsheet from c. 1450 to 1825* (Berkeley and Los Angeles: Univ. of California Press, 1973), pp. 230–31.

18. For convincing evidence that Shakespeare based his play on folkloric sources, see Jan Harold Brunvand, "The Folktale Origin of *The Taming of the Shrew*," *Shakespeare Quarterly* 17 (1966): 345–59.

19. "The Most Obedient Wife," in *Danish Fairy Tales*, comp. Svend Grundtvig, trans. Gustav Hein (London: George G. Harrap, 1914), pp. 175–83.

20. Brunvand's unpublished dissertation lists over three hundred variant forms of the tale. See "*The Taming of the Shrew*: A Comparative Study of Oral and Literary Versions" (Ph.D. diss., Indiana Univ., 1961). An abbreviated form of the dissertation appears in Jan Harold Brunvand, *The Study of American Folklore* (New York: Norton, 1968), pp. 360–71. That essay contains most of the variants cited in this paragraph. The reference to the britches appears in "He Counted up to Three," in *Sticks in the Knapsack and Other Ozark Folk Tales*, collected by Vance Randolph (New York: Columbia Univ. Press, 1958), pp. 71–73. The illustration of the obedient wife in harness appears in *American Folk Tales and Songs*, collected by Richard Chase (New York: Signet, 1956), pp. 226–27.

21. *Perrault's Complete Fairy Tales*, pp. 100–14. The translation renders the verse narrative into prose and abridges it. For the full text, see "Griselidis: Nouvelle," in Perrault, *Contes*, pp. 9–50. In the original, "a domineering will of her own" is "point de volonté" ("without any will at all").

22. *The Decameron of Giovanni Boccaccio*, trans. Frances Winwar (New York: Modern Library, 1930), pp. 649–59.

23. Geoffrey Chaucer, "The Clerk's Tale," in *The Canterbury Tales*, trans. Nevill Coghill (London: Penguin, 1951), pp. 338–73.

24. "The Bad Wife" and "The Mayoress," in Afanasev, *Russian Fairy Tales*, pp. 56–57, 141.

25. Afanasev, *Russian Fairy Tales*, p. 280.

26. Perrault, préface to *Contes*, p. 3.

27. On interpretations of "Bluebeard," see my *Hard Facts of the Grimms' Fairy Tales*, pp. 157–64. The equation of the forbidden chamber with the vaginal area is made by Alan Dundes, "The Psychoanalytic Study of the Grimms' Tales with Special Reference to 'The Maiden Without Hands' (AT 706)," *Germanic Review* 62 (1987): 56. Modern rewritings of the tale by Angela Carter and by Max Frisch are analyzed by Kari E. Lokke, "*Bluebeard* and *The Bloody Chamber*: The Grotesque of Self-Parody and Self-Assertion," *Frontiers* 10 (1988): 7–12.

Even when female disobedience is not tainted with sexual transgression, it spells trouble for everyone. The Italian story "The North Wind's Gift" (*Italian Folktales*, comp. Calvino, pp. 301–4) provides an interesting study in contrasts between the consequences of male disobedience and female disobedience. A farmer named Geppone receives a magical box from the North Wind along with precise instructions to tell no one about it. But as soon as he arrives home, he reveals the secrets of the box to his wife and children. The wife tells the prior, who coerces Geppone into giving him the box. Geppone, the narrator reports, was "as badly off as ever, and all because of his wife, mind you." The husband's failure to heed the North Wind's instructions is not even taken into account—only his wife is responsible for the box's loss.

28. "A Son of Adam," in *English Fairy Tales*, comp. Jacobs, pp. 215–16.

29. "The She-Bear," in Basile, *The Pentamerone*, 1:170–78.

30. "Griselidis," in Perrault, *Contes*, p. 22.

31. On deceit as a "traditional female survival tactic" and on its use by "defenceless child protagonists," see Paul, "Enigma Variations," pp. 186–201.

32. Infidelity and licentiousness are, for our purposes, variants of the single sin of adultery: the one aligns transgression of conjugal boundaries with self-assertion, the other with self-indulgence.

33. On variants of the tale, see Walter Anderson, *Der Schwank vom alten Hildebrand: Eine vergleichende Studie* (Dorpat: n.p., 1931). A dramatic variant of the plot, along with visual representations of the story, is discussed by Leopold Schmidt, "Das steirische Schwankspiel vom Bauern und seinem Weib im Rahmen der Volksüberlieferung vom Meister Hildebrand," in *Festschrift für Eduard Castle* (Vienna: Notring der wissenschaftlichen Verbände Österreichs, 1955), pp. 13–32. An American version of "Old Hildebrand" is recorded by Isabel Gordon Carter in "Mountain White Folk-Lore: Tales from the Southern Blue Ridge," *Journal of American Folklore* 38 (1925): 366–68. Hans Christian Andersen's "Little Claus and Big Claus" (*Eighty Fairy Tales*, pp. 17–26) gives us a cleaned-up version of the story.

34. "The Blind Man's Wife," in *The Bawdy Peasant*, comp. Alexander N. Afanasev, ed. Giuseppe Pitré (London: Odyssey, 1970), pp. 28–29.

35. Afanasev, *The Bawdy Peasant*, pp. 98–106.

36. In an introduction to a collection of American bawdy tales, Rayna Green points out that women in those tales "enjoy sex as much as men . . . and will go to as much trouble to satisfy sexual desires as men." See *Pissing in the Snow and Other Ozark Folktales*, comp. Randolph, p. 20.

37. Kunzle, *The Early Comic Strip*, p. 236.

38. "Jump into My Sack," in *Italian Folktales*, comp. Calvino, p. 712.

39. Robert Darnton, "Peasants Tell Tales: The Meaning of Mother Goose," in *The Great Cat Massacre and Other Episodes in French Cultural History* (New York: Basic Books, 1984), p. 34.

40. "And Seven!" in *Italian Folktales*, comp. Calvino, p. 14.

41. On punishments and executions in the Grimms' collection, see Bottigheimer, *Grimms' Bad Girls & Bold Boys*, pp. 81–100. Bottigheimer observes that "obedience is necessary for females but not for males. Girls and women are regularly punished in *Grimms' Tales*, and the punishment itself often seems to take precedence over the transgression that is supposed to have occasioned it, as does an apparent inner drive to incriminate females" (p. 94).

42. Bechstein, "Der Zornbraten," *Deutsches Märchenbuch*, in *Märchen*, pp. 96–106.

43. "Animal Talk and the Nosy Wife," in *Italian Folktales*, comp. Calvino, p. 641.

44. "Solomon's Advice," in *Italian Folktales*, comp. Calvino, pp. 668–69.

45. "The Three Snake Leaves," in *The Complete Fairy Tales of the Brothers Grimm*, pp. 64–67.

46. "The Lion's Grass," in *Italian Folktales*, comp. Calvino, p. 695.

CHAPTER VI

1. "The Maiden without Hands," in *The Complete Fairy Tales of the Brothers Grimm*, pp. 118–23.

2. For an analysis of the motivation underlying the substitution, see John M. Ellis, *One Fairy Story Too Many: The Brothers Grimm and Their Tales* (Chicago: Univ. of Chicago Press, 1983), pp. 77–78.

3. "Olive," in *Italian Folktales*, comp. Calvino, pp. 255–61.

4. Dundes, "The Psychoanalytic Study of the Grimms' Tales," pp. 50–65.

5. On the church ritual, see Lynda E. Boose, "The Father's House and the Daughter in It: The Structures of Western Culture's Daughter-Father Relationships," in *Daughters and Fathers*, ed. Lynda E. Boose and Betty S. Flowers (Baltimore: Johns Hopkins Univ. Press, 1989), pp. 19–74.

6. Margaret R. Miles discusses a painting that depicts one of Saint Barbara's executioners slicing off her left breast and observes that Saint Agnes was subjected to a similar fate—both her breasts were cut off. See her *Carnal Knowing*, p. 156.

7. For a fascinating analysis of the episode in Ovid and the way in which weaving and spinning become the literal and metaphorical equivalents of storytelling for

women who are literally or metaphorically silenced, see Karen E. Rowe, "The Female Voice in Folklore and Fairy Tale," in *Fairy Tales and Society: Illusion, Allusion, and Paradigm,* ed. Ruth B. Bottigheimer (Philadelphia: Univ. of Pennsylvania Press, 1986), pp. 53–74.

8. "The Girl with Maimed Hands," in Basile, *The Pentamerone,* 1: 232–41.

9. Thelma S. Fenster has argued that the self-mutilation of another heroine "ensures that Joïe is no longer a perfect copy of her mother, and is therefore no longer participating in the doubling" (49). See "Beaumanoir's *La Manekine*: Kin D(r)ead: Incest, Doubling, and Death," *American Imago* 39 (1982): 41–58.

10. For elaboration on this point, see Lynda E. Boose, "The Father's House and the Daughter in It," p. 32.

11. "If social organization had a beginning," Lévi-Strauss writes, "this could only have consisted in the incest prohibition, since . . . the incest prohibition is, in fact, a kind of remodeling of the biological conditions of mating and procreation (which know no rule, as can be seen from observing animal life) compelling them to become perpetuated only in an artificial framework of taboos and obligations. It is there, and only there, that we find a passage from nature to culture, from animal to human life." See his essay "The Family," in *Man, Culture, and Society,* ed. Harry Shapiro (New York: Oxford Univ. Press, 1956), p. 278. Freud's most complete statement on the cultural implications of the incest prohibition appears in *Totem and Taboo: Some Points of Agreement between the Mental Lives of Savages and Neurotics,* vol. 13 of the *Standard Edition.* Robin Fox disputes the notion of incest taboos as "the great gateway and bridge to culture" (14). See *The Red Lamp of Incest* (New York: E. P. Dutton, 1980).

12. For an extensive discussion of the nature/culture opposition and of de Beauvoir's observations, see Sherry B. Ortner, "Is Female to Male as Nature Is to Culture?" in *Woman, Culture, and Society,* ed. Michelle Zimbalist Rosaldo and Louise Lamphere (Stanford: Stanford Univ. Press, 1974), pp. 67–87.

13. Dundes, "The Psychoanalytic Study of the Grimms' Tales," p. 61. Dundes even goes so far as to assert that *King Lear,* since it is based on a folkloric source, must entail "*a projection of incestuous desires on the part of the daughter.* In this sense, the plot revolves around Cordelia, not Lear" (p.236; Dundes' emphasis). For Dundes, Lear is truly "a man more sinn'd against than sinning." See also Jack Zipes's critique of Dundes' reasoning in "Recent Psychoanalytical Approaches with Some Questions about the Abuse of Children," in *The Brothers Grimm: From Enchanted Forests to the Modern World,* pp. 110–34.

14. Nancy Chodorow astutely observes that the "absence of actual paternal seduction is not the same thing as absence of seductive fantasies toward a daughter or behavior which expresses such fantasy." Similarly, fairy tales about paternal seduction may have as much to do with seductive behavior as with actual paternal seduction. See *The Reproduction of Mothering: Psychoanalysis and the Sociology of Gender* (Berkeley and Los Angeles: Univ. of California Press, 1978), p. 160.

15. As Judith Lewis Herman observes, "the relationship between father and daughter, adult male and female child, is one of the most unequal relationships imaginable. It is no accident that incest occurs most often precisely in the relation-

ship where the female is most powerless." See her study conducted with Lisa Hirschman: *Father-Daughter Incest* (Cambridge: Harvard Univ. Press, 1981), p. 4.

16. On incest in Shakespeare, see Diane Elizabeth Dreher, *Domination and Defiance: Fathers and Daughters in Shakespeare* (Lexington: Univ. Press of Kentucky, 1986). I am grateful to Elizabeth Archibald, who sent me the typescript of a talk given at Harvard University on women and incest in medieval literature. In it, she refers to the passage in *Pericles* and also draws attention to the late medieval morality play *Dux Moraud* in which is found an exception to the rule of evil father and innocent heroine in father-daughter incest plots. The maiden without hands, as Archibald makes clear, is a prominent figure in medieval romance as well as in folklore.

17. Cox was the first to undertake a systematic study of Cinderella variants. In *Cinderella: Three Hundred and Forty-five Variants of Cinderella, Catskin, and Cap o' Rushes*, ed. Andrew Lang (London: David Nutt, 1893), Cox uses the three names in her subtitle as categories for collecting tales about an "ill-treated heroine" ("Cinderella"), an "unnatural father" who forces the heroine to flee ("Catskin"), and a "King Lear judgment" that turns the heroine into an outcast ("Cap o' Rushes"). Cox's three groups were modified by Anna Birgitta Rooth (*The Cinderella Cycle* [Lund: Gleerup, 1951]).

18. For a full discussion of the Oedipal dimensions of the plot, see Bettelheim, *The Uses of Enchantment*, pp. 236–77.

19. "The Girl without Hands," in *Folktales of Germany*, ed. Kurt Ranke, trans. Lotte Baumann (Chicago: Univ. of Chicago Press, 1966), pp. 84–89.

20. On this point, see my *Hard Facts of the Grimms' Fairy Tales*, pp. 137–55.

21. A. L. Grimm, *Lina's Märchenbuch: Eine Weynachtsgabe* (Frankfurt: Wilmans, 1816), pp. 191–216.

22. The phrase comes from *A Midsummer Night's Dream*, when Duke Theseus counsels Hermia to marry the man chosen by her father (I.i.47).

23. "Donkey-Skin," in *Perrault's Complete Fairy Tales*, pp. 92–99. On the tale, see Réné Démoris, "Du littéraire au littéral dans *Peau d'Ane* de Perrault," *Revue des sciences humaines* 43 (1977): 261–79.

24. "La Peau d'Anon," in *Le Conte populaire français*, ed. Delarue and Tenèze, pp. 256–60.

25. Critics have been quick to use these cues from the tellers of tales to blame mothers for the heroine's misfortune. W.R.S. Ralston, for example, notes that "Rashie-Coat's degradation is consequent upon her dying mother's unfortunate imprudence," and in the Sicilian tale of "Betta Pilusa," the marriage from which the heroine flees "would never have been suggested to her had not her mother obtained a promise from her husband on her death-bed that he would marry again whenever any maiden was found whom her ring would fit." See Ralston's essay "Cinderella," in *Cinderella: A Casebook*, ed. Alan Dundes (New York: Garland, 1982; Madison: Univ. of Wisconsin Press, 1988), pp. 30–56. The phrase about the fit comes from a Brazilian "Catskin." See "Dona Labismina," in *The Cinderella Story: The Origins and Variations of the Story Known As "Cinderella,"* ed. Neil Philip (London: Penguin, 1989), pp. 70–73.

26. Straparola, *The Facetious Nights*, pp. 79–103.

27. On the seductive daughter and the collusive mother, see Herman, *Father-Daughter Incest*, pp. 36–49.

28. "Catskin," in *English Fairy Tales*, comp. Jacobs, pp. 268–71.

29. *English Fairy Tales*, comp. Jacobs, p. 341.

30. "The White Duck," in Afanasev, *Russian Fairy Tales*, pp. 342–45.

31. *Brüder Grimm. Kinder- und Hausmärchen*, ed. Heinz Rölleke (Stuttgart: Reclam, 1980), vol. 3, pp. 117.

32. As Alan Dundes points out, "the 'love like salt' plot appears to be a weakened form of the folktale plot in which a 'mad' father tries to marry his own daughter." See his essay "'To Love My Father All,'" in *Cinderella: A Casebook*, pp. 229–44.

33. "The She-Bear," in Basile, *The Pentamerone*, 1:170–78.

34. Bettelheim, *The Uses of Enchantment*, p. 308.

35. Dreher, *Domination and Defiance*, p. 108.

36. "All Fur," in *The Complete Fairy Tales of the Brothers Grimm*, pp. 259–63. Since the title of this tale has been translated in so many different ways, I have chosen to retain the Grimms' original title to identify the tale.

37. Elizabeth Butler Cullingford discusses the literary topos of the virgin in the tree in "W. B. Yeats and Sylvia Plath," in *Daughters and Fathers*, ed. Boose and Flowers, pp. 233–55.

38. Sylvia Plath, *Collected Poems*, ed. Ted Hughes (New York: Harper & Row, 1981), pp. 81–82.

39. Claude Lévi-Strauss, *The Elementary Structures of Kinship*, rev. ed., trans. James Harle Bell, John Richard von Sturmer, and Rodney Needham, and also ed. Rodney Needham (Boston: Beacon Press, 1969), p. 481. The effectiveness of the loss of exchange value as a barrier to father-daughter incest is recognized by Jane Gallop, who writes that "the father must not desire the daughter, for to do so would threaten to remove him from the homosexual commerce in which women are exchanged between men, for the purpose of power relations and community for the men" (47). See "The Father's Seduction," in *The (M)other Tongue: Essays in Feminist Psychoanalytic Interpretation*, ed. Shirley Nelson Garner, Claire Kahane, and Madelon Sprengnether (Ithaca: Cornell Univ. Press, 1985), pp. 33–50.

40. G. Devereux, "The Social and Cultural Implications of Incest among the Mohave Indians," *Psychoanalytical Quarterly* 8 (1939): 510–33.

41. Peter Brooks describes the story as representing the move from "one desire that we . . . know to be prohibited, to a legitimate desire whose consummation marks the end of the tale." See his *Reading for the Plot: Design and Intention in the Narrative* (New York: Random House, Vintage Books, 1984), p. 8. Marianne Hirsch challenges Brooks' reading by calling attention to the tale's "fundamental power structure" and revealing "possible responses to it." See "Ideology, Form, and 'Allerleirauh': Reflections on *Reading for the Plot*," *Children's Literature* 14 (New Haven: Yale Univ. Press, 1986), pp. 163–68. Finally, Sandra M. Gilbert finds that the "two kings are one, paternal figures from both of whom the 'fair princess' tries to escape, though not, perhaps, with equal vigor" (275). See "Life's Empty Pack: Notes toward a Literary Daughteronomy," in *Daughters and Fathers*, ed. Boose and Flowers, pp. 256–77.

42. Heinz Rölleke, "Allerleirauh: Eine bisher unbekannte Fassung vor Grimm," *Fabula* 13 (1972): 153–59.

43. "The Cat Cinderella," in Basile, *The Pentamerone*, pp. 56–63.

44. "Catskin," in *English Fairy Tales*, comp. Jacobs, pp. 268–71.

45. Richard Schickel, *The Disney Version: The Life, Times, Art and Commerce of Walt Disney* (New York: Simon and Schuster, 1968), p. 220.

CHAPTER VII

1. "East o' the Sun and West o' the Moon," in *The Blue Fairy Book*, comp. Andrew Lang, ed. Brian Alderson (Harmondsworth: Penguin, Puffin Books, 1987), p. 2; "Night the Second, First Fable" ("The Pig King"), in Straparola, *The Facetious Nights*, p. 139; "The Small-Tooth Dog," in *Folktales of England*, ed. Katharine M. Briggs and Ruth L. Tongue (Chicago: Univ. of Chicago Press, 1965), pp. 3–5; "The Serpent," in Basile, *The Pentamerone*, 1:163. For a list of variants of the tale type, see Ludwig Friedländer, "Das Märchen von Amor und Psyche," in *Darstellungen aus der Sittengeschichte Roms*, ed. Georg Wissowa (Aalen: Scientia, 1964), pp. 122–24. For a full analysis of the tale type, see Betsy Hearne, *Beauty and the Beast: Visions and Revisions of an Old Tale* (Chicago: Univ. of Chicago Press, 1989).

2. Apuleius's tale was based on folk sources. That the literary tale reentered the oral tradition becomes evident from "Die Königstochter und der Drache," a version of the tale recorded by Künzig and Werner in *Ungarndeutsche Märchenerzähler II*, pp. 40–50.

3. *The Transformations of Lucius Otherwise Known as The Golden Ass*, trans. Jack Lindsay (Bloomington: Indiana Univ. Press, 1960), pp. 107–8. All further citations will be to this translation of the original. For a translation with the Latin text on facing pages, see Apuleius, *The Golden Ass, Being the Metamorphoses of Lucius Apuleius*, trans. W. Adlington, rev. S. Gaselee (London: Heinemann, 1915).

4. Lady Mary Chudleigh's poem "To the Ladies" is cited by Lawrence Stone, *The Family, Sex and Marriage in England*, pp. 340–41.

5. William Cobbett, *Advice to Young Men, and (incidentally) to Young Women, in the Middle and Higher Ranks of Life* (London: Mills, Jowett, and Mills, 1829), p. 157.

6. Erich Neumann, *Amor and Psyche: The Psychic Development of the Feminine. A Commentary on the Tale by Apuleius*, trans. Ralph Manheim (Princeton: Princeton Univ. Press, Bollingen, 1956), p. 62. For Bruno Bettelheim, the funeral procession that leads Psyche to her husband represents "the death of maidenhood" (*The Uses of Enchantment*, p. 293).

7. On martial metaphors, see Denis de Rougemont, *Love in the Western World*, rev. ed., trans. Montgomery Belgion (New York: Harper & Row, 1940), pp. 244–45.

8. "The Search for the Lost Husband" (AT 425) is followed in the tale type index by "The Monster (Animal) as Bridegroom" ("Cupid and Psyche") (AT 425A) and by "Beauty and the Beast" (AT 425C). For the sake of convenience, I will refer to both of these subclasses of AT 425 as "The Search for the Lost Husband."

9. Angela Carter, "The Courtship of Mr. Lyon," in *The Bloody Chamber and Other Stories* (Harmondsworth: Penguin, 1979), pp. 41–51.

10. "The Enchanted Pig," in *The Red Fairy Book*, ed. Andrew Lang (London: Longman's, Green, 1909), pp. 104–15.

11. Mme Leprince de Beaumont, "Beauty and the Beast," in *The Classic Fairy Tales*, ed. Iona Opie and Peter Opie (New York: Oxford Univ. Press, 1974), pp. 182–95.

12. Afanasev, "The Snotty Goat," in *Russian Fairy Tales*, pp. 200–202. "The Mouse with the Long Tail," in *Italian Folktales*, comp. Calvino, pp. 653–56.

13. "Ricky of the Tuft," in *Perrault's Complete Fairy Tales*, pp. 47–57.

14. While the princess of Perrault's tale learns a lesson, the heroine of Mlle Catherine Bernard's "Riquet with the Tuft" is taught a lesson. Her heroine's beauty is also marred by her stupidity, and she too promises to marry Ricky in exchange for the gift of intelligence. But "Mama," as she is called, falls in love with a young man named Arada before her wedding to Ricky. Mama begins a daytime love affair with Arada while she is married to Ricky, who tries unsuccessfully to sabotage the relationship by making his wife intelligent only at night. Finally, Ricky is forced to take full revenge by turning Arada into his physical twin: the wife can no longer distinguish the husband from the lover. See "Riquet with the Tuft," in *Beauties, Beasts and Enchantment*, trans. Jack Zipes (New York: New American Library, 1989), pp. 95–100. Jack Zipes finds that this tale "states unequivocally that women must be placed under constant surveillance even when they are endowed with reason to temper their appetites: they are potentially destructive and may be harmful to civil order." See his *Fairy Tales and the Art of Subversion: The Classical Genre for Children and the Process of Civilization* (New York: Wildman, 1983), p. 36. For a discussion of the story in the context of French variants of the tale type, see Jacques Barchilon, "Beauty and the Beast: From Myth to Fairy Tale," *Psychoanalysis and the Psychoanalytic Review* 46 (1959): 19–29.

15. "Bellinda and the Monster," in *Italian Folktales*, comp. Calvino, pp. 197–202.

16. "The Singing, Springing Lark," in *The Complete Fairy Tales of the Brothers Grimm*, pp. 317–21.

17. Bachofen read the scene of illumination in a similar way. "Sexual enjoyment," he wrote, "shrouded in darkness, is replaced by a yearning to possess the god recognized in all his glory." And more dramatically, he observed that "darkness and chaos give way to light and order, and unregulated hetaerism to a yearning for conjugal union." See "The Lamp in the Myth of Amor and Psyche," in *Myth, Religion, and Mother Right: Selected Writings of J. J. Bachofen*, trans. Ralph Manheim (Princeton: Princeton Univ. Press, Bollingen, 1967), pp. 44–47.

18. Mary Anne Ferguson takes a different view when she writes that the story "seems to say that for a god or a male, love involves seeing and knowing but that for a woman the satisfaction of curiosity is destructive of love for both lovers" (230). Curiosity may lead to separation of the lovers, but it does not destroy Psyche's love. See "The Female Novel of Development and the Myth of Psyche," in *The Voyage In: Fictions of Female Development*, ed. Elizabeth Abel, Marianne Hirsch, and Elizabeth Langland (Hanover: Univ. Press of New England, 1983), pp. 228–43.

19. By contrast, Lee R. Edwards sees each task as "a concrete marker of an increase in psychic range, a claim of consciousness to apprehend and use what was

formerly forbidden and inaccessible" (39). See "The Labors of Psyche: Toward a Theory of Female Heroism," *Critical Inquiry* 6 (1979): 33–49.

20. Jan-Öjvind Swahn points out that the modest request does not always simply underscore the humble nature of the heroine. In some cases, for example, the heroine wishes for something that seems ordinary (e.g., a rose), but that is in fact "fabulous" because of the qualification attached to it (a rose that grows in winter, one that talks, or one that has no thorns). See Swahn, *The Tale of Cupid and Psyche (Aarne-Thompson 425 & 428)* (Lund: Gleerup, 1955), p. 217.

21. *The Transformations of Lucius Otherwise Known as The Golden Ass*, trans. Robert Graves (New York: Farrar, Straus and Giroux, 1951), p. xix.

22. "The Frog King, or Iron Heinrich," in *The Complete Tales of the Brothers Grimm*, pp. 2–5.

23. "The Well of the World's End," in *English Fairy Tales*, comp. Jacobs, pp. 134–36.

24. That narrative fact has not escaped the attention of critics in Germany, who are perplexed that disenchantment comes about without any real effort ("Leistung") on the part of the princess. See Alfred Clemens Baumgärtner, "'Ach, du bists, alter Wasserpatscher . . .': Zur aktuellen Rezeption Grimmscher Märchen," in *Mythen, Märchen und moderne Zeit: Beiträge zur Kinder- und Jugendliteratur*, ed. Alfred Clemens Baumgärtner and Karl Ernst Maier (Würzburg: Königshausen and Neumann, 1987), pp. 43–55.

25. Swahn, *The Tale of Cupid and Psyche*, p. 241.

26. For a catalog of tasks, see Ernst Tegethoff, *Studien zum Märchentypus von Amor und Psyche*, Rheinische Beiträge und Hülfsbücher zur germanischen Philologie und Volkskunde, no. 4 (Bonn: Kurt Schroeder, 1922), pp. 42–44.

27. Aarne, *The Types of the Folktale*, pp. 128–29, 140.

28. Torberg Lundell, "Gender-Related Biases in the Type and Motif Indexes of Aarne and Thompson," in *Fairy Tales and Society: Illusion, Allusion, and Paradigm*, ed. Ruth B. Bottigheimer (Philadelphia: Univ. of Pennsylvania Press, 1986), p. 155.

29. This too might not be so odd if it were not the case that the episodic structure of AT 425 could easily be reformulated in the following way to stand in a relation of perfect symmetry to the description of AT 400.

The Woman on a Quest for Her Lost Husband
   I. The Heroine
   II. The Enchanted Prince
   III. Her Visit Home
   IV. Loss of the Husband
   V. The Search
   VI. The Recovery

30. "The King of the Golden Mountain," in *The Complete Fairy Tales of the Brothers Grimm*, pp. 338–42.

31. "A Tale about the Boy Who Went Forth to Learn What Fear Is," in *The Complete Fairy Tales of the Brothers Grimm*, pp. 12–20. "The Youth Who Wanted to Learn What Fear Is" (AT 326) is in fact a subtype of "Enchanted Princesses and Their Castles" rather than a separate tale type.

32. Bettelheim, *The Uses of Enchantment*, p. 281.

33. "Yann the Fearless," in *Folktales of France*, ed. Massignon, pp. 3–8.

34. Not every version of the tale type makes the ability to feel fear a prerequisite for marriage. In one variant, for example, the hero, after learning what fear is when a cannon is shot off, goes back home. See Johannes Bolte and Georg Polívka, *Anmerkungen zu den Kinder- und Hausmärchen der Brüder Grimm* (Leipzig: Dieterich, 1913), vol. 1, pp. 22–37. In an Icelandic tale, the hero nearly goes "crazy with terror" when he discovers that his head is on backwards ("The Boy Who Knew No Fear," *Icelandic Folktales and Legends*, trans. Jacqueline Simpson [Berkeley and Los Angeles: Univ. of California Press, 1972], pp. 122–31).

CHAPTER VIII

1. "Herr Korbes," in *The Complete Fairy Tales of the Brothers Grimm*, pp. 157–58.

2. Bolte and Polívka, *Anmerkungen zu den Kinder- und Hausmärchen der Brüder Grimm*, 1:375. See also Claudia Schittek, "Der Herr Korbes: Die Sprache der Märchen in den Reimen und Sprüchen der Brüder Grimm," *Aufmerksamkeit: Klaus Heinrich zum 50. Geburtstag* (Frankfurt a.M.: Roter Stern, 1979), pp. 396–402.

3. "Riffraff," in *The Complete Fairy Tales of the Brothers Grimm*, pp. 40–41.

4. On the role of inanimate objects in stories, see H. Joseph Schwarcz, "Machine Animism in Modern Children's Literature," in *A Critical Approach to Children's Literature*, ed. Sara Innis Fenwick (Chicago: Univ. of Chicago Press, 1967), pp. 78–95.

5. James B. Twitchell, *Preposterous Violence: Fables of Aggression in Modern Culture* (New York: Oxford Univ. Press, 1989).

6. "The Old Woman Who Was Skinned," in Basile, *The Pentamerone*, 1:94–102. For other versions, see "The King Who Wanted a Beautiful Wife," in *Italian Popular Tales*, comp. Crane, pp. 97–100, and "The Three Crones," in *Italian Folktales*, comp. Calvino, pp. 80–83. Crane's misguided effort to view this tale as a close cousin of "The Kind and Unkind Girls" shows how easy it is to fall into the trap of classifying the story as a cautionary tale. "This story," he writes, "leads quite naturally to the class in which gifts, good and bad, are bestowed by the fairies on two persons, one of whom is deserving of good fortune; the other, of punishment or reproof" (100).

7. "The Rejuvenated Little Old Man," in *The Complete Fairy Tales of the Brothers Grimm*, pp. 502–3.

8. Ruth B. Bottigheimer makes the point that the conclusion serves as an "attempt to socialize the story's violence." See *Grimms' Bad Girls & Bold Boys*, p. 147.

9. On the sources for the Grimms' tale, see Hermann Hamann, *Die literarischen Vorlagen der Kinder- und Hausmärchen und ihre Bearbeitung durch die Brüder Grimm* (Berlin: Mayer & Müller, 1906), pp. 51–52.

10. "Put the Old Woman in the Furnace," in *Italian Folktales*, comp. Calvino, pp. 595–96.

11. In "The Lord, St. Peter, and the Blacksmith," collected by Thomas Frederick Crane, a blacksmith who tries to replicate God's miracles ends by learning a lesson in humility. "There are gentlemen in Venice and professors in Padua, but I am a

bungler," he declares at the end of his story. See *Italian Popular Tales*, comp. Crane, pp. 188–89.

12. On the body as target of power, see Michel Foucault, *Discipline and Punish*, p. 136.

13. *Märchen aus Sibirien*, ed. Hugo Kunike (Jena: Eugen Diederichs, 1940), p. 104.

14. A few of these tales have remained popular, though not in this country. "The Table, the Ass, and the Stick," for example, remains a classic children's story in Germany.

15. "The Magic Table, the Gold Donkey, and the Club in the Sack," in *The Complete Fairy Tales of the Brothers Grimm*, pp. 134–47.

16. "Von dem Tischgen deck dich, dem Goldesel und dem Knüppel in dem Sack," in *Kinder- und Hausmärchen* (1986), 1:161–71.

17. "Tischchen deck dich, Goldesel und Knüppel aus dem Sack," in *Brüder Grimm. Kinder- und Hausmärchen*, ed. Heinz Rölleke (Köln: Eugen Dieterichs, 1982), vol. 1, pp. 129–36. This passage is not altered substantially in subsequent revisions.

18. "Two out of the Sack," in Afanasev, *Russian Fairy Tales*, pp. 321–24.

19. The hero's magnanimous nature is emphasized in many folktales, but especially in the Italian "Jump into My Sack," which shows the hero using his power to give a selfish doctor his comeuppance. A devil who lures poor souls into a life of gambling gets the same treatment. See "Jump into My Sack," in *Italian Folktales*, comp. Calvino, pp. 708–17.

20. "The North Wind's Gift," in *Italian Folktales*, comp. Calvino, pp. 301–4.

21. "The Ass that Lays Money," in *Italian Popular Tales*, comp. Crane, pp. 123–27.

22. "Von der Serviette, dem Tornister, dem Kanonenhütlein und dem Horn," in *Kinder- und Hausmärchen* (1986), pp. 172–76.

23. "The Knapsack, the Hat, and the Horn," in *The Complete Fairy Tales of the Brothers Grimm*, pp. 204–209.

24. J.K.A. Musäus, "Richilde," in *Volksmärchen der Deutschen* (Munich: Winkler, 1976), p. 115.

25. An English translation of "The Three Gifts" appears in Darnton, "Peasants Tell Tales: The Meaning of Mother Goose," pp. 69–72. The French original ("Les Trois Dons") appears in *Le Conte populaire français*, ed. Delarue and Tenèze, 2:492–95.

26. "The Jew in the Thornbush," in *The Complete Fairy Tales of the Brothers Grimm*, pp. 398–402.

27. Darnton, "Peasants Tell Tales: The Meaning of Mother Goose," p. 52.

28. The phrase is Ruth B. Bottigheimer's. See her *Grimms' Bad Girls & Bold Boys*, p. 139.

29. In the version of the tale as it was first recorded by the Grimms, the boy is presented as a crafty rogue who tells that judge that the money in question is rightfully his, for the Jew promised him a bag of money for playing the fiddle. Only in a later edition does the servant actually tell the truth to the judge, declaring that the Jew gave him the money so that he would *stop* playing the fiddle. The first edition

describes the Jew simply as an "old" man, not as a person with a long goatee who is immediately labeled a thief. Only in later editions does he curse incessantly ("You miserable musician! You beer-house fiddler! You tramp!"), worship his ducats, and wear shabby clothes despite his wealth. In the first edition, the Jew is described as "naked and pathetic" after the servant's cruel prank, not as rabid with rage. He may be described in stereotypical terms as someone who has gotten his money by "cheating a Christian," but his words and actions in the tale itself portray him as a man who wants nothing more than legal restitution for a wrong inflicted on him.

30. Bottigheimer takes note of some of these contradictions in her analysis. See *Bad Girls & Bold Boys*, p. 139.

31. The master who cheats his servant no longer "escapes reproach," as Bottigheimer puts it; it is more than "malice pure and simple" that leads the servant to torture the Jew—revenge also plays a role; the servant's allusion to the Jew's fleecing of others is then based on experience rather than speculation; and the "honest" servant's victimization of the Jew loses its capricious character and has a certain logic—however twisted—to it.

32. In his *Altdeutsche Wälder*, Jacob Grimm's meditations on the colors red, white, and black give a clear sense of the intensity of the anti-Semitism behind the revisions in "The Jew in the Thornbush": "Red stands for the wounds of the Savior—white for the purity of Jesus—black for the baseness of the Jews." See *Altdeutsche Wälder*, ed. Wilhelm Schoof (Darmstadt: Wissenschaftliche Buchgesellschaft, 1966), vol. 1, pp. 1–30.

33. "Nachwort," in Grimm and Grimm, *Kinder- und Hausmärchen*, p. 294.

34. "The Dog and the Sparrow," in *The Complete Fairy Tales of the Brothers Grimm*, pp. 222–24.

35. *Some Thoughts Concerning Education*, vol. 9 in *The Works of John Locke* (London: W. Otridge and Son, 1812), p. 112. On Locke and his influence, especially on didactic tales about cruelty toward animals, see Pickering, *John Locke and Children's Books*, pp. 3–39.

36. Darton, *Children's Books in England*, p. 158.

37. Sarah Kirby Trimmer, *Fabulous Histories, or, The History of the Robins. Designed for the Instruction of Children, respecting Their Treatment of Animals*, vol. 3 in *Masterworks of Children's Literature*, ed. Robert Bator (New York: Stonehill/Chelsea House, 1983), pp. 296, 351.

38. Andersen, "The Storks," in *Eighty Fairy Tales*, pp. 277–81.

39. "The Death of the Cock," in Afanasev, *Russian Fairy Tales*, pp. 17–19.

40. "The Death of the Hen," in *The Complete Fairy Tales of the Brothers Grimm*, pp. 290–91.

41. "The Louse and the Flea," in *The Complete Fairy Tales of the Brothers Grimm*, pp. 117–18.

42. *The Oxford Dictionary of Nursery Rhymes*, ed. Opie and Opie, p. 231.

43. *The Oxford Dictionary of Nursery Rhymes*, p. 392, records "Solomon Grundy." The other examples are taken from Aarne, *The Types of the Folktale*, pp. 523–24.

44. "Misfortune," in *The Complete Fairy Tales of the Brothers Grimm*, p. 706.

45. "How Some Children Played at Slaughtering," in *The Complete Fairy Tales of the Brothers Grimm*, pp. 650–51.

46. "Three Tales by Three Sons of Three Merchants," in *Italian Folktales*, comp. Calvino, pp. 588–91.

CHAPTER IX

1. Maurice Sendak, "An Informal Talk," in *Caldecott & Co.*, pp. 213–14.

2. "The Land of the Young," *Time*, 29 Dec. 1980, p. 66.

3. Maurice Sendak, *Where the Wild Things Are* (New York: Harper & Row, 1963).

4. Otto Fenichel, "The Dread of Being Eaten," in *The Collected Papers of Otto Fenichel* (New York: Norton, 1953), pp. 158–59. Freud discusses the dread of being eaten in his essay "Female Sexuality," vol. 21 in the *Standard Edition*, pp. 223–43.

5. "Isaac Bashevis Singer on Writing for Children," *Children's Literature* 6 (1977): 9–16.

6. P. L. Travers, "Only Connect," in *Only Connect*, ed. Egoff et al., p. 201.

7. See Michael Harner, "The Ecological Basis for Aztec Sacrifice," *American Ethnologist* 4 (1977): 117–35. On cannibalism from a psychogenetic point of view, see Eli Sagan, *Cannibalism: Human Aggression and Cultural Form* (New York: Harper & Row, 1974). W. Arens denies that cannibalism was ever a "prevalent cultural feature." For him the significant question hinges "not on why people eat human flesh, but why one group invariably assumes that the others do." See *The Man-Eating Myth: Anthropology and Anthropophagy* (New York: Oxford Univ. Press, 1979). Peggy Reeves Sanday rebuts that view in her *Divine Hunger: Cannibalism as a Cultural System* (London: Cambridge Univ. Press, 1986).

8. "The Knapsack, the Hat, and the Horn," in *The Complete Fairy Tales of the Brothers Grimm*, pp. 204–9.

9. "The Children of Famine," in *The Complete Fairy Tales of the Brothers Grimm*, pp. 704–5.

10. Jean-Pierre Peter, "Ogres d'Archives," *Nouvelle Revue de Psychanalyse* 6 (1972): 249–67.

11. The Armenian tale appears in *The Cinderella Story*, ed. Philip, pp. 47–51. Cox's versions can be found in *Cinderella: Three hundred and forty-five variants*.

12. "Tom Thumb," in *Perrault's Complete Fairy Tales*, pp. 26–41.

13. "Hansel and Gretel," in *The Complete Fairy Tales of the Brothers Grimm*, pp. 58–64.

14. "When the children give in to untamed id impulses, as symbolized by their uncontrolled voraciousness, they risk being destroyed," Bettelheim observes in his analysis of "Hansel and Gretel." See *The Uses of Enchantment*, p. 162.

15. Bettelheim, *The Uses of Enchantment*, p. 165.

16. "Jack and the Beanstalk," in *The Classic Fairy Tales*, ed. Opie and Opie, pp. 210–26.

17. Michael Patrick Hearn, *The Annotated Wizard of Oz* (New York: Clarkson N. Potter, 1973), p. 86.

18. W. Arens cites this fact in *The Man-Eating Myth*, p. 148.

19. To Marie Bonaparte, Freud wrote in 1932: "The situation with incest is just the same as with cannibalism. There are of course real grounds in modern life against slaying a man in order to devour him, but no grounds whatever against eating human flesh instead of animal flesh. Still most of us would find it quite impossible." Cited by Ernest Jones, *The Life and Work of Sigmund Freud* (New York: Basic Books, 1953–57), vol. 3, p. 454. See also Otto Fenichel, "The Dread of Being Eaten," p. 159.

20. "Vasilisa the Beautiful," in Afanasev, *Russian Fairy Tales*, pp. 439–49.

21. For a fuller discussion of such tales, see Caroline Scielzo, "An Analysis of Bába-Yagá in Folklore and Fairy Tales," *American Journal of Psychoanalysis* 43 (1983): 167–75.

22. "Baba Yaga," in Afanasev, *Russian Fairy Tales*, pp. 363–65.

23. Freud, *Totem and Taboo*, p. 141.

24. On Freud's repression of the mother in general, see Madelon Sprengnether, *The Spectral Mother: Freud, Feminism, and Psychoanalysis* (Ithaca: Cornell Univ. Press, 1990).

25. Melanie Klein, "Weaning," in *Love, Guilt and Reparation & Other Works, 1921–1945* (N.p.: Delacorte Press, 1975), pp. 290–305.

26. Susan Rubin Suleiman, "Writing and Motherhood," in *The (M)other Tongue*, ed. Garner, et al., pp. 352–77.

27. Masson, *The Assault on Truth*, p. 113.

28. Alice Miller makes a similar point about Oedipus in "Oedipus: The 'Guilty' Victim," in *Thou Shalt Not Be Aware: Society's Betrayal of the Child*, trans. Hildegarde Hannum and Hunter Hannum (New York: Farrar, Straus and Giroux, 1984), pp. 145–59. David C. Taylor also calls attention to the fact that the parents of Oedipus "attempted to kill, wound, expose, and limit the freedom and the inheritance of their child." See "Oedipus' Parents Were Child Abusers," *British Journal of Psychiatry* 153 (1988): 561–63.

29. Darnton, "Peasants Tell Tales," in *The Great Cat Massacre*, p. 34.

30. "Cinderello," in *Folktales of Greece*, ed. Georgios A. Megas, trans. Helen Colaclides, (Chicago: Univ. of Chicago Press, 1970), pp. 99–104.

31. "The Tabby Who Was Such a Glutton," in *Norwegian Folktales*, comp. Asbjørnsen and Moe, pp. 161–67.

32. "The Cat and the Parrot," in *World Folktales: A Scribner Resource Collection*, ed. Atelia Clarkson and Gilbert B. Cross (New York: Charles Scribner's Sons, 1980), pp. 223–25.

33. "Master Francesco Sit-Down-and-Eat," in *Italian Folktales*, comp. Calvino, pp. 604–6.

34. "The Seven Lamb Heads," in *Italian Folktales*, comp. Calvino, pp. 609–11.

35. "Baba Yaga and the Brave Youth," in Afanasev, *Russian Fairy Tales*, pp. 76–79.

36. "The Garden Witch," in *Italian Folktales*, comp. Calvino, pp. 650–53.

37. See the notes to "The Wolf and the Three Girls," in *Italian Folktales*, comp. Calvino, pp. 720–21.

38. Walter Scherf, "Family Conflicts and Emancipation in Fairy Tales," *Chil-*

dren's Literature 3 (1983): 77–93. The translator did not quite succeed in producing an idiomatic version of the game, which would probably end with children shouting "me" rather than his grammatically correct "I" (which I have replaced with "me").

39. Cited in *World Folktales*, ed. Clarkson and Cross, p. 245, which also reprints the tale published in the May 1875 issue of *St. Nicholas Magazine*.

CHAPTER X

1. Since the woman in the story is mother to one child and stepmother to the other, I designate her consistently as the step/mother.

2. "The Juniper Tree" is tale number 47 in the *Nursery and Household Tales* and appears in English translation in *The Complete Fairy Tales of the Brothers Grimm*, pp. 171–79. (The verse translation is my own, otherwise I cite from Zipes's translation.) Michael Belgrader discusses tale variants in *Das Märchen von dem Machandelboom (KHM 47)* (Frankfurt a.M.: Peter D. Lang, 1980). For a full description of the tale type, see Aarne and Thompson, *The Types of the Folktale*, pp. 249–50. Arland Ussher and Carl von Metzradt refer to "The Juniper Tree" as "the greatest of all fairy tales." See *Enter These Enchanted Woods* (Dublin: Dolmen, 1957), p. 37. P. L. Travers's observations on the story appear in "Only Connect," in *Only Connect*, ed. Egoff et al., pp. 183–206. For J.R.R. Tolkien's reference to the tale, see "On Fairy-Stories," in *The Tolkien Reader* (New York: Ballantine, 1966), p. 31.

3. Heinz Rölleke notes that the tears and helplessness of many fairy-tale heroes elicit assistance in the form of benefactors or gifts. He observes that the infant's experience of feeling needy, crying, and getting help may well be the realistic model for this pattern. See "Nachwort," in Grimm and Grimm, *Kinder- und Hausmärchen*, 3:614.

4. Miller, *For Your Own Good*.

5. In an engaging analysis of Donald Duck's adventures in *Walt Disney's Comics & Stories*, James A. Freeman observes that Donald "consistently exhibits traits which any schoolboy recognizes as defining a parent." For that very reason, the constant assaults to his dignity and his perpetual failures have a special appeal for children. See "Donald Duck: How Children (Mainly Boys) Viewed Their Parents (Mainly Fathers), 1943–1960," *Children's Literature* 6 (1977): 150–64.

6. The version in the *Nursery and Household Tales* naturalizes the decapitation episode to some extent by putting a "big, sharp iron lock" on the chest, though most versions do not.

7. Both Vilma Mönckeberg and Louis L. Snyder discuss the responses of children to fairy-tale readings. See *Das Märchen und unsere Welt: Erfahrungen und Einsichten* (Düsseldorf: Diederichs, 1972), pp. 14–15, and *Roots of German Nationalism* (Bloomington: Indiana Univ. Press, 1978), p. 49. My own observations bear out their findings.

8. "Pippety Pew," in *The Well at the World's End: Folk Tales of Scotland*, retold by Norah Montgomerie and William Montgomerie (Toronto: The Bodley Head, 1956), pp. 56–59.

9. "The Rose-Tree," in *English Fairy Tales*, comp. Jacobs, pp. 13–15.

10. Carl-Heinz Mallet, for example, finds that the tale stages the biblical scene of temptation, with the mother as Eve and the boy as Adam. His interpretation does not, however, account for numerous deviant textual details. See his *Kopf ab! Gewalt im Märchen*, pp. 214–15.

11. That a connection exists between the apple offered to the boy and the one peeled by the biological mother at the start of the tale is not wholly improbable. Both apples are linked to an act of mutilation: the mother cuts her finger while peeling an apple; the son is decapitated while reaching for an apple. They function as the object of (limited) desire that sets in motion a train of events leading to death. And their colors (red/white is the conventional association with the fruit) harmonize with the "red as blood / white as snow" motif (itself strongly linked with the notion of mortality).

12. "Jacob Grimm: Sechs Märchen," in *Briefe der Brüder Grimm an Savigny*, ed. Ingeborg Schnack and Wilhelm Schoof (Berlin: Erich Schmidt, 1953), p. 430.

13. Lutz Röhrich points out that dismemberment has a dual function in fairy tales: it stands as a murderous act of violence, but also forms part of a ritual for rejuvenating the weak, ill, or aged. See "Die Grausamkeit im deutschen Märchen," pp. 176–224.

14. Cited by John A. Phillips, *Eve: The History of an Idea* (San Francisco: Harper & Row, 1984), p. 49. The association between Eve and death is a common one. St. Jerome writes, for example, that "Death came through Eve, but life has come through Mary" (cited by Julia Kristeva, "Stabat mater," in *The Female Body in Western Culture: Contemporary Perspectives*, ed. Susan Rubin Suleiman [Cambridge: Harvard Univ. Press, 1985], p. 103).

15. On the opening paragraph, see Belgrader, *Das Märchen von dem Machandelboom*, p. 330. Of the 495 tale variants examined by Belgrader, only the version in the *Nursery and Household Tales* describes the child's birth in such detail. Reinhold Steig attributes this detail to the "self-conscious artistic intentions" of its author. See his "Zur Entstehungsgeschichte der Märchen und Sagen der Brüder Grimm," *Archiv für das Studium der neueren Sprachen* 107 (1901): 277–301.

16. "The Juniper Tree" made its literary debut in Achim von Arnim's *Journal for Hermits* (*Zeitung für Einsiedler*) some four years before its appearance between the covers of the *Nursery and Household Tales*. Arnim, who had always been generous with the literary property of his friends, gave copies of the tale to the Grimms, who published it in their collection, and to Friedrich Heinrich von der Hagen, who passed it on to Johann Georg Büsching, who in turn published it in 1812 in his own collection of tales ("Von dem Mahandel Bohm," in *Volkssagen, Märchen und Legenden* [Leipzig: Reclam, 1812], pp. 245–58). On the varied fortunes of Runge's tale, see especially Steig, "Zur Entstehungsgeschichte der Märchen," pp. 277–84.

17. Dorothy Dinnerstein, *The Mermaid and the Minotaur: Sexual Arrangements and the Human Malaise* (New York: Harper & Row, 1976), pp. 106–14.

18. Sigmund Freud, *The Future of an Illusion*, vol. 21 in the *Standard Edition*, pp. 15–16.

19. Aarne/Thompson, *The Types of the Folktale*, pp. 249–50.

20. On this point, see Tatar, *The Hard Facts of the Grimms' Fairy Tales*, pp. 179–92.

21. Eugen Weber, "Fairies and Hard Facts: The Reality of Folktales," *Journal of the History of Ideas* 42 (1981): 93–113. For a compelling analysis of the traumatic effect on a child of a mother's death in childbirth, see Carol A. Mossmann, "Targeting the Unspeakable: Stendhal and Figures of Pregnancy," *Nineteenth-Century French Studies* 16 (1988): 257–69.

22. It is important to note here that many versions of "The Juniper Tree" cast a girl in the role of victim—the boy consequently becomes her savior. Belgrader finds that the roles are almost equally distributed between males and females (p. 320), but my own statistical sample reveals a preponderance of male heroes. Belgrader does not cite a single version in which the murderous parent is a father, though Jacques Geninasca asserts the existence of such a variant (without citing it). See his "Conte Populaire et identité du cannibalisme," in *Nouvelle Revue de Psychanalyse* 6 (1972): 220.

23. Adrienne Rich, *Of Woman Born: Motherhood as Experience and Institution* (New York: Norton, 1976), p. 166. Louis Adrian Montrose observes, in the context of *A Midsummer Night's Dream*, that "in order to be freed and enfranchised from the prison of the womb, the male child must *kill* his mother: 'She, being mortal, of that boy did die.'" See his "'Shaping Fantasies': Figurations of Gender and Power in Elizabethan Culture," in *Representing the English Renaissance*, ed. Stephen Greenblatt (Berkeley and Los Angeles: Univ. of California Press, 1988), pp. 31–64.

24. In nearly every version of the bird's song, the boy is slain by his mother and not his stepmother. This suggests that the splitting of the mother into a good biological mother and a sinister stepmother came only as a later development in the tale's evolution. Songs are generally held to preserve the original diction and motifs of a folktale more faithfully than the texts in which they are anchored.

25. On this point, see Bruce Lincoln, *Myth, Cosmos, and Society: Indo-European Themes of Creation and Destruction* (Cambridge: Harvard Univ. Press, 1986).

26. Chodorow, *The Reproduction of Mothering*, p. 97.

27. Chodorow, *The Reproduction of Mothering*, p. 82.

28. Rank, *Myth of the Birth of the Hero*, p. 84.

29. The translation is my own, since many translators—unaware of the folktale—dilute the strength of the original German. See for example, Walter Arndt's version: "My mother, the whore / Who smothered me, / My father, the knave / Who made broth of me! . . ." (*Faust: A Tragedy*, trans. Walter Arndt, ed. Cyrus Hamlin [New York: Norton, 1976], p. 112).

30. "Vasilisa the Beautiful," in Afanasev, *Russian Fairy Tales*, p. 447; "The Cloven Youth," in *Italian Folktales*, comp. Calvino, p. 102; "Tom Thumb," in *Perrault's Complete Fairy Tales*, p. 41.

EPILOGUE

1. The phrase "new matrix" is from Betsy Hearne, who finds among scholars "a reluctance, almost an embarrassment, in associating fairy tales with children's literature." See her *Beauty and the Beast*, p. 149.

2. Greenblatt, introduction to *Representing the English Renaissance*, p. viii.

3. Carolyn G. Heilbrun, "What was Penelope Unweaving?" in her *Hamlet's Mother and Other Women* (New York: Columbia Univ. Press, 1990), p. 109.

4. Carol Gilligan, "Oedipus - Psyche: Two Stories about Love," paper presented at MLA Convention, December 1989. I was not at that presentation, but heard a modified form of the paper at a seminar at Harvard University.

5. Rudy Behlmer has pointed out that "there was never any material written or drawn and photographed for the film showing Snow White's real mother, who dies in childbirth, although references or drawings of this and other embellishments were made up for authorized book versions and comic strips." See his "They Called It 'Disney's Folly': Snow White and the Seven Dwarfs (1937)," in *America's Favorite Movies: Behind the Scenes* (New York: Ungar, 1982), pp. 40–60.

6. The configuration of female characters in "Snow White" closely parallels that of the most recent large-scale Disney production for children, "The Little Mermaid." There, the good mother is totally effaced from the screen as a cinematic presence to make room for a ghoulishly repulsive sea-witch who becomes steadily demonized in her efforts to acquire the heroine's soul. Here too the heroine relies on her father and on father-substitutes (the good-natured, if somewhat doltish, Sebastian) to protect her from the perils posed by female figures. Disney's observation was made during a story conference on 10 March 1937.

7. Bettelheim, *The Uses of Enchantment*, p. 204.

8. "The Sleeping Prince," a Spanish tale, appears in English translation in *Clever Gretchen and Other Forgotten Folktales*, retold by Alison Lurie, illus. Margot Tomes (New York: Thomas Y. Crowell, 1980), pp. 74–83.

9. Alison Lurie makes the point that the editors of the great nineteenth-century fairy tale collections also favored stories like "Snow White," "Cinderella," "Sleeping Beauty," and "Little Red Riding Hood" over tales with "strong, brave, clever, and resourceful" heroines. See her *Clever Gretchen and Other Forgotten Folktales*, pp. xi-xiii.

10. *The Complete Fairy Tales of the Brothers Grimm*, pp. 196–204.

11. *55 Favorite Stories Adapted from Disney Films* (Golden Book, Western Publishing, 1960).

12. The phrase about the dwarfs is from *Snow White*, illus. Rex Irvine and Judie Clarke, Superscope. The description of Snow White comes from *Storytime Treasury*, McCall, 1969.

13. These are the thoughts that Walt Disney put in Snow White's mind in a story conference of October 1935.

14. *New York Times*, 14 January 1938, p. 21.

15. Brüder Grimm, *Kinder- und Hausmärchen*, rpt. of the first edition (Göttingen: Vandenhoeck & Ruprecht, 1986), pp. 238–50.

16. *New York Times*, 2 May 1938.

17. Miles, *Carnal Knowing*, p. 190.

18. Bettelheim, *The Uses of Enchantment*, pp. 17–19.

19. *New York Times*, 24 November 1990, p. 26.

20. While this version of "Snow White" inspired gales of laughter in the ten children that I observed watching it and seemed to have successfully attenuated the threat from the stepmother, it seemed also to go wrong in certain respects. At the very same time that vanity is parodied through the figure of the stepmother, the importance of physical appearances is repeatedly emphasized through the revulsion

exhibited by each character who encounters the queen as old hag and through the instant adoration directed at the lovely Snow White. The hate-at-first-sight and love-at-first-sight reactions send a clear message about the degree to which looks count and override any surface indictment of vanity. Story conferences for Disney's film reveal that the wicked queen was originally to be presented as "verging on the ridiculous" (22 October 1934) and as a "sort of vain—batty—self-satisfied, comedy type" (30 October 1934).

21. *Cinderella*, as told by Russell Shorto, illus. T. Lewis (New York: Birch Lane, 1990). See also, in the same series, *Jack and the Beanstalk*, as told by Tim Paulson, illus. Mark Corcoran (New York: Birch Lane, 1990).

22. The story is reprinted in Zipes, *Breaking the Magic Spell*. For further thoughts on rewriting fairy tales, see Zipes's *Fairy Tales and the Art of Subversion*, pp. 170–94.

23. Jane Yolen, *Sleeping Ugly*, illus. Diane Stanley (New York: Coward, McCann & Geoghegan, 1981.

24. Feminists have tried to resurrect some forgotten tales as reading matter for children. See especially *Womenfolk and Fairy Tales*, ed. Rosemary Minard, illus. Suzanna Klein (Boston: Houghton Mifflin, 1975); *Tatterhood and Other Tales*, ed. Ethel Johnston Phelps, illus. Pamela Baldwin Ford (Old Westbury, N.Y.: Feminist Press, 1978); and *The Maid of the North: Feminist Folktales from around the World*, ed. Ethel Johnston Phelps, illus. Lloyd Bloom (New York: Henry Holt, 1981). For creative rewritings, see especially Jay Williams, *The Practical Princess*, illus. Friso Henstra (New York: Parents' Magazine Press, 1969), and Harriet Herman, *The Forest Princess*, illus. Carole Petersen Dwinell (Berkeley: Over the Rainbow Press, 1974).

✿ SELECT BIBLIOGRAPHY ✿

Aarne, Antti. *The Types of the Folktale: A Classification and Bibliography*. Trans. and enlarged by Stith Thompson. Helsinki: Academia Scientiarum Fennica, 1981.

"Accusations of Abuse Haunt the Legacy of Dr. Bruno Bettelheim." In the *New York Times*, 4 November 1990. The Week in Review.

Afanasev, Alexander. *The Bawdy Peasant*. Ed. Giuseppe Pitré. London: Odyssey, 1970.

————. *Russian Fairy Tales*. Trans. Norbert Guterman. New York: Pantheon, 1945.

Andersen, Hans Christian. *The Fairy Tale of My Life: An Autobiography*. New York: Paddington, 1975.

————. *Hans Christian Andersen: Eighty Fairy Tales*. Trans. R. P. Keigwin. New York: Pantheon, 1982.

Anderson, Walter. *Der Schwank vom alten Hildebrand: Eine vergleichende Studie*. Dorpat: n.p., 1931.

Apuleius, Lucius. *The Golden Ass, Being the Metamorphoses of Lucius Apuleius*. Trans. W. Adlington. Rev. S. Gaselee. London: Heinemann, 1915.

Arens, W. *The Man-Eating Myth: Anthropology and Anthropophagy*. New York: Oxford University Press, 1979.

Arnim, Friedmund von, comp. *Hundert neue Märchen im Gebirge gesammelt*. Charlottenburg: Egbert Bauer, 1844.

Asbjørnsen, Peter Christen, and Jørgen Moe, comp. *Norwegian Folktales*. Trans. Pat Shaw and Carl Norman. New York: Pantheon, 1960.

Avery, Gillian. *Nineteenth-Century Children: Heroes and Heroines in English Children's Stories, 1780–1900*. London: Hodder and Stoughton, 1965.

Bachofen, J. J. *Myth, Religion, and Mother Right: Selected Writings of J. J. Bachofen*. Trans. Ralph Manheim. Princeton: Princeton University Press, Bollingen, 1967.

Bakhtin, Mikhail. *Rabelais and His World*. Trans. Helene Iswolsky. Cambridge: MIT Press, 1968.

Bang, Ilse. *Die Entwicklung der deutschen Märchenillustration*. München: Bruckmann, 1944.

Barchilon, Jacques. "Beauty and the Beast: From Myth to Fairy Tale." *Psychoanalysis and the Psychoanalytic Review* 46 (1959): 19–29.

Basile, Giambattista. *The Pentamerone*. Trans. and with an introduction by Benedetto Croce. Ed. N. M. Penzer. 2 vols. New York: John Lane, 1932.

Bastian, Ulrike. *Die "Kinder- und Hausmärchen" der Brüder Grimm in der literatur-pädagogischen Diskussion des 19. und 20. Jahrhunderts*. Giessen: Haag und Herchen, 1981.

Bator, Robert J. "Eighteenth-Century England versus the Fairy Tale." *Research Studies* 39 (1971): 1–10.

Baum, L. Frank. Introduction to *The Wonderful Wizard of Oz*. New York: Dover, 1960.

Baumgärtner, Alfred Clemens. "'Ach, du bists, alter Wasserpatscher . . .': Zur aktuellen Rezeption Grimmscher Märchen." *Mythen, Märchen und moderne Zeit: Beiträge zur Kinder- und Jugendliteratur*. Ed. Alfred Clemens Baumgärtner and Karl Ernst Maier. Würzburg: Königshausen und Neumann, 1987. 43–55.

Bechstein, Ludwig. *Märchen*. Stuttgart: Parkland, 1985.

Behlmer, Rudy. "They Called It 'Disney's Folly': Snow White and the Seven Dwarfs (1937)." In *America's Favorite Movies: Behind the Scenes*. New York: Ungar, 1982.

Beit, Hedwig von. *Symbolik des Märchens: Versuch einer Deutung*. 3 vols. 2d ed. Bern: Francke, 1960.

Belgrader, Michael. *Das Märchen von dem Machandelboom (KHM 47)*. Frankfurt a.M.: Peter D. Lang, 1980.

Ben-Amos, Dan, ed. *Folklore Genres*. Austin: University of Texas Press, 1976.

Benjamin, Walter. *Illuminations*. Trans. Harry Zohn. New York: Harcourt, Brace and World, 1968.

———. *Über Kinder, Jugend und Erziehung*. Frankfurt a.M.: Suhrkamp, 1969.

Benzel, Ulrich, and Walter Kniepert, eds. *Sudetendeutsche Volkserzählungen*. Marburg: Elwert, 1962.

"'Bettelheim Became the Very Evil He Loathed.'" *New York Times*. 20 November 1990, A20.

Bettelheim, Bruno. "Hänsel und Gretel, mein Lieblingsmärchen." In *Das Märchen -ein Märchen? Psychoanalytische Betrachtungen zu Wesen, Deutung und Wirkung der Märchen*. Ed. Jochen Stork, 137–60. Stuttgart: frommann-holzboog, 1987. 137–60.

———. *The Uses of Enchantment: The Meaning and Importance of Fairy Tales*. New York: Knopf, 1976; New York: Random House, Vintage Books, 1977.

Bloch, Dorothy. *"So the Witch Won't Eat Me": Fantasy and the Child's Fear of Infanticide*. Boston: Houghton Mifflin, 1978.

Bloom, Harold. "Driving out Demons." Review of *The Uses of Enchantment*, by Bruno Bettelheim. *New York Review of Books*, 15 July 1976, 10, 12.

Boccaccio, Giovanni. *The Decameron*. Trans. Frances Winwar. New York: Modern Library, 1930.

Böklen, Ernst. *Sneewittchenstudien: Fünfundsiebzig Varianten im engern Sinn*. Leipzig: Hinrich, 1910.

Bolte, Johannes, and Georg Polívka. *Anmerkungen zu den Kinder- und Hausmärchen der Brüder Grimm*. Leipzig: Dieterich, 1913.

Boose, Lynda E. and Betty S. Flowers, eds. *Daughters and Fathers*. Baltimore: Johns Hopkins University Press, 1989.

Boswell, John. *The Kindness of Strangers: The Abandonment of Children in Western Europe from Late Antiquity to the Renaissance*. New York: Pantheon, 1988.

Bottigheimer, Ruth B., ed. *Fairy Tales and Society. Illusion, Allusion and Paradigm*. Philadelphia: University of Pennsylvania Press, 1986.

———. *Grimms' Bad Girls & Bold Boys: The Moral & Social Vision of the Tales*. New Haven: Yale University Press, 1987.

Brackert, Helmut, ed. *Und wenn sie nicht gestorben sind. . . . Perspektiven auf das Märchen*. Frankfurt a.M.: Suhrkamp, 1980.

Bredsdorff, Elias. *Hans Christian Andersen*. New York: Scribner's, 1975.

Brémond, Claude. "Les Bons récompensées et les méchants punis." In *Sémiotique narrative et textuelle*. Ed. Claude Chabrol, 96–121. Paris: Larousse, 1973.

Brooks, Peter. *Reading for the Plot: Design and Intention in the Narrative*. New York: Random House, Vintage Books, 1984.

Brüggemann, Theodor, and Hans-Heino Ewers, eds. *Handbuch zur Kinder- und Jugendliteratur von 1750–1800*. Stuttgart: Metzler, 1982.

Brunvand, Jan Harold. "The Folktale Origin of *The Taming of the Shrew*." *Shakespeare Quarterly* 17 (1966): 345–59.

———. *The Study of American Folklore*. New York: Norton, 1968.

———. "*The Taming of the Shrew*: A Comparative Study of Oral and Literary Versions" Ph.D. diss., Indiana University, 1961.

Bunyan, John. *A Book for Boys and Girls: or, Country Rhimes for Children* [facsimile of first edition]. London: Elliot Stock, 1890.

Büsching, Johann Georg. *Volkssagen, Märchen und Legenden*. Leipzig: Reclam, 1812.

Calvino, Italo, comp. *Italian Folktales*. Trans. George Martin. New York: Pantheon, 1980.

Carroll, Lewis. *Alice's Adventures in Wonderland & Through the Looking-Glass*. Toronto: Bantam, 1981.

Carsch, Henry. "The Role of the Devil in Grimms' Tales: An Exploration of the Content and Function of Popular Tales." *Social Research* 35 (1968): 466–99.

Carter, Angela. *The Bloody Chamber and Other Stories*. Harmondsworth: Penguin, 1979.

Carter, Isabel Gordon. "Mountain White Folk-Lore: Tales from the Southern Blue Ridge." *Journal of American Folklore* 38 (1925): 366–68.

Cass, Joan E. *Literature and the Young Child*. London: Longmans, 1967.

Chase, Richard, comp. *American Folk Tales and Songs*. New York: Signet, 1956.

———, comp. *The Jack Tales*. New York: Houghton Mifflin, 1943.

Chaucer, Geoffrey. *The Canterbury Tales*. Trans. Nevill Coghill. London: Penguin, 1951.

Child's Instructor, The; intended as a first book, for children. London: Thorp and Burch, 1828.

Chodorow, Nancy. *The Reproduction of Mothering: Psychoanalysis and the Sociology of Gender*. Berkeley and Los Angeles: University of California Press, 1978.

Chutes and Ladders. Milton Bradley Co. 1979.

Clarkson, Atelia, and Gilbert B. Cross, eds. *World Folktales: A Scribner Resource Collection*. New York: Charles Scribner's Sons, 1980.

Clifford, Lucy Lane. *Anyhow Stories, Moral and Otherwise*. London: Macmillan, 1882.

Clifford, Mrs. W. K. *The Last Touches and Other Stories*. New York: Macmillan, 1892.

Cobbett, William. *Advice to Young Men, and (Incidentally) to Young Women, in the Middle and Higher Ranks of Life*. London: Mills, Jowett, and Mills, 1829.

Collodi, Carlo. *The Adventures of Pinocchio*. Trans. E. Harden. New York: Knopf, 1988.

Cott, Jonathan. *Pipers at the Gates of Dawn: The Wisdom of Children's Literature*. New York: Random House, 1981.

Cott, Jonathan, et al., eds. *Masterworks of Children's Literature*. 10 vols. New York: Chelsea House, 1984.

Cox, Marian Roalfe. *Cinderella: Three Hundred and Forty-five Variants of Cinderella, Catskin, and Cap o' Rushes*. Ed. Andrew Lang. London: David Nutt, 1893.

Crago, Hugo. "The Roots of Response." *Children's Literature Association Quarterly* 10 (1985): 100–104.

Crane, Thomas Frederick, comp. *Italian Popular Tales*. Boston: Houghton Mifflin, 1885.

Croce, Benedetto. Introduction to *The Pentamerone of Giambattista Basile*. 2 vols. Ed. N. M. Penzer. London: John Lane, 1932.

Cruikshank, George, ed. and illus. *Cinderella and the Glass Slipper*. London: David Bogue, 1853.

———, ed. and illus. *The History of Jack & the Bean-Stalk*. London: David Bogue, 1854.

———, ed. and illus. *Hop-o'-my-Thumb and the Seven-League Boots*. London: David Bogue, 1853.

Darnton, Robert. "Peasants Tell Tales: The Meaning of Mother Goose." In *The Great Cat Massacre and Other Episodes in French Cultural History*. New York: Basic Books, 1984.

Darton, F. J. Harvey. *Children's Books in England: Five Centuries of Social Life*. Cambridge: Cambridge University Press, 1932.

Darton, William. *Little Truths, for the Instruction of Children*. London: Darton and Harvey, 1802.

Dasent, George Webbe. *Popular Tales from the Norse*. New York: Putnam's, 1888.

Davis, Arthur Paul. *Isaac Watts: His Life and Work*. New York: Dryden, 1943.

Dawkins, R. M., comp. and trans. *Modern Greek Folktales*. Oxford: Clarendon, 1953.

Dégh, Linda. *Folktales and Society: Storytelling in a Hungarian Peasant Community*. Trans. Emily M. Schossberger. Bloomington: Indiana University Press, 1969.

Delarue, Paul. "Les Contes Merveilleux de Perrault et la tradition populaire: I. Le Petit Chaperon Rouge." *Bulletin folklorique d'Ile-de-France* (1951): 221–28, 251–60, 283–91; (1953): 511–17.

———, ed. *Borzoi Book of French Folktales*. Trans. Austin E. Fife. New York: Knopf, 1956.

Delarue, Paul, and Marie-Louise Tenèze, eds. *Le Conte populaire français*. 3 vols. Paris: Editions G.-P. Maisonneuve et Larose, 1976.

Démoris, Réné. "Du littéraire au littéral dans *Peau d'Ane* de Perrault." *Revue des sciences humaines* 43 (1977): 261–79.

Devereux, G. "The Social and Cultural Implications of Incest among the Mohave Indians." *Psychoanalytical Quarterly* 8 (1939): 510–33.

de Vries, Leonard, ed. *Flowers of Delight*. London: Dennis Dobson, 1965.

Dickens, Charles. "Frauds on the Fairies." *Household Words: A Weekly Journal*, 97–100. New York: McElrath and Barker, 1854.

Dinnerstein, Dorothy. *The Mermaid and the Minotaur: Sexual Arrangements and the Human Malaise*. New York: Harper & Row, 1976.

Disney, Walt. *55 Favorite Stories Adapted from Disney Films*. Golden Book, Western Publishing, 1960.

Doderer, Klaus, ed. *Walter Benjamin und die Kinderliteratur: Aspekte der Kinderkultur in den zwanziger Jahren*. Munich: Juventa, 1988.

Dorfman, Ariel. *The Empire's Old Clothes*. New York: Pantheon, 1983.

Dundes, Alan. "Bruno Bettelheim's Uses of Enchantment and Abuses of Scholarship," *Journal of American Folklore* 104 (1991): 74–83.

————. "The Psychoanalytic Study of the Grimms' Tales with Special Reference to 'The Maiden Without Hands' (AT 706)." *Germanic Review* 62 (1987): 50–65.

————, ed. *Cinderella: A Casebook*. New York: Garland, 1982; Madison: University of Wisconsin Press, 1988.

————, ed. *Little Red Riding Hood: A Casebook*. Madison: University of Wisconsin Press, 1989.

Edwards, Lee R. "The Labors of Psyche: Toward a Theory of Female Heroism." *Critical Inquiry* 6 (1979): 33–49.

Egoff, Sheila, and G. T. Stubbs, and L. F. Ashley, ed. *Only Connect: Readings on Children's Literature*. Toronto: Oxford University Press, 1969.

Elias, Norbert. *The History of Manners*. Trans. Edmund Jephcott. New York: Pantheon, 1978.

Ellis, John M. *One Fairy Story Too Many: The Brothers Grimm and Their Tales*. Chicago: University of Chicago Press, 1983.

————. "What Really is the Value of the 'New' Grimm Discovery?" *German Quarterly* 58 (1975): 87–90.

Enzyklopädie des Märchens. Berlin: Walter de Gruyter, 1975- .

Farrer, Claire R., ed. *Women and Folklore*. Austin: University of Texas Press, 1975.

Favat, F. André. *Child and Tale. The Origin of Interest*. Urbana, Ill.: National Council of Teachers of English, 1977.

Federspiel, Christa. *Vom Volksmärchen zum Kindermärchen*. Vienna: Notring, 1968.

Fenichel, Otto. *Collected Papers*. New York: Norton, 1953.

Fenster, Thelma S. "Beaumanoir's *La Manekine*: Kin D(r)ead: Incest, Doubling, and Death." *American Imago* 39 (1982): 41–58.

Ferguson, Mary Anne. "The Female Novel of Development and the Myth of Psyche." In *The Voyage In: Fictions of Female Development*. Ed. Elizabeth Abel, Marianne Hirsch, and Elizabeth Langland. Hanover: University Press of New England, 1983. 228–43.

Fiedler, Leslie A. "Fairy Tales—Without Apologies." Review of *The Uses of Enchantment*, by Bruno Bettelheim. *Saturday Review*, 15 May 1976.

Fink, Gonthier-Louis. "Les Avatars de Rumpelstilzchen: La Vie d'un Conte Populaire." *Deutsch-Französisches Gespräch im Lichte der Märchen*. Ed. Ernst Kracht. Münster: Aschendorff, 1964.

Fish, Stanley. *Is There a Text in This Class? The Authority of Interpretive Communities*. Cambridge: Harvard University Press, 1980.

Folktales of England. Ed. Katharine M. Briggs and Ruth L. Tongue. Chicago: University of Chicago Press, 1965.

Folktales of Norway. Trans. Pat Shaw Iversen. Ed. Reidar Christiansen. Chicago: University of Chicago Press, 1964.

Foucault, Michel. *Discipline and Punish: The Birth of the Prison*. Trans. Alan Sheridan. New York: Random House, Vintage Books, 1977.

———. *The History of Sexuality*. Trans. Robert Hurley. New York: Random House, Vintage Books, 1978.

Freeman, James A. "Donald Duck: How Children (Mainly Boys) Viewed Their Parents (Mainly Fathers), 1943–1960." *Children's Literature* 6 (1977): 150–64.

Freud, Sigmund. "Female Sexuality." Vol. 21 of *The Standard Edition of the Complete Psychological Works of Sigmund Freud*, pp. 223–43. Trans. James Strachey. London: Hogarth, 1961.

———. *The Future of an Illusion*. Vol 21 of the *Standard Edition*.

———. *The Interpretation of Dreams*. Vol. 4 of the *Standard Edition*.

———. *Totem and Taboo: Some Points of Agreement between the Mental Lives of Savages and Neurotics*. Vol. 13 of the *Standard Edition*.

Friedländer, Ludwig. "Das Märchen von Amor und Psyche." *Darstellungen aus der Sittengeschichte Roms*. Ed. Georg Wissowa. Aalen: Scientia, 1964.

Früh, Sigrid, ed. *Die Frau, die auszog, ihren Mann zu erlösen: Europäische Frauenmärchen*. Frankfurt a.M.: Fischer, 1985.

Garner, Shirley Nelson, Claire Kahane, and Madelon Sprengnether, eds. *The (M)other Tongue: Essays in Feminist Psychoanalytic Interpretation*. Ithaca: Cornell University Press, 1985.

Geninasca, Jacques. "Conte Populaire et identité du cannibalisme." *Nouvelle Revue de Psychanalyse* 6 (1972): 215–30.

Gerstl, Quirin. *Die Brüder Grimm als Erzieher: Pädagogische Analyse des Märchens*. Munich: Ehrenwirth, 1964.

Gilbert, Sandra M., and Susan Gubar. *The Madwoman in the Attic: The Woman Writer and the Nineteenth-Century Literary Imagination*. New Haven: Yale University Press, 1979.

Gilligan, Carol. *In a Different Voice: Psychological Theory and Women's Development*. Cambridge: Harvard University Press, 1982.

———. "Oedipus - Psyche: Two Stories about Love." MLA Convention. San Francisco, Dec. 1989.

Godden, Rumer. *Hans Christian Andersen: A Great Life in Brief*. New York: Knopf, 1955.

Goethe, Johann Wolfgang von. *Faust: A Tragedy*. Trans. Walter Arndt. Ed. Cyrus Hamlin. New York: Norton, 1976.

Gonzenbach, Laura. *Sizilianische Märchen*. Leipzig: Wilhelm Engelmann, 1870.

Graves, Robert, trans. *The Transformations of Lucius, Otherwise Known as The Golden Ass*. New York: Farrar, Straus and Giroux, 1951.

Green, Roger Lancelyn. *Tellers of Tales*. Leicester, England: Edmund Ward, 1946.

Greenacre, Phyllis. "Hans Christian Andersen and Children." *Psychoanalytic Study of the Child* 38 (1983): 617–35.

Greenblatt, Stephen. *Representing the English Renaissance*. Ed. and with an introduction by Stephen Greenblatt. Berkeley and Los Angeles: University of California Press, 1988.

Grimm, A. L. *Lina's Märchenbuch: Eine Weynachtsgabe*. Frankfurt: Wilman's, 1816.

Grimm, Jacob. *Altdeutsche Wälder*. Ed. Wilhelm Schoof. Darmstadt: Wissenschaftliche Buchgesellschaft, 1966.

Grimm, Jacob, and Wilhelm Grimm. *Brüder Grimm. Kinder- und Hausmärchen* [2d edition of 1819]. 2 vols. Ed. Heinz Rölleke. Köln: Eugen Dieterichs, 1982.

———. *The Complete Fairy Tales of the Brothers Grimm*. Trans. Jack Zipes. Toronto: Bantam, 1987.

———. *German Fairy Tales*. Ed. Helmut Brackert and Volkmar Sander. New York: Continuum, 1985.

———. *Kinder- und Hausmärchen* [1857 edition]. 3 vols. Ed. Heinz Rölleke. Stuttgart: Reclam, 1980.

———. *Kinder- und Hausmärchen gesammelt durch die Brüder Grimm* [3d edition of 1837]. Ed. Heinz Rölleke. Frankfurt a.M.: Deutscher Klassiker Verlag, 1985.

———. *Kinder- und Hausmärchen. Gesammelt durch die Brüder Grimm* [1st edition]. 2 vols. Ed. Heinz Rölleke. Göttingen: Vandenhoeck & Ruprecht, 1986.

———. *Kinder- und Hausmärchen gesammelt durch die Brüder Grimm: Kleine Ausgabe von 1858*. Ed. Heinz Rölleke. Frankfurt a.M.: Insel, 1985.

Grimm, Wilhelm. *Dear Mili*. Trans. Ralph Manheim. Illus. Maurice Sendak. New York: Farrar, Straus and Giroux, 1988.

Grundtvig, Svend, comp. *Danish Fairy Tales*. Trans. Gustav Hein. London: George G. Harrap, 1914.

Grylls, David. *Guardians and Angels: Parents and Children in Nineteenth-Century Literature*. London: Faber and Faber, 1978.

Halpert, Herbert. "Folklore and Obscenity: Definitions and Problems." *Journal of American Folklore* 75 (1962): 190–94.

Hamann, Hermann. *Die literarischen Vorlagen der Kinder- und Hausmärchen und ihre Bearbeitung durch die Brüder Grimm*. Berlin: Mayer & Müller, 1906.

Hanks, Carole, and D. T. Hanks, Jr. "Perrault's 'Little Red Riding Hood': Victim of the Revisers." *Children's Literature* 7 (1983): 68–77.

Harner, Michael. "The Ecological Basis for Aztec Sacrifice." *American Ethnologist* 4 (1977): 117–35.

Hays, H. R. *The Dangerous Sex: The Myth of Feminine Evil*. New York: Putnam, 1964.

Hearn, Michael Patrick. *The Annotated Wizard of Oz*. New York: Clarkson N. Potter, 1973.

Hearne, Betsy. *Beauty and the Beast: Visions and Revisions of an Old Tale*. Chicago: University of Chicago Press, 1989.

Heilbrun, Carolyn G. "What was Penelope Unweaving?" *Hamlet's Mother and Other Women*. New York: Columbia University Press, 1990.

Heisig, James W. "Bruno Bettelheim and Fairy Tales." *Children's Literature* 6 (1977): 93–114.

Herman, Harriet. *The Forest Princess*. Illus. Carole Petersen Dwinell. Berkeley, Calif.: Over the Rainbow Press, 1974.

Herman, Judith Lewis. *Father-Daughter Incest*. Cambridge: Harvard University Press, 1981.

Hirsch, Marianne. "Ideology, Form, and 'Allerleirauh': Reflections on *Reading for the Plot*," *Children's Literature* 14. New Haven: Yale University Press, 1986. 163–68.

History of Little Goody Two-Shoes, The; Otherwise called, Mrs. Margery Two-Shoes. London: John Newbery, 1765.

Hoffmann, Heinrich. *Der Struwwelpeter* (Volksausgabe). N.p.: n.p., n.d.

Holbeck, Bengt. *The Interpretation of Fairy Tales: Danish Folklore in a European Perspective.* Helsinki: Academia Scientiarum Fennica, 1987.

Horn, Katalin. *Der aktive und der passive Märchenheld.* Basel: Schweizerische Gesellschaft für Volkskunde, 1983.

————. "Motivationen und Funktionen der tödlichen Bedrohung in den Kinder- und Hausmärchen der Brüder Grimm." *Schweizerisches Archiv für Volkskunde* 74 (1978): 20–40.

Hoyme, James B. "The 'Abandoning Impulse' in Human Parents." *The Lion and the Unicorn* 12 (1988): 32–46.

Huck, Charlotte. *Princess Furball.* Illus. Anita Lobel. New York: Greenwillow Books, 1989.

Hughes, Felicity A. "Children's Literature: Theory and Practice." *ELH* 45 (1978): 542–61.

Hunt, Peter, ed. *Children's Literature: The Development of Criticism.* London: Routledge, 1990.

Hürlimann, Bettina. *Three Centuries of Children's Books in Europe.* Trans. and ed. Brian W. Alderson. London: Oxford University Press, 1967.

Hurst, Mary Jane. *The Voice of the Child in American Literature: Linguistic Approaches to Fictional Child Language.* Lexington: University of Kentucky Press, 1990.

Isadora, Rachel. *The Princess and the Frog.* New York: Greenwillow Books, 1989.

Jackson, Mary V. *Engines of Instruction, Mischief, and Magic: Children's Literature in England from Its Beginnings to 1839.* Lincoln: University of Nebraska Press, 1989.

Jacobs, Joseph, comp. *English Fairy Tales.* London: The Bodley Head, 1968.

Janeway, James. *A Token for Children: Being an Account of the Conversion, Holy and Exemplary Lives, and Joyful Deaths of Several Young Children.* London: Francis Westley, 1825.

Johnson, A. E., trans. *Perrault's Complete Fairy Tales.* New York: Dodd, Mead, 1961.

Jolles, André. *Einfache Formen.* Halle: Max Niemeyer, 1929.

Jones, Ernest. *The Life and Work of Sigmund Freud.* 3 vols. New York: Basic Books, 1953–57.

Jones, Gwyn, comp. *Scandinavian Legends and Folk-tales.* Illus. Joan Kiddell-Monroe. London: Oxford University Press, 1956.

Kamenetsky, Christa. *Children's Literature in Hitler's Germany: The Cultural Policy of National Socialism.* Athens: Ohio University Press, 1984.

Karlinger, Felix, ed. *Wege der Märchenforschung.* Darmstadt: Wissenschaftliche Buchgesellschaft, 1973.

Kilner, Dorothy. *The Village School; A Collection of Entertaining Histories, for the Instruction and Amusement of All Good Children.* London: John Harris, 1831.

Kilner, Mary Ann. *The Memoirs of a Peg-Top.* London: Marshall, 1781.

————. *William Sedley: or, The Evil Day Deferred.* London: n.p., 1783.

Klein, Melanie. *Love, Guilt and Reparation & Other Works, 1921–1945.* N.p.: Delacorte Press, 1975.

Kloss, Robert J. "Fantasy and Fear in the Work of Maurice Sendak." *Psychoanalytic Review* 76 (1989): 567–79.

Klotz, Volker. *Das europäische Kunstmärchen.* Stuttgart: Metzler, 1985.

————. "Weltordnung im Märchen." *Neue Rundschau* 81 (1970): 73–91.

Kolbenschlag, Madonna. *Kiss Sleeping Beauty Good-Bye: Breaking the Spell of Feminine Myths and Models.* New York: Doubleday, 1979.

Könneker, Marie-Luise, ed. *Kinderschaukel: Ein Lesebuch zur Geschichte der Kindheit in Deutschland, 1756–1860.* Darmstadt: Luchterhand, 1976.

Kristeva, Julia. "Stabat mater." *The Female Body in Western Culture: Contemporary Perspectives.* Ed. Susan Rubin Suleiman. Cambridge: Harvard University Press, 1985.

Kunike, Hugo, ed. *Märchen aus Sibirien.* Jena: Eugen Diederichs, 1940.

Künzig, Johannes, and Waltraut Werner, eds. *Ungarndeutsche Märchenerzähler II.* Freiburg: Rombach and Co., 1971.

Kunzle, David. *The Early Comic Strip: Narrative Strips and Picture Stories in the European Broadsheet from c. 1450 to 1825.* Berkeley and Los Angeles: University of California Press, 1973.

Laiblin, Wilhelm, ed. *Märchenforschung und Tiefenpsychologie.* Darmstadt: Wissenschaftliche Buchgesellschaft, 1969.

Lambertz, Maximilian, trans. *Die geflügelte Schwester und die Dunklen der Erde: Albanische Volksmärchen.* Eisenach: Erich Röth, 1952.

"Land of the Young, The." *Time,* 29 Dec. 1980, 66.

Lanes, Selma G. *The Art of Maurice Sendak.* New York: Harry N. Abrams, 1980.

————. *Down the Rabbit Hole: Adventures & Misadventures in the Realm of Children's Literature.* New York: Atheneum, 1971.

Lang, Andrew, comp. *The Blue Fairy Book.* Ed. Brian Alderson. Harmondsworth: Penguin, Puffin Books, 1987.

————, ed. *The Red Fairy Book.* London: Longman's, Green, 1909.

Legman, G. "Toward a Motif-Index of Erotic Humor." *Journal of American Folklore* 75 (1962): 227–48.

Lévi-Strauss, Claude. *The Elementary Structures of Kinship.* Rev. ed. Trans. James Harle Bell, John Richard von Sturmer, and Rodney Needham, ed. Boston: Beacon Press, 1969.

————. *Man, Culture, and Society.* Ed. Harry Shapiro. New York: Oxford University Press, 1956.

Lieberman, Marcia. "Some Day My Prince Will Come: Female Acculturation through the Fairy Tale." *College English* 34 (1972): 383–95.

Liebs, Elke. *Kindheit und Tod: Der Rattenfänger-Mythos als Beitrag zu einer Kulturgeschichte der Kindheit.* Munich: Fink, 1986.

Lincoln, Bruce. *Myth, Cosmos, and Society: Indo-European Themes of Creation and Destruction.* Cambridge: Harvard University Press, 1986.

Lindsay, Jack, trans. *The Transformations of Lucius Otherwise Known as The Golden Ass.* Bloomington: Indiana University Press, 1960.

Locke, John. *Some Thoughts Concerning Education. The Works of John Locke.* Vol. 9. London: W. Otridge and Son, 1812.

Lokke, Kari E. "*Bluebeard* and *The Bloody Chamber*: The Grotesque of Self-Parody and Self-Assertion." *Frontiers* 10 (1988): 7–12.

Löwis of Menar, August von, ed. *Finnische und estnische Volksmärchen.* Jena: Eugen Diederichs, 1922.

Luce, Clare Boothe. "Frogs and Freudians." Review of *The Uses of Enchantment*, by Bruno Bettelheim. *National Review*, 20 August 1976: 908–9.

Lurie, Alison, comp. and ed. *Clever Gretchen and Other Forgotten Folktales.* Illus. Margot Tomes. New York: Thomas Y. Crowell, 1980.

———. *Don't Tell the Grown-ups: Subversive Children's Literature.* Boston: Little, Brown, 1990.

———. "The Haunted Wood." Rev. of *The Uses of Enchantment*, by Bruno Bettelheim. *Harper's*, June 1976: 94, 96–97.

Luther, Martin. *Dr. Martin Luthers Grosser Katechismus.* Ed. Gotthilf Hermann. Gütersloh: Gerd Mohn, n.d.

Lüthi, Max. *The European Folktale: Form and Nature.* Trans. John D. Niles. Philadelphia: Institute for the Study of Human Issues, 1982.

———. *The Fairy Tale as Art Form and Portrait of Man.* Trans. Jon Erickson. Bloomington: University of Indiana Press, 1985.

Mackensen, Lutz, ed. *Handwörterbuch des deutschen Märchens.* Berlin: de Gruyter, 1930–1940.

Mallet, Carl-Heinz. *Kennen Sie Kinder? Wie Kinder denken, handeln und fühlen, aufgezeigt an vier Grimmschen Märchen.* Hamburg: Hoffmann and Campe, 1981.

———. *Kopf ab! Gewalt im Märchen.* Hamburg: Rasch und Röhring, 1985.

Massignon, Geneviève, ed. *Folktales of France.* Trans. Jacqueline Hyland. Chicago: University of Chicago Press, 1968.

Masson, Jeffrey Moussaieff. *The Assault on Truth: Freud's Suppression of the Seduction Theory.* New York: Farrar, Straus and Giroux, 1984.

Mattenklott, Gundel. *Zauberkreide: Kinderliteratur seit 1945.* Stuttgart: Metzler, 1989.

Megas, Georgios A., ed. *Folktales of Greece.* Trans. Helen Colaclides. Chicago: University of Chicago Press, 1970.

Mieder, Wolfgang. "Modern Anglo-American Variants of the Frog Prince (AaTh 440)." *New York Folklore* 6 (1980): 111–35.

———, ed. *Disenchantments: An Anthology of Modern Fairy Tale Poetry.* Hanover: University Press of New England, 1985.

———, ed. *Grimmige Märchen: Prosatexte von Ilse Aichinger bis Martin Walser.* Frankfurt a.M.: R. G. Fischer, 1986.

Mikkelsen, Nina. "Sendak, *Snow White*, and the Child as Literary Critic." *Language Arts* 62 (1985): 362–73.

Miles, Margaret R. *Carnal Knowing: Female Nakedness and Religious Meaning in the Christian West.* Boston: Beacon Press, 1989.

Miller, Alice. *For Your Own Good: Hidden Cruelty in Child-rearing and the Roots of Violence.* Trans. Hildegarde Hannum and Hunter Hannum. New York: Farrar, Straus and Giroux, 1983.

———. *Thou Shalt Not Be Aware: Society's Betrayal of the Child*. Trans. Hildegarde and Hunter Hannum. New York: Farrar, Straus and Giroux, 1984.

Miller, D. A. *The Novel and the Police*. Berkeley and Los Angeles: University of California Press, 1988.

Minard, Rosemary, ed. *Womenfolk and Fairy Tales*. Illus. Suzanna Klein. Boston: Houghton Mifflin, 1975.

Mitchell, Lucy Sprague. *Here and Now Story Book*. New York: Dutton, 1921.

Mönckeberg, Vilma. *Das Märchen und unsere Welt: Erfahrungen und Einsichten*. Düsseldorf: Diederichs, 1972.

Montgomerie, Norah, and William Montgomerie, comp. and ed. *The Well at the World's End: Folk Tales of Scotland*. Toronto: The Bodley Head, 1956.

Montrose, Louis Adrian. "'Shaping Fantasies': Figurations of Gender and Power in Elizabethan Culture." *Representing the English Renaissance*. Ed. Stephen Greenblatt. Berkeley and Los Angeles: University of California Press, 1988.

Mossmann, Carol A. "Targeting the Unspeakable: Stendhal and Figures of Pregnancy." *Nineteenth-Century French Studies* 16 (1988): 257–69.

Musäus, J.K.A. *Volksmärchen der Deutschen*. Munich: Winkler, 1976.

Ness, Evaline, illus. *Mr. Miacca: An English Folktale*. New York: Holt, Rinehart and Winston, 1967.

Neumann, Erich. *Amor and Psyche: The Psychic Development of the Feminine. A Commentary on the Tale by Apuleius*. Trans. Ralph Manheim. Princeton: Princeton University Press, Bollingen, 1956.

Newell, William Wells, comp. *Games and Songs of American Children*. New York: Harper & Bros., 1884.

Opie, Iona and Peter Opie, comps. *The Classic Fairy Tales*. New York: Oxford University Press, 1974.

———, eds. *The Oxford Dictionary of Nursery Rhymes*. Oxford: Oxford University Press, 1951.

Ortner, Sherry B. "Is Female to Male as Nature Is to Culture?" In *Woman, Culture, and Society*. Ed. Michelle Zimbalist Rosaldo and Louise Lamphere. Stanford: Stanford University Press, 1974. 67–87.

Paul, Lissa. "Enigma Variations: What Feminist Theory Knows about Children's Literature." *Signal* 54 (1987): 186–201.

Paulson, Tim. *Jack and the Beanstalk*. Illus. Mark Corcoran. New York: Birch Lane, 1990.

Péju, Pierre. *La Petit Fille dans la forêt des contes*. Paris: Robert Laffont, 1981.

Perrault, Charles. *Contes*. Ed. Gilbert Rouger. Paris: Garnier Frères, 1967.

———. *Perrault's Complete Fairy Tales*. Trans. A. E. Johnson, et al. New York: Dodd, Mead, 1961.

Peter, Jean-Pierre. "Ogres d'Archives." *Nouvelle Revue de Psychanalyse* 6 (1972): 249–67.

Phelps, Ethel Johnston. *The Maid of the North: Feminist Folktales from around the World*. Illus. Lloyd Bloom. New York: Henry Holt, 1981.

———, ed. *Tatterhood and Other Tales*. Illus. Pamela Baldwin Ford. Old Westbury, N.Y.: Feminist Press, 1978.

Philip, Neil, ed. *The Cinderella Story: The Origins and Variations of the Story Known As "Cinderella."* London: Penguin, 1989.

Philippson, Ernst. *Der Märchentypus von König Drosselbart.* Greifswald: Academia Scientiarum Fennica, 1923.

Phillips, John A. *Eve: The History of an Idea.* San Francisco: Harper & Row, 1984.

Piaget, Jean. *The Moral Judgment of the Child.* New York: Free Press, 1965.

Pickard, P. M. *I Could a Tale Unfold: Violence, Horror and Sensationalism in Stories for Children.* London: Tavistock, 1961.

Pickering, Samuel F., Jr. *John Locke and Children's Books in Eighteenth-Century England.* Knoxville: University of Tennessee Press, 1981.

Plath, Sylvia. *Collected Poems.* Ed. Ted Hughes. New York: Harper & Row, 1981.

Plumb, J. H. "The New World of Children in Eighteenth-Century England." *Past and Present* 67 (1975): 64–93.

Pogrebin, Letty Cottin, ed. *Stories for Free Children.* New York: McGraw-Hill, 1982.

Pourrat, Henri, comp. *French Folktales.* Trans. Royall Tyler. New York: Pantheon, 1989.

Propp, Vladimir. *Morphology of the Folktale.* Trans. Laurence Scott. 2d rev. ed. Austin: University of Texas Press, 1968.

———. *Theory and History of Folklore.* Trans. Ariadna Y. Martin and Richard P. Martin. Ed. Anatoly Liberman. Minneapolis: University of Minnesota Press, 1984.

Pyles, Marian S. *Death and Dying in Children's and Young People's Literature: A Survey and Bibliography.* Jefferson, N.C.: McFarland & Co., 1988.

Randolph, Vance, comp. *Pissing in the Snow and Other Ozark Folktales.* Urbana: University of Illinois Press, 1976.

———, comp. *Sticks in the Knapsack and Other Ozark Folk Tales.* New York: Columbia University Press, 1958.

Rank, Otto. *The Myth of the Birth of the Hero and Other Writings.* Ed. Philip Freund. New York: Knopf, 1932; New York: Random House, Vintage Books, 1964.

Ranke, Kurt. *Die zwei Brüder: Eine Studie zur vergleichenden Märchenforschung.* Helsinki: Academia Scientiarum Fennica, 1934.

———, comp. *Folktales of Germany.* Trans. Lotte Baumann. Chicago: University of Chicago Press, 1966.

———, comp. *Schleswig-Holsteinische Volksmärchen.* Kiel: Ferdinand Hirt, 1958.

Rich, Adrienne. *Of Woman Born: Motherhood as Experience and Institution.* New York: Norton, 1976.

Richter, Dieter. *Das fremde Kind: Zur Entstehung der Kindheitsbilder des bürgerlichen Zeitalters.* Frankfurt a.M.: Fischer, 1987.

Richter, Dieter, and Johannes Merkel. *Märchen, Phantasie und soziales Lernen.* Berlin: Basis, 1974.

Ritz, Hans, ed. *Die Geschichte vom Rotkäppchen: Ursprünge, Analysen, Parodien eines Märchens.* Emstal: Muriverlag, 1981.

Roberts, Leonard. "The Gold in the Chimney." *Midwest Folklore* 6 (1956): 76–78.

Roberts, Warren E. *The Tale of the Kind and the Unkind Girls: A-Th 480 and Related Tales.* Berlin: Walter de Gruyter, 1958.

Röhrich, Lutz. "Die Grausamkeit im deutschen Märchen." *Rheinisches Jahrbuch für Volkskunde* 6 (1955): 176–224.

———. "Märchen mit schlechtem Ausgang." *Hessische Blätter für Volkskunde* 49/50 (1958): 219–45.

———. *Wage es, den Frosch zu küssen! Das Grimmschen Märchen Nummer Eins in seinen Wandlungen.* Köln: Diederichs, 1987.

Rölleke, Heinz. "Allerleirauh: Eine bisher unbekannte Fassung vor Grimm." *Fabula* 13 (1972): 153–59.

———. "Tales from Grimm—Pictures by Maurice Sendak: Entdeckungen und Vermutungen." In *Brüder Grimm Gedenken.* Ed. Ludwig Denecke. Marburg: N. G. Elwert, 1975. 242–45.

———. *"Wo das Wünschen noch geholfen hat": Gesammelte Aufsätze zu den Kinder- und Hausmärchen der Brüder Grimm.* Bonn: Bouvier, 1985.

Rooth, Anna Birgitta. *The Cinderella Cycle.* Lund: Gleerup, 1951.

Rose, Jacqueline. *The Case of Peter Pan or The Impossibility of Children's Fiction.* London: Macmillan, 1984.

Rosenman, Stanley. "The Myth of the Birth of the Hero Revisited: Disasters and Brutal Child Rearing." *American Imago* 45 (1988): 1–44.

Rougemont, Denis de. *Love in the Western World.* Rev. ed. Trans. Montgomery Belgion. New York: Harper & Row, 1940.

Rumpf, Marianne. "Caterinella: Ein italienisches Warnmärchen." *Fabula* 1 (1957): 76–84.

———. "Spinnstubenfrauen, Kinderschreckgestalten und Frau Perchta." *Fabula* 17 (1976): 215–42.

Rustin, Margaret, and Michael Rustin. *Narratives of Love and Loss: Studies in Modern Children's Fiction.* London: Verso, 1987.

Rutschky, Katharina, ed. *Schwarze Pädagogik: Quellen zur Naturgeschichte der bürgerlichen Erziehung.* Berlin: Ullstein, 1977.

Sagan, Eli. *Cannibalism: Human Aggression and Cultural Form.* New York: Harper & Row, 1974.

Sale, Roger. *Fairy Tales and After: From Snow White to E. B. White.* Cambridge: Harvard University Press, 1978.

Sanday, Peggy Reeves. *Divine Hunger: Cannibalism as a Cultural System.* London: Cambridge University Press, 1986.

Schenda, Rudolf. "Märchen erzählen - Märchen verbreiten: Wandel in den Mitteilungsformen einer populären Gattung." In *Über Märchen für Kinder von heute: Essays zu ihrem Wandel und ihrer Funktion.* Ed. Klaus Doderer. Weinheim: Beltz, 1983. 25–43.

———. *Volk ohne Buch.* Frankfurt a.M.: Klostermann, 1970.

Scherf, Walter. *Die Herausforderung des Dämons: Form und Funktion grausiger Kindermärchen.* Munich: K. G. Saur, 1987.

———. "Family Conflicts and Emancipation in Fairy Tales." *Children's Literature* 3 (1983): 77–93.

———. *Lexikon der Zaubermärchen.* Stuttgart: Alfred Kröner, 1982.

Schickel, Richard. *The Disney Version: The Life, Times, Art and Commerce of Walt Disney.* New York: Simon and Schuster, 1968.

Schittek, Claudia. "Der Herr Korbes: Die Sprache der Märchen in den Reimen und Sprüchen der Brüder Grimm." *Aufmerksamkeit: Klaus Heinrich zum 50. Geburtstag.* Frankfurt a.M.: Roter Stern, 1979. 396–402.

Schlumbohm, Jürgen. "'Tradionale' Kollektivität und 'moderne' Individualität: Einige Fragen und Thesen für eine historische Sozialisationsforschung." *Bürger und Bürgerlichkeit im Zeitalter der Aufklärung.* Ed. Rudolf Vierhaus. Heidelberg: Lambert Schneider, 1981.

Schmidt, Leopold. "Das steirische Schwankspiel vom Bauern und seinem Weib im Rahmen der Volksüberlieferung vom Meister Hildebrand." *Festschrift für Eduard Castle.* Vienna: Notring der wissenschaftlichen Verbände Österreichs, 1955.

Schnack, Ingeborg, and Wilhelm Schoof, eds. *Briefe der Brüder Grimm an Savigny.* Berlin: Erich Schmidt, 1953.

Schwarcz, H. Joseph. "Machine Animism in Modern Children's Literature." *A Critical Approach to Children's Literature.* Ed. Sara Innis Fenwick, pp. 78–95. Chicago: University of Chicago Press, 1967.

Scielzo, Caroline. "An Analysis of Bába-Yagá in Folklore and Fairy Tales." *American Journal of Psychoanalysis* 43 (1983): 167–75.

Sendak, Maurice. *Caldecott & Co.* New York: Farrar, Straus and Giroux, Michael di Capua, 1988.

————. *Where the Wild Things Are.* New York: Harper & Row, 1963.

————, illus. *The Juniper Tree and Other Tales from Grimm.* Trans. Lore Segal and Randall Jarrell. New York: Farrar, Straus and Giroux, 1973.

Sherwood, Martha Butt. *History of the Fairchild Family.* By Martha Sherwood. Vol. 2 of *The Works of Mrs. Sherwood.* New York: Harper, 1864.

Shorto, Russell. *Cinderella.* Illus. T. Lewis. New York: Birch Lane, 1990.

Simpson, Jacqueline, trans. *Icelandic Folktales and Legends.* Berkeley and Los Angeles: University of California Press, 1972.

Singer, Isaac Bashevis. "Isaac Bashevis Singer on Writing for Children." *Children's Literature* 6 (1977): 9–16.

Sloane, William. *Children's Books in England & America in the Seventeenth Century.* New York: King's Crown, 1955.

Snow White. Illus. Rex Irvine and Judie Clarke. N.p.: Superscope, n.d.

Snyder, Louis A. *Roots of German Nationalism.* Bloomington: Indiana University Press, 1978.

Solms, Wilhelm, and Charlotte Oberfeld, eds. *Das selbstverständliche Wunder: Beiträge germanistischer Märchenforschung.* Marburg: Hitzeroth, 1986.

Soriano, Marc. "From Tales of Warning to Formulettes: The Oral Tradition in French Children's Literature." *Yale French Studies* 43 (1969): 24–56.

————. *Les Contes de Perrault. Culture savante et traditions populaires.* Paris: Gallimard, 1968.

Sprengnether, Madelon. *The Spectral Mother: Freud, Feminism, and Psychoanalysis.* Ithaca: Cornell University Press, 1990.

Steig, Reinhold. "Zur Entstehungsgeschichte der Märchen und Sagen der Brüder Grimm." *Archiv für das Studium der neueren Sprachen* 107 (1901): 277–301.

————, ed. *Achim von Arnim und Jacob und Wilhelm Grimm.* Stuttgart: Cotta, 1904.

Stone, Harry. "Dickens, Cruikshank, and Fairy Tales." *Princeton University Library Chronicle* 35 (1973–74): 212–47.

Stone, Kay F. "The Misuses of Enchantment: Controversies on the Significance of Fairy Tales." In *Women's Folklore, Women's Culture*. Ed. Rosan A. Jordan and Susan J. Kalcik. Philadelphia: University of Pennsylvania Press, 1985.

Stone, Lawrence. *The Family, Sex and Marriage in England, 1500–1800*. New York: Harper & Row, 1977.

Straparola, Giovanni Francesco. *The Facetious Nights*. 4 vols. Trans. W. G. Waters. London: Society of Bibliophiles, 1901.

Sulzer, Johann Georg. *Pädagogische Schriften*. Ed. Willibald Klinke. Langensalza: Hermann Beyer, 1922.

Swahn, Jan-Öjvind. *The Tale of Cupid and Psyche (Aarne-Thompson 425 & 428)*. Lund: Gleerup, 1955.

Tabbert, Reinbert, ed. *Maurice Sendak: Bilderbuchkünstler*. Bonn: Bouvier, 1987.

Tatar, Maria. *The Hard Facts of the Grimms' Fairy Tales*. Princeton: Princeton University Press, 1987.

Taylor, David C. "Oedipus' Parents Were Child Abusers." *British Journal of Psychiatry* 153 (1988): 561–63.

Tegethoff, Ernst. *Studien zum Märchentypus von Amor und Psyche*. Rheinische Beiträge und Hülfsbücher zur germanischen Philologie und Volkskunde, Series 4. Bonn: Kurt Schroeder, 1922.

Thompson, Stith. *The Folktale*. New York: Holt, Rinehart and Winston, 1946.

———, ed. *One Hundred Favorite Folktales*. Bloomington: Indiana University Press, 1968.

Todd, Richard. "In Praise of Fairy Tales." Review of *The Uses of Enchantment*, by Bruno Bettelheim. *Atlantic*, June 1976: 103–5.

Tolkien, J.R.R. *The Tolkien Reader*. New York: Ballantine, 1966.

Travers, P. L. *About the Sleeping Beauty*. New York: McGraw-Hill, 1975.

———. "On Not Writing for Children." *Children's Literature* 4 (1975): 15–22.

Tucker, Nicholas. "How Children Respond to Fiction." In *Writers, Critics, and Children*, 177–78. New York: Agathon, 1976.

———. "Lullabies and Child Care: A Historical Perspective." In *Opening Texts: Psychoanalysis and the Culture of the Child*, 17–27. Ed. Joseph H. Smith and William Kerrigan. Baltimore: Johns Hopkins University Press, 1985.

Twain, Mark. *The Adventures of Huckleberry Finn*. Ed. John Seeyle. London: Penguin, 1985.

Twitchell, James B. *Preposterous Violence: Fables of Aggression in Modern Culture*. New York: Oxford University Press, 1989.

Updike, John. Review of *The Uses of Enchantment*, by Bruno Bettelheim. *New York Times Book Review*, 23 May 1976, 1–2.

Upton, William. "The School Girl: A Poem." London: William Darton, 1820.

Ussher, Arland, and Carl von Metzradt. *Enter These Enchanted Woods*. Dublin: Dolmen, 1957.

Waller, Jennifer R. "Maurice Sendak and the Blakean Vision of Childhood." *Children's Literature* 6 (1977): 130–40.

Wardetzky, Kristin. "The Structure and Interpretation of Fairy Tales Composed by Children." *Journal of American Folklore* 103 (1990): 157–76.

Watts, Isaac. *Divine and Moral Songs for Children*. New York: Hurd and Houghton, 1866.

Weber, Eugen. "Fairies and Hard Facts: The Reality of Folktales." *Journal of the History of Ideas* 42 (1981): 93–113.

Williams, Jay. *The Practical Princess*. Illus. Friso Henstra. New York: Parents' Magazine Press, 1969.

Wülfing, Isabella. *Alter und Tod in den Grimmschen Märchen und im Kinder- und Jugendbuch*. Herzogenrath: Murken-Altrogge, 1986.

Yolen, Jane. *Sleeping Ugly*. Illus. Diane Stanley. New York: Coward, McCann & Geoghegan, 1981.

Young, Doris. "Evaluation of Children's Responses to Literature." *A Critical Approach to Children's Literature*. Ed. Sara Innis Fenwick, pp. 100–109. Chicago: University of Chicago Press, 1967.

Zipes, Jack. *Breaking the Magic Spell: Radical Theories of Folk & Fairy Tales*. Austin: University of Texas Press, 1979.

——. *The Brothers Grimm: From Enchanted Forests to the Modern World*. New York: Routledge, Chapman and Hall, 1988.

——. *Fairy Tales and the Art of Subversion: The Classical Genre for Children and the Process of Civilization*. New York: Wildman, 1983.

——. "A Second Gaze at Little Red Riding Hood's Trials and Tribulations." *The Lion and the Unicorn* 7/8 (1985): 78–109.

——, ed. *Don't Bet on the Prince: Contemporary Feminist Fairy Tales in North America and England*. New York: Methuen, 1986.

——, ed. *The Trials and Tribulations of Little Red Riding Hood: Versions of the Tale in Sociocultural Context*. South Hadley, Mass.: Bergin & Garvey, 1983.

✄ INDEX ✄